STRESEMANN
AND THE
DNVP

RECONCILIATION OR REVENGE
IN GERMAN FOREIGN POLICY
1924-1928

ROBERT P. GRATHWOL

THE REGENTS PRESS OF KANSAS
Lawrence

Library of Congress Cataloging in Publication Data
Grathwol, Robert P   1939-
Stresemann and the DNVP.
Bibliography: p.
Includes index.
1. Stresemann, Gustav, 1878-1929. 2. Deutschnationale Volkspartei—History.
3. Germany—Foreign relations—1918-1933. I. Title.
DD231.S83G7   943.085'092'4   79-28199
ISBN 0-7006-0199-6

TO THE MEMORY OF MY PARENTS
AND FIRST TEACHERS

JOHN EGAN GRATHWOL

AND

BOŽENA McKEON GRATHWOL

CONTENTS

Preface		ix
List of Acronyms Used in Text		2
1	The Conjunction of Forces at the Outset	3
2	Coalition or Opposition	21
3	From the Dawes Plan to the December Elections	42
4	The Security-Pact Memorandum	58
5	Practical Politics	76
6	The Invitation to Locarno	102
7	Locarno and the Breakup of the Coalition	121
8	Foreign Policy versus Coalition Politics	145
9	Overcoming Ideology	163
10	The Fruits of Pragmatism	180
11	The Conjunction of Forces on Balance	204
Appendix: DNVP Personnel		223
Notes		227
Bibliography		267
Index		293

PREFACE

At the end of World War I, Germany faced a critical choice akin to that which Hamlet had posed for himself: to bear the ills she had, or to fly to others that she knew not of—to reconcile herself to her fortune, or to take arms (quite literally) against her sea of troubles and to seek revenge. From 1919 to 1939 it was between these two antipodal points—reconciliation to postwar realities and revenge against outrageous fortune—that Germany's foreign policy moved. For many Germans the choice was as cosmic as Hamlet's own: To be, or not to be.

My own interest in the German question goes back to two very memorable years that I spent in France at the University of Strasbourg during the early 1960s. Both my courses of study and the life around me made me conscious of the pivotal nature to the future of Europe of the relationship between France and Germany. Influenced by the events of the day, I turned my study of history to the Locarno era. Here was an early attempt to reconcile those two great nations whose histories are so obviously joined in the daily life of Strasbourg. The Locarno era provided an opportunity to observe two powerful forces that continued to dominate politics in the 1960s: traditional nationalism and a broader conception of national advantage that saw international cooperation as a necessary component in the pursuit of national interest.

It was evident from the outset that both France and Germany had been limited in their conduct of foreign affairs during the 1920s by strong nationalistic forces within the body politic. Less evident was precisely how this influence had worked itself out in practice. This was the context, therefore, in which this book began.

Actual research was undertaken with a relatively simple question in mind: What role had the German National Peoples' Party (Deutsch-nationale Volkspartei, or DNVP) played in the formation, the limitation, and the conduct of Gustav Stresemann's foreign policy of rapprochement with France and England? The question centered naturally upon the relationship between the DNVP and the German foreign minister, because the Nationalists were strong, vocal proponents of a traditional spirit of nationalism in German politics and were publicly hostile to Stresemann's conduct of German foreign policy. As a result of the elections of May 1924, they emerged as the strongest party in the Reichstag, and throughout the rest of the 1920s they represented the strongest nonsocialist electoral force in German politics. In 1925 and again in 1927 they joined cabinets. One might therefore assume that the government would have been able to conduct a policy of reconciliation with the enemies of the recent war—a policy that was rejected viscerally by many German Nationalists—only with the most scrupulous attention to the attitudes of that party which possessed such political strength.

Stresemann's foreign policy of reconciliation and adjustment was oriented towards the restoration of Germany's position of power. German Nationalists could have no quarrel with this goal. But they longed for a frank reassertion of Germany's prewar position, an objective that could only be reached if one were to repudiate the international system based on the results of the World War and the treaties of 1919. The Nationalists were prepared to extend the recent war by means of a diplomacy of resistance in order to reclaim Germany's place in the sun: one does not treat with the enemy; one forces conditions upon him.

Stresemann understood that this tactic was not only impossible but was unnecessary as well, and thus worse than pointless. For him, revision meant, not the restoration of the past greatness and glory of the German state, but the integration of the existing German state into the new European constellation of power. This goal was not simply a possibility; it was a necessity to which Germany's diplomatic protagonists could subscribe. This was the clash which underlay the relations between Stresemann and the DNVP.

As my research progressed, however, it became increasingly evident that the relationship between the DNVP and the government concerning the conduct of foreign policy was a reciprocally active one. As the party sought to influence foreign policy, it became more and more conscious of the exigencies of that policy. In its pursuit of political power and influence it was forced to confront the realities of the postwar world. Thus, the original question had to be recast to take into account the party's own conditioning in the dynamic relationship with the government.

What has emerged is therefore a study of the interaction between foreign and domestic policy, rather than a study of either singly. It attempts to focus on specific groups: the German cabinet, the German Foreign Office —and in particular upon the foreign minister in both of these institutions of government—and the leadership group within the Deutschnationale Volkspartei. This study attempts to describe some of the domestic forces that circumscribed Stresemann's conduct of foreign policy, as well as the manner in which he defended and advanced that policy in the face of opposition.

In an effort to keep the book within manageable proportions, I had to limit certain possible subthemes. Factionalism within the DNVP, the composition of the interest groups that stood behind the party and supported it, the structure and organization of the party itself—all of these are explored only to the extent that they help to explain the immediate relationship between the government and the party's leadership. The research also touches only lightly on many of the questions that arise concerning the loss of control of the party by the moderates in late 1928 in their struggle with the radicals of the Right. It does suggest, however, that neither the victory of the radicals nor the direction they took was the inevitable culmination of the political evolution that was then most apparent among German conservatives. These problems, and the socioeconomic profile of the DNVP that their elucidation would entail, deserve a study of their own, as I became acutely aware in my own research. However, I was forced to the conclusion that to try to pursue them in depth at this point would involve even greater delays in the completion of the study that I had originally undertaken.

There are several ways in which I hope this book will contribute to a better understanding of the Weimar Republic. First, it suggests that Stresemann had a degree of success in winning converts for his foreign policy of reconciliation and adjustment, even in camps that by disposition were hostile to such a policy. This is a matter which has frequently been misjudged even in the more recent literature on Stresemann, as I have pointed out in the text and notes. Second, it illustrates a growing political pragmatism on the part of German conservatives, which led to an increasing accommodation to the political rules of the game under the Weimar Constitution. This set of phenomena suggests that German conservatism's relationship to republican institutions was more dynamic than one-dimensionally hostile and thus, I would hope, opens for subsequent research a set of hypotheses which deserves further exploration. Too often our view of the Weimar Republic is conditioned by an inescapable fact which C. V. Wedgwood describes in her biography of William the Silent: "History is lived forwards but it is written in retrospect. We know the end before we consider the beginning and we can never wholly recapture what it was to know the beginning only." Without offering an apologia or justifications for men whose politics I do not find particularly appealing in most instances, I do hope that this study will contribute to a more sensitive understanding of the all-too-human dilemmas they faced. Not endowed with that knowledge of the end which Wedgwood speaks of, they could not know the terrible fate that their failures were preparing. In trying to recapture the beginning we who know the end must bear this in mind.

Beyond the problems immediately related to Weimar are certain echoes of current events. Much of my research was completed before the term "linkage" became politically topical. And yet the nature of the argument between Stresemann and the leaders of the DNVP is very close to the argument that exists in current debates on the foreign policy of détente. Should negotiations with a protagonist in international competition involve explicit or implicit quids pro quo? The Nationalists took the position that linkage should be explicit; Stresemann, that it should be implicit. The argument continues today. Or again, what does one do in the face of a political party whose tradition is judged to be hostile to the existing constitutional framework but which commands such political strength that it cannot be ignored? Should one seek to domesticate it, as Stresemann thought to do with the Nationalists? Should one encourage its moderate elements, as the German government tried to do with the Nationalist leadership group? Should one allow it to share power in the hope that responsibility will bring it to heel? Or should one spurn it adamantly? No situation today is comparable to that faced in the 1920s in Germany. Still, living in Italy, one hears the echoes persistently.

No one walks the path of scholarship unaccompanied. The help of many companions along the way can only be acknowledged in a general manner. I hope my teachers over the years will see at least an indirect tribute to themselves in my dedication. But there are those who have come so far with me that I cannot now fail to let them know explicitly how important their continuing encouragement has been. Three of my mentors from the University of Chicago have continued through the years to offer me their support and assistance: Peter N. Stearns, William H. McNeill, and Leonard Krieger. Two foundations, the Foreign Area Fellowship Program and the Alexander von Humboldt Stiftung, provided financial and moral support for extended stays in Germany so that I could undertake and complete this research. Smaller grants were received from the American Philosophical Society's Penrose Fund and from the summer stipend program of the National Endowment for the Humanities. Various libraries and archives, listed in the bibliography, have generously opened their facilities to me, for which I thank them. I also wish to thank Dr. Götz von Boehmer for permission to consult the papers of Alfred Hugenberg, and Prof. Dr. Herbert von Einem for permission to use the papers of Karl Jarres. Dr. Friedrich Freiherr Hiller von Gaertringen repeatedly assisted me by mail and in person with the location of material in his own collection, the Westarp Papers, as well as in other archives throughout Germany. The Institut für Europäische Geschichte in Mainz, directed by Prof. Karl Otmar Freiherr von Aretin, provided me with office space and excellent library facilities for the better part of two years. Finally, during the first half of 1975 the Benedictine priests and brothers of the Sankt Jakobsberg Monastery above Ockenheim, West Germany, provided me with a refuge when I needed time in order to reflect and to write. To all of these and to the many others whom I have not named but who have helped, I am most grateful.

To my wife and my three children, the latter of whom have had to learn two new languages and to endure even more changes of residence during the gestation of this book, a "thank you" is by far too small. With them in mind, I recall a line from Virgil, which my father often mentioned: "Forsan et haec olim meminisse iuvabit" ("For some day perchance it may be pleasing to remember even these things"; *Aeneid* 1. 203).

Bologna, Italy
April 1979

STRESEMANN AND THE DNVP

LIST OF ACRONYMS
USED IN TEXT

ADV   Alldeutscher Verband—Pan-German League
BVP   Bayerische Volkspartei—Bavarian People's Party
DDP   Deutsche Demokratische Partei—German Democratic Party
DNVP   Deutschnationale Volkspartei—German National People's Party
DVP   Deutsche Volkspartei—German People's Party
IMCC   Interallied Military Control Commission
KPD   Kommunistische Partei Deutschlands
MICUM Mission interalliée de contrôles des usines et des mines—Interallied Mission for Control of Factories and Mines
RDI   Reichsverband der Deutschen Industrie—National Federation of German Industry
RLB   Reichslandbund—Reichsland Federation
SPD   Sozialdemokratische Partei Deutschlands—German Social Democratic Party
VDI   Vereinigung deutscher Industrieller—German Manufacturer's Union

political reality. The struggle took place in two different spheres. In the realm of international affairs, Stresemann sought to convince Germany's diplomatic protagonists, who were skeptical at best of German intentions, that the interests of all could be met most satisfactorily by mutual understanding and adjustment. In the domestic sphere, Stresemann sought to convince German political leaders and the public that this same policy offered the only path to Germany's recovery of any semblance of her prewar stature, influence, and strength.

This study concentrates both upon the domestic dimension of the struggle to implement and execute the foreign policy of reconciliation in the period 1924 to 1928 and, more specifically within this framework, upon the relationship between the government and the German National People's Party (Deutschnationale Volkspartei, or DNVP), which was the strongest non-Socialist party in the German Reichstag in this period and had twice been a coalition partner in the government. This is not, therefore, purely a study of the diplomacy of the government, nor is it a sociohistorical study of the DNVP. It focuses rather upon the interaction between government and party. The three groups that hold its attention are the cabinet and the Foreign Office—in both especially the foreign minister—and the leadership of the DNVP. Before dealing with this relationship, however, certain points—such as the meaning of "policy of reconciliation," the men and offices involved in its conduct, and the organization of the DNVP—bear preliminary examination.

Gustav Stresemann stamped the policy of reconciliation with his personality. He did not either conceive or execute it alone, but his political stature and his long tenure as foreign minister made pursuit of it possible, and his conceptions allowed others the scope to contribute to it. The basic aim of the policy was to have Germany reemerge as a fully sovereign power in the European state system.[2] That system had been fundamentally disrupted by the war and was being artificially held in an abnormal balance by the Treaty of Versailles. For Germany to regain her sovereignty and power the Versailles system had to be revised. But a realistic recognition of the distribution of power within postwar Europe convinced Stresemann that any revision that would be to Germany's advantage could take place only on the basis of a policy of adjustment *within* the existing international order.

For Stresemann, Germany's prewar claim to great-power status and the basis for her reemergence after the war lay in her economic strength and potential. Even before the war he had perceived that this strength was highly vulnerable to destruction if Germany were closed off from foreign markets on which her export economy depended. He had therefore favored

THE CONJUNCTION OF FORC
AT THE OUTSET

Gustav Stresemann moved slowly toward the long rec
took his accustomed seat at its center, the members o
corps, who had gathered on this late September after
that this informal coffee hour was just like the
become an institution during Stresemann's six yea
fact, they could see that the man was dying.
Louis Lochner, the director of the Associated
coffee was served. Lochner listened as Stresema
felt after his recent convalesence-cure, and lied
Stresemann looked better. The informal exch
remained superficial. None of the correspor
man's strength with a truly penetrating
sought to conclude the interview. He spoke
his "few words" lengthening into a fervent
pursued for six years. Beads of sweat bro
pallid and flushed and with increasingly
unshakeable faith in reason and law in
about twenty minutes before exhausti
from his staff, he rose and left the
mann, who had been Germany's for
dead at the age of fifty-one.[1]

Stresemann's life and early dea
life and death of the Weimar Re
from 1923 to 1929, Stresemann h
gling to translate his faith in p

P
r
P
no
bec
stu
of t
and
Fore
circle
facto
agenc
prelim
Gu
sonality
acumen
and his
aim of th
in the E
rupted by
by the T
power, the
the distribu
any revision
by means
framework.
For Stre
key to her
potential. Ev
fragile, subjec
kets, upon wh

a peaceful world economic policy before the war, but had accepted the possibility that war would be necessary in order to protect Germany's position.[4] During the war, Stresemann saw victory as the only guarantee that Germany's economy would survive. But he went much further than a desire for simple economic security could justify, demanding extensive annexations and compensations.[5] Stresemann's stance as a militant national annexationist and enthusiastic supporter of the military dictatorship of Hindenburg and Ludendorff constitutes his least defensible political position.

The war ended all hope of Germany's obtaining economic security by means of military conquest. Stresemann began to perceive the lesson that Frederick the Great had learned but that most of his later German admirers had not: namely, that the use of force may end in destruction and defeat rather than in glory and victory. The perception forced Stresemann to acknowledge Germany's disaster and to demand that his countrymen also accept and bear the consequences of defeat.[6] At the same time it allowed him to recognize that France's victory was not so clear as Germany's defeat, that France's dominant position in Europe remained artificial and insecure.

These perceptions brought Stresemann back to his earlier appreciation of the economic necessity of peaceful adjustment of interests. As early as 1920 his political analysis had defined the four cardinal points around which he would build his future policy: (1) direct negotiations with France, (2) the balancing potential of England, (3) the vital interests of the United States in a stable and high-consumption market in Europe, and (4) the Western powers' antipathy and sense of anxiety regarding Bolshevist Russia.[7] From these points, Stresemann conceived the necessity of a foreign policy aimed at the simultaneous "recognition (as a consequence of the lost war) and revision (as the desirable aim of any national German foreign policy) of the Treaty of Versailles."[8]

Within the framework of this policy of simultaneous recognition and revision, Stresemann pursued a balance between East and West, believing that Germany's long-range opportunities lay in the tensions between Soviet Russia and the capitalistic powers. Stresemann wanted to have good relations with Russia, for they presented economic and political advantages. Stresemann never acknowledged the validity of the territorial settlement on Germany's eastern border. But he saw the path to any revision, even of the Polish-German border, as passing through the capitals of the West rather than through Moscow. In the East he aimed, at least proximately, to keep the possibility of revision open while he came to terms with France. At the same time, however, he saw his Western policy as furthering his Eastern; for as the Western powers accepted Germany's insistence that the Eastern question must remain open, they implicitly acknowledged that revision in the East was possible.[9] Still, any settlement of the Eastern question had to wait until Germany's sovereignty and economic leverage had been fully restored. Thus, in the short run, relations in the West demanded tactical priority to those with either Russia or Poland. The keys to the solution of Germany's immediate desires lay in the West: namely, relief from payment of reparations and an end to the military occupation of German soil. Stresemann had graphically stated his case to Crown Prince William, urging that Germany keep first things first: "We must at least have the hangman off our necks before we begin to plan for the days of our reprieve."[10]

Western policy thus enjoyed both a logical and a sequential priority which the daily conduct of politics reflects. However, this aspect of Stresemann's policy provoked more determined resistance and criticism within Germany than did any other. It is therefore primarily to Germany's policy regarding the West that the term "policy of reconciliation" and related expressions are applied in this study.

For all his force of personality and his political perception, Stresemann was neither the sole originator nor the sole implementor of Germany's policy of reconciliation. Both among the German Foreign Office's professional staff in Berlin and among the diplomatic representatives in Germany's missions abroad, Stresemann found able and willing supporters. Within the Foreign Office the key assistants were certainly Carl von Schubert and Friedrich Gaus.

Schubert combined a command of general policy with an attention to detail and a zeal for work that were surpassed by none. First as director of Department III (Great Britain and the Americas) and then, from December 1924, as state secretary in the Foreign Office, he exercised a decisive influence on the policy of reconciliation, to which he was firmly committed. Schubert, who was less facile than Ago von Maltzan, his predecessor as state secretary, achieved a higher degree of influence because of his harmony with Stresemann. Maltzan, too, however, accepted and promoted Stresemann's policy of reconciliation during his tenure as state secretary from December 1922 to December 1924. Indeed, his own Eastern policy assumed that there must be a prior understanding with England in the West.[11]

One guiding maxim governed the German Foreign Office during the 1920s: "The Versailles Treaty is our Bible. We must know it thoroughly."[12] As head of the Foreign Office's Legal Department, Friedrich Gaus epitomized this rule. Gaus's legal memoranda formed the basis of every important step in the policy of reconciliation, which was after all a policy of revision of the Versailles Treaty. Particularly in the drafting of Germany's negotiating positions on the Locarno accords, Gaus's role was crucial. Indeed, the basic formula for that treaty, which was a mutual guarantee of the existing territorial disposition on the Rhine, came from an unsuccessful proposal that Gaus and Schubert had devised early in 1923, before Stresemann had entered the Foreign Office.[13]

In both of the key German embassies, in Paris and in London, the policy of reconciliation found able supporters. Germany's ambassador to France, Leopold von Hoesch, achieved universal recognition as one of the most intelligent and effective diplomats of the 1920s. Hoesch, the son of a Rhenish industrial family who had chosen a career in his country's foreign service, was first sent to Paris in 1920. He assumed full responsibility as chargé d'affaires when the German ambassador was withdrawn in protest against the French seizure of the Ruhr in 1923. In this difficult situation, he so impressed the French premier, Raymond Poincaré, with his tact and skill that the premier supported the appointment of Hoesch as ambassador in January 1924. Throughout his service, Hoesch contributed not only to the implementation but to the continuing evolution of policy by his incisive and suggestive reports on French politics and on French reaction to German policy.[14]

In London, Friedrich Sthamer held the position of ambassador throughout most of the Weimar years. Sthamer had been mayor of Hamburg, where his reserved personality, honesty, and tactfulness had developed. These qualities served him and his country well in his ambassadorial post by helping to allay British resentment immediately after the war. From the time of his appointment in 1920 he established good contacts and rapport with British business and political leaders, and he provided the German Foreign Office with solid information on the situation in London. He was less inclined toward personal initiative than Hoesch, but essentially this was a minor liability, since initiative emanated for the most part from Berlin.[15]

Two other administrative offices deserve mention in a study of the interaction of German foreign and domestic politics: the Reichschancellery and the Office of the President. Both played important roles in the communications among the party, the government, and the Foreign Office and, thus, in the domestic dimension of foreign policy. Three state secretaries served in the Reichschancellery during the period 1924 to 1928: Franz Bracht, Franz Kempner, and Hermann Pünder. Both Kempner and Pünder moved up to the office from the second post in the hierarchy (that of *Ministerialdirektor*), so that a certain continuity persisted throughout the four years. Kempner's role became particularly important in the summer of 1925, when relations between Chancellor Hans Luther and Stresemann reached their nadir as a direct result of attacks by the DNVP on Stresemann's foreign policy. Kempner, acting as Luther's trusted go-between, helped to restore a working relationship between the two.[16] As Luther's position weakened, so did

Kempner's; and Pünder's influence began to rise, without, however, destroying the cordial working relationship that he and Kempner had established. After the change of chancellors in May 1926—from Luther to the Center Party's leader Wilhelm Marx—Pünder replaced Kempner as state secretary. None of the three state secretaries played a fundamentally decisive role in the policy of reconciliation, but by virtue of their central position, all figured in the domestic struggle that surrounded the policy.[17]

Another state secretary, Otto Meissner, played a similar central role and tried at least to use it to influence both the policy of reconciliation and the domestic tugs of war that it provoked. He occupied this key position as the senior civil servant in the Office of the President. Meissner's role became particularly significant after the death of the republic's first president, Friedrich Ebert, and the election of Ebert's successor, Paul von Hindenburg. Meissner's role exceeded that of simply maintaining lines of communication for the new president. He was not a mere advisor but became an extremely active agent in attempts to shape both foreign and domestic political developments.[18]

Administrative support from the executive agencies could not single-handedly sustain the policy of reconciliation. In order to remain the government's foreign policy it had to command support from the political parties as well. Here the key dissident was the German National People's Party. From the Social Democratic Party (Sozialdemokratische Partei Deutschlands, or SPD) on the Left to the German People's Party (Deutsche Volkspartei, or DVP) on the Right, the government could expect support for a policy of reconciliation, to which the parties assented on the basis of ideology and/or pragmatism. The DNVP, however, stood in sharp contrast to the other politically tractable parties on the question of foreign policy. Its attitude was dictated by its conservatism and its nationalism, both of which had been traumatized by the shock of defeat in 1918. Its conservatism, in the traditional German conception, elevated the foreign political role of the state: power is the state's essential characteristic. Its nationalism exalted the honor of the state, expressed particularly through the state's primacy in foreign affairs, which was an achievement and basic characteristic of Bismarck's Reich. Any admission of weakness or any failure to assert the state's primacy thus constituted an affront to the fundamental principles of the Nationalist political philosophy.

Of course, 1918 represented a massive affront, indeed a destruction of the bases in reality for any such political conception. As Stresemann trenchantly described the psychological shock: "We thought we were the Romans, but we turned out to be the Carthaginians."[19] To help them repress this fact, which Stresemann had recognized, the Nationalists constructed an

8

elaborate world of myth in which fact and reality were both consciously and unconsciously transmuted. It began with the mythical redefinition of Wilson's Fourteen Points as a plan to achieve by means of the peace settlement what Germany had failed to win on the battlefield. It continued with the closely related myths of the "undefeated army," the "stab in the back," and the "November traitors," who had betrayed the historic roots of the German state and had introduced the alien concepts of democracy and Marxism.

The Versailles Treaty provided these myths with a convenient political focus. For the Nationalists, the peace was clearly vindictive, a "Carthaginian" peace. The territorial clauses, disarmament, reparations, and especially the imputation of German guilt for the war all arose from the Allied desire to rob Germany of her nationhood. Any acquiescence to the treaty amounted to a negation of Germany's national identity and honor. Thus, what the Nationalists valued as Germany's essence as a nation—namely, her power and primacy among European states—became layered over with the myths of the unlost war and of the traitorous betrayal that had led to the acceptance of the dictated and dishonorable peace.

The Nationalist myths served two immediate functions. On a psychological level they protected individuals from facing harsh realities personally, and they allowed a comforting "flight" from the disaster of 1918. On a more practical level they defined certain elements of German foreign policy. Any compromise regarding these elements, therefore, undermined the defense against reality. Conversely, however, to the extent that the Nationalists compromised on these issues at the practical level, they had to make adjustments at the psychological level. Since the conservative conception of the nation-state that was shared by the Nationalists viewed the exercise of power in the international arena as the state's essential function, the Weimar Republic could win credibility insofar as it could demonstrate its ability to advance Germany's interests internationally. Thus, to the extent that a policy of reconciliation was perceived by the Nationalists as a permissible or even effective means to the reemergence of Germany as a European power, they would be drawn toward acknowledging the legitimacy of the existing state. Moreover, to the extent that the Weimar Republic gained legitimacy, the myths surrounding the defeat of 1918 would become less efficacious, less persuasive, and less insulating from reality. As a result, the strength of irrational forces in German and European politics could be reduced. Given this general conservative-nationalist mentality, foreign policy played a potentially legitimizing role in the attitudes toward the Weimar Republic in a way that interest politics did not. For this reason, the DNVP's response to the foreign policy of reconciliation offers a crucial insight into the evolution of

German politics during the most stable—and thus most normal—years of the Weimar Republic.

Of course, the phrase "stable years" is relative; scratch any stable year, and you will find a revolution in ferment.[20] Still, the period 1924 to 1928 allows one to examine the institutions of the republic at a point when these were relatively free from the threat of immediate external or internal destruction. The dangers of imminent revolution and of separatism had been overcome; the territorial and administrative integrity of the Reich had been reendorsed by the Western powers with their promotion of a negotiated settlement of the reparations question; and the state and its economy had begun to function once again. This situation would prevail until the world economic crisis strained the structure and institutions of many countries, among them the German Republic. Nevertheless, although the stability is indeed relative, Weimar's political institutions operated at that time in their most normal manner and thus offer the best basis for one to judge their potential strengths and weaknesses.

These same years also offer the best opportunity for examining the relation between the DNVP and the government. In the four years from the elections of May 1924 to those of May 1928, the DNVP was the largest non-Marxist party in the German Reichstag; and for one brief period it displaced the SPD as the party with the greatest number of seats. Thus the DNVP represented a substantial bloc of parliamentary votes that had to be taken into account in any political calculation. After the elections of May 1928 the party's numerical strength in the Reichstag slipped significantly. More importantly, the substantial gains by the SPD shifted the parliamentary center of gravity towards the Left, and it became impossible to construct a government that would exclude the Socialists, at least in the short run. This study therefore concentrates on these middle years of the Weimar Republic, because they offer relatively stable political conditions and thus a unique opportunity to examine interaction between the Nationalists and the government.

The DNVP was not, of course, a philosophical society dedicated to the elaboration of conceptions of the state, such as those described earlier. It was, rather, a conglomerate of individuals and groups which coalesced in 1918 and 1919 on the political Right in opposition to the revolution of 1918. The inner core of the party consisted of landowners, industrialists, professionals, upper-level civil servants, and officers of the imperial era. These groups, which were small in number, continued to be overrepresented in key offices of the party throughout its history. But such groups alone do not account for the 15 to 20 percent of the popular vote that the DNVP commanded in Reichstag elections through 1928. These numbers came from the ranks of the modest to small proprietors in the towns and in the country, such as small landholders, artisans, small tradesmen, and merchants; from those who had been dependent upon the state under the empire, such as the lesser functionaries and the noncommissioned and junior officers; from the "half-proletarians," who still honored private property although they possessed none, such as preachers, teachers, and small-town doctors and lawyers; and from the working class, both white- and blue-collar. The mass following of the party was thus exceptionally heterogeneous.[21]

Several organized interest groups stood in a more or less close association with the DNVP. Among the working class the United Alliance of German Christian Trade Unions (Gesamtverband der christlichen Gewerkschaften Deutschlands) acted as a Nationalist recruiter. Its vice-chairman, Franz Behrens, long enjoyed a privileged position in the DNVP. The German National Labor Federation (Deutschnationaler Arbeiterbund), under Emil Hartwig and its executive secretary (*Hauptgeschäftsführer*), Wilhelm Lindner, also represented a Nationalist effort to penetrate the working classes. The German National Federation of Clerks (Deutschnationaler Handlungsgehilfenverband) was primarily a union of commercial employees and was less a political organization; but through its executive secretary, Walter Lambach, who sat as a Nationalist member of the Reichstag, it had close ties with the DNVP.[22]

At the other end of the social spectrum stood such groups as the Reichsland Federation (Reichslandbund, or RLB), the National Federation of German Industry (Reichsverband der deutschen Industrie, or RDI), and the German Manufacturers' Union (Vereinigung deutscher Industrieller, or VDI), which represented the major forces of agriculture and industry. The ties between these groups and the DNVP were largely personal rather than organizational, and their support for the party varied according to its willingness to accept their economic interests as its political goals; nevertheless, they were generally considered close to the Nationalists. One observes their potential influence, in the fact that 56 of the DNVP's 110 delegates in the third Reichstag (1924–28) belonged to the agrarian Reichslandbund, although not all 56 derived their principal income from agriculture. In addition, certain organizations tended toward the DNVP immediately after the war for purely ideological reasons—the United Societies for the Fatherland (Vereinigte Vaterländische Verbände), the Pan-German League (Alldeutscher Verband, or ADV), and the Steel Helmet (Stahlhelm), the veterans' association.[23]

From the inception of the DNVP, all these groups vied with one another for control and influence within the party. Essentially, they fell into two fundamentally opposed and contradictory attitudes. The intransigent

11

radicals saw the DNVP as the political vehicle for the counterrevolution and demanded that it unconditionally oppose the republican regime and all its pomps and works, a "republic cursed and condemned by God."[24] The opposite demand motivated the party moderates, who felt a responsibility to the state independently of the regime and who therefore favored cooperation with the existing government, even within the system, but aimed at the reorientation and reform of the state so that it would fit conservative tradition.[25] In between stood the vast majority of the party. Material interests pushed them toward the moderates, but their myths made them susceptible to the rhetoric of the radicals.

Trying to hold these divergent forces together was the task of the Nationalist party leadership. Theoretically, policy-making power was ultimately vested in the party convention (*Parteitag*), then in the party's expanded executive committee (*Parteivertretung*), which included the chairmen of the regional party committees (*Landesverbände*), in the executive committee (*Vorstand*), the leadership committee (*Parteileitung*), and finally in the party chairman and his personal assistants (*politische Beauftragten*). In actuality, to the extent that decision-making with regard to policy followed organizational lines at all, it ran in just the opposite direction: from party chairman to the increasingly larger and less effective bodies. Not only was there the structure of the national party organization; the DNVP's Reichstag delegation (*Fraktion*) had its own organization, which included its chairman (*Fraktionsvorsitzender*) and an executive committee (*Fraktionsvorstand*), which selected from its midst a steering committee of six.[26] In both structures, however, decisions arose much more from personal consultations than from formal administrative soundings.

Oskar Hergt had been chairman of the DNVP since its organization and from 1920 on had been chairman of the party's Reichstag delegation as well. Although he had had no significant political experience prior to the defeat of 1918, Hergt had pursued a career as a bureaucratic administrator, which had culminated in his appointment as Prussian finance minister in 1917. Hergt served in both party offices until late 1924. He was succeeded as party chairman by Friedrich Winckler and as chairman of the Reichstag delegation by Count Kuno von Westarp. When Winckler resigned as party chairman in March 1926, Westarp assumed that office also, thus reuniting the positions of party and delegation chairman in one person. Even prior to Winckler's resignation, however, Westarp had the greater influence.[27]

Like Hergt, Westarp had progressed in his early career through the Prussian administrative structure. Unlike Hergt, however, he brought considerable practical political experience to the party offices he held. Elected to the imperial Reichstag in 1908, he rose quickly within the German Conservative Party, and in 1912 he assumed the chairmanship of its Reichstag delegation. During the war he favored an annexationist policy and rejected all suggestions for a peace of understanding. He opposed and despised the revolution, and initially he saw the DNVP as a possible vehicle against it. He resisted all efforts to introduce a moderate, cooperationist program into the party's counsels in 1919 and 1920. When the ultranationalist Wolfgang Kapp began to plan for his putsch to overthrow the republic, Westarp was deeply involved. When the putsch collapsed after only four days in March 1920, however, Westarp managed to maintain a public distance. The extent of his complicity remained generally unknown, and his political career was not impaired. In the aftermath of the putsch, he continued to oppose the attempts by moderates within the party to promote cooperation with the existing state and government. Unlike Hergt, then, whose ministerial background in the Prussian government made him sympathetic to the moderates' desire to participate in the state, Westarp stood squarely, in the early years, with the right-wing opponents of the republic. Still, Westarp's personal qualities and his talent for compromise within the party won him the respect of the moderates as well, a factor that made him an acceptable successor to Hergt.[28]

In addition to the offices of chairman in the national and the party organizations, the position of political assistant to the party chairman (*politischer Beauftragte des Parteivorsitzenden*) carried great practical importance. The office was held successively by Hans-Erdmann von Lindeiner-Wildau, to February 1925, and by Gottfried Treviranus, through 1929, when it was eliminated. Both men figured significantly in the contacts between the party and the government. Both were considered political moderates, although Treviranus began as a protégé of the man who would emerge as the leader of the DNVP's radical right wing, Alfred Hugenberg.[29]

Other party members played a role in decision-making and implementation that was less connected with any particular office than with their expertise. Max Wallraf and Hans Schlange-Schöningen both filled the office of vice-chairman of the party during the middle years of the republic. Each one owed his influence less to this office, however, than to other factors. Wallraf's position as president of the Reichstag in 1924 suggests his prestige. Throughout the period he continued to be a confidant and advisor to Westarp and a *bête noire* to the party's right-wing radicals. Schlange began as a member of the party's right wing,[30] but he modified this position after the party's experience in government in 1925. As a representative of the important Pomeranian Regional Committee, Schlange's influence increased within the party from 1926 onward.

On questions of foreign policy, the DNVP possessed two academic experts. Both were university professors, but they stood at opposite ends of the spectrum of opinion. Axel Freiherr von Freytagh-Loringhoven represented the radical right wing within the party. As cochairman of the DNVP's standing "racial" committee, he held a position that allowed him access to inner-party counsels. His expertise made him a logical choice as an occasional party spokesman in the Reichstag and in its Foreign Affairs Committee for the party's views on foreign policy. Otto Hoetzsch was also a member of the Reichstag and of its Foreign Affairs Committee, and he also acted as the party's occasional spokesman on foreign-policy questions. As a moderate, he also had excellent contacts with the government and with important members of the Berlin diplomatic corps. It is difficult to measure the influence of either man directly. Both, however, consistently contributed their opinions to the party leadership, and in certain instances these opinions emerged as party policy in virtually unchanged form.

One agency tried to hold the party together on a day-to-day basis: the party's central business office in Berlin, which consisted of the *Hauptgeschäftsstelle* and the *Schriftenvertriebsstelle*, roughly translated as the administrative and public information (propaganda) offices. From 1921 on, the dominant figure in this administrative team was Max Weiss, the executive secretary (*Hauptgeschäftsführer*) of the office. He saw his post in Berlin as providing the link between the leadership and the rank and file. He assumed the responsibility for making "the will of the top, the party leadership," known to each member.[31] This function entailed the preparation and circulation of newsletters, political-information outlines, party newspapers, and releases.[32]

The struggle within the DNVP between moderate and intransigent opinion received extra stimulus as a result of the evolution of politics after 1920, with domestic politics pushing the Nationalists one way and foreign policy pushing them another. Domestically the pressure resulted from the search for a basis on which to form a stable majority coalition government. The foreign political pressure resulted from the constellation that favored a policy of reconciliation in European affairs, which arose in the wake of the crises of 1923 concerning reparations.

The first elections to the German Reichstag in June 1920 had produced an inherently unstable political situation. The "Weimar Coalition," consisting of the SPD, the German Democrats (Deutsche Demokratische Partei, or DDP), and the Center Party (Zentrum), had controlled 75 percent of the seats in the National Assembly at Weimar and had written the constitution. But the coalition emerged with less than 50 percent of the seats in the new Reichstag. As a result, majority government became dependent upon an opening either to the Right or to the Left. Since the parties to the

SPD's left were unwilling to cooperate, it soon became apparent that control of possibilities for a coalition had passed from the Weimar Coalition to a "middle bloc," consisting primarily of the German Democrats, the Center Party, and the German People's Party. If this bloc moved toward the Left, a majority Grand Coalition from the SPD to the DVP would emerge. If it moved to the Right, it would constitute a *bürgerliche Koalition*—a national "civic" alignment that would exclude the Marxist Socialists from the government. This anti-Marxist turn, which could be achieved through a *bürgerliche Koalition*, appealed particularly to the DNVP, which had inherited Imperial German society's aversion to Marxian Socialists; but its appeal reached far beyond any single party to include much of the German bourgeoisie.[33]

The DNVP had been organized in fundamental opposition to the republic, and throughout 1919 it constituted a focal point for antidemocratic forces.[34] This antidemocratic penchant became strikingly evident in March 1920, when the party assumed an ambivalent attitude toward the putsch led by Wolfgang Kapp, for which many prominent Nationalists openly declared their support. The party leaders, although they were more circumspect, were slow to repudiate the usurpers.[35] Their antidemocratic stance thus excluded the Nationalists from the government, and the early cabinets of the Weimar Republic, with or without formal majority coalitions, looked to the Left for support.

A change occurred with the appointment of Wilhelm Cuno as chancellor in November 1922. Cuno's reputation as an astute man of affairs had brought him to the chancellorship, where his relative political independence —he had no party affiliation—allowed him to win an initial Reichstag vote of confidence which reached from the SPD to the DNVP. The predominant influence on the Cuno cabinet, however, came increasingly from the Right, through the personal ties that certain prominent German Nationalist leaders established with the government.[36] Cuno's resignation in August 1923 and the subsequent formation of the Grand Coalition, from the SPD to the DVP, by Gustav Stresemann ended this special relationship. The DNVP returned to its more accustomed stance of acerbic opposition.[37]

This sharp reversion to opposition belied, however, the forces of compromise that were still at work within the DNVP and between the Nationalists and the other parties, particularly the DVP.[38] This became evident when the Nationalists adopted a more accommodating attitude towards the reorganization of the Stresemann cabinet in October 1923, in which they hoped to replace the SPD. But the German Democrats and the Centrists were not yet willing to form a civic *(bürgerliche)* government that would preclude Socialist cooperation. Nor was Stresemann anxious to have his

15

new cabinet labeled right wing, and although he did appoint a German Nationalist, Count Gerhard von Kanitz, to the Foods and Agriculture Ministry, the DNVP was left out and in turn refused to give the government its support.

Nationalist ambitions were frustrated once again in November 1923, when Stresemann ultimately fell; Reichspresident Friedrich Ebert declined to call upon the DNVP to form the new cabinet, although the party leadership was eager to assume the task.[39] In fact, the cabinet that emerged from this crisis was based on a minority coalition, which, although it was inadequate as a long-term solution to the parliamentary problem, managed to govern until March 1924 by resorting to a limited emergency law. When this law came up for renewal, however, Chancellor Wilhelm Marx failed to find the parliamentary support that he needed, and he was forced to ask President Ebert to dissolve the Reichstag.[40]

The resultant elections of May 6, 1924, represented an overwhelming success for the DNVP, whose strength in the Reichstag increased dramatically from 66 to 96 seats. Even though the DNVP was outpolled by the SPD, which garnered 100 seats, the DNVP controlled the additional 10 mandates won by the agrarian Reichslandbund, which had run candidates independently but which chose to sit as an integral part of the Nationalist parliamentary delegation. This brought the DNVP count to 106, making it the strongest party in the new Reichstag and giving it the privilege and prestige of seeing one of its members, Max Wallraf, elected president of that assembly.[41] The DNVP's domestic fortunes seemed assured; a rightist coalition appeared inevitable.

But at this juncture, Germany's foreign political situation impinged upon its domestic development. As coalition negotiations began in the spring of 1924, the most important issue facing the German nation was the question of war reparations. Germany's default on reparations deliveries to France in 1922 had occasioned France's occupation of the German industrial heartland in the Ruhr.[42] The Ruhr occupation, which had begun on January 11, 1923, in conjunction with Belgium and Italy but over the protests of Great Britain, brought Germany to the point of collapse; and the specters of runaway inflation, French-encouraged separatism, and revolt from the Right and the Left—all still haunted the German voters as they went to the polls in May 1924.[43]

The German policy of passive resistance to the French military and civil administration in the Ruhr had ended in September 1923, and Germany's plight had been alleviated slightly as a result of the diplomatic intervention of less Germanophobic powers such as Great Britain and the United States. But France had remained in the Ruhr and, through special treaties negoti-

16

COALITION POSSIBILITIES IN THE SECOND REICHSTAG, MAY 4, 1924, TO DECEMBER 1924 (ACTUAL CABINET SUPPORT INDICATED)

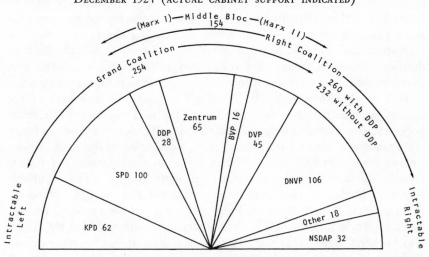

472 Delegates; 237 = Majority
Adapted from *dtv-Atlas zur Weltgeschichte* (Munich: Deutsche Taschenbuch Verlag, 1966), vol. 2, p. 150.

COALITION POSSIBILITIES IN THE THIRD REICHSTAG, DECEMBER 7, 1924, TO MAY 1928 (ACTUAL CABINET SUPPORT INDICATED)

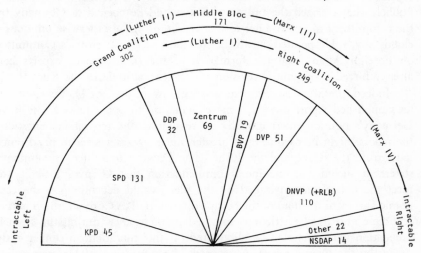

493 Delegates; 247 = Majority
Adapted from *dtv-Atlas zur Weltgeschichte* (Munich: Deutsche Taschenbuch Verlag, 1966), vol. 2, p. 150.

17

ated in 1923 at the depths of the German financial crisis, had controlled the major part of Germany's industrial potential.[44] These accords—referred to as the MICUM treaties, after the commission that represented France in the Ruhr (Mission interalliée de contrôles des usines et des mines)—had not been contracted with the German government, but with the Rhineland industries directly, as though they constituted an independent entity—a fact that disturbed those Germans who were concerned about France's long-range designs on the Rhineland. Only through a negotiated settlement of the reparations question that would be acceptable to France could Germany hope to regain control of her own destinies along the Rhine and in the Ruhr.

France had gone far toward accepting negotiation of the issue in principle in November 1923, when she had agreed to a general study of reparations by an international committee of economic experts. The committee had been formed of two financial experts from each of five countries—France, Great Britain, Belgium, Italy, and the United States—and had begun its work in January 1924 in Paris under the chairmanship of the American banker Charles G. Dawes. In February the Dawes Committee visited Berlin to investigate Germany's actual financial situation. And on April 9, in the middle of the German Reichstag election campaign, it released its report, which contained recommendations with regard to a feasible schedule for reparations payments.[45]

The investigations and their political implications had long been the subject of intense discussion within the cabinet.[46] Stresemann had already publicly characterized the prospects that would be opened to Germany by the committee's mere existence as a silver lining in an otherwise ominously cloudy sky.[47] He pointed out to the members of the Reichstag's Committee on Foreign Affairs that the formation of the committee of experts had already forced a substantial revision of France's attitude in the Ruhr.[48]

Indeed, the Marx government was well aware that the Dawes Committee's published report presented more than just an opportunity to improve Germany's position internationally by regulating the reparations question; the report might be used to even greater advantage as a lever to pry France loose from the Rhine and the Ruhr. The Dawes Committee's preliminary statement included a one-line recommendation that Germany's ability to meet the obligations envisaged by the plan would depend upon the economic and fiscal freedom of the occupied territories. As a result, the punitive economic and fiscal restrictions imposed in these areas during the French occupation would have to be eliminated. If this condition, so conveniently set up by the Dawes report, were made the touchstone of German policy in the negotiations over reparations, France would be placed in a difficult position. She would have either to restore full economic and political control of the Ruhr to Germany or answer to the charge of obstructing the experts' proposed solution to the reparations problem. But the Marx cabinet realized that immediate and unconditional acceptance of the Dawes report was imperative if this advantage were to be exploited. In the political briefings covering the diplomatic situation, the government argued that France was well aware of the potential embarrassment that the Dawes report could cause to her Rhineland plans and that she was therefore working hard to revise the committee's recommendations. Any delay or equivocation in the German response to the Dawes proposals might make it possible for France to modify or scuttle the report and might also give credence to the Gallic contention that Germany could only be dealt with by means of an ultimatum.[49]

The cabinet, in addition to seeking foreign political advantage, was being prompted toward quick acceptance of the Dawes plan by domestic considerations. It hoped to eliminate campaign rhetoric as an influence upon this policy decision by making a binding commitment to the plan before the elections took place.[50]

Such a commitment was vigorously opposed by the German Nationalists. Since the end of the war, the DNVP had consistently rejected the idea of cooperating with the former enemy powers, asserting that German foreign policy should be aimed in every instance at freeing the country from "the slavery of the peace of Versailles."[51] Now it rejected the government's suggestion that the Dawes plan might offer such an opportunity. Moreover, in a meeting on April 14, 1924, between government representatives and the DNVP leadership—just five days after the publication of the Dawes plan in Paris—party spokesman Count Kuno von Westarp formally objected that the government had no power to contract an obligation that would in effect present any future cabinet with a *fait accompli* on so important an affair: the government lacked a majority in the Reichstag, and the imminent elections could very well produce a cabinet of a markedly different composition. Any decision, he argued, should be left until after a new cabinet had been formed, until after the elections. Reichschancellor Marx, however, refused to admit that his cabinet did not have the power to act.

The two points of view remained unresolvedly opposed, but the German Nationalists were in no position to block the cabinet's initiative.[52] Thus, with the approval of the state governments and of the leaders of several Reichstag delegations, the German government delivered a note to the reparations commission in Paris on April 16, 1924, notifying the Allies of its willingness to accept the Dawes Committee's recommendations as the basis for the negotiations of a reparations settlement.[53]

The cabinet's action only served to intensify Nationalist campaign activity against the experts' plan. Two days after the government sent its note, an article appeared—written by the DNVP's prominent financial authority Karl Helfferich, whose death in a rail accident just a few days later robbed the Nationalists of one of their most effective leaders—which attacked the Dawes proposals as a "second Versailles."[54] This succinct condemnation of the government's policy of reconciliation through an evocation of the humiliation at Versailles became the keynote of the Nationalist campaign.

The cabinet also based its election appeal forthrightly on the reparations issue, requesting that the voters return a Reichstag that would be favorable to the Dawes plan.[55] But the Nationalists rode the stronger tide of discontent to a resounding electoral success. Their flamboyant slogan, however, was to prove less acceptable in the coming coalition negotiations than it had been in the election campaign.

2

COALITION OR OPPOSITION

The elections of May 4, 1924, were a resounding success for the DNVP, but they underscored the party's basic dilemma, for they forced it to face two crucial questions. The first was a matter of principle: Could the party work for and within a state that it formally rejected as being unhistorical and illegitimate? The second was practical: How far could the Nationalists go in making concessions to potential partners?[1]

Despite its dilemma, the DNVP quickly attempted to capitalize on its electoral gains. Rightist newspapers began to clamor for the formation of a national "civic" bloc, headed by the DNVP and composed of all the non-socialist parties.[2] But within the party itself, opinion about how best to exploit the situation remained divided. The militant, intransigent radicals, who found support among the conservative die-hards, the Pan-Germans, the racist *deutschvölkische,* and representatives of war-veterans' associations, still rejected all participation in the government and particularly opposed the Dawes report and any accommodation with the "enemy."[3] The moderates, on the other hand, who felt they had the support of Chairman Oskar Hergt and his political lieutenant, Hans-Erdmann von Lindeiner-Wildau, favored entry into the government, even at the cost of certain concessions. Their aim continued to be the reform of the state from within. Between these two extremes stood a third group within the party, for which Count Kuno von Westarp became the chief proponent during the summer of 1924. Westarp did not reject entry into the government out of hand, but he did question the timing. The party could hardly hope to change the outcome of the negotiations over the Dawes plan by its presence in the cabinet, whereas if it were associated with the conclusions reached in the negotiations, its nationalistic image would be tarnished.[4] Because of his long association with the highly orthodox German Conservatives (Deutschkonservativen), Westarp enjoyed the confidence of most of the men on the Right. Because of his willingness to tolerate, at least in private, the idea of participation within the Republican system, he enjoyed the confidence of those in the more moderate camp as well. But the fact that the two extremes tried to pull the party first one way, then the other, heightened the unpredictability of an already unstable political situation.

The moderate aim of a coalition of the Right enjoyed the prospect of success in May 1924. The radical Right within the DNVP had suffered a severe setback because of its association with Hitler's recent abortive putsch in Munich.[5] Its stance of unqualified opposition to the government was accordingly compromised, and the influence of moderates upon the direction of the party increased.

Also enhancing the position of the DNVP moderates was the pressure from an influential segment of the German People's Party, which favored an accommodation with the DNVP.[6] Even the DVP's chairman, Stresemann, ever ready to face political reality, was willing to accept the inclusion of the Nationalists in the government, though they had denounced his foreign policy throughout the campaign and had slandered his personal integrity.[7] Despite these attacks, Stresemann had voiced the hope during the campaign that the DNVP could bring itself to participate in the postelection government, for he was convinced that in a matter of weeks the Nationalists would see how differently things looked when viewed under the weight of responsibility.[8] Shortly after the election he privately expressed the opinion that the Nationalist party's successes would exert a moderating influence; the party would no longer be able to avoid taking clear positions even if it remained in the opposition. "Size," wrote Stresemann, "creates responsibility."[9]

The DNVP, for its part, was anxious to enter the government. The proponents of cooperation encouraged the party's leaders to soften their position on the Dawes plan. DNVP Chairman Oskar Hergt accordingly issued a policy statement on May 7, which indicated that the Nationalists did not stand in unalterable opposition to the experts' recommendations and to the Allied invitation to negotiations, but that they did insist that certain concessions from the Allies were absolutely indispensable.[10] Even Pan-Germanist Professor von Freytagh-Loringhoven, who was a prominent figure in the most radical party circles and was an untiring proponent of an extreme nationalistic political course, publicly subscribed to this tactical retreat from campaign polemics.[11]

The Marx cabinet, which had been charged with the conduct of government business until the formation of a new government, was understandably leery of the DNVP's sudden change of heart and failed to take action to include the DNVP in the government with the alacrity that the Nationalist leaders felt was appropriate. As a result, on May 15 the DNVP's Executive Committee published a demand for the immediate resignation of the Marx cabinet so as to clear the way for a national bloc government. In a cabinet meeting that same day, however, Foreign Minister Stresemann argued against complying with the DNVP's demand. Stresemann informed the cabinet that the DNVP's recent insistence upon certain concessions as preconditions of negotiations with the Allies had provoked the mistrust of the international financial community, whose good will was essential both to the realization of the experts' plan and to the international loan to Germany of 800 million gold marks, which was the cornerstone of the plan.[12] Stresemann urged his colleagues to continue in office, since their resignation would seriously disrupt the negotiations that were already in progress on the Dawes plan. Delay in negotiations, he avowed, could provoke a disastrous economic crisis for Germany which would be enough to wipe out the gains that had been made since the refunding of the mark. Instead, Stresemann proposed that the cabinet immediately announce plans to resign in about ten days, shortly before the Reichstag was to reconvene. This, Stresemann asserted, would force the parties to exert all their efforts to avoid a vacuum of power at a critical moment. The fundamental condition of any new cabinet must of course be a continuation of the present foreign policy, including the commitment to the reparations settlement. The Nationalists would have to decide whether or not they were willing to accept the Dawes Committee's recommendations.[13]

Stresemann's colleagues in the cabinet agreed that the DNVP Executive Committee's demand that they resign called for an immediate public reply. The tactical approach to the cabinet's eventual resignation provoked a divergence of opinion, however. Stresemann's suggestion that a hiatus in the government could best be avoided by fixing a date for the resignation, thus opening the way for coalition negotiations before the cabinet actually resigned, was opposed by Chancellor Marx and his Centrist colleague Minister of Labor Heinrich Brauns. Both hoped that the formation of a strong middle bloc might obviate the necessity of having the present cabinet retreat.[14]

The cabinet's reply, which was published on May 15, 1924, only hours after the DNVP had demanded that the cabinet resign, carefully ignored the question of its eventual dissolution, dwelling instead upon its obligation to remain in power to prevent the grave danger of economic crisis which any interruption of the Dawes negotiations might provoke. The reply not only pointed out that a solid majority of the new Reichstag supported these negotiations but also demanded from the DNVP a clear and definitive statement regarding its willingness to accept the Dawes proposals, which had become the central point of German foreign policy.[15]

In the week that followed, negotiations continued between the cabinet and the DNVP over the critical question of the Dawes plan. The cabinet was not the only organization to issue a public communiqué; the parties supporting the Marx government, the "middle bloc," prepared a statement outlining their minimum demands on foreign policy: in effect they amounted to the acceptance of the Dawes Committee's report and recommendations as an indivisible whole with no reservations about preconditions to be met before negotiations could begin. The statement—which at this point was confidential—pointed out the advantages of such a course of action. It would bind the Allies, as well as Germany, to a strict acceptance of the experts' proposals. Of particular interest to the government and its supporters, of course, were the proposals that called for the complete economic and political freedom of German territory as a prerequisite for the proper implementation of the reparations plan.[16]

The DNVP responded to the statements by suggesting that all differences regarding policy be subordinated to the more basic question of leadership. A sufficiently prestigious personality as chancellor, they argued, could inspire a confidence that would go beyond mere party loyalty and that would certainly allow the realization of a satisfactory governmental program.[17] The Nationalists thereupon suggested Admiral Alfred von Tirpitz as such an appropriate "personality above the parties." The fact that Tirpitz was an acknowledged German Nationalist struck the middle parties as singularly inappropriate, however. The German Nationalists remained recalcitrant, and on May 24 they rejected the Dawes proposals, claiming that they provided an inadequate basis for negotiations with the Allies. The party again suggested that a governmental program that would be satisfactory to all could still be worked out if Admiral von Tirpitz were granted the chancellorship. But the middle parties closed ranks over this point and refused to accept DNVP leadership of a new cabinet.[18]

For a brief instant during this first week of negotiations to build a new cabinet, the common front assumed by the middle parties showed signs of breaking. Certain elements appeared momentarily to be willing to concede the Nationalists' demand that final acceptance of the Dawes proposals be made conditional upon the simultaneous conclusion of an international treaty that would incorporate Germany's political demands, such as the release of prisoners, the readmission of exiles into the Ruhr, and the evacuation of certain occupied areas. Alarmed, Stresemann warned the cabinet that if acceptance of the Dawes solution were subordinated to such political demands, there would be disastrous consequences for Germany. He spoke out strongly against any suggestion that side issues, however important they might be to Germany, be raised as conditions of Germany's participation in a reparations settlement. His admonition was strongly seconded by Chancellor Marx and the Center Party's spokesman, Heinrich Brauns. Both warned of the dangers inherent in any departure from the cabinet's present foreign policy.[19]

The demand for prior—or at least simultaneous—concessions by the Allies, which paralleled the Nationalists' approach to the negotiations on the Dawes plan, found a more sympathetic hearing from Stresemann's party colleague Vice-Chancellor Karl Jarres, however. The laws that Germany would eventually need in order to implement the experts' proposed plan would have to pass the Reichstag, where some sign of Allied accommodation on occupation and amnesty within the Rhineland and Ruhr areas would aid the government's cause. Jarres feared that if such accommodations were not formally recorded in an international protocol—if, in other words, Germany really held to its present policy of accepting the reparations solution unconditionally—no real amelioration would follow. Jarres admitted that he could readily understand the Nationalists' position, and accordingly he felt that these important political questions ought to be included in negotiations regarding the Dawes plan.[20]

While Jarres sought a rapprochement between the cabinet and the Nationalists, radical forces on the Right sought to pull the DNVP farther away by denouncing any accommodation with the government. In a meeting held on May 24, 1924, the executive committee of the rightist Societies for the Fatherland (Vaterländische Verbände) discussed with great apprehension the rumor that a part of the German Nationalist Reichstag delegation wanted to sacrifice its categorical rejection of the experts' report in return for inclusion in the new cabinet. These delegates, the committee charged, had succumbed to the government's argument that rejection of the Dawes proposals would cause the collapse of the German economy by limiting the foreign capital and credit that Germany needed for its continued development. The radical organization's executive committee circulated its strongly worded protest against this faltering by the "esteemed legislators," contending that its own experience ("many of us have very close ties with foreign [business] circles") indicated just the opposite and that it thus expected the Nationalist delegation to spare no effort in blocking the acceptance of the Dawes plan.[21]

Despite dissent in both camps, negotiations regarding coalition lumbered on between the middle bloc and the DNVP. Within the German People's Party, which was the necessary link between the DNVP and the remaining middle parties, there ran a strong current to bring the Nationalists into the government; and this gave the DNVP a chance even after its May 24 rejection of the coalition parties' statement on foreign policy. On May 26 the DVP published a decision that had been reached by its Reichstag delegation, calling for the resignation of the Marx cabinet in order to free the way for formal, constitutionally correct negotiations for the formation of a government that would be more nearly representative of the "new parliamentary conditions."[22] The DNVP, however, continued to prejudice its own cause. It chose this moment to address a letter to the leader of the DVP delegation in the Reichstag, Ernst Scholz, in which the DNVP reiterated its demands for a predominant position in any new cabinet, renamed Tirpitz as a person who deserved universal trust and therefore would be appropriate as a candidate for chancellor, and renewed its insistence that any cabinet program state clearly that a final decision regarding "any accord arising out of the negotiations over current economic and political questions" be reserved to the future and be dependent on the concrete results of these negotiations.[23]

The Nationalists' letter produced an immediate response. Representatives of the middle parties met on the evening of May 26 to formulate their reply. In agreement with the attending cabinet representatives, who included Marx and Stresemann, they decided to publish not only their statement on foreign policy, which they had earlier circulated confidentially among the parties as the basis for cabinet negotiations, but also the DNVP letter to Scholz, thus exposing to everyone the incompatibility of the two positions and making clear that no basis for further negotiations existed for the moment between the DNVP and the middle parties. A few hours later, the cabinet met and, in conformity with its earlier decision to step down on the eve of the reassembling of the Reichstag, voted to submit its resignation that evening.[24]

Up to this point, negotiations had been carried on among the parties in an extraconstitutional manner, while the Marx government continued to hold office officially. Now that the cabinet had resigned, Reichspresident Ebert commissioned Marx, in the constitutionally prescribed manner, to form a new government on the broadest possible base, even to include the DNVP if their "honorable" cooperation could be secured. Reports from the Reichstag indicated that strong sentiment within the Nationalist Party's parliamentary delegation still favored its entering the government.[25] Marx thereupon sought out the German Nationalists' chairman, Oskar Hergt. In an interview between the two on May 28, Hergt demanded that the government's foreign policy begin to press questions touching on Germany's honor, especially that of Germany's war guilt, more vigorously. Hergt continued to insist on a preponderance of Nationalist influence in any new government. After a lengthy discussion, Marx concluded that continuing the negotiations in this vein was futile. He proposed, instead, to formulate a tentative governmental program, which he would submit to the German Nationalist delegation to see if some accord could be reached. Hergt accepted this procedural suggestion, and within two days, Marx had submitted his draft for a program and had received a reply from the Nationalists. In their response, which quite unexpectedly shifted the whole basis of the discussion, the Nationalists agreed to accept Marx's proposed program, including its foreign policy stipulations, with only minor modifications, and to accept Marx as chancellor. But they demanded concessions from the middle parties in heretofore unmentioned areas: namely, the reorganization of the Prussian state cabinet, so that it would include Nationalists and exclude the Social Democrats; the replacement of Stresemann as foreign minister; and a "change in course" on foreign policy, which would lead to a "middle line" that would be reached through compromises made by both the government and the Nationalists.[26]

Marx expressed doubt to Hergt that any point would be conceded by the middle bloc. He was surprised, however, by the readiness with which the middle parties were willing to abandon Stresemann. The German Democrats declared that they had never considered that it was absolutely essential for Stresemann to be retained; they were far more concerned that his foreign policy be continued. The Center Party showed equally little concern for Stresemann's presence in the cabinet, much less concern, Marx admitted, than he himself felt. The chancellor's party labeled as secondary in nature the question of whether the foreign minister were to be replaced. Only Stresemann's own DVP expressed its willingness to insist upon Stresemann's presence in the cabinet as foreign minister as long as he himself wanted the position. And even this was a less forthright stand than it seemed; it constituted, in fact, an invitation to Stresemann that he resign rather than remain the only obstacle to a majority nonsocialist coalition.[27] Still, none of the government parties was ready to subvert the Grand Coalition in Prussia to Nationalist interests, and thus the negotiations foundered once again. In the face of this unfulfillable demand from the DNVP, the DVP decided regretfully to abandon its role as mediator between the political Center and the German Nationalists. Marx was appointed by Ebert to re-form the minority cabinet which had just resigned. On June 4, 1924, the new-old cabinet presented itself before the Reichstag. Four days later it survived a vote of confidence, gaining, in addition to the votes of the coalition parties—the DDP, the Center Party, the DVP, and the BVP (Bayerische Volkspartei, or Bavarian People's Party)—the support of the Social Democrats, who always voted with the government when it faced critical situations in foreign affairs.[28]

The German Nationalist leadership had shown remarkable ineptitude in the cabinet negotiations. It had failed to capitalize on either its tremendous election successes or the very strong pressure within the DVP which urged Nationalist participation upon the government. The German Nationalists had not redirected foreign policy, despite a softening within the middle parties, nor had they even demonstrated a very resolute position of their own on the Dawes plan. At the eleventh hour they had seemed to be prepared to abandon their intransigent opposition to the government's foreign policy if only two things could have been engineered—namely Stresemann's removal and a favorable reorganization in Prussia.

This gesture ultimately proved most costly. The flip-flop undermined the confidence of people in the provinces—both within the DNVP's organization and among the rank and file—in the directorate and in the leaders based in Berlin. These incipient doubts about the orthodoxy of the Berlin leadership provided fertile ground over the next four years for the rightist radicals within the party in the growing contest with the moderates for control of the DNVP. In addition, the party's suggestion of compromise encouraged the government to think that the Nationalists might eventually be split over the issue of the Dawes plan.[29]

In contrast to the DNVP, the transitional government had handled itself well during the cabinet negotiations. The latter had resisted the weakening of resolve among its parliamentary supporters with regard to foreign policy and had maintained its insistence upon the unconditional acceptance of the Dawes plan. In so doing, it had made the negotiations on the Dawes plan the basis for German foreign policy in the months ahead. The cabinet, and particularly Stresemann, felt justified in this course of action because of the belief that the plan was more than just the key to Germany's economic stability. It was seen, rather, as the first opportunity that Germany had had since the armistice to participate in the settlement of one of the war-born issues that were so vital to her destiny. The plan might be used to curtail France's freedom of action in the Rhineland and the Ruhr and, perhaps, to restore this area to real German control.[30] Reconciliation with the Allies could mean a real improvement in Germany's overall situation, as the government saw it; but to achieve this, cooperation in the reparations settlement was essential. The difference between the government's and the DNVP's positions was not simply one of degree, as is frequently maintained;[31] rather, it involved totally different ways of thinking about foreign policy. True, the government hoped to obtain from the Allies many of the same concessions that the DNVP demanded so ostentatiously; but the government refused to make these concessions the precondition of its willingness to negotiate concerning the Dawes plan. In the diplomatic vocabulary of the 1970s, it was prepared to settle for implicit rather than explicit "linkage." This difference—between the Nationalists' demand for prior concessions and the government's willingness to take a chance on the ramifications that would result from a policy of consistent reconciliation and adjustment of interest with the Allies—constitutes an essential factor in the judgment of the policy of reconciliation in both its diplomatic and domestic dimensions. This difference also provides a leitmotif in the relations between the government and the party throughout the period 1924 to 1928.

Determined not to lose the advantages that the Dawes proposals offered, the new Marx cabinet hastened to reaffirm publicly its acceptance of the plan in the presentation of its governmental program to the Reichstag on June 4, 1924. In addition to making this reaffirmation, Marx appealed to the Reichstag to subordinate all issues of domestic and party politics to this most urgent necessity: the solution to the reparations problem on the basis of the Dawes plan and in the interests of the German economy and the relief of the Rhineland.[32]

At the same time, Germany's Foreign Office sought to turn the failure of the cabinet negotiations to its diplomatic advantage. The middle parties, it emphasized, had been willing to accept the DNVP into the government in order to help stabilize the German democracy. The failure of the negotiations created a perilous situation for the democratic parties, however: namely, the threat of an antigovernment front among the Communists, the Nationalists, and the racists. This situation could be eased and Germany's democratic forces could be strengthened by meaningful gestures from the Western powers, especially by French concessions regarding prisoners and persons who had been expelled from occupied territories as a result of the Ruhr incursion, and by an easing of the Allied position on military control of Germany.[33]

The DNVP's failure to gain access to the government during the cabinet negotiations of the preceding weeks left the party leaders with two alternatives. Either they could set the party's course in continued opposition to the foreign policy of conciliation and to its immediate corollary, the Dawes plan, thus sacrificing any immediate prospect of power within the government, or they could attempt to contain the party's emotional nationalism and seek some compromise on foreign policy that would induce the middle parties to broaden the new minority government to the Right.

At first it seemed clear that the party had chosen the more militant course. Speaking in the Reichstag for the DNVP in response to Chancellor Marx's defense of the new cabinet's policies, Count Westarp demanded a

29

complete reorientation of German foreign policy to correspond with the election results of May 4. He insisted further, as had Hergt in the final phases of the cabinet negotiations, that the German government take decisive diplomatic steps to repudiate the imputation of war guilt to the German nation. He contended that republican parliamentary democracy was not capable of freeing Germany from the foreign political pressure under which she suffered. In the name of his party, he condemned the Reichspresident and Chancellor Marx for having connived to keep the mandate for a new cabinet from the Reichstag's strongest party, despite continued manifestations by the DNVP of its willingness to cooperate and of its readiness to compromise on issues of both leadership and policy.[34]

In reply to the DNVP's challenge that the government was incapable of defending Germany's interests, Stresemann enunciated, even more forcefully than had Marx, the new cabinet's objectives in the Dawes negotiations. He named the Allied military occupation as an obvious obstacle to Germany's capacity to pay reparations. In order to conform to the Dawes plan, all such limitations would have to be removed. He excluded, however, any introduction into the diplomatic debates of questions touching on Germany's honor (*Ehrenfragen;* e.g., the question of war guilt). No agreement could be reached, Stresemann insisted, if each nation sought to pick only the raisins out of the cake; if Germany were to raise demands touching her honor, France would raise demands touching her security, and France was decidedly on the "longer end of the stick." German policy could not be conducted by the same spirit that animates parades and public rallies, concluded Stresemann, but had to be pursued responsibly and skillfully.[35]

The two positions seemed to be irreconcilable, but it soon became evident that Westarp's Reichstag speech did not represent the DNVP's final word. Out of the public eye, in the meeting of the Reichstag's Foreign Affairs Committee on June 17, 1924, the Nationalist representatives gave the distinct impression that if the government could meet certain minimum conditions in the negotiations with the Allies, the DNVP might still throw its support behind the legislation that would be needed in order to implement the Dawes plan. The Nationalist attitude was in sharp contrast to Westarp's speech.[36]

The Marx cabinet had never, in fact, been overly apprehensive about Nationalist opposition. Despite Westarp's speech in the Reichstag, the ministers knew that certain Nationalists were attracted by the advantages to be gained by acceptance of the Dawes plan. Chancellor Marx doubted that these delegates would sacrifice obvious interest for narrow party obstructionism, especially if their votes as individuals became the margin between adoption and rejection of the plan. The cabinet, moreover, was laying a plan of action that would put the moderate DNVP delegates in just this uncomfortable position. The Dawes proposal called for foreign participation in the administration of the German railroads as one measure of control over Germany's economy that would be needed in order to ensure her financial security. One argument contended that the legislation to implement this demand amounted to a constitutional amendment and thus would require a two-thirds majority in the Reichstag. Such a majority would only be possible, however, if some of the DNVP delegates were to vote with the government. If the government demanded the two-thirds vote and if government negotiators could score some success in matters touching upon German honor—the area of foreign policy that struck the most sensitive chord among the Nationalists—Marx was confident that the necessary votes would emerge.[37]

Moreover, the cabinet was well aware that influential agrarian circles within the DNVP were anxious to have agricultural tariffs set that would protect their interests. Government accommodation, it had been inferred, might encourage a concerted effort to modify the DNVP's rigid public opposition to the Dawes plan. Stresemann recognized the potential of the agricultural tariffs issue; therefore he proposed to the cabinet that the question be treated in the Reichstag only after the Dawes plan had been approved. This would force the influential agrarian league, the Reichslandbund, to urge the DNVP to accept the plan in order to secure advantageous tariffs.[38] Finally, throughout June and July, conversations were being carried on between several of the more influential DNVP moderates and members of the government and the army to find a means of broadening the cabinet to the Right.[39]

But to secure either the cooperation or the votes of even the DNVP moderates, Marx expected that the government would have to win some concessions from the Allies on matters concerning Germany's honor. Here the outlook was more propitious than at any time since the war. Early in 1924, new governments had been formed in France and England, under Edouard Herriot and Ramsay MacDonald, respectively. In both cases, the new governments had evinced a willingness to settle their differences with Germany through negotiations. The change was particularly significant in France, where Herriot had replaced Raymond Poincaré, the architect of the Ruhr action and the chief proponent in French politics of an intransigent policy toward Germany.[40] Stresemann considered the change to be of the utmost importance to Germany. His ultimate aim in the pursuit of a reparations settlement was the liberation of German soil. He knew that, even with Herriot, such an achievement would demand the most careful diplomacy. He expressed his conviction to the cabinet, however, that Herriot was already prepared to make certain concessions to Germany, such as the readmission of those who had been expelled from the Rhineland since the beginning of the Ruhr occupation. And he suggested that an evacuation settlement might even be secured, if Germany would accept the assurances of the other Western powers, rather than a formal accord, that France would in fact withdraw her troops once a reparations agreement had been reached.[41]

The prospect of gaining these concessions, which were needed in order to bring the wavering Nationalists around, was seriously compromised by a diplomatic note concerning German disarmament that was issued jointly by Herriot and MacDonald on June 22, 1924. The disarmament issue, which had lain dormant during the Ruhr occupation, had been raised by Raymond Poincaré as he was forced by both diplomatic and domestic pressure to abandon the direct application of force in the Ruhr. Throughout the winter and spring of 1924 the German government and the Allied Conference of Ambassadors, over which Poincaré presided, exchanged a series of notes concerning the resumption of military control and inspection in Germany. The German government continually insisted that Germany had already satisfied the disarmament clauses in the Versailles Treaty, that the Interallied Military Control Commission (IMCC) had made what amounted to a final inspection of German armaments in 1922 and had subsequently suspended its activity, and that, as a result, the only body that was now competent to reactivate inspection was the League of Nations. The Conference of Ambassadors rejected the German interpretation that the IMCC had concluded its work and thus could not be reactivated. It also maintained that so much time had elapsed since the last inspection of German armaments that another examination of several months' duration would now be necessary. Finally, in the last note issued under Poincaré's signature on May 28, 1924, the Conference of Ambassadors warned that any failure by Germany to accept and expedite the demanded inspection would force "the strict application of the [Versailles] Treaty" and insisted that the German government reply before June 30, 1924.[42]

The Marx government's plans to woo the Nationalists were thus complicated by this Allied insistence upon renewed inspection and military control. Any reply that seemed to be too intransigent ran the risk of undermining the Dawes negotiations. On the other hand, the government faced the certainty of attack from Nationalist quarters because of a putative abasement of German honor if it accepted the Allied demands. Any affront to the Nationalists' sense of German honor would make it much more difficult for the DNVP moderates and the government to reach a compromise on the Dawes plan.

With all this very much in mind, Stresemann had adopted a policy of delay after he had received the May note from the Conference of Ambassadors, while he made every effort to convince the chief of the army command, General Hans von Seeckt, that acceptance of the Allied demands was the only sane course of action for Germany.[43] Seeckt's approval was crucial, for his position as head of the German army made it essential that he cooperate with the Allied inspection and control teams. Moreover, he had very close ties with Nationalist circles, which he had used in an important fashion in the recent coalition negotiations, urging the DNVP to enter the government.[44]

The Herriot-MacDonald statement of June 22 precluded further delay on Stresemann's part. It intimated that rumors that Germany might reject the May note of the Conference of Ambassadors had reached the French and English governments. In addition, it referred to "most disquieting reports" that nationalist and militarist associations were continuing, indeed were increasing, their illegal military activity. Failure to disarm, the note warned, would jeopardize the application of the Dawes plan. The Allied prime ministers implored the German government to cooperate with the Interallied Military Control Commission and declared that, if this were done, they would earnestly work to remove the commission itself as fast as satisfaction on the outstanding points would make it possible to do so.[45]

The note demanded immediate German action. A rejection of the inspection was out of the question, but a direct acceptance would have dangerous domestic ramifications. The cabinet decided upon a reply that would reject the contention that activities in Germany threatened European peace in any way and would insist that Germany was in fact disarmed but would offer, as a sign of Germany's good will, to accept the specific inspection to which the Allies held, with the stipulation that the methods to be employed during the inspection be the subject of a prior understanding between the Allied governments and Germany. By reserving the methods of inspection for negotiation, the cabinet hoped to prevent inspection of the army's barracks facilities and its organization of cadres. Seeckt expressed dissatisfaction with the cabinet compromise, for he foresaw that the German conditions would be rejected. He asked if, in this eventuality, the government would be prepared to oppose Allied inspection altogether. The cabinet members tried very hard to beg his questions, but it was clear that ultimately they would acquiesce to the Allied demands.[46]

Despite Seeckt's objections, the German note was delivered to the Conference of Ambassadors on June 30, 1924. The Allied answer confirmed Seeckt's prediction. The reply, which was issued on July 8 under Herriot's signature, noted with satisfaction that Germany had accepted the inspection but denied that the Allies had any obligation to discuss with the German government either the time of the inspection or the means to be used. The inspection would begin as soon as possible and would employ methods that would be consonant with the spirit of understanding that had prompted the Herriot-MacDonald note. All suggestions advanced by the German government would be examined and observed to the extent the Allies deemed possible.[47]

Stresemann's efforts to defuse Nationalist criticism by attaching Seeckt to the government's response to the Allied demands for an inspection had failed. The Nationalists now sharpened their attacks upon the government's foreign policy. Acting as the party's spokesman during Chairman Hergt's absence from Berlin, Count Westarp had prepared a denunciation of the Herriot-MacDonald note of June 22, but he had not released it for publication.[48] The Allied answer of July 8, however, offered an opportunity to mount a personal attack against Stresemann which could not be passed up. Accordingly, Westarp prepared and published an open letter from the DNVP Reichstag delegation to the foreign minister, charging him with having failed to carry to a successful conclusion the policy that had been outlined by the cabinet in its note of June 30 to the Ambassadors Conference: Stresemann's earlier assurances—namely, that bearing the affront to German honor, which military control denoted, would bring advantage in the Dawes negotiations, especially in the Ruhr and Rhineland—had proved without foundation. "Herr Minister, the hour has come," the letter challenged, "to free Germany from the disgrace of military control. . . . We challenge the government . . . not to permit the control operation." The letter further warned that responsibility for the domestic repercussions and for incidents that would surely accompany any permission to make an inspection would rest solely upon Stresemann.[49]

Westarp was fully aware that this letter contradicted the private negotiations that were being carried on between members of the moderate wing of the party and the government. But he believed that until negotiations regarding the Dawes plan had been completed, it would be difficult to realize the present ambitions and machinations aimed at bringing the DNVP into the government. Even though Westarp had heard that "Stresemann and his people, Maltzahn [*sic*], Schubert, and Kypke [*sic*]," who were leading foreign-office personnel, were favorably disposed to the inclusion of the DNVP, he did not believe that the party could get a guarantee that Stresemann and the new chancellor, or even the Center Party, would reject the Dawes plan in the event that the military evacuation were not achieved. It was highly improbable that the evacuation could be won, Westarp thought, and he doubted that DNVP participation in the cabinet could improve the prospects for it.[50]

The public attack by the DNVP was well timed to embarrass Stresemann and to disrupt the cabinet's efforts to win the support of the moderate wing of the DNVP for the Dawes negotiations, because events of the few days preceding the publication of the party's open letter to the foreign minister had materially weakened Germany's diplomatic position. Ever since the Herriot-MacDonald note, French nationalists had been protesting that Herriot had been tricked by Britain's prime minister into abandoning the sacrosanctity of the Treaty of Versailles. Just two days before the publication of the DNVP's letter, Poincaré had led an attack upon Herriot in the French Senate, insisting that even under the Dawes plan, no French government could surrender its right to take independent action in the face of a future German default in its reparations obligations. His speech had the ring of the logic behind the Ruhr action. Under Poincaré's influence, the French Senate passed a motion expressing its "confidence" that the Herriot government would insist upon complete fidelity to the Treaty of Versailles in its negotiations regarding the reparations and security settlements.[51]

The action of the French Senate undermined the German position both at home and in the diplomatic arena. Herriot's own domestic position was so threatened that Stresemann informed his cabinet colleagues that Herriot seemed to have lost his nerve regarding reconciliation with Germany. The French premier claimed to be engaged in a fight for survival against attacks on him by Poincaré. He insisted that any declaration on his part concerning evacuation of the Ruhr was absolutely out of the question. Furthermore, his government could never survive the slightest hint that the Dawes negotiations represented a modification of the Versailles settlement. The plan was solely a new method of payment to be administered by the existing Allied reparations commission. Herriot also indicated that the German government would be invited to negotiations in London concerning the Dawes plan only after the Reichstag had approved the laws that would be necessary in order to enact that plan.[52]

If the German government were forced, as Herriot wished, to seek Reichstag approval of the domestic legislation necessary for the implementation of the Dawes plan, it would be robbed of one of its strongest arguments in its campaign to gain the support of the moderate Nationalists. The government had already laid plans to draft the necessary legislation as soon as possible but to delay the introduction of it into the Reichstag until after the government had negotiated the Dawes agreements with the Allies. In this manner, Stresemann would be in a position to go to the London conference and say, in effect, to the Allies: "You have the German *govern-*

ment's unconditional acceptance of the Dawes plan in principle, but this is of little practical value unless the legislation necessary to implement the plan passes the Reichstag; we must return with significant concessions concerning matters touching German honor in order to command the votes we need." Thus the burden of choice between intransigence and compromise would be placed upon the Allies, whereas the logic of a mutual adjustment of interests would work to Germany's advantage. By the same token, if the concessions were granted, the cabinet could point in its Reichstag negotiations to its positive accomplishments on the questions of honor and could perhaps force a split in the DNVP by placing the moderates in a position in which defeat of the legislation necessitated by the Dawes plan would forfeit the gains associated with it. To demand a vote on the draft legislation before going to London would not only cost the government the additional leverage that it sought in its negotiations with both the Allies and the DNVP; this action would also expose the government to the risk that the Reichstag would burden the German negotiators with political conditions to be met by the Allies in London, a factor that would seriously jeopardize any settlement.[53]

The diplomatic delays arising from Herriot's position and the efforts by Germany, Great Britain, and the United States to overcome the renewed French obstinacy forced the German cabinet to revise its tactics with regard to the domestic debate and presented the DNVP with an additional opportunity to harass the government. Stresemann had expected that Germany would be invited to London for the final negotiations on the Dawes plan with the Allies in mid July and that he would return—after having satisfactorily negotiated the political demands that he would argue were necessary in order to obtain Reichstag approval of the plan—in time to present the draft legislation to the Reichstag before the end of the month. The parties in the Reichstag had been informed of this schedule, and consultations between them and the government had been arranged accordingly, when Stresemann learned that France was insisting upon delaying the invitation to Germany until complete concord had been restored among the Allies. The German cabinet was suddenly faced with Reichstag consultations that were extremely ill-timed, since they would come before Germany actually received the invitation to join the Allies in London, and in a situation that would make it seem as though the Allies were once again lining up together to present Germany with a nonnegotiable package that she would either have to accept or reject.[54]

The cabinet, in an effort to head off the full-scale debate on foreign policy in the Reichstag that it had scheduled for the end of July, met with party leaders on July 22 amidst new pressure from the DNVP to modify the direction of its foreign policy. In the course of the consultations, DNVP Chairman Hergt insisted that the government's delegation take parliamentary directives with it to London. His immediate concern, he pointed out, was with the inclusion of his party's demands relative to such directives. He granted that the Nationalists might be willing to forego a Reichstag debate on these demands if they could be assured that German negotiators would accept the demands without such a debate. He observed, however, that if there were determined opposition in the Reichstag, this might strengthen the government's bargaining position in London more than would the more muted opposition that compromise outside the assembly would bring.[55]

Hergt's suggestion concerning the value of vocal opposition seems to parallel rather closely Stresemann's own expressed intention, because of the necessity to swing votes, to demand concessions from the Allies.[56] The difference between them lies once again in the German Nationalists' desire to impose preconditions for the negotiation of the Dawes settlement. The cabinet was quite explicit about its insistence that satisfaction regarding the issue of evacuation was an aim of the negotiations, not a prerequisite. The government refused to be placed in the position of insisting that the occupied territories be evacuated before Germany would implement the Dawes legislation.[57]

The DNVP demands to which Hergt had alluded were not long in appearing in the public forum. Published in the press simultaneously with the government's report on the consultations with the parties, the demands covered seven points:

1. Germany must refuse to participate in any way in the London conference unless the Allies recognized her as a fully equal partner in all discussions.

2. France must grant total amnesty in the occupied territories to all prisoners whose offenses had grown out of the Ruhr action.

3. Economic and military withdrawal from the so-called sanction areas must take place immediately.

4. German administrative sovereignty in the occupied Rhineland must be restored, and recognition must be given that the occupation dated from January 10, 1920. (France contended that, due to German default in her other treaty obligations, the term of occupation had not yet begun.)

5. Assurances must be given that there would be no future imposition of sanctions by the Allies.

6. Demands that were unrealizable or that constituted affronts to German dignity or independence must be rejected.

7. The war-guilt clauses of the treaty must be disavowed.[58]

Acceptance of the DNVP demands would have meant a complete surrender of the diplomatic flexibility that Stresemann and the government had been trying to maintain. Stresemann thus sought to head off an open discussion of the DNVP program by replying to it point by point in the secret proceedings of the July 23 meeting of the Reichstag's Foreign Affairs Committee.[59] He indicated that the party's first point (*Gleichberechtigung*, or equality of rights) was part and parcel of the government's policy. This was undeniable. The cabinet had already agreed, at Stresemann's own suggestion, that Germany would accept an invitation to come to the London meeting only if she were to be treated as a partner in the official negotiations.[60] By this time, moreover, Stresemann was confident that American and British pressure was forcing Herriot to make some accommodation and that Germany would be accorded the equal treatment that the Nationalists were demanding.[61] As for the rest of the DNVP's demands, Stresemann insisted that the Nationalists would have to trust in the discretion of the German negotiators to raise them should this be possible under the circumstances prevailing in London when the German delegation arrived. He assured the Nationalists, however, that their demands stood "in so inseparable a connection with the experts' report that we could place our signature on this report only in the event that we have complete clarity on these points."[62]

Stresemann then outlined the government's position on each of the six remaining demands. The government and all the Reichstag parties were of one mind on the point that, with the acceptance of the Dawes plan, all political prisoners would have to be released (point 2). For the ultimate realization of a settlement, military evacuation (point 3) was also an essential factor. Stresemann had consistently insisted that evacuation be pressed in the negotiations as a concession that the Allies would have to make before the Reichstag would pass legislation to implement the Dawes plan. He knew that the London negotiations gave Germany a certain added leverage, because the Allies wanted "a voluntary signature" from Germany and would go far to achieve this aim.[63] Moreover, he now informed the Foreign Affairs Committee that the American financial representatives at London had taken up Germany's cause and had insisted that Germany leave the matter in their hands. Stresemann pointed out that the Americans, whose financial power would influence all the parties at London, could plead Germany's case with the greatest chance of success if Germany herself refrained from arousing the nationalistic sensitivities of the French. He assured the Nationalists that the government had made its interest in this question clear to all the participating parties. He maintained, nevertheless, that the American approach represented Germany's best hope. In relation to the Nationalists' sixth demand—that Germany reject all unrealizable or disgraceful obligations—Stresemann observed that the legislation to implement the Dawes plan, which the government would lay before the Reichstag, could only be accepted or rejected *in toto,* just as was the case with commercial treaties. It could not be picked over in an effort to isolate its more or less favorable aspects. Stresemann assured the Nationalists that the fourth demand, regarding the beginning date of the occupation of the Rhineland areas that had been designated by the treaty, would be cleared up in London. Finally, the German government had made it perfectly clear to the Allies that by accepting the Dawes plan, Germany would not thereby be admitting any war guilt, which the Versailles Treaty accused her of. The government planned to demand in London that an international tribunal be formed to study the question of war guilt, but the form and manner of this demand had to be left to the discretion of the government's delegation.[64]

Stresemann's explanations failed to placate the Nationalists. Hergt rejected the foreign minister's defense of the government's policy as being inadequate in view of the demands of his party. He noted particularly that Stresemann had failed to give a forthright assurance that the Dawes plan would be rejected if Germany's conditions—by which he meant the DNVP's conditions—were not met *prior* to the enactment of the plan. He also accused the Marx cabinet of an inability or unwillingness to seize the initiative in the negotiations with the Allies.[65]

Faced with this seeming intransigence on the part of the DNVP, the cabinet tried to map a strategy by which it could avoid public debate. Its plan was to try to convince the SPD to join the government parties in tabling the Reichstag discussion for the time being. The cabinet even raised the possibility of invoking Article 48 of the Weimar Constitution, which would have allowed the government both to by-pass the Reichstag and to continue to govern by presidential decree.[66]

An open Reichstag debate became unavoidable, however. So the governmental parties prepared a statement which was designed to steal some of the Nationalists' thunder. Delivered in the Reichstag by Centrist delegate Fehrenbach on July 25, the statement expressed approval of the cabinet's foreign policy of seeking a reparations settlement on the basis of the Dawes report. The statement continued:

> If the goal [of settlement] is to be achieved, then the report cannot be put into effect only to the extent that it imposes new burdens on Germany. Rather, allowances must be made for those considerations which the report takes of Germany's situation.
>
> As a prerequisite of Germany's ability to pay, the experts designated the reestablishment, throughout the entire state, of economic and

financial sovereignty. Therefore, the territories occupied beyond the limits of the Treaty of Versailles must be evacuated economically and militarily, the Treaty accords must be reestablished in the older occupied territories, the prisoners must be freed, the banished must be reinstated, and security against further arbitrary interventions in German sovereignty . . . must be given. . . . We have confidence that the government will enter upon the London negotiations in this spirit, and [we] are ready to support her with all our power in the continuation of her policies pursued so responsibly thus far.[67]

It must have been with a certain glee that the German Nationalists listened to Fehrenbach's speech. In reply, Professor Otto Hoetzsch of the DNVP noted, with evident satisfaction, the deep indebtedness of the speech to the seven demands of his own party. Hoetzsch continued by reiterating these and insisting that each demand constituted a *"conditio sine qua non* [which] must be regulated beforehand; otherwise the entry into negotiations [in London] is not possible." He further insisted that his party held fast to the necessity of a two-thirds majority in order to pass the legislation designed to implement the Dawes plan. He referred to the parliamentary situation, which made DNVP votes indispensable to such a majority, and he concluded with the promise that his party would stand united in opposition to any accord that did not include the DNVP's "minimum demands."[68]

The DNVP's decision to insist upon a two-thirds vote for the enacting legislation corresponded to the cabinet's own choice in the matter. The question of whether or not any of the proposed legislation effected a change in the constitution had been under discussion all summer long. It was clear from reports made by Reichsbank president Hjalmar Schacht as early as May 3, 1924, and from Stresemann's diplomatic soundings that both the international financial community, particularly the British and American representatives, and the French political leaders put great stock in seeing the Dawes legislation enacted with overwhelming Reichstag support.[69] Diplomatic pressure was thus all in favor of the two-thirds vote.

The question of the constitutional necessity for a weighted majority vote was less clear. The state secretary of the Ministry of Justice could only observe that a simple majority would leave serious question about the constitutionality of the enabling law.[70] When the issue was raised by the German Nationalists in a June meeting of the Reichstag's Foreign Affairs Committee, Stresemann was either unable or unwilling to give a straight answer. He expressed his personal inclination toward the view that a two-thirds vote was necessary, but he noted that judicial opinion was divided on the matter. In any event, he declared, the cabinet's final decision would come only after the specific legislation had been drafted.[71]

When this decision did come, on July 21, 1924, it was motivated more by political than by constitutional considerations. Schacht's insistence upon the importance of the two-thirds vote in securing the loan that would come with the Dawes plan was the determinative factor. But the cabinet was also aware that it could turn this foreign political necessity to its own domestic advantage. Marx was still banking on the likelihood that certain DNVP delegates would vote for the plan if the two-thirds vote were demanded, rather than see the plan rejected[72]. The cabinet's final decision was therefore based on the unanimous view that a two-thirds majority was politically imperative because of both domestic and foreign considerations, regardless of whether it was judicially necessary.[73]

The government's willingness, even eagerness, to face a two-thirds vote on the Dawes legislation took some of the force out of the DNVP's attack in the Reichstag. The Nationalists, in fact, were in far more trouble than they realized. Throughout the summer, the DNVP's leaders had failed to give their party adherents a clear-cut choice between the policy of accommodation with the government and the policy of intransigent opposition. The party had alternately struck one pose, then another. Neither the seven demands nor the final Reichstag rhetoric could conceal this basic failure of the party leadership. The government, on the other hand, had worked consistently to apply pressure to the moderates in the DNVP, hoping to gain their support in the showdown vote on the Dawes plan. The government's consistence and diligence were to pay off when the German negotiators returned from London.

3

FROM THE DAWES PLAN
TO THE DECEMBER ELECTIONS

The Dawes Conference began for Germany—at long last—on August 5, 1924, when the German delegation, led by Marx, Stresemann, and Finance Minister Hans Luther, was greeted upon its arrival in London by the British prime minister, Ramsay MacDonald. The conference had opened on July 16, but the early days had been devoted to negotiations among the Allies themselves. This had awakened the anxiety among the Germans that they would face, in effect, a new ultimatum. The cordiality of MacDonald's welcoming speech dispelled these fears, however, and inspired immediate confidence that Germany, as a fully sovereign and independent equal in the negotiations, was to be accorded the treatment that was so important to her sense of honor.[1]

The overriding problem in the minds of the German negotiators at London was the question of the evacuation of the Ruhr. For the German nation, acceptance or rejection of the entire Dawes plan was likely to hinge upon this point.[2] In the negotiations among the Allies that had preceded the invitation to Germany to come to London, French Premier Herriot had sought assurances that the Ruhr issue would not be raised because of the domestic difficulties that discussion of it would cause him. But the German delegation was determined to bring the matter up, and MacDonald had encouraged the Germans to do so, if only in private conversations with Herriot.[3] In these initial conversations, which were conducted outside the official sphere of the conference negotiations, Herriot urged that the Germans postpone any open request for the evacuation of the Ruhr until after the Allies had concluded their military inspection and control, which was then just beginning. Such a procedure was necessary so that Herriot could confidently assure his countrymen, especially his political critics, that French security was not threatened by Germany in her present state of disarmament. At the same time, he raised the possibility of a broader discussion of mutual guarantees of Rhineland security, such as Germany had suggested under the Cuno government at the beginning of the Ruhr action.[4] The Germans could not postpone the Ruhr issue, however, and MacDonald's sympathy with their point of view made it impossible to exclude the question from the more formal negotiations of the Dawes plan. The German delegation's insistence stemmed in large part from the realization that it would be impossible to obtain political approval of the Dawes plan, especially by any part of the DNVP, unless Germany gained a secure commitment to evacuate the Ruhr.

Herriot's diplomatic flexibility was limited by his domestic situation in much the same way as was Germany's. Herriot himself argued with his cabinet that France had always defended her Ruhr action by claiming that it was aimed at securing economic guarantees from Germany. To maintain the military occupation of the Ruhr, when the Dawes plan was designed to ensure just such economic guarantees, would expose France to the charge of hypocrisy and would bring down on her the hostility of the entire international community.[5] But the group that held the prevalent view within the French cabinet was directly opposed to Herriot on this matter. Supported by the military and the French nationalists, this group argued that France could not afford to evacuate the Ruhr until she had established effective control over the future potential of that area to produce war materials. This would involve linking eventual evacuation to continuing military inspection and control.[6] The French premier was thus bound, by instructions from his cabinet, to press for a close association between the Ruhr occupation, on the one hand, and French security, on the other.

The German negotiators, however, were compelled to reject any coupling of the Ruhr evacuation with either military control or French security. Such discussions would be "parliamentarily impossible" for any German government.[7] Marx and Stresemann, who were anxious to see evacuation begin immediately, had long been aware that logistics and politics might delay the termination of the occupation of the Ruhr. They were therefore prepared to accept, as politically tolerable, the fact that the complete and final liberation of the Ruhr might be postponed for a period of from five to an absolute maximum of nine months. The Germans thus appeared thunderstruck when Herriot proposed that a full year elapse before the Ruhr withdrawal even be started and that evacuation be completed by stages over the course of a second year. More he could not offer. Emotionally, he pleaded for the other delegates to understand that any further concession would bring down his government, a fall that would be a grave misfortune for the cause of European peace and reconciliation. Unmoved, Stresemann declared that the proposal was wholly unacceptable. He insisted that such an agreement would never command, for legislation to implement the Dawes plan, the two-thirds majority that it would require in order to be passed by the Reichstag. (Stresemann insisted upon the legal, and avoided mention of the political, necessity.) Despite the sharpness of his protest, Stresemann strove to preserve the friendly and conciliatory spirit that had characterized the negotiations thus far. In fact, he appealed to this spirit of conciliation in a manner that was well designed both to flatter Herriot's own predilections toward international peace and to allay the fears of the French nationalists. Stresemann spoke of the greater significance of the negotiations regarding the Dawes plan, which he claimed to have made the touchstone of his defense of the cabinet's foreign policy. He had argued constantly before the skeptics in his own country that the plan's merits lay less in the resolution of the questions of finance than in its establishment of a new basis for the relations among peoples. The maintenance of the military occupation of the Ruhr, however, would rob him of this, his strongest defense of reconciliation. Some compromise had to be worked out, he avowed, "because we must be able to prove to the German people that the Dawes plan does not mean a new stage in the struggle, but rather a return to peace *on the basis of the Versailles Treaty*."[8] Stresemann's invocation of the Treaty of Versailles seems to have startled no one.

The negotiations had reached a climactic and critical impasse. Hour after hour, in conferences that succeeded one another in rapid order, Herriot insisted that he had gone as far as he could, while the Germans insisted that this was not far enough. MacDonald commiserated with the Germans but declared that he was powerless to offer anything more than tacit moral support. Reichschancellor Marx informed a news conference that the breaking point was near.[9]

But the German position was more flexible than it appeared to be. For although the cabinet in Berlin, having been informed of the proposals, had publicly telegraphed its approval of the delegation's stand that one year was an unacceptable extension of the Ruhr occupation, it had secretly communicated its unanimous decision that the Dawes negotiations should not be broken off over the issue of the date of evacuation so long as a binding commitment to the fact of evacuation could be secured.[10] The situation built to a tense climax on August 14. The Germans proposed to accept the French formula of a "maximum [NB] delay of one year" if that year were calculated from April 9, 1924, the date of the completion of the Dawes Committee's report. Herriot rejected this proposal but countered by agreeing to date the year from the completion of the London Conference rather than from the date on which the plan would take effect—a prospective gain of about two months for Germany. Then Herriot went even further: in a tête-à-tête with Marx, he promised that France would evacuate certain cities and river ports along the Rhine, which had been occupied in conjunction with the Ruhr action. The French premier insisted, however, that this gesture of his good will be kept secret at all costs. With perhaps unbecoming candor, Marx pointed out that the restriction of secrecy would rob Herriot's gesture of any value in the German cabinet's attempts to gain the Nationalists' support for the Dawes plan in the Reichstag.[11]

Despite these concessions, the German delegation decided to send Finance Minister Luther back to Berlin to consult with the Reichspresident and the cabinet and to seek instructions. The announcement of this intention caused considerable consternation within the Allied camp. The French realized that such an interruption of the negotiations might be interpreted as a sign of the failure of the Dawes plan that would be attributable to their intransigence. MacDonald, suffering perceptibly from nervous strain, feared that even if negotiations were to resume, the resultant delay would leave him no time for the repose and vacation that his doctor so urgently recommended that he take.[12] All parties who were directly involved urged Marx to reconsider, holding out as an inducement the possibility of an immediate evacuation of the limited Rhineland areas mentioned by Herriot only that afternoon. In view of this, the German negotiators agreed to forego Luther's return and to contact their government in Berlin by telegram.[13]

The reaction in Berlin to the French offer of an immediate token evacuation was favorable. Vice-chancellor Jarres, who had the most conservative voice in the cabinet and was closest to the DNVP, noted with satisfaction that the conference results thus far exceeded his expectations. Still, several concessions would have to be pursued further. The cabinet therefore formulated a telegram which, "with heavy heart," approved acceptance of the French offer but urged that negotiations be continued in order to secure an internationally binding commitment on a date for evacuation of the Ruhr; a reduction in the total troop strength in the Rhineland that would be equal to the number of men withdrawn from the areas named by Herriot, as well as a general improvement in the administration of the occupation; and the guarantee that the ten-month extension of the Ruhr occupation would not be lengthened by a disloyal *(schikanöse)* handling of the question of military control or by other excuses. A number of lesser demands were included as well.[14]

The crisis was past. From the moment the German delegation received this telegram, the successful conclusion of the conference was assured. The cabinet's list of additional concessions could not be met in full, as both the government and the delegation realized. But the essential commitment to evacuation of the Ruhr was secured. An exchange of letters between the chancellors of France, Belgium, Germany, and England, which were published as annexes to the London Conference accords, gave formal expression to the agreement regarding evacuation of the Ruhr.

Before the final plenary session of the conference, the German delegation met to prepare Marx's closing speech and to include in it a statement on the issue of war guilt, another "point of honor" that the DNVP had raised. But Marx passed over this section in delivering his speech, because he had not had the occasion to discuss the matter privately with MacDonald during the final session as had been planned, a procedure that the German negotiators had followed on all the touchy diplomatic issues of the conference and that Marx felt he would be ill-advised to ignore as the negotiations approached a successful conclusion. Marx therefore decided to reserve the declaration for a private letter addressed to the British prime minister as chairman of the conference. The letter was prepared jointly by members of the delegation during their return trip to Berlin, and it was mailed en route. It was a more forceful and effective statement than the passage that had been prepared for the speech, expressing Germany's desire to have the question of the responsibility for the war submitted to an international tribunal, just as disputes arising out of the reparations question were now to be arbitrated. But the full impact of the delegation's rejection of Germany's sole guilt was diminished by the request that the letter "be treated confidentially for the time being."[15]

Now the way was clear for the battle in the Reichstag. Untrammeled by any fixed "preconditions" to negotiations such as the German Nationalists had tried to impose, the German delegation had conducted its diplomacy rather well. Germany had been accepted in London as a fully equal party to the negotiations. Despite strong opposition from within the French government, she had secured from Herriot a promise regarding the evacuation of the Ruhr, a promise that had also been endorsed by England. The negotiators had raised the questions, contained in the July demands published by the DNVP, concerning an amnesty for inhabitants of the Ruhr and a general amelioration of the administration of occupation in the Rhineland. Even the issue of war guilt had been raised and denounced in Marx's letter to MacDonald, albeit sotto voce. The delegation had gone to the limits of the possible and had conceded only when it seemed that further demands might break up the conference, thereby forfeiting what had already been gained. But the domestic problem remained: Was the possible enough to satisfy the DNVP?

Even after the German Nationalists' minimum conditions had been published late in July, the cabinet had remained confident that the DNVP would provide enough votes to pass the legislation for implementing the Dawes plan. After all, Stresemann argued, the very fact that the demands had been stated represented a change of attitude, from one of absolute opposition to the financial obligations of the plan to one that admitted the possibility of acceptance but demanded the satisfaction of German "honor" as its price.[16] Certainly, if this optimism were to be realized, it would be necessary to cultivate carefully those Nationalists who were either influential or favorably disposed, or both.[17] Accordingly, the government devoted considerable attention to keeping the Nationalists abreast of the negotiations even during the London Conference. The first secretary in the German Foreign Office, Baron Ago von Maltzan, met daily with the DNVP's foreign-policy specialist, Otto Hoetzsch.[18] Indeed, Maltzan was initially encouraged by his conversations with Hoetzsch over the party's reaction to the progress of the conference.[19] But as the London discussions of the Ruhr evacuation approached a deadlock, it became evident that the DNVP considered a year-long extension of the Ruhr occupation to be unacceptable.[20] Even within Stresemann's own German People's Party, the extension was causing considerable difficulty.[21]

Despite the DNVP's official posture, the government continued to be convinced that the necessary votes could be found. Its case was well served by the fact that while Marx was in London, Jarres, whose sympathies for the Nationalist point of view were known, was the cabinet's spokesman during the conference. In addition, the favorable attitude of German financial and industrial circles towards acceptance of the plan tended to make it more difficult to maintain a monolithic Nationalist opposition.[22]

Indicative of the tendency towards compromise within the DNVP leadership was a meeting that took place on August 15 between "two German Nationalist leaders" and one of the secretaries from the Reichschancellor's office, Franz Kempner. The Nationalists, who had sought out Jarres earlier in the day, presented Kempner with a number of "wishes" that they hoped to see fulfilled. The list closely paralleled the DNVP's earlier "minimum program." The two Nationalists pointed out that, of these wishes, the first two—a shortening of the duration of the Ruhr occupation and an international guarantee of a terminal date for it—would be decisive for the coming vote.[23]

At this point, opinion within the party ranged from absolute rejection of the Dawes plan to reserved acceptance of it as representing a distinct improvement in Germany's situation, both actually and potentially.[24] Even Admiral von Tirpitz, whose credentials as a nationalist seemed to be irreproachable, urged the party leadership to approach its final decision with great caution.[25]

Despite this wide variance of opinion, the party preserved a semblance of unity in its caucus of August 21, which was called in preparation for the Reichstag debates on the subject of what the government had accomplished in London. Here it voted nearly unanimously to reject the results of the London Conference as being unsatisfactory and to maintain its insistence upon its seven-point minimum program.[26]

Count Westarp, to whom the intransigent opponents of the plan looked as their ally in the leadership circle, believed that the party would have to defeat the government in the final vote. He saw little chance to obtain concessions that would be significant enough to change the resolve of his party's delegation. But party chairman Hergt continued to pursue the possibility of concessions, either from the government or from the foreign powers, which he thought might be pressured into modifying the accords on the Dawes plan so as to make them acceptable to the DNVP. He had broached the latter idea at a cocktail party with the American ambassador in Berlin, Alanson Houghton, and had been told, in broken but emphatic German, "Wenn Sie nicht accept the Dawes plan, hat Amerika kein Interesse mehr an Germany." Houghton added that renewed negotiations such as Hergt hoped to provoke were out of the question.[27] Still, Hergt continued to give the impression that the party might be won over if the proper price were paid, much to the chagrin of the intransigents and to the embarrassment of Count Westarp.[28]

The cabinet and the government parties recognized the divergence of tendencies within the German Nationalist Party. They were even encouraged by the DNVP statement of August 21, which some saw as a less adamant position than might have been expected. They therefore set out to cajole and threaten alternately, in an effort to win the needed votes from the Nationalists.[29] Both the DVP and the Center Party approached the DNVP with offers of a rightist coalition in return for passage.[30] On the other hand, the government threatened to dissolve the Reichstag and to hold new elections if the needed legislation failed to gain the necessary majority. Moreover, the cabinet announced that it planned to sign the final accords for the Dawes plan on August 30 in London even without a two-thirds Reichstag vote on the legislation.[31]

The government pressures began to produce movement within the Nationalist ranks. At the last minute, the conservative agricultural association, the Reichslandbund, which was still seeking government support for its proposals regarding protective tariffs, urged the DNVP to ratify the Dawes legislation and to join the government.[32] Attracted by the prospects of foreign credit and of a rightist coalition over which its influence would be strong, the Reichslandbund released its members from any obligation to oppose the Dawes legislation during the Reichstag vote. Since 52 of the DNVP's 106 delegates belonged to this agrarian organization, the Reichslandbund's recommendation was bound to have an important impact.[33]

Also from high within the army, that bastion of nationalistic respectability, came pressures to move the Nationalists toward approval of the Dawes plan. Both Seeckt and his political liaison officer, Schleicher, who had been involved throughout the summer in consultations to bring the DNVP into the government, actively worked to persuade enough Nationalist delegates to vote for approval so as to ensure the needed two-thirds majority. Seeckt was convinced not only that the plan had financial merits but, more relevantly, that rejection of it would seriously complicate the army's dealings with the Interallied Military Control Commission, which was renewing its activity.[34]

Despite the growing pressure, Hergt still, as a matter of policy, opposed having any of the DNVP's Reichstag delegates approve the legislation unless the party could win further concessions to its official point of view. He hoped to disarm the Nationalist moderates, who were pressing the party to compromise, by indicating in his conversation with the government that his party's position was not one of totally unconstructive rejection of any and all accord with the victors of 1918, but rather was one of constructive opposition to this particular accord, which so offended Germany's dignity and economic self-interest. Hergt wanted to establish the impression that it was the government's intransigence—its refusal to hold out for necessary and legitimate concessions from the Allies—that was at fault.[35] But Hergt only succeeded in further beclouding the situation for his own party's followers by provoking the extreme wing and by fostering the moderates' hope that compromise was still possible.

Hergt's Reichstag speech of August 25 established no clearer course than had his conduct of confidential exchanges. True, it formally rejected the Dawes plan as it stood, but it also contained an expressed and strongly implied ambivalence toward this decision, which encouraged renewed efforts to win the DNVP over.[36]

Until August 27, both Hergt and Westarp remained unaware of how far out of hand this vacillation by the party between policies of fundamental opposition and possible acceptance had allowed the situation to get. On that morning, just two days before the crucial vote on the Dawes legislation was to take place, a delegation from the moderate group informed Hergt that about thirty of the DNVP's representatives in the Reichstag, including every one from the occupied territories and a number who were connected with influential economic organizations, were prepared to approve the plan.[37]

Still, Hergt seems not to have believed that these delegates would defy party discipline, if it were demanded on the Reichstag floor, unless enough other votes could be mustered from within the DNVP's ranks to ensure the two-thirds majority needed to pass the enabling legislation for the Dawes plan. He was, however, alarmed enough to seek immediate approval within the DNVP of a procedure that would prevent a further erosion of party unity. Hergt—who was still committed to the plan of trying to force a renewal of the international negotiations, a tactic that was now accepted by Count Westarp as well[38]—suggested, in a meeting of provincial party leaders, that the DNVP propose an amendment to the Dawes legislation that would make the execution *(Inkraftsetzen)* of the legislation dependent upon the acceptance by the Allies of the party's old "indispensable conditions." If the amendment were rejected by the government, the DNVP representatives could vote unanimously against the legislation. The onus of intransigence would thus have been shifted to the cabinet. Hergt's suggestion won overwhelming endorsement from the chairmen of the local party committees *(Landesverbandsvorsitzende)*. But in the meeting with the party's Reichstag delegation it became evident that the new procedure was less enthusiastically embraced. Still, Hergt's impression was that an "overwhelming majority" of the delegation approved his compromise tactics.[39] On the next day, however, August 28, the German People's Party intervened with a letter to the Nationalist delegation, formally renewing an earlier offer to bring the party into the government in exchange for cooperation on the passage of the legislation to implement the Dawes plan. Later that same day, representatives of the Center Party reiterated their own similar offer.[40]

Hergt felt that he could not simply ignore these new developments. More was at stake, he later argued in his own defense, than simply mollifying moderate opinion, since even the elements in the party that took it for granted that the delegation would reject the Dawes plan were urging that subsequent accommodation be made in order to permit quick entry into the cabinet after the vote.[41] Hergt therefore decided to discuss the proposals made by the DVP and the Center Party, although he doubted that the moment was propitious. But to secure the sort of preponderant influence that he deemed to be necessary, Hergt demanded that both the chancellorship and the Prussian government be delivered to the Nationalists. This remained, however, more than the coalition parties were willing to concede.[42]

Simultaneously, Hergt was engaged in talks with Stresemann, who seemed to be prepared to issue a public renunciation of the charge of Germany's war guilt and to accept certain other Nationalist principles regarding foreign policy.[43] The army may have been instrumental in setting up these talks;[44] but here, too, Hergt's reach exceeded his grasp, although he seems not to have realized this. He thought that he had secured a promise from Stresemann that the issue of war guilt would be raised again in London by the German ambassador; but, in fact, Stresemann had only agreed to discuss that possibility with the cabinet, whose ultimate decision was that the matter should be brought up by means of a Reichstag declaration from the chancellor after the vote on the Dawes plan rather than through more formal diplomatic channels.[45] The declaration that Marx issued immediately after the vote on the Dawes plan was a disappointment to the Nationalists both in its content and in the manner of its publication.[46]

Hergt's machinations continued down to the very day of the crucial vote. That morning he once again asked Marx if the latter were prepared to meet the DNVP's conditions. Marx's negative reply evoked Hergt's assurance that the Nationalist delegation would defeat the Dawes legislation and that this would bring down the government. Hergt quickly called a caucus to instruct the party representatives that all efforts to win concessions had failed and that it was thus their duty to vote against the plan.[47]

The August 29 vote on the Dawes legislation—in particular the balloting on the railroad law, for which a two-thirds majority had been demanded —was one of the most "dramatically charged votes ever experienced in the German Reichstag."[48] The outcome remained uncertain throughout the proceedings. The German Nationalists emerged from their caucus just as the assembly was being reconvened for the final series of votes. All the other delegates, the press, and the galleries focused their attention on the Nationalists alone. As the president of the assembly announced the commencement of the final round of voting, a strained silence filled the hall. First the amendment proposals were voted upon; then votes were taken on each piece of legislation that the government had laid before the Reichstag. The railroad bill was the seventh in this package. In each case, the voting was to proceed by roll call. During the first six roll-call votes, all of which gave the government bills comfortable simple majorities, the onlookers tried to calculate how many extra votes would be needed in order to carry the railroad law by a two-thirds vote of the delegates present. The question in every mind was: Would the DNVP delegation provide enough votes, or would it perhaps send enough representatives out of the hall so that the legislation could be passed by the reduced assemblage? During the preliminary voting, the Nationalists held repeated consultations within their delegation. Straw votes showed them that a united front was impossible.[49] The agitation within the Nationalist delegation increased and ran throughout the hall.

The tension reached its peak as the vote on the railroad bill began. Each delegate deposited his personal ballot—red for no; white for yes. At first, only red ballots were seen as the German Nationalists voted. Only as the balloting was ending did the white cards appear, one after the other, "a true symphony in white, held shamefully hidden down to the last second." So rapidly had the white cards appeared that the onlookers were unable to take a count. The National Socialists and the Communists began to clamor uproariously. Scornful jeers were hurled at the Right, "where the German Nationalists stood with lowered gaze."[50]

The total number of delegates who had deposited ballots was 441, making 294 votes necessary for passage. The moment the results were read —314 affirmative votes—the assembly burst into disorder. Communists and National Socialists brayed insults at the DNVP; mocking cries arose from the Social Democrats. Only the German National People's Party sat mute. Of its 100 delegates present, 48 had voted for adoption.

Once again, as in May, the DNVP had allowed a position on foreign policy to obstruct its domestic development. Once again the party leadership had failed to profit from a position of apparent strength. The absence of a clear-cut policy in times of crisis and the ostensible readiness to compromise without a concomitant realization of the limits of the terms that would make compromise possible had encouraged a split within the Nationalist delegation that could not be repaired by simple appeals to party solidarity. The truly radical nationalists would never have voted for the plan, even if the caucus had gone against them.[51] The moderates, for their part, refused to see their hopes—so long fostered by the negotiations with the government—dashed at the last instant.

Imperatives of foreign policy had preempted the domestic balance, allowing the government to exploit the situation to its own advantage in a way that the DNVP seemed to be incapable of doing. The necessity of a two-thirds vote for the railroad law had been at best constitutionally questionable. But the demands by the Allied financiers for a sign of overwhelming endorsement as a tacit condition of the Dawes loan, plus the chance to force upon the German Nationalists some of the weight of responsibility for an unpopular but necessary decision regarding foreign policy, made the two-thirds vote a tactical measure that was universally accepted within the cabinet. Since the opposition of the DNVP could not be avoided, it might as well be used. Indeed, it was not unwelcome to Stresemann, as long as it did not either bind the German delegation to a rigid posture in negotiations or threaten the final acceptance of the Dawes plan. He could not, of course, be sure beforehand whether these pitfalls would be avoidable. Opposition was useful inasmuch as it added an element of urgency to demands that represented fundamental aims of his own foreign policy: namely, the evacuation of the Ruhr and the Rhineland and the abandonment of unilateral sanctions. In fact, Stresemann had dramatically timed a request for additional concessions from France as the August Reichstag debates drew to a close. Just two days before the vote, he had telegraphed Paris, arguing that some further timely gesture of French good will was needed in order to gain the few votes that were still necessary for passage of the legislation.[52] Although the pressure of the need for Nationalist votes in the Reichstag did not get Stresemann all that he wanted, both he and the entire cabinet believed that Germany had gained the maximum that was compatible with the preservation of the international atmosphere of understanding that encouraged accommodation rather than confrontation.

That atmosphere was almost destroyed by one point, however, the issue of war guilt; and the situation was rescued only by the resolute inaction of one man: State Secretary Ago von Maltzan. In the waning hours of its struggle to win DNVP support in the Reichstag, the cabinet had agreed to issue a statement that would reject the imputation that Germany was guilty of starting the war and had promised that foreign governments would receive an official notification of the German position.[53] Stresemann and the cabinet had assumed that the notification would take place immediately upon the release of the statement, and Stresemann had left Berlin on vacation with that understanding. But the statement was released to the press late in the evening of August 29 and did not appear until the next day, in the Saturday-morning newspapers. Maltzan, who was in charge of the Foreign Office during Stresemann's absence, ordered the preparation of the necessary dispatches to Germany's diplomatic delegations, but he found "technical and diplomatic reasons" for delaying the actual execution of the step. Vindication of the wisdom of Maltzan's decision came swiftly. On Sunday, the French Foreign Office issued a press notice that any German note regarding war guilt would provoke "the necessary official answer." The French press raised its own cry against the German announcement of an impending note. The French, English, Italian, and Belgian representatives in Berlin counseled the Germans against making the move. On Monday, September 1, Maltzan sent a letter to Stresemann, requesting that he be permitted a short delay before notifying the foreign governments officially, and Stresemann telegraphed his approval the next day. Maltzan then forwarded the note to the embassies in London, Paris, Rome, and Brussels; but it was to be communicated to those governments only a week later, on September 8. In the meantime, in an effort to restore diplomatic calm, he urged Chancellor Marx to send personal and private letters to both Herriot and MacDonald in order to explain the necessity for the step. The effect was quite the opposite. In reply, MacDonald stated, even more strongly than in his earlier letter of August 22,[54] that everything that he had sought to achieve for the betterment of Germany's international position would be "knocked on the head" by a German note concerning war guilt. He urgently requested that the German government reconsider this step, "which would be a catastrophe for Germany and for the world." In the face of the mounting pressure against the note, the cabinet authorized Maltzan to delay the diplomatic communication again, this time indefinitely. Despite subsequent pressure from the Nationalists and from the Bavarian state government, the matter remained dormant for some time.[55] Maltzan's determined dilatoriness thus prevented a major diplomatic faux pas.

The DNVP derived no benefit, however, from the government's failure to press the issue of war guilt. The party remained preoccupied by the instability and uncertainty within its own midst which had been provoked by the split over the Dawes plan. Nationalists stood divided into two camps: the *Ja-Sager* ("yes-sayers"), who had voted for the plan, and the *Nein-Sager* ("no-sayers"), who had voted against it. Charges were leveled from the party's right wing that the leadership had connived to ensure that there would be enough yes votes for passage, while maintaining its public posture of opposition.[56] Hergt's leadership was fully discredited. Confidence between the party organization in the provinces and the Reichstag delegation in Berlin was so shaken that it was never completely restored. The Nein-Sager considered leaving the party to form their own organization. Indeed, the Pan-German League, while rejecting an open break, set out, as a result of the Dawes vote, to "purify" the party. Its leaders planned to establish their own influence in the local party committees, hoping eventually to force a transfer of power from the central party organization in Berlin, where the influence of the moderates was pronounced, to the provincial committees, which they would control, a tactic that they exploited during the Locarno crisis of October 1925.[57]

Hergt tried to placate his critics by forming a temporary committee to allow "all wishes and tendencies within the party and the *Fraktion* a voice" in coming decisions. It consisted of Max Wallraf, Wilhelm Laverrenz, Hans von Goldacker, and Walther von Keudell. The moderates, however, still hoped to gain some compensation from the government for their defection. They continued to press for entry into the cabinet, not only because of their desire to oversee the execution of the Dawes plan and to reorient government policy in a more nationalistic sense, but also because of a belief that the DNVP could not be held together any longer if it remained in "unqualified opposition."[58]

Count Westarp still maintained his position between the two wings of the party. Though he had been intimately involved in the negotiations that led to the disastrous split, he had voted against the Dawes plan, and many of the Nein-Sager preserved their confidence in him. In answer to their attacks on Hergt, he urged them to wait for a clearer explanation of events and to honor, at least for the time being, that "principle of authority" which was so fundamentally a part of the nationalistic outlook.[59] At the same time, he was courted by the party moderates, urged not to deny the party and the country his services, and requested to accept the Ministry of the Interior if the negotiations with the government bore fruit.[60] Westarp expressed serious reservations and skepticism concerning coalition negotiations at this time. He doubted that the government would now be willing to make the sort of concessions to nationalist influence that it had refused to make before the vote on the Dawes plan. The trumps were all played out. Westarp agreed with the moderates that the party must follow the path of power and that it was necessary for the party to recognize the legislation that had already been passed. But he felt that the party could not publicly embrace the present foreign policy and must therefore continue for the moment to oppose the "impossible and insupportable burdens" that this policy imposed.[61]

In contrast to Westarp, the majority of the DNVP's Reichstag delegates still thought that cooperation with the government from inside the cabinet was the most effective means of exercising a powerful nationalistic influence on German policy.[62] In an effort to prepare the way for coalition negotiations, the DNVP delegation issued a statement, which acknowledged the Dawes legislation as "binding laws that must be carried out" and which asserted its own obligation "to assure itself influence in the interpretation, operation, and improvement of these laws."[63]

The government parties were as divided among themselves on the advisability of an opening to the Right as the DNVP was divided within itself. Some reproached Hergt and Westarp because of what they considered to be their inexcusable duplicity in posing as intransigent opponents of the plan when they had expressed themselves to be quite willing to accept it if only the price were right.[64] This mistrust was most manifest in the left wings of the Center and the German Democratic parties. The German People's Party, however, viewed the rightist coalition as the only combination that was likely to secure a Reichstag majority. It therefore presented Chancellor Marx with a party resolution urging a widening of the cabinet to include the DNVP.[65]

The negotiations that followed the DVP *démarche* fell into two distinct phases. In the first, conducted between October 1 and 9, Marx sought to include the Social Democrats as well as the German Nationalists. With the approval of the cabinet, he formulated a number of guidelines which were to be the basis of the program of the broadened coalition. The list contained an affirmation of the Weimar Constitution and of the foreign-policy objectives of the existing cabinet. Although the DNVP voiced its willingness to accept the Dawes plan and the general direction of the cabinet's foreign policy, the effort to realize this "Very Grand Coalition" proved fruitless when the SPD failed to be as flexible as the DNVP over certain other conditions.[66]

With the SPD's rejection of the coalition bid, Act One, as Marx observed, was over. Little practical choice remained, so Marx, encouraged by the DVP if not by all quarters of the Center Party and the DDP, opened negotiations with the DNVP only. The new move gained Stresemann's guarded support, because he realized that DNVP participation in the government might be less of a burden to his foreign policy than the party's unqualified opposition would be.[67]

As talks with the DNVP got under way, Finance Minister Luther offered a suggestion that was aimed at overcoming the reluctance, within both the government parties and the DNVP, to a strict political coalition. As an alternative to the dissolution that would be necessary if these negotiations failed—and the prospect of new elections was unwelcome to all—Luther proposed that the various party delegations simply name three candidates whose reputations would command sufficient votes in the Reichstag to ensure majority support for the cabinet.[68] But Luther's plan failed to establish the desired alignment. When the Nationalists proposed two Nein-Sager as ministerial candidates, the DDP, which viewed the opening to the Right with great misgivings at best, absolutely refused its support and declared its active opposition to any cabinet that would be formed with the participation of expressed opponents of the Dawes plan.[69]

The Democrats' defection from the government ranks would have left even a coalition that included the DNVP with an unreliable majority (see first chart on p. 17). As a result, the Reichstag was dissolved, and new elections were called, with an appeal being made to the people to return a Reichstag in which a majority combination would be possible.[70]

The elections of December 7, 1924, changed the numerical balance of the Reichstag only slightly. The results were about what had been expected: losses at the extreme Right and Left, clear gains for the Social Democrats, and modest gains for the coalition parties. The only real surprise was the showing of the DNVP. Rather than suffering modest losses, as the coalition leaders had predicted that it would, the DNVP actually gained a number of seats.[71]

Despite its strong showing in the elections, the DNVP had forfeited much of its advantage over the year. It had failed to attain power in spite of its preeminent position in the Reichstag—an advantage that it had now lost to the Social Democrats, who emerged from the December elections as the assembly's strongest party, with 131 seats. And the government had not been intimidated by the Nationalists' opposition: It had pursued the negotiations concerning the reparations settlement according to its own plan. It had refused to be bound by the Nationalists' insistence that the Allies fulfill certain preconditions before the negotiations over the Dawes plan were even begun. The concessions that the government had sought in London would have been demanded even if the Nationalist votes had been less critical. It had pressed for compromise only within the limits that it deemed to be compatible with a successful completion of the Dawes conference.

The DNVP's abysmal failure in its contest with the government over the Dawes plan was somewhat obscured by its success in the December elections. The party still hoped to exert an effective nationalistic influence from within the government. Both its own readiness to accept the *fait accompli* of the Dawes plan and the essentially unchanged distribution of parliamentary strength were to give it this chance in 1925.

4

THE SECURITY-PACT
MEMORANDUM

Germany's diplomatic and domestic situations were both precarious as 1925 began. Domestically the problem is simply stated: the search for a majority coalition. In foreign policy, even stating the problem is complex.

On January 5, 1925, the Allied governments informed Germany that the first Rhineland zone of occupation around the bridgehead city of Cologne would not be evacuated on January 10, as the Versailles Treaty permitted, provided Germany had faithfully fulfilled her obligations under that treaty. The ostensible justification was Germany's lack of fulfillment, specifically concerning disarmament. The real reason lay in France's concern for her security.

Since the end of the war, French foreign policy had been dominated by a concern for security against any future German attack. French military and political leaders had proposed a variety of plans to achieve this. But essentially, the Versailles settlement had offered three guarantees of French security: the Anglo-American guarantee treaty, German disarmament, and occupation of the Rhineland. By mid 1924 all three of these had become uncertain. The Anglo-American treaty had never come into effect because of the repudiation of the Versailles Treaty by the American Congress. Occupation was temporary, so long as Germany fulfilled her obligations under the treaty. And disarmament was only a security so long as the French could control and verify it. During the summer of 1924 the Interallied Military Control Commission (IMCC) had begun a general inspection of Germany to determine the state of her disarmament. The Allied note of January 5, 1925, referred to the incomplete findings of this general inspection, concluding that Germany had not disarmed and thus could not benefit from the reduced duration of occupation provisionally afforded by the Versailles Treaty. In fact, some French argued that, because of this nonfulfillment, the fifteen-year term of occupation had not even begun.

The decision had been predicted months before. In late October and early November 1924 Ambassador Leopold von Hoesch had informed Stresemann from Paris that he feared the French would use the general inspection as a means to justify the extension of the Rhineland occupation. Even earlier, at the London Conference on the Dawes plan, Ramsay MacDonald had pointedly mentioned to the Germans that disarmament was the condition of the early evacuation of the Cologne zone.[1]

Disarmament was less the problem, then, than French security. This was no new perception. As early as February 1924, in a meeting of the Reichstag's Foreign Affairs Committee, Stresemann had linked the resolution of France's desire for security to the elimination of Germany's foreign political problems. The London Conference had underscored this connection and had demonstrated the limits of French premier Edouard Herriot's ability to prevail against the French hard liners who wanted to extend the occupation of Cologne. MacDonald, to whom the Germans had turned in London for aid and comfort, offered scant encouragement. The occupation of the Rhineland, he had observed, depended, not on his view, but upon the decision that the majority of Allied ambassadors would reach in their conference concerning the state of Germany's disarmament.[2]

The question was, What to do? Labor Minister Heinrich Brauns had asked it in a cabinet meeting in mid summer, just prior to the London Conference. Chancellor Marx had emphasized it in his presentation a few weeks later to the presidents of the state governments. Now that the calamity of nonevacuation had come to pass, spokesmen of the German Democratic Party and the Socialists broached the same question in a meeting of the Reichstag Foreign Affairs Committee: Could not Germany seize the diplomatic initiative by proposing a Rhineland settlement based upon reciprocal guarantees of existing frontiers? The Geneva Protocol, which had been designed by the League of Nations to allay France's fears concerning her security by means of an institutionalization of compulsory arbitration, was clearly headed for failure; the new Conservative cabinet in Britain, formed in November 1924, was certain to reject it. In light of these circumstances, might this not be a propitious moment for Germany to act?[3]

The January meeting of the Foreign Affairs Committee of the Reichstag exemplified the extent to which the domestic problem concerning who should govern was affected by the foreign political dilemma of what to do. Count Westarp received Stresemann's report on the foreign political situation with singular moderation. "Obviously," observed Bavaria's state representative in his report on the meeting, "this is traceable to the DNVP hope of joining the government as a result of the present governmental crisis and to their willingness to tolerate Stresemann as foreign minister" under the circumstances.[4]

The government crisis, which the Nationalists now were eager to resolve in their favor, had begun with the passage of the Dawes plan. After inconclusive consultations between the parties and the government, new elections became necessary. Called for December 1924, they had failed to clarify the parliamentary situation. Because of the stridency of the DNVP campaign, moreover, Marx had little desire to bring the party into the government. The German People's Party, on the other hand, insisted upon a rightist coalition. And whereas, prior to the Dawes plan, Stresemann had been lukewarm to the idea, he now saw that the inclusion of the Nationalists might be an advantage. The new cabinet would have to deal with the nonevacuation of the Cologne zone. Having the Nationalists in the government, where they would be compelled to share the responsibility for the hard decisions ahead, would be better than having them in the opposition, where they would be free to attack any measures the government took.[5] Moreover, Stresemann hoped that participation in the cabinet might strengthen the moderates within the DNVP and eventually might lead the whole party to a more responsible attitude politically. The hope was encouraged when the Nationalist delegations in the Reichstag recognized the Dawes-plan laws as binding and when the moderate Martin Schiele was elected to succeed Oskar Hergt as chairman of the Reichstag delegation.[6]

The DNVP had reasons of its own for wanting to join the government. Aside from all the reasons evoked by the split over the Dawes plan and the realization, in the abstract, that permanent opposition held little prospect of healing that split, the party hoped that, by joining the cabinet, it could influence key issues which were bound to be faced in 1925. One of these was compensation for losses due to inflation, an issue on which the DNVP had picked up many of its votes in December. Another was the restructuring of the tax laws. A third was tariffs, which would all be up for renegotiation in 1925, the year when the special trade arrangements dictated by the Treaty of Versailles would expire. Indeed, the economic interest groups that were behind the party sometimes used such exaggerated political demands when they urged a coalition that the party leadership encouraged all members to observe strict discipline and warned them not to burden the negotiations for a new cabinet with "ill-considered comments."[7]

The Marx minority government, which had led Germany since the fall of Stresemann's cabinet in November 1923, resigned on December 15, 1924. Negotiations with the party leaders showed quickly that, as in October, the rapid formation of a new cabinet was out of the question. The effort was then suspended until the new year.[8]

The new year brought great activity but, initially, little change in positions. Marx abandoned his efforts, and the task then fell to Hans Luther, who had been finance minister since 1923. Luther's initial inquiries seemed no more encouraging than Marx's had been. The Center Party refused, on the basis of these inquiries, to participate in the cabinet that Luther envisaged. At the same time, however, the party made it clear that its objection was not to Luther himself. With the door to success thus left still slightly ajar, Luther resurrected an idea that he had raised back in October but that had been around for even longer: the creation of a "cabinet of personalities," whose personal stature alone would command sufficient respect to assure the government a working majority in the Reichstag. Confidence in the individuals would take precedence over party differences regarding a political program. The idea had much in common with the German Nationalists' proposal in May 1924 that Tirpitz be a chancellor candidate "above party." The parliamentary impasse was to be resolved by the convenient fiction that the parties would be bound to the cabinet by a spokesman rather than by commitment to a formal government coalition. The Center Party agreed to send Heinrich Brauns, minister of labor; and the DNVP agreed to send Martin Schiele, a party moderate who had just succeeded Oskar Hergt as chairman of the Nationalist delegation in the Reichstag, as minister of the interior. Stresemann would stay on as foreign minister and spokesman for the German People's Party. In addition, Karl Stingl would represent the Bavarian People's Party. Otto Gessler would remain as minister of defense but not as the spokesman of the DDP, which preferred to disassociate itself from the opening to the Right without actually opposing the Luther cabinet. On January 22, 1925, Luther's program received a vote of "approval" from the Reichstag, and the long cabinet crisis thus came to an end.

The rightist combination was at last a reality, even though Luther's cabinet claimed to be a nonparty government. Moreover, inclusion of the Nationalists had been accompanied by some encouraging signs, which Stresemann immediately began to emphasize in his diplomatic dispatches. The DNVP spokesman, Martin Schiele, was an acknowledged moderate within the party, a representative of both landed and industrial interests. Throughout the negotiations, the DNVP leadership had repeated its acceptance of the Dawes-plan legislation as binding. Luther's presence assured the continuity of foreign policy. In addition, the reserved reaction of the Nationalists with regard to the nonevacuation of Cologne augured well for the development of its more constructive participation in that policy.[9]

Stresemann needed this hoped-for amelioration in Nationalist behavior, for by the time that Luther's rightist cabinet had won its parliamentary vote, the foreign minister had already secretly launched his proposal for a Rhineland security pact which was to dominate his foreign policy for the next several years. In the discussion of nonevacuation held in the meeting of the Reichstag's Foreign Affairs Committee on January 9, Stresemann had devoted most of his reply to the suggestion that Germany take the initiative diplomatically by making some offer for a Rhineland security pact. It was evident that he found merit in the idea.[10] Nor was the Foreign Affairs Committee the only place in which the idea had been raised in these weeks of crisis. The British ambassador, Edgar Vincent, Lord D'Abernon, in a conversation with State Secretary Schubert in late December 1924, had praised former Chancellor Wilhelm Cuno's proposal for a nonaggression treaty and had urged that the Germans reexamine it. The German Foreign Office on the Wilhelmstrasse, preoccupied with the impending nonevacuation of Cologne, had not taken up D'Abernon's hint immediately, but it had constructed its reply to the Allied notification of the extension of occupation in such a way as to retain maximum diplomatic flexibility. The German reply note of January 6, 1925, purposely avoided labeling nonevacuation as a violation of the Versailles Treaty, in order to circumvent a diplomatic discussion of purely technical points. In such a discussion, the Allies could always find technicalities within the treaty that Germany had failed to fulfill. Instead, the Germans' note played on the theme that their Foreign Office had been emphasizing since December 1924. The evacuation was the first instance in which the Versailles Treaty called upon the Allies, rather than Germany, to act in a very specific manner to promote peace and understanding. If the Allies failed to act, they risked destroying the confidence in a policy of reconciliation that had been growing in Germany and Europe since the London Conference.[11] The German note asserted that the continued occupation of the Cologne zone was disproportionate to any minor difficulties that might remain concerning German disarmament. Over the fulfillment of a treaty, which had not been the product of negotiations from the start, one might expect differences to arise. But these difficulties should not be allowed to frustrate the policy of peaceful understanding upon which Germany had entered. The note concluded with a call upon the Allies to cooperate in this spirit of understanding.

The Germans thus hoped to shift the diplomatic emphasis from the narrow consideration of the disarmament clauses, which the French could use indefinitely to extend their military control of the Rhine, toward the more general problem of Rhineland security. The broader plan offered far greater possibilities. Stresemann could assume that influential personalities within the Conservative government in Britain would be sympathetic to a German diplomatic step to resolve the impasse.[12] In the light both of Lord D'Abernon's encouragements and of the broad support that the Foreign Affairs Committee meeting of January 9 had suggested might exist for a German initiative toward a security pact in the Rhineland, the atmosphere for action seemed right.

The first step came within days of the meeting of the Foreign Affairs Committee. On January 14, 1925, D'Abernon and Schubert met and, in a wide-ranging discussion, tentatively explored the possible approaches to the security question. D'Abernon counseled against an immediate formal approach to Paris, suggesting instead an informal sounding out of British opinion by means of a general memorandum. During the next week, the German Foreign Office drafted such a memorandum for the British government, outlining the possible content of a Rhineland security pact that Germany was prepared to enter into. As Luther shaped his cabinet, he was consulted also, and the Wilhelmstrasse suggested that he include certain remarks on the issue in his inaugural speech to the Reichstag as chancellor. On January 20, 1925, D'Abernon received and dispatched the memorandum to London, with the request for strict secrecy in the matter.[13]

The German memorandum to London referred to the connection in the French mind between France's security and the questions of disarmament and evacuation, which had become diplomatically acute with the non-evacuation of Cologne. It suggested that the two latter problems might be easier to resolve if combined with a more general accord to assure peace between Germany and France. Such a security pact might take a form similar to the Cuno proposal of December 1922. A number of approaches appeared possible to the German government: the powers which had an interest in the Rhine could renounce war under guarantee of the United States; arbitration treaties could be drawn to cover both judicial and political conflicts; there could be a guarantee of the present territorial distribution (*"gegenwärtigen Besitzstand,"* a phrase that would become important later); and the demilitarization of the Rhineland could be guaranteed. Still other possibilities existed, and the ideas that formed the bases of Germany's examples could be combined in a variety of ways; but, the note concluded, these suggestions ought to demonstrate that such a security pact was at least a feasible goal.[14] Although the German Foreign Office's memorandum to London was a closely guarded secret—D'Abernon claimed that outside of the diplomatic officers directly involved, only Luther had seen the text—public discussion of the security question was prevalent in Germany and in Europe more generally.[15] A French newspaper even published a report of imminent German proposals concerning the security of the Rhineland.[16]

The Nationalists also gave the issue attention, and in a way that boded well for the DNVP's cooperation in the policy regarding a security pact. In an article entitled "Das Ausland und das Kabinett Luther," the party's newsletter, *Korrespondenz der Deutschnationalen Volkspartei*, spoke of the surprise and disappointment that certain foreign circles must be feeling with regard to the Luther cabinet. Many had expected the Nationalists to begin pounding the table with their fists to demonstrate their resolve. Luther's comments on foreign policy gave them less grist for their propaganda mills than food for thought. His foreign-policy proposals connected Germany's continued loyal fulfillment of her reparations obligations with the comparable "loyalty of our treaty protagonists. Thus no more the one-sided demonstration of good will, but rather fulfillment step-by-step [by both sides]." The problems the government faced were surely serious: critical decisions in the East concerning access to East Prussia and relations with Poland, military control, "the evacuation question and, in connection with it, the projects that one labels with the slogan 'security question,' economic negotiations"—all would demand a strong government. The article concluded simply by asserting that only time would reveal whether the Luther cabinet could meet these demands.[17] The article is striking because of its moderation and because of the specific mention of the problem of security and its connection with the occupation of the Rhineland—the same points that Stresemann's memorandum to London had made.

Initial reaction to that memorandum in London was mixed. Britain's foreign secretary, Austen Chamberlain, who was unable to respond immediately because of personal illness, met with the German ambassador, Friedrich Sthamer, on January 30, 1925. At first objecting to the German insistence on strict secrecy, Chamberlain argued that England could not negotiate the security question behind France's back. He appeared wholly mollified, however, when Sthamer indicated that Germany intended to communicate her views to France as well and that the prior consultation with Great Britain was simply a preliminary sounding. Thus assured that Germany had no intentions to divide Britain and France on the issue, Chamberlain expressed his warm enthusiasm for the spirit of the German proposal, which showed a definite attention to France's sensitivity about her security. He hoped the initiative would quiet public apprehension in France. He himself could accept the German note as a basis for eventual discussions of the security question. But for all that, he considered the diplomatic initiative premature.[18]

At this point, the French had heard nothing more than rumors of German proposals regarding Rhineland security. Their reaction to these was decidedly colored by the state of the negotiations about military control and disarmament which were then in progress. The French tended to consider the rumors of German suggestions for a security pact as a ruse to deprive France of the guarantee of the occupation which she was exerting in the Cologne zone in the face of German violations of the treaty.[19] On January 28 Premier Edouard Herriot voiced this suspicion in a speech during the debate in the Chamber of Deputies over Germany's treaty violations and France's security. French occupation of the Rhine was the essential "and, alas, the last condition of our security." Peace in Europe was his wish, but the first condition of that peace must be the security of his own country.[20]

Herriot's speech caused considerable consternation in Germany. But it provided an occasion for Luther to emphasize publicly Germany's readiness to negotiate the status of the Rhineland. In a speech before the foreign press in Berlin on January 30, in which he evoked the Geneva Protocol, Herriot's speech, and France's desire for security, Luther noted that the German government would immediately cooperate in any effort to reach security agreements in areas in which the need was "felt to be immediately acute."[21]

The German Foreign Office followed up Luther's public statement with its offer of a security pact to France. In an eleven-page letter of instructions sent with the memorandum to the German ambassador in Paris, Leopold von Hoesch, Stresemann outlined the government's motives and aims. He instructed Hoesch to communciate the memorandum on security to Herriot with the utmost secrecy.[22]

The German views were duly presented to Herriot on February 9, 1925: Germany wanted to find a solution to the security problem in cooperation with all interested parties; she had no intention of playing one off against another. The Luther cabinet, which had aroused mistrust in France because of the inclusion of German Nationalists, was singularly fitted to develop a security pact. Due precisely to its connection with the Right, it could speak for the whole German people, and not just for the Left or the Middle, as had been the case with prior cabinets. The examples of possible solutions that the German government proposed in the memorandum were not made in an effort to avoid the obligations of disarmament but were prompted by a genuine concern for the importance that France attached to the question of security.

Herriot listened intently. He replied that France was indeed greatly concerned over the matter of security. His own policy had always been one directed toward European peace, as his conduct in Geneva and London—notably the promised evacuation of the Ruhr—had illustrated. He would therefore examine the proposals of the German memorandum with great care.[23]

Herriot was impressed. Indeed, he immediately sought out the president of the Republic, interrupting his attendance at the theater, to present the German note to him. Both looked upon the proposal as a welcome alternative to the Geneva Protocol for mutual security, which seemed destined for rejection in Britain. Thus, on February 20, after further conversations with Ambassador Hoesch, the French government replied that it was prepared to consider the memorandum, in consultation with its allies, as the basis for possible negotiations of a security pact for the Rhineland.[24]

Up to this point, the diplomatic exchanges had been free from any domestic pressure. Luther's speech of January 30 and his mention of Germany's willingness to enter into negotiations to ensure European security had caused no stir. The DNVP's newsletter for party functionaries took no notice of it in its review of foreign policy. Its intraparty newspaper contented itself with rejection of Socialist demands for entry into the League of Nations and counseled a policy that would fall between the extremes of surrender—such as the Socialists recommended—and war.[25]

The bond of secrecy that Stresemann had urgently requested for the discussions on the security pact began to break down in late February 1925. First, Herriot felt compelled to mention the German proposals before the Foreign Affairs Committee of the French Senate, then before the Paris diplomatic corps, with a demand for utmost secrecy, which was honored in the breach. The Paris press immediately took the matter up in its columns. Shortly thereafter, Chamberlain referred to the proposals in the Commons during the open debate of March 5 on European security.[26]

These revelations forced Stresemann to acknowledge the German initiative publicly.[27] He convened a confidential press conference on March 7, 1925. Speaking for the cabinet, and thus ostensibly for his colleagues from the DNVP as well, he traced the background of the security proposals, the content of the memorandum, and the political significance of the initiative. The German Foreign Office had proceeded in secrecy with the proposals regarding a security pact in order to allow dispassionate discussions of the issues involved. Public debate introduced the danger that French opponents of accommodation would raise a cry of protest and upset the calm pursuit of a mutual understanding. The strident negative reaction in some circles in France, as well as in Poland, to Herriot's recent revelation of the pact plan demonstrated the wisdom of secrecy. Stresemann chose not to mention the likelihood that the secrecy maintained by the German Foreign Office was motivated by fear as much of domestic as of foreign reaction. He explained that the origins of the proposal predated the formation of Luther's cabinet; they had grown out of an analysis of the crisis regarding non-evacuation of the Cologne zone. Obviously, the fundamental difficulty had resulted, not from the state of German disarmament, but from France's fears for her security. The German Foreign Office therefore had to consider ways in which this French fear of some future German aggression through the Rhineland, which so prejudiced French policy, might be allayed once and for all.

In these circumstances the German Foreign Office had taken up a proposal that had already been the subject of intensive German diplomatic efforts twice before, under Chancellor Cuno and again under Stresemann himself. The government had communicated a note—first to the British government, then to France, Belgium, and Italy—outlining a number of ways in which the problem of French security, to which the question of German disarmament and Rhenish occupation were so closely linked, could be approached so as to resolve all three issues.

From this sketch of the diplomatic background, Stresemann turned to the content and significance of the German proposals. A pact would certainly entail a renunciation of Alsace-Lorraine, he admitted openly, but no one could seriously believe that the German people would ever be willing to follow a government into a war of aggression against France the sole purpose of which would be the reacquisition of Alsace-Lorraine. In any event, a guarantee of the Rhineland such as the proposed pact should contain would not be one-sided. The real danger on the Rhine was less to France than to Germany, because France, due to her imperialism, refused to countenance a retreat from the German Rhineland. A pact would secure Germany against any state that would fail to respect the present territorial arrangement along the Rhine. In addition, the pact would end the need for continued military occupation of the Rhine. A shortening of the remaining ten years of occupation would be a logical consequence of a pact.

The question of whether Germany had recognized her eastern borders had figured prominently in press comments in France and Poland. Stresemann denied that any such recognition had been intimated in the German proposal. The suggestion had been that Germany was prepared to enter into treaties of arbitration with any nation, including France's eastern allies, and thereby to obligate herself to a peaceful settlement of differences. But Germany was not prepared to offer an official guarantee of the eastern boundaries; on the contrary, the path to a peaceful revision of them had to remain open. Indeed, Article 19 of the Versailles Treaty specifically provided that treaties that had become inapplicable or that failed to contribute to peace could be revised.

These comments to the journalists represented the policy on eastern borders that Stresemann had clearly outlined to Ambassador Hoesch in Paris when he had sent the memorandum concerning the security pact. He had instructed Hoesch to emphasize that any treaty that even suggested a renewed and free recognition of the eastern boundaries would be intolerable to Germany. To this extent, a difference had to be maintained between the treatment of the problems in the West and the East. However, Hoesch was also instructed to emphasize to Herriot that the German government, with Poland specifically in mind, had included the suggestion that there be arbitration treaties, which would offer an absolutely reliable guarantee of the maintenance of peace.[28]

Such, said Stresemann, was the state of affairs. He reminded the assembled journalists that it was beyond his powers to predict how the negotiations would advance, but he was clearly optimistic. He urged the reporters to read "between the lines of the [Commons] speech by Mr. Chamberlain," in which the British foreign secretary had suggested that Poland would perform a great service to European peace by voluntarily entering into discussions about border revisions. Public opinion in England, Italy, and Belgium, and official reaction in France as well, was favorable to the German initiative. The breach of secrecy was unfortunate, because confidential negotiations still offered the best opportunity for the conclusion of a treaty, which Stresemann felt would signify a tremendous advance for Germany. Because he believed this, he had readily undertaken the first steps, and he accepted responsibility for them. If the SPD organ *Vorwärts* felt that his foreign policy had become more reasonable since the entry of the German Nationalists into the government, he was flattered. It was appropriate that the latest German proposal regarding a security pact came from a government whose political support closely resembled that enjoyed by the Cuno cabinet, from which the original security offer had emanated. Stresemann expressed his satisfaction at *Vorwärts*'s left-handed recognition that if a foreign minister had to choose between having the German Nationalists oppose or cooperate, he might not be wrong in accepting their cooperation.

Finally, Stresemann urged that extreme care be taken in the public treatment of the security-pact proposals. Too great an emphasis on the advantages that Germany hoped to gain would only serve to excite French opposition and to decrease the likelihood of concessions. Discussions of a revision of the eastern borders with Poland should be left to the British press for the time being. If the London *Times* wished to continue its insistence that Poland's boundaries were untenable, so much the better. The German press ought, by contrast, to emphasize its government's offer to settle disputes by peaceful means. For those to whom this was distasteful, Stresemann added another word of caution: German military strength was too often overrated by people who ought to know better. During his own chancellorship, he had had occasion to ask General von Seeckt about Germany's military potential in the East. The general's answer was no secret: Even in a purely defensive action, Germany would not be able to preserve her frontiers. An offensive effort was therefore absolutely beyond Germany's military capacity. Those who dreamed of producing the cannon must keep in mind that Germany would still lack the munitions to charge them. In war, he remarked pointedly, the superiority of race meant nothing against the superiority of technology. No German government could contemplate urging the nation on to such a hopeless war.

Stresemann's extensive defense of his security-pact proposal is significant for a number of reasons. To begin with, it was the first discussion of the pact outside the confidentiality of government circles, and although the briefing of the Berlin press corps was itself semiconfidential, the motives that Stresemann offered for the government's actions were intended to make their way into the daily papers, and they did. Second, Stresemann made a conscious effort to portray the diplomatic initiative as the policy of the entire cabinet, the DNVP included. In later days, both the thoroughness of the briefings that Stresemann had offered and the extent of the DNVP's knowledge of and responsibility for the initiative would become objects of controversy. Finally, the briefings at this point contained a very open admission that Alsace-Lorraine, at least, was lost for all practical purposes. This was to become a point of attack.

In the days immediately after his briefing of the press, Stresemann repeated his review of the origins, progress, prospects, and implications of the security-pact suggestions that had been presented to the Foreign Affairs committees of the Reichsrat and the Reichstag, as well as to his own party's parliamentary delegation, broadening his arguments to include several additional points. He indicated that a real danger had existed in January that an Allied security pact among England, France, and Belgium might have been concluded. Such a pact would have excluded Germany from participating in the determination of the ultimate fate of the Rhineland—a participation that would be ensured by the government's initiative—and would have been directed implicitly against Germany. Nor could the related danger be ignored, namely, that the German Rhenish provinces might abandon their attachment to the German nation and, in an attempt to rid themselves of Allied occupation, agree to the formation of an independent Rhenish state under French patronage.[29]

Before each of these groups, Stresemann returned insistently to his theme that the security-pact proposals represented the policy of a united coalition government. Indeed, before the Reichsrat's Foreign Affairs Committee, Stresemann explicitly contended that with the exception of the radical extremes—the Communists and the Racists—"all the parties of the Reichstag" stood behind the government's actions, a comment that, as the

Bavarian representative in the Reichsrat observed privately, if it were allowed to pass, would truly vindicate Stresemann's previous insistence that the DNVP be included in the government.[30]

The next day, March 11, in the meeting of the Reichstag's Foreign Affairs Committee, Stresemann's vindication seemed at hand, as the German Nationalists' spokesman, Otto Hoetzsch, proceeded to voice his party's disquietude "with muffled drums."[31] His party feared that Stresemann's proposals went far beyond those of Chancellor Cuno. They would abandon Alsace-Lorraine forever; they would involve a voluntary acceptance of the terms of the Versailles Treaty, which had formerly been forced upon Germany; they also would entail even further obligations. Hoetzsch hoped that the government had not bound itself in any way to the terms of Stresemann's memorandum. He also objected that the pact proposal had not been made conditional on the evacuation of the Cologne zone and the shortening of the duration of the Rhineland occupation. Stresemann had avoided these very conditions in order to prevent the immediate dismissal of the German initiative as a mere ploy to circumvent the difficulties that had arisen in January; he had also included this explanation in his presentation to the committee. For all his concern, however, Hoetzsch offered no denunciation or repudiation of the Foreign Office's initiative, although the four days that had elapsed since Stresemann's report to the Berlin press corps should have allowed the party leaders enough time to prepare one if they had chosen to do so. In fact, the DNVP spokesman even endorsed the idea of a pact, on the condition that Russia and the United States participate. Indeed, the only denunciation came, as Stresemann had predicted, from the Communists, in a speech that might have come from the mouth of a German Nationalist had the composition of the cabinet been different.[32]

The DNVP leaders hardly welcomed a crisis over foreign policy so early in the life of the Luther cabinet. They had serious reservations, to be sure, about Stresemann's proposals; but they were prepared, at this early stage, to acquiesce in his initiative and to accept—or, at least, not to reject—the link that he had drawn between the party and the political responsibility for the cabinet's actions. Oskar Hergt, who had formerly held the party's top offices and was now chairman of the Reichstag's Foreign Affairs Committee, went so far as to admit—be it only in intraparty exchanges—that the government's proposals bound the DNVP to a certain extent, despite the leadership's reservations concerning them.[33] But the leaders faced a dilemma: provincial party officials, the Societies for the Fatherland, and the Pan-German League all began to make concerned inquiries, thus displaying far less readiness to accept Stresemann's lead in diplomacy. Moreover, Stresemann himself seemed anxious for an open debate in order to force the

DNVP leaders to take a public position on the security-pact suggestions before hostility toward compromise deepened within the party.[34]

The DNVP dealt first with the cabinet. In a meeting between Luther, Stresemann, and Martin Schiele, the party's cabinet spokesman, Schiele warned that if the security-pact proposal came up for open discussion in the Reichstag, the Nationalists would have to "protect themselves against attacks from the more radical Right and would find it most difficult to continue to cooperate in the government." Avoidance of a debate would permit the Nationalists to continue to participate in the cabinet. The idea of an open debate was dropped.[35]

The DNVP's Reichstag delegation came next. With Westarp ill and absent from Berlin, it seemed uncertain of the course it should take. About forty of the one hundred Nationalist deputies met on March 19, 1925—an attendance that the party considered "good"—hoping to define their position more clearly. The moderate Otto Hoetzsch, who had spoken for the party in the meeting of the Foreign Affairs Committee, reported on the explanations that Stresemann had given there. He recommended that the party approach the matter with caution rather than outright hostility. Developments toward a security pact were inevitable, and the government's seizure of the initiative was therefore not necessarily disadvantageous. Freytagh-Loringhoven, a spokesman for the far right wing of the party and, like Hoetzsch, a member of the Foreign Affairs Committee, argued that Stresemann's diplomatic initiative had failed in any event, since it remained unanswered, and that therefore the DNVP need not take any immediate action. The discussion continued into the next day, when a delegation of six representatives was chosen to approach Stresemann for more specific information concerning his memorandum. Stresemann entertained them to a lively three-quarter hour's defense of his policies, in which the Nationalists learned that the Allies had requested clarification of the February proposals, that Stresemann expected to exclude discussion of eastern borders from the current negotiations, and that he was prepared to concede Alsace-Lorraine. He hoped to gain the evacuation of the Cologne zone, and he would refuse to sign any pact before this was assured. He was skeptical about the advisability of connecting the evacuation of the remaining two Rhineland zones to the conclusion of a pact, but he was persuaded by the Nationalist delegates to promise to make such an effort. In any event, the conclusion of some sort of security pact, Stresemann assured his visitors, was inevitable.[36]

The discussion within the Nationalist delegation in the Reichstag continued that evening, March 20. Hoetzsch's suggestion of cautious toleration of the foreign minister's initiative was now opposed by more intransigent elements, who called for a repudiation of both the proposal and the foreign minister. The role of compromiser fell, surprisingly, to Freytagh-Loring-hoven. He proposed that Stresemann's views, expressed that morning to the Nationalist deputation, be incorporated into a letter from the party to the foreign minister, expressing the DNVP's serious misgivings concerning both the past and the possible future negotiations toward a security pact and reserving explicitly the party's right to reject any accord based on the spirit of Stresemann's proposals. The letter, by demanding that all future conduct of foreign affairs be taken only with the direct consent of the chancellor and in constant consultation with the various party spokesmen in the cabinet, also represented an attempt to undermine Stresemann's authority. The party thus tried to dissociate itself from the foreign minister's proposals, characterizing them as Stresemann's sole responsibility, undertaken independently of both cabinet and chancellor. By doing this, they hoped to drive a wedge between Luther and his foreign minister. As Schiele put it, not Stresemann, but Luther, was to become the determinative personality in the cabinet's foreign policy as far as the DNVP was concerned.[37]

Schiele and his colleagues in the party had badly misjudged, however, the extent to which Luther was prepared to play their game. Luther reacted decisively to the letter, which, because of the absence of Westarp, was drawn up by the acting chairman of the party's Reichstag delegation, Schultz-Bromberg, who sent it to Stresemann on March 21, 1925. The chancellor met with the Nationalist leaders the following day and energetically rejected the DNVP's implication that the foreign minister had the sole responsibility for the recent orientation and conduct of foreign policy. He himself, as well as the foreign minister, carried the responsibility. His competence encompassed the guidelines and strategy, if not always the tactics, of foreign policy. In this case he had gone into even the tactical aspects of the security proposals extensively and had thoroughly read all the documents now under discussion. The DNVP's written rejection of the continued pursuit of foreign policy "in the same spirit" as heretofore could be interpreted to mean either that the chancellor had failed to live up to his declared governmental program or that the DNVP was no longer willing to support this program. Luther thus converted the attack on Stresemann into a challenge to his own authority and to the continued existence of the rightist coalition that the Nationalists still wanted to preserve. So, the Nationalists gave way. Schiele insisted that the party had at no time entertained the slightest lack of confidence in Luther. Certain delegates merely objected to the secrecy with which the German Foreign Office shrouded its conduct of diplomacy. The letter had been an expression of this apprehension. The confrontation ended when Schiele and his colleagues agreed to let their party's letter be interpreted in a way that would in effect disarm their attack on Stresemann.[38]

On the following day, March 23, Luther answered Schultz-Bromberg with a letter of his own. He asserted that he and the foreign minister had each exercised his full constitutional responsibility in the conduct of foreign affairs and that, in full accord with the suggestions raised in the Nationalists' letter, they would continue to do so. Furthermore, Luther intended to maintain close contact with party spokesmen in the government regarding important matters of foreign policy. The Nationalist insistence upon the right to withhold approval of any accord that would be concluded on the basis of a "continuation of negotiations in the same spirit" could only have represented an objection to the secrecy of the early security-pact negotiations, which had been maintained by the government even in relation to the coalition parties, rather than an objection to the nature of those negotiations. The Nationalists leaders, who had accepted the text of the letter the day before it was actually sent, offered no objections.[39]

The crisis being over, Luther suggested a more extensive discussion between the DNVP leaders, himself, and Stresemann regarding the cabinet's foreign-policy aims—a shrewd good-will gesture which he made in order to offer the Nationalists some consolation. Thus, on April 2, 1925, Stresemann addressed himself directly to the points raised in Schultz-Bromberg's letter. He pointed out that his earlier reference to a total liberation of the Rhineland ought not to be construed as a promise that the entire area would immediately be evacuated as the result of a security pact. Evacuation was, however, a logical and attainable consequence of the security pact, since the pact would reaffirm the clauses in the Versailles Treaty that governed the demilitarization of the Rhineland zone. This was a point that the Nationalists had not been aware of. Stresemann answered question after question posed by the Nationalist delegation. He portrayed the direct advantages that he expected to obtain from the security pact: a guarantee against any unilateral imposition of territorial sanctions by France—such as had taken place in the Ruhr—and the prevention of a three-power pact that would have been directed specifically against Germany. Already, he pointed out, Germany's claim to the right of revision of her eastern border had been given new support as a direct result of the security-pact proposals. He referred to British Foreign Secretary Chamberlain's recent speech before the House of Commons. The Nationalists showed some skepticism over Stresemann's rather optimistic view regarding the direction of the negotiations, but they refrained from voicing any fundamental objections to the continued pursuit of the policy. They asked only to be consulted before the government moved into any new stage in the negotiations. They accepted Stresemann's proposal to delay publication of the memorandum until the Allies had replied, which he expected them to do in the next week. If the exceedingly thorough briefing had not satisfied them, at least it had mollified them for the moment.[40]

Luther's forthright support of Stresemann's foreign policy forced the Nationalists' parliamentary leaders to choose between disrupting or preserving the coalition. Despite their discomfiture, they chose to accept a degree of responsibility for Stresemann's foreign policy. Indeed, their conduct in the face of the revelation of Stresemann's secret initiative had been exceedingly mild. They had resisted the efforts of the Pan-German League, which had published its own condemnation of Stresemann for his betrayal of German honor, to arouse the Nationalist press. They had managed to keep the right-wing press in check, a success that the president of the Pan-German League deplored and castigated. The party's own newsletter, *Korrespondenz der Deutschnationalen Volkspartei*, had studiously avoided mention of either the Reichstag delegation's letter to Stresemann or the resultant consultations between the party and the government. The only article that was devoted to the revelations on the German memorandum welcomed Stresemann's initiative as an appropriate means of avoiding the imposition of a diplomatic solution, such as the Allies might seek to impose. Party circulars to the provincial organizations reflected the same reserve.[41]

Stresemann could be reasonably satisfied both with his defense of his policy and with his seemingly successful tactic of bringing the Nationalists into the cabinet in order to neutralize their opposition and to school them in responsibility. He had survived the breach of secrecy surrounding his security-pact initiative by giving the party leaders in the Reichstag a very thorough paraphrase of his February memorandum and an extensive explanation of its origins and aims. A comparison of the text of the memorandum with the minutes of the various briefings that Stresemann conducted confirms this. He had perhaps deemphasized the less tangible advantages that he saw in the pact—the transformation of the tenor of foreign policy from confrontation to adjustment—and had emphasized the more concrete gains to be made—namely, the evacuation of Cologne and the shortening of the term of occupation for the other zones; protection against French sanctions; and the preemption of a situation in which an anti-German security pact might have been formed. Still, he was neither abandoning the less tangible cornerstone of his policy nor inventing motives for his initiative where they had not previously existed in order to meet Nationalist criticism.[42] Implicit in the circumstances that had surrounded the origins of the memorandum had been the threat of a Rhineland, or even a European, security pact without, and therefore against, Germany. D'Abernon had taken this threat into account in recommending the German initiative. The Belgians and the French had actively considered such a pact, and Czechoslovakia's Edward Beneš also favored it. Even the British under MacDonald had appeared ready to accept the Continental obligations of the Geneva Protocol. Germany's foreign-policy planners had no assurance that their passivity would end this threat of a security arrangement that would exclude Germany and be to her disadvantage. And so they acted.[43]

With the revelation of Stresemann's proposals regarding a security pact, the DNVP's whole relationship to the politics of the Weimar Republic began to change. Its entry into the government had certainly been a tactical accommodation, hedged about with mental reservations. The Nationalists insisted that they had not surrendered either their future goals or their convictions when they agreed to participate in Luther's cabinet.[44] Now, however, they were brought face-to-face with a conflict between their world of nationalist ideals and the world of political reality. Stresemann's foreign-policy initiative challenged one of their fundamental, visceral truths—national honor above all else. They were being asked, in effect, to suspend a whole complex of myths, which they had constructed in order to make the defeat of 1918 psychically bearable, and to accept instead the possibility of resolving conflicts with the "enemy" over the *Diktat*—the rape of German land, the lawless occupation—not by some manly act of defiance, but by negotiation, accommodation, compromise.[45] So far, the negotiations were still just a possibility, whereas their possession of governmental influence and power was a reality. For the first time, but not for the last, the leaders of the DNVP suspended their myths and opted for reality. Their decision did not go unchallenged within the party. They were forced to explain, to defend, to justify their choice. The psychological impact of such a process is to confirm the original choice. Acceptance of Stresemann's pursuit of a Rhineland security pact was but a first step in a process of which the men involved were hardly conscious.

Since it was but a first step, Stresemann's concern that the hostility among the party's rank and file would deepen if the party's leadership did not make a clear-cut public stand was well founded. Even as the consultations between Stresemann, Luther, and the DNVP leaders were taking place, provincial Nationalists and local organizations, which were free from the responsibility of preserving the coalition, were becoming increasingly restive. Whether their restiveness could be contained would be a key factor in determining whether the compromise concerning Stresemann's policy could be preserved.

5

PRACTICAL POLITICS

The German Nationalists had entered Luther's cabinet for practical reasons: taxes, trade, revaluation of the inflation mark. All of these incentives remained when the security-pact memorandum became known. In addition, the death of Reichspresident Friedrich Ebert on February 28, 1925, added another: the election of a new president. The Nationalists hoped to work in harmony with the middle parties for the election of a nonsocialist, preferably a "national-minded," candidate. Destroying the coalition because of Stresemann's independent conduct of foreign policy would have jeopardized Nationalist influence in all these issues.[1]

Throughout the spring of 1925, however, two factors worked against the preservation of the compromise that the DNVP had accepted regarding the security-pact initiative. The first of these was the long delay in the official Allied response to Germany's February memorandum. This diplomatic delay contributed to the impact of the second factor, an increasingly vocal dissatisfaction among the radical Nationalists about the compromise within the cabinet over the responsibility for the security-pact policies that Stresemann and Luther had worked out with the DNVP leaders.

That compromise had not been reached without opposition. With the first revelations of the security-pact proposal, the party leaders had begun to receive protests urging the repudiation of Stresemann and, if necessary, the abandonment of the government. The earliest protest came from the party's right wing: from Gottfried Traub, editor of the *München-Augsburger Abendzeitung* and *Eiserne Blätter*; from the Fatherland Societies (Vaterländische Verbände); from members of the Pan-German League and, publicly, from the league's own executive committee. Criticism centered around

76

the supposed "renunciation" of German populations and land along the western border.

Initially the party leadership temporized. Answers to protestors insisted that the initiative predated the DNVP's entry into the government, referred to Hoetzsch's objections in the Foreign Affairs Committee, and assured that the party would continue to protect the "honor and dignity of our nation."[2]

The volume and stridency of the protest within the DNVP increased steadily as the wait for an answer from the Allies to Stresemann's proposals lengthened. The protestors voiced their chagrin at any sign of patience with Stresemann's policies or of tolerance of his person. Playing upon the debacle of the previous year's vote on the Dawes plan, they warned the Berlin leadership against another "August 29" and urged a return to opposition rather than a compromise of national and party honor. They demanded, in effect, the surrender of power and the preservation of myth.[3] This clamor from those who were rabidly nationalistic found an outlet largely in intra-party debate. In the April 7, 1925, meeting of the DNVP's Central Committee, Reinhold Quaatz, a former member of the German People's Party and now a DNVP delegate to the Reichstag, roundly denounced the foreign minister's security-pact proposals. Although the party committee made no formal decisions on the policy, Quaatz began to circulate his own view among the provincial committees as evidence of the party's vigorous opposition to the security-pact initiative: the DNVP's Reichstag delegation had learned of the contents of the February note on Rhineland security only after it had been sent; since then, the leadership had remonstrated continually against the new policy. Within the leadership circle itself, Quaatz decried the silence of the Nationalist press and urged stronger public action. But his appeal met with little response.

Throughout April and May the leadership sought to preserve the compromise with the cabinet.[4] Comment in the *Korrespondenz der Deutschnationalen Volkspartei* remained reserved to the utmost. The paper, which was supportive of Luther, avoided all direct attacks on Stresemann. The only sharp rhetoric appeared in the publication of a resolution passed by the DNVP district committee of Potsdam.[5] Party instructions to the provinces continued to insist that the truce with the German People's Party be maintained and that Stresemann be left in peace.[6]

Still, Stresemann recognized that there was growing nationalistic hostility to his policy of reconciliation. Despite the relative equanimity with which the DNVP leaders had accepted his conduct of these policies since March, a real danger to the successful pursuit of these policies existed in the stubborn opposition of the DNVP's right wing. He had not calculated on a long delay before the Allies would respond to his proposals, nor could he hasten their response by initiatives of his own.

Stresemann thus had to be content throughout the spring of 1925 with diplomatic activity on lesser issues: Germany's boundaries on the east and the west, the special status of Eupen-Malmédy, and entry into the League of Nations. These issues bogged down progress toward a broader security pact, thus allowing time for the Nationalist opposition to ferment. On the other hand, the issues could hardly be avoided.

Stresemann knew that France would try to induce Germany to contract agreements within a security pact that would entail a virtual recognition of Poland's borders. He had thus drawn a distinction from the beginning between the East and West.[7] When, in mid March, France suggested that the arbitration proposal that Germany had made in the security-pact memorandum be broadened to include the Polish-German boundaries, Stresemann parried immediately: such a suggestion went far beyond the range that Germany had anticipated for treaties of arbitration. What France proposed amounted to a de facto acceptance of the eastern boundaries, a concession that neither his personal inclination nor domestic politics would permit. He reiterated time and again, however, that the arbitration treaties, as he envisaged them, would preclude war as a means of revising Germany's borders.[8] Even this simple renunciation of force as a means of revision in the East represented a guarantee that the German Nationalists were loath to offer.

The issue of "renunciation" in the West raises questions concerning the quality of the concessions that the German Foreign Office was prepared to make—distinctions that both France and the German Nationalists tried to ignore, for very different reasons. Whereas Stresemann and his advisors refused to recognize the eastern boundaries, they had specifically proposed a recognition of the territorial distribution in the West. In his earliest diplomatic message on the security pact, State Secretary Carl von Schubert had pointed out that one element that ought to impress the French was the "free-will confirmation of the German renunciation of Alsace-Lorraine."[9]

Although the German memorandum used the phrase "guarantee the current state of possessions (*gegenwärtigen Besitzstand*) on the Rhine," rather than the legally more far-reaching phrase "status quo," Stresemann's reiteration of this willing renunciation of Alsace-Lorraine, in the briefings that he conducted in March, tends to confirm Germany's original intention to abandon all pretensions to Alsace-Lorraine (see chapter 4). The phrase became significant, however, when the German Foreign Office learned from Luther that conversations had taken place between Belgian and German financial representatives concerning the possible return of Eupen-Malmédy to Germany in exchange for the German redemption of the debt that the

Belgian government had incurred in retiring German marks circulated in Belgium during the occupation from 1914 to 1918.[10]

Eupen and Malmédy had been imperial German territories for centuries and Prussian since 1815. They had passed to Belgian sovereignty under the terms of the Treaty of Versailles but had remained poorly integrated into the political life of that state. Strésemann had overlooked them in his early thinking on the security memorandum, and he ignored them in his defense of his policies in March. Once he became aware that it might be possible to gain Belgian consent to their recovery, he tried to keep the diplomatic path to such a settlement open. When France's Ambassador de Margerie inquired about the two territories in late March, Stresemann insisted that a security pact should not exclude a peaceful return of these districts to Germany by a mutual agreement between Germany and Belgium. At the same time, however, he counseled Germany's diplomatic representatives against extensive discussion of the Eupen-Malmédy issue before the final stages of the security-pact negotiations had taken place. Any Belgian-German deal would be dependent on French approval, and any attempt to force the pace of discussions could endanger the whole security-pact offer, "because it could make a false impression if we insist ostentatiously so early upon a formulation of the pact so advantageous to us."[11] In any choice, the policy of adjustment with France would be more important than the return of the provinces. The possible renunciation of Alsace-Lorraine and Eupen-Malmédy continued to be an issue of domestic politics, however; for while it was a question of pragmatic concern to Stresemann, it remained a matter of national honor to his critics on the Right.

Nearly as sensitive for the German government and its critics as territorial "renunciation" was its relationship to the League of Nations. It became apparent in the spring of 1925 that both England and France would insist upon Germany's entry into the league as a part of any security pact. Since the league's charter was an integral part of the Versailles Treaty, discussion of Germany's entry raised all the passions that had been directed against that treaty. Germany's entry had been actively discussed since the Dawes-plan negotiations of 1924. In September of that year, the German government released a memorandum stating its position—principally its reservations—concerning membership in the league. The German communiqué, which was sent to the league's ten permanent council members, outlined the factors upon which the government's participation would depend. The first asserted Germany' right to a permanent seat on the council. The second, in relation to Article 16 of the league's charter, involved what Germany termed special consideration due to her unique status because of disarmament and her geographic position. Article 16 called for all members to impose military and economic sanctions upon any nation that had formally been declared an aggressor by the league. Germany's geographic position in the middle of Europe made her particularly vulnerable to retaliation by an aggressor because of her imposition of any form of sanctions, and her disarmament made defense against such retaliatory action impossible. Thus, she contended, the league must recognize the necessity of a special discretionary right for Germany in the application of Article 16. Third, if Germany were to enter into the organization, she would have to be freed from any implication that she thereby accepted moral guilt for the war. Finally, her entry would entail the recognition that Germany was worthy of administering colonies.[12] As the security pact came under discussion, Germany continued to emphasize her reservations and to insist that they be taken into account before she made any formal request for entry.[13]

These points—renunciation of German land, the special situation of Eupen-Malmédy, and Germany's entry into the league—continued to be factors of both domestic and foreign policy throughout the spring of 1925. On all of them, the standpoint of the German government had been made clear both to the Nationalist partners in the cabinet, who would later raise objections on all three points, and to the diplomatic representatives of the Allies. In addition, the problem that had started the year's troubles for Germany remained unresolved: the Interallied Military Control Commission had ended its inspection in February 1925, but the Allied note on German disarmament, which should have justified the continued occupation of Cologne, had not yet been delivered.[14]

Still, none of these questions constituted a major factor impeding a more rapid development of the German proposal for a security pact. The delay resulted less from German differences with the Allies than from political developments within these countries and from differences among them. On April 10, 1925, the Herriot government, with which negotiations on the security pact had been begun, fell and was succeeded by a cabinet which was led by Paul Painlevé and included Aristide Briand as foreign minister, a post that he would hold without interruption until shortly before his death in 1932. The new French government was content to wait for the results of the second round of the German presidential elections, a factor that caused further delay in the negotiations on the security pact until after the victory of Paul von Hindenburg in late April 1925. Moreover, differences between France and Poland, on the one hand, and Great Britain, on the other, over the nature of possible guarantees in the Rhineland and in the East had to be ironed out. The Belgian government expressed concern over possible German designs on Eupen-Malmédy and sought to determine more precisely the status of those provinces in the Allied discussions.[15]

Whatever the reasons for it, the unanticipated delay strained the compromise between Stresemann and the DNVP leadership. Expecting a reply to his initiative in early April,[16] Stresemann had promised the German Nationalists on April 2 that he could soon publish the text of the German memorandum with the Allies' note of reply. As the delay lengthened, however, Stresemann considered making the German memorandum public independently. In favor of such an action stood the fact that the memorandum of February 9 contained nothing that was not already known. On the other hand, militating against its publication was the reaction that it might provoke among those political forces which were already hostile to or suspicious of the government's conduct or who could interpret the release of the memorandum as an attempt to pressure the Allies into hasty action. Stresemann discussed these views with Count Westarp just before the Reichstag assembly of May 18, 1925, pointing out that Luther was especially concerned about possible hostile reaction.[17]

Still acting to preserve the March compromise between the party and the cabinet, Westarp assented to Stresemann's plan to discuss the proposals in the Reichstag without actually quoting the text of the memorandum. At the same time, however, Stresemann made copies of the memorandum available to Westarp and to the Nationalists' expert on foreign policy, Otto Hoetzsch.[18] Chancellor Luther, too, sought to promote the working relationship between the Nationalists and the cabinet. On the same day as Stresemann's discussion with Westarp, he received two DNVP representatives from East Prussia to discuss the security pact and Germany's possible entry into the League of Nations. Luther tried to dispel the Nationalists' suspicions with the assurance that no circumstances could induce the government to recognize the existing eastern borders. On the contrary, the government aimed, through the security-pact negotiations, to win acceptance for the German insistence that these boundaries were not final.[19]

Count Westarp further attested to the continued endurance of the March compromise in his Reichstag reply of May 19 to Stresemann's foreign-policy speech of the previous day. Westarp objected to the dilatoriness of the Allies in the pact negotiations, but he acknowledged that there was no occasion for Germany to offer some new statement or renew its previous proposals. He declined to launch a general discussion regarding the origins of the German offer. His concern was rather that his party, as the largest of the parties supporting the government, exert its influence on the diplomatic handling of the issue in the future. To that end, he specified certain fundamental points of view. For negotiations to take place, the Allies would have to recognize Germany's equality and dignity as a nation. He noted with satisfaction the foreign minister's assurances that the government had no intention of recognizing the existing Polish-German border and that it hoped, in fact, for a favorable evolution of that problem under the terms of the arbitration treaties that it envisaged. But Westarp expressed far less optimism; the prospects of satisfactory arbitration with Poland seemed minimal in the light of recent public statements from Warsaw. As for German entry into the League of Nations, it could only take place after the evacuation of the Cologne zone; after the conclusion of a security pact; after the suspension of any obligations, under the terms of Article 16 of the League Covenant, to participate in economic or military sanctions; and only on condition that there be an official renunciation of Article 231, the "war-guilt clause." Westarp then concluded that his party accepted the obligations that had been contracted by the German government before the party's entry into the cabinet, and further, that negotiations begun "with or without our assistance, against our criticism and opposition or not," must be carried to conclusion. He insisted only that his presentation ought to indicate the direction that such negotiations should take if the DNVP's aspirations were to be satisfied.[20]

To judge that this first public discussion of the security pact between the government and the DNVP was indicative of the impossibility of their mutual cooperation is to miss the significance of the first five months of the Nationalist Party's participation in the cabinet.[21] Westarp's speech confirmed rather than challenged the compromise that the party leaders had struck with Stresemann and Luther. It contained no surprises for the government. It included, rather, a public acceptance of the obligation to pursue the security-pact negotiations further, although its rhetoric was directed more at quieting the party's right wing than at calming international fears. Far from suggesting that the DNVP could not or would not support Stresemann's foreign policy,[22] Westarp's speech raised every expectation that the party was willing to proceed within the coalition despite its reservations on foreign policy. Thus, whether these reservations could be overcome remained an open question.

This impression of a will to cooperate was confirmed by the DNVP news circular *Korrespondenz der Deutschnationalen Volkspartei*. On May 19, the same day as Westarp's speech in the Reichstag, the *Korrespondenz* published an article on the security problem which described the efforts that France was making to diminish the "world-wide psychological plus" that Germany had won with her proposal and which observed that the international situation demanded initiative from Germany and "the ability to cooperate (*mitspielen*)."[23] On the following day, the paper carried a summary of Stresemann's foreign-policy speech of May 18, which praised it as "proceeding from the domestic platform characterized by the spirit of Hin-

denburg," high praise from the party that considered the new Reichspresident its personal hero.[24] The paper even claimed, some days later, that
Stresemann's speech on foreign policy revealed a decided movement toward
the Nationalist—and away from the Marxist—position on the conduct of
diplomacy.[25] To be sure, there were still important differences between
Stresemann and even the moderate Nationalists over the conduct of German
diplomacy, and these would emerge as the summer lengthened. But for the
moment, at least, the cabinet and the party had agreed to go in the same
direction.

The DNVP's right wing recognized that the party's leadership was
willing to compromise with the government, but it abhorred this fact. The
executive committee of the old German-Conservative Party issued a public
rejection of Stresemann's policy of "renunciation" and a not so indirect
rebuff to the DNVP leadership for tolerating it. The chairman of the
DNVP's local committee in the electoral district of Potsdam-I invited other
"right-oriented local committees to a common undertaking against any
'policy of renunciation.'" Similar protests were directed to the party's leadership in Berlin. All received the same reply, which was formulated in essence
by Freytagh-Loringhoven and seems to have been automatically reproduced
by Westarp's political office. The reply stated that the DNVP delegation
had learned of the security-pact initiative only after it had been taken and
that the text of the memorandum had not yet been revealed to the party—an
inaccuracy which suggests that the confidentiality between Stresemann and
the party leaders who had received the text was being preserved. The auto-
matic answer concluded that the best possible outcome—a likely one by all
indications—would be if the German initiative were to fail because of
France's intransigence. In any event, no further action would be undertaken
by the government without the prior approval of the party.[26] In addition to
making the disarming replies, the party leadership sought to identify and
quiet the voices of dissent from the Fatherland Societies that were trying to
promote direct political activity by these groups because the Nationalist
Party had abdicated its true responsibility.[27]

Even the Allied note on disarmament, which finally arrived on June 4,
1925, did not shake the DNVP leadership from its willingness to give
Stresemann time to pursue the security pact and also to give itself time to
exercise its nationalistic influence. Publicly it characterized the disarmament
note as childish and as a sign of France's designs to extend the occupation
of the Rhine for an indefinite period. Privately, in an intraparty circular, it
demanded proof of "mutual fulfillment" before any resolution of the disarmament issue, and it counseled patience. The content of the Allied answer
to the security-pact proposal would provide a barometer of the willingness

to recognize Germany's equal status. The party's foreign political program remained as Westarp had outlined it in May. Before Germany would accept any new obligations, the Allies must fulfill theirs: first, they must evacuate the Ruhr and Cologne; second, they must put an end to military control. Then the Nationalists would be prepared to enter into security-pact negotiations, but only on the basis of equality and reciprocity. The final step would be to negotiate for Germany's entry into the league. This program was different from Stresemann's, but it did not reject the direction that Stresemann had set. It sought only to set preconditions that the Allies would have to fulfill before there would be any negotiations. And the party leaders were still trying to control their dissidents. The situation in foreign policy was serious, and it created dangers to domestic stability which made it necessary for every "politician who loves his fatherland and is conscious of his responsibility" to avoid insignificant disagreements which might lead to divisions or serious altercations within the nationalist movement. The worst possible development would be for "the enemies" to succeed, through their demands concerning the disarmament and security questions, in returning the Social Democrats to the government in the Reich. Clearly, a strong "national" foreign policy was more important to the DNVP leadership than was an understanding with France; but "trade treaties," "tariff policy," and "tax laws" were, for the moment, more important than either.[28]

Still, the party leaders did not simply ignore the criticism from the Right. Instead, they sought to allay it by arguing that continued DNVP participation in the cabinet could not only win concessions on tariffs, taxes, and trade but could prevent the German Foreign Office from making unacceptable concessions to the Allies in the security-pact negotiations. In the rhetoric that was necessary in order to mollify the Right, the policy became: stay in the cabinet to prevent a leftist-Marxist coalition, to win concessions for nationalist interests in domestic policy, and to frustrate and undermine Stresemann's foreign policy.[29]

Despite Stresemann's recognition of the growing nationalistic hostility to his policy of reconciliation, he was impressed by the calm that prevailed til mid June. Even the meeting of the Reichstag's Foreign Affairs Committee that was devoted to the Allied note of June 4, 1925, regarding disarmament had not broken this calm. Stresemann realized, of course, that the seeming equanimity with which the DNVP leaders had accepted his conduct of foreign policy since March did not remove the real danger to the pursuit of reconciliation that existed in the stubborn opposition of the DNVP's right wing. The real test of the compromise between the party and the government would arise only when the French would finally reply to the February memorandum.[30]

That reply came on June 16, 1925, much delayed by the political crisis in France that had brought Aristide Briand to France's Foreign Office, the Quai d'Orsay, by the election of Hindenburg as Germany's new president, and by the negotiations between France and Great Britain over the wording of the reply.[31]

The French note was in general conciliatory, and its tone was conducive to further negotiations. It was exploratory in nature, intending to focus on those questions that had been raised by the German memorandum so that the German government could clarify certain points. At the same time, the note represented a brilliantly conceived attempt by Briand to rewin for France the moral advantage that Germany had gained from her original proposal and to regain the diplomatic initiative in order to preserve France's position of superiority under the Versailles Treaty. To these ends, the French note made the conclusion of the security pact conditional upon Germany's entry into the League of Nations. The pact, the French insisted, could neither imply any modification of the peace settlement nor have the practical effect of such modification, especially concerning rights to oppose any nonfulfillment of the peace treaties; this represented a clear effort to reserve the right of sanctions. Nor could the pact affect the clauses in the Versailles Treaty that governed the occupation of the Rhineland. The treaties of arbitration that were proposed in the German memorandum would have to be contracted with all states desiring them, and the signatory powers of the Rhineland pact would have the privilege of acting as guarantors of these treaties, a provision that would allow France to protect her eastern allies in any dispute with Germany. By carefully implying that the French interpretation of these conditions was consistent with the suggestions already put forward in the German proposal, Briand tried to create a situation in which Germany could not reject those conditions without appearing to retreat from the initiative toward reconciliation that the February memorandum had represented.[32]

The diplomatic implications of the French reply were devastating. Although its tone was conciliatory, it broadened the German concept of treaties of arbitration far beyond the scope that Stresemann had envisaged. France's retention of a right to guarantee such treaties amounted to extending the Rhineland settlement to Germany's frontier with Poland, a development that Stresemann had no intention of accepting. Moreover, the note indicated France's refusal to entertain any modification of the Rhineland occupation; and this ran counter to one of the very motives that had prompted Stresemann's offer.[33]

Stresemann immediately set to work to regain the diplomatic advantages for Germany that the note jeopardized. He informed the French ambassador that Germany could only enter the league if her views on Article 16 were taken into account. He objected to the note's attempt to apply the Rhineland guarantee also to the eastern borders, and he protested that the note would give France the right to act as both guarantor and judge in relation to possible Polish-German disputes.[34]

Equally as important as the diplomatic implications of the French note was the political activity it touched off in Germany. The cabinet discussion of June 24 revealed the extent of the impact the French reply had had. The meeting opened with sketches of the disarmament situation, the security-pact negotiations, and Russo-German relations; but the second point dominated the discussion. Stresemann outlined the points on which he thought German diplomacy should concentrate: the French role in Polish-German arbitration treaties, the French insistence upon the right of sanctions, and Germany's entry into the league. In opening the discussion, however, Minister of Justice Joseph Frenken raised a new issue: the renunciation of Eupen-Malmédy. A free acknowledgment of the western borders might be permissible in relation to Alsace-Lorraine, but the abandonment of the population of Eupen-Malmédy, which had been German before the Belgian state had even existed, would be a betrayal of German land, people, and honor. Since the negotiations had already been started, Frenken saw no way to avoid continuing them, but he urged that the cabinet proceed with the clear—if unstated—intention of abandoning the original German memorandum. In reply, Stresemann revealed that Belgium might be interested in returning Eupen-Malmédy to Germany if Germany would redeem the occupation marks; he also disclosed his efforts to ensure that such a peaceful accord would not be excluded by a security pact. As for the suggestion that the memorandum be abandoned as the basis for Germany's negotiating position, Stresemann rejected this idea out of hand and threatened to resign if the cabinet accepted it. This threat did nothing to quiet the criticism.

General Hans von Seeckt was the next person to level his guns at the foreign minister. He had been asking himself for weeks what advantage Germany could possibly derive from the security-pact proposal. The answer, he had found, was none. Advantages aplenty he could see for France; but none for Germany. Stresemann's assertion that Eupen-Malmédy could be recovered by peaceful agreement ran counter to the lessons of history: borders are never altered by treaties, only by force of arms. As for Alsace-Lorraine, Seeckt urged Germany to adopt the French formula: Never mention it, but think exclusively of reconquest. He, like Frenken, would be delighted to see the negotiations toward a security pact fail. The Nationalist minister of economics, Albert Neuhaus, said amen. His party colleague and minister of the interior, Martin Schiele, added that Germany was caught in

a web of the foreign minister's weaving. The security pact was supposed
to allow Germany to gain freedom of action in the East; but the text of the
memorandum—which, Schiele pointedly remarked, had only recently become known—contradicted this contention, because it suggested that Germany was prepared to conclude treaties of arbitration with all neighboring
states, including Poland and Czechoslovakia. Schiele thus insinuated that
his objections concerning the eastern borders could only take form now that
the text of the memorandum had been published, ignoring that Stresemann's
thorough summaries of the memorandum in March and later had adequately discussed the arbitration treaties and the eastern boundaries. Schiele's
remarks also ignored the fact that the DNVP had been offered a copy of
the memorandum in mid May.[35]

Even the generally moderate Centrist minister of labor, Heinrich
Brauns, added his voice to the chorus of skeptics that Stresemann faced. But
the foreign minister refused to submit to the suggestion that further negotiations be aimed at sabotaging the security-pact proposal. He admitted that
the reservations—which he himself had always maintained in his pursuit of
the pact—concerning the eastern boundaries and Germany's entry into the
League of Nations might ultimately prevent a pact from being concluded.
But he insisted that these reservations were consistent with—in fact, were
inherent in—the original German memorandum. Continued reference to
the memorandum as the basis for further negotiations would be enough
protection against the unacceptable implications of the French note. Any
departure from it would make it impossible for him to continue as foreign
minister.

Once again, as in March, when the DNVP had attacked the foreign
minister, Chancellor Luther came to Stresemann's aid. Those who suggested
the abandonment of the security-pact negotiations offered as an alternative a
policy of passivity in the face of the Treaty of Versailles and foreign political
pressure. Such a policy was absolutely unacceptable. If the pact presented
some difficulties, so did inaction: "Politics does not stand still." The threat
that a tripartite security pact might be directed specifically against Germany
in the West was no fantasy. Remaining an inactive object of international
policy offered no defense. The German Foreign Office's initiative aimed to
restore Germany as an active party in international affairs; and the fact that
at the moment both France and Russia (who feared any accommodation
between Germany and the capitalistic western powers) were eagerly courting Germany attested to the success of these efforts. Moreover, the German
initiative had had a pronounced effect on the United States. "North America is a cool-headed observer," Luther noted. "It has money to spare and is
looking for secure investments in a quiescent Europe, and just now America

is beginning to perceive that the calm it needs in Europe is threatened by France's troublesome attitude," rather than by Germany. The concern that the German Foreign Office's actions aroused relative to the eastern borders was understandable. "But after all," Luther remarked, "we could not start off by saying publicly that one of the inner motives for the German memorandum is the reestablishment of our former eastern boundaries." The balance struck by the Foreign Office appeared to be quite successful. The government must follow through with the negotiations, because the consequences of inaction would be overwhelming. The approach suggested by some—namely, to negotiate, with the aim of destroying the groundwork laid by the memorandum—was as unacceptable to him as it was to the foreign minister.

Luther's strong endorsement of Stresemann's policies was reinforced by Minister of Defense Otto Gessler and by Minister of Transport Rudolf Krohne. The latter openly challenged Schiele's implied disavowal of the February initiative by remarking that very shortly after the formation of the present cabinet, Stresemann, in the very room that they now occupied, had conducted a lengthy briefing on the German memorandum and the proposals regarding an arbitration treaty. That briefing, noted Krohne, had evoked no opposition; had the objections just heard existed then, they certainly could have been raised. The implication of Krohne's remarks was clear: the DNVP was manufacturing objections now in order to escape its political responsibility.

The support that Stresemann had gained seemed to turn the tide. Schiele suddenly averred that the decisive factor for him was the "inner energy" with which the negotiations would be pursued. If the reservations were maintained—war guilt, entry into the league, and Article 16—on which the cabinet's discussion had revealed a unanimity among the ministers, Schiele conceded that he would have "no objections against continuation of the negotiations."

But Schiele's attempt to undermine Stresemann's position within the cabinet had not ended. Luther concluded the meeting by suggesting that a small committee, composed of himself, Stresemann, Brauns, Schiele, and Frenken prepare a short communiqué for release to the press. The communiqué would cover the origins of the German initiative concerning security and the current state of the negotiations. The proposal for such a communiqué had, however, originated with Schiele rather than with Luther. In a clear attempt to divorce the DNVP from responsibility for the security-pact policies in their early phases, Schiele presented Luther with the following short statement, which he proposed that the cabinet adopt:

Subsequent to the foreign minister's suggestion—through oral declarations by the [German] Ambassador [in Paris], which were supported
by an *aide-memoire*—of a reciprocal security pact, and after having received the [reply] note from the French government, the cabinet has
now addressed itself to the foreign minister's suggestions of February 9,
1925, and the note issued in relation to them.[36]

Both Luther and Stresemann immediately realized the implications of
Schiele's draft: another attempt, as in March, to impute the sole responsibility for the security-pact initiative to Stresemann. Luther suggested to
Schiele that a reference to Luther's speech of January 30, 1925, be added to
the communiqué. This, he told Stresemann privately, would confirm the
chancellor's role and would blunt the inference that the foreign minister
alone was responsible for the initiative. Stresemann acknowledged that this
constituted an improvement, but he also realized that it would still allow
the DNVP to disclaim any responsibility of its own. Consultation with his
principal aides in the German Foreign Office, Carl von Schubert and Friedrich Gaus, confirmed Stresemann's conviction that any formula which
suggested that the German memorandum had been the initiative of the
German Foreign Office alone, and not of the German government, was
unacceptable. Gaus therefore prepared several draft statements for consideration by the cabinet committee. Stresemann insisted that the cabinet communiqué must end with an expression of readiness to pursue negotiations
on the basis of the February memorandum. Thus, Gaus's drafts always concluded with a mention of continuing negotiations "in the spirit of the
memorandum." Schiele and Frenken accepted this phrase in committee, but
it was later modified in the cabinet debate on June 25 to state that negotiations ought to proceed with the aim of concluding an accord on the basis
of full reciprocity. Stresemann agreed that this expressed the fundamental
thought of the original memorandum.

In its final form the cabinet communiqué was a far cry from the draft
that Schiele had originally proposed. In addition to the closing reference, in
which the German government welcomed negotiations that might lead to a
reciprocal security pact, it contained a full description of the diplomatic
circumstances in which the note had originated and a strong affirmation of
the eagerness and readiness for peace to which the German initiative attested.
Nonetheless, the communiqué did not represent a clear-cut victory for
Stresemann. In specific reference to the February memorandum, which was,
after all, the crux of the matter, the cabinet communiqué stated that as a
result of the overall foreign political situation, it had "appeared appropriate
to the [German] Foreign Office to inform the Allied governments of the
bases on which the German government could cooperate in the resolution

of the question of security." The possibility of implying a distinction between the actions of the government, the cabinet, and the German Foreign Office thus had not been forthrightly countered.[37]

Because the communiqué was still ambiguous, the Executive Committee of the German People's Party (DVP) raised sharp protests against having it published by the cabinet. The DVP leaders were convinced that the ambiguity gave the Nationalists too great an opportunity to shirk all prior responsibility for the initiative, something that the DVP found politically unacceptable, since its efforts had been aimed consistently at compelling the Nationalists to share responsibility for foreign policy. Stresemann defended the compromise before his party colleagues, pointing to the final sentence of the communiqué, which affirmed the government's resolve to proceed with the security-pact negotiations. He also emphasized that Schiele had promised his utmost effort to win the entire delegation of German Nationalists in the Reichstag over to united support of positive cooperation with the government. The Executive Committee of the DVP remained dissatisfied, however. The chairman of the DVP's Reichstag delegation, Ernst Scholz, telephoned Luther to express this dissatisfaction. A meeting was arranged between Scholz, Schiele, and Luther. Here, Schiele again gave the same assurances to Scholz that he had earlier given to Stresemann: namely, that the German Nationalists would ignore the question of who was responsible for the memorandum and would simply proceed with the work at hand. Scholz demanded the additional assurance that Schiele would instruct the DNVP press to desist in its attempts to exonerate the Nationalist Party. Schiele agreed.

Schiele, however, was not in sole command of the situation. On the preceding day, June 25, six district committees from northwest Germany had met and issued a sharply anti-Stresemann declaration, demanding that he resign and that the DNVP reject the foreign policy that he had initiated "without the approval of the cabinet." The Nationalist press took up the call.[38] Two days later, the DNVP's Executive Committee (*Parteivorstand*) met with the chairmen of all the district committees. Here the leadership managed to pass a unanimous resolution, which insisted on the necessity of staying in the cabinet, now more than ever, to protect the "vital interests and dignity of the German Reich."[39]

But the cabinet in which the DNVP thus chose to stay did not necessarily have to include Stresemann. In the same issue of the party's news circular that published the Executive Committee's decision to remain in the government, a long article appeared on the cabinet's communiqué of June 26, which pointedly distinguished between the responsibility of the German Foreign Office and foreign minister, on the one hand, and the cabinet on the other. On the same day that the party had passed its resolution to stay in the government, Westarp and Lindeiner-Wildau, the political secretary of the Nationalist Party, furnished the *Deutsche Zeitung* with material for a direct attack on Stresemann, demanding his resignation as well as those of Schubert and Gaus, his co-workers in the Foreign Office.[40] The disposition within the DNVP leadership had certainly changed. As late as June 20, Westarp had written of the February initiative as the "German memorandum"; on June 23, 51 of the DNVP's 111 delegates in the Reichstag had signed a protest demanding that Stresemann be removed. By June 24 the memorandum had become Stresemann's sole responsibility. The truce with Stresemann had ended.[41]

The Nationalist attacks provoked the German People's Party into action. With Stresemann's approval, the DVP issued a call for a full parliamentary debate on foreign policy to clarify the question of responsibility. This declaration was released on June 30.

The next day, July 1, 1925, Stresemann briefed the Reichstag's Foreign Affairs Committee. He reported that France's reply went far beyond the German memorandum regarding the eastern borders and that it was in many other ways unsatisfactory, but that negotiations should nonetheless be pursued. Stresemann had expected the moderate Otto Hoetzsch to answer for the DNVP, but instead Count Westarp took the floor. No basis for negotiations could exist, he asserted, as long as the Cologne zone remained occupied. He then made a sharp distinction between *discussions* (*Erörterungen*) and *negotiations* (*Verhandlungen*). Any discussions that might eventually take place on the basis of the cabinet's communiqué of June 26 would be quite distinct from the February memorandum, for which the foreign minister bore the sole responsibility. The cabinet's responsibility dated only from the communiqué. Germany was thus in no way bound to the original memorandum. The diplomatic activity of the present must consist in nothing more than *prediscussions* (*Vorerörterungen*) concerning subsequent procedural measures. The question of eventual negotiations remained open. In fact, for the DNVP, the entire situation remained open. The security-pact proposal held no advantage for Germany; negotiations on the proposal could therefore only evolve unfavorably. Nonetheless, Westarp's party would reserve final judgment until the current "discussions" were completed.[42]

Westarp's attack and his attempt to isolate the foreign minister evoked an immediate reaction from the noncoalition parties of the Left—the SPD and the DDP. First, the Social Democrat Rudolf Breitscheid spoke, saying that the memorandum was in no way the private work of the foreign minister; the entire cabinet shared in the responsibility. The Nationalists were simply conniving to dump Stresemann while preserving their own position in the cabinet in order to push through protective tariffs. The Democratic representative echoed the protest against Westarp's obvious attempt to dodge any responsibility.

Stresemann defended himself with a detailed presentation of the relationship between the chancellor, the German Foreign Office, and the cabinet during the evolution of the policy regarding the security pact. But the decisive voice had to be Luther's. The real question was whether the distinction drawn by the DNVP between the responsibility of the foreign minister and that of the cabinet had even the remotest political reality—whether, in effect, the memorandum still enjoyed the support of the full cabinet. Luther had arrived at the meeting late, but in time to hear Stresemann's detailed review concerning the origins of the memorandum. Repeatedly, delegates from all parties demanded that he speak to the issue.

Suddenly, the pattern of behavior that Luther had followed since January changed. In January he had approved the memorandum. In February he had reviewed it with Stresemann (and with Schiele, according to Stresemann),[43] on the day after the French had formally acknowledged having received it. In March, when the DNVP had attacked Stresemann for his independent action and his secrecy, Luther had shouldered joint responsibility for the memorandum and had forced the Nationalists back into line. In May he had assured individual Nationalist leaders who had attacked the foreign minister's policy that all was well under his leadership. As late as the cabinet meetings of June 24 and 25 he had worked toward compromise on the communiqué, with which the DNVP spokesman had tried once again to isolate Stresemann as the sole advocate of the security pact. The chancellor had even remarked ironically on the apparent expectation that "we will once again some day have a great army, and that until then we [can] sit with our hands in our laps and hope that God will send us a miraculous elixir to protect us against our enemies."[44] Now, all this changed. Here, before the Foreign Affairs Committee of the Reichstag, amidst cries from all sides that he declare himself with regard to Stresemann's assertion that he, Luther, had known of and supported the memorandum from the beginning, the chancellor remained silent.

After the meeting, Luther approached Stresemann to declare that he did not recall seeing the relevant documents from the German Foreign Office before February 21 and could not accept responsibility for what he did not recall. He then retired to prepare a letter that would lay this lapse of memory—or repudiation of responsibility for the origins of the security pact—openly before the cabinet and possibly the political public. Stresemann was understandably livid.[45] But why did Luther suddenly change?

Westarp's change of course was only slightly less dramatic. In January and February the DNVP's newsletter carried nothing that was hostile to the man who was the Nationalists' new coalition partner and chairman of the German People's Party. It did carry one or two articles on foreign policy, which observed the "disappointment" that hostile foreign circles must feel at the Nationalists' objective but firm approach to diplomacy and which mentioned the "complex of problems commonly referred to as the 'security question'" that the cabinet would have to face in the near future. When, in early March, the first protests over the actual security-pact proposal began to reach Westarp from the provinces, his office had replied that it viewed the rumors concerning an initiative by the foreign minister with the greatest concern, especially since the Nationalists themselves shared responsibility for the foreign policy of the cabinet in which they participated. In March and April, not a word about the party's effort to isolate Stresemann, or about its failure and the resultant compromise, appeared in the official newsletter. In May, Westarp agreed with Stresemann that, for diplomatic and domestic reasons, the memorandum should not be published, but he did accept Stresemann's offer to make copies available to select members of the DNVP. With the arrival of the disarmament note, there began to be a subtle shift away from this rather benign toleration of Stresemann's foreign policy. Westarp began to argue for a split approach: substantive, issue-oriented criticism of Stresemann's policy in public, coupled with an effort to isolate the foreign minister within the government. By June 27 Westarp's attacks had become highly personal, if indirectly engineered. He had provided the information that had helped the *Deutsche Zeitung* to launch its open attack on Stresemann. This attack was intensified on July 1 with the printing of a private letter from Martin Schiele, dated May 22, in which he denied that, even as of that date, he had been informed of the contents of the February memorandum. The obvious conclusion, which the *Deutsche Zeitung* drew for its readers, was that Stresemann had misled and deceived his colleagues in the cabinet. The attack was perfectly timed with the sudden lapse of Luther's memory and support. Why the sudden change?

Explanations of this crisis have heretofore concentrated on the relationship between Luther and Stresemann. If one keeps Westarp's actions in mind, a new explanation suggests itself.

Luther had seen Stresemann virtually isolated in the cabinet meeting of June 24, when first Frenken, then Seeckt (whose ties with the Nationalists in these weeks were particularly close), then the DNVP ministers had all attacked the foreign minister's security-pact policy in vitriolic terms. Perhaps Luther asked himself whether the cabinet might not be able to get along without this independent, strong-willed, powerful personality as foreign minister. Perhaps, at that moment, Westarp and Lindeiner-Wildau found this a consummation devoutly to be wished. After all, the Nationalists had many reasons to continue to support a *Luther* cabinet, which had many important domestic projects still to complete. The Nationalists were not even opposed to negotiating the security question; they simply preferred to negotiate it on their own terms, rather than on Stresemann's. Perhaps the presidency of Paul von Hindenburg made it possible to think about new cabinet combinations. Perhaps the DVP's resolution to demand a potentially embarrassing foreign political debate, an action that was taken without prior consultation with Luther, had piqued the chancellor enough so that on July 1 his previously vigorous support of Stresemann suddenly dissolved. Even a politician who had no great ambition might be tempted by the possibility of becoming the political domesticator of the strongest nonsocialist party in the Reichstag, a formidable political force to which both the Reichspresident and the commander of the Reichswehr would be sympathetic. Without Luther's support, any effort to unseat Stresemann—who was no negligible political force himself—had no hope of success. With his support, a change in personnel in the German Foreign Office might seem quite attainable.

On the other hand, perhaps in July, Luther simply forgot what he had done in January and had remembered in March. Perhaps Westarp or Lindeiner-Wildau, coming quite accidentally in late June upon a letter that Schiele had written a month earlier, decided that it was still newsworthy. Perhaps the sudden shift in tactics in several places at once was coincidental.[46] More likely, it was not.

Whatever the explanation for the intense crisis, it was short-lived. Stresemann briefly considered Luther's proposal to lay a letter before the cabinet, but on the morning of July 2 he telephoned Luther's secretary in the Reichschancellery, Franz Kempner, and told him that he, Stresemann, was fed up with singlehandedly carrying the full burden of responsibility for foreign policy. He refused to go along with the formal exchange of letters that Luther had envisaged or even with a cabinet discussion of the matter. If Luther wanted to persist in issuing his own statement, Stresemann would reply to it, but from the floor of the Reichstag, no longer as foreign minister, but as a simple delegate. Luther quickly dropped the idea of a formal statement, and in a cabinet meeting that had already been scheduled for July 2, he simply declared that although Stresemann's comments before the Foreign Affairs Committee did not correspond in all details with his own recollections, they correctly reflected the fact that he continued to espouse the same point of view as the foreign minister. The next day, Westarp also dropped the attack.[47]

The problem of the DVP's call for an open debate on foreign policy remained to be dealt with. The idea met with universal disfavor from Stresemann's cabinet colleagues. To this, Stresemann responded with what constituted a major concession to Nationalist sensitivities by indicating that a debate on foreign policy would serve the useful purpose of uniting all the parties of the Reichstag (with the standard exception of the Communists) behind a statement that certain outstanding points of contention between Germany and the Allies, especially the evacuation of the Ruhr and Cologne, would have to be resolved before any security treaty could be concluded. Such a declaration would not be a repudiation of the memorandum, Stresemann insisted, but would reemphasize the problems that had occasioned it; therefore, it would be most welcome to the German Foreign Office. This was a reversal of the position that Stresemann had maintained throughout the spring, when he had steadfastly refused to make such a formal connection between his proposals concerning security and the issue of evacuation for fear that he would alienate the Allies from the outset and thus lose the moral leverage he hoped the initiative would gain for Germany. Now he seemed to be prepared to change his tactics in order to tempt the DNVP leaders not only to break with the right wing of the party but also to opt for continued participation in the government.

But the rest of the cabinet still found the prospect of a full debate in the Reichstag unacceptable. As a result of the discussion, the cabinet decided to initiate consultations between Luther and the DVP leaders in an effort to persuade the latter to delay their Reichstag interpellation. The meeting, which took place right after the cabinet session, was marked by sharp exchanges between Luther and the DVP representatives. The chancellor protested the fact that a coalition party had announced its intention to present an important interpellation without consulting him. DVP chairman Scholz countered by objecting that the chancellor had published the cabinet's communiqué, which lay at the root of the trouble, without having consulted the DVP. The party still feared that this communiqué would allow the DNVP to disclaim any political responsibility for the memorandum. Despite the extremely high tension—Stresemann speaks of Luther's having nearly lost his composure—a compromise emerged. Luther agreed to hold a debate on foreign policy later in July, before adjournment of the current Reichstag session, whereupon the DVP agreed to issue a statement that would affirm the party's solidarity with the chancellor. Luther gave further assurances that the government intended to proceed as rapidly as possible in drafting an answer to the French note.[48] He had made similar recommendations in the cabinet meeting of July 2, in effect to move into a "new stage" in the negotiations with France, thus moving out of the current domestic crisis.[49]

Stresemann's readiness to force a debate on foreign policy had brought the DNVP and the chancellor to heel. Luther, who was convinced that pursuit of the issue of responsibility would cause the cabinet to break up, happily accepted the chance to postpone the debate until after Germany's answer to the French note of June 16 had been dispatched. The Nationalist leaders, for their part, accepted the compromise, because advantageous and important tariffs could only be secured if they stayed in power. In effect, they perceived that they stood to lose a great deal by breaking up the coalition and, in political terms, stood to gain nothing at all by it; perhaps they would even be paving the way for a return of the Socialists. Another factor entered the political calculation. In a showdown vote on whether or not to support Stresemann's foreign policy and thus preserve the coalition, the right wing of the party, led by Freytagh-Loringhoven, would have been outvoted but would not have been reconciled to the outcome; and this would have had disastrous consequences for the unity of the delegation. To avoid this, the leaders chose compromise rather than an intraparty showdown. They spread the word that the attack on Stresemann, which they had endorsed in late June, had to be suspended for the time being. The party would continue its surveillance of foreign policy, however, seeking the propitious moment to retake the offensive against Stresemann. If this strategy failed, Westarp assured his colleagues on the Right, the party would withdraw from the government.[50]

General von Seeckt also realized that the effort to unseat Stresemann had miscarried and would have to be abandoned for the moment. He had actively supported the Nationalist onslaught against Stresemann in the cabinet meetings of June 24 through June 26; he may even have coordinated his attack with the Nationalists beforehand. He still spoke of an eventual clearing of the way for a new foreign policy, but he justified the delay by the suggestion that it was unwise to change jockeys in mid race.[51]

The postponement of the discussion on the security proposals angered the parties that were outside the government, however. The Socialists, in particular, charged that the delay was designed so that the agrarian interests would have time to make their gains before their strength was broken because of the disruption of the rightist coalition. Rudolf Breitscheid taunted the Nationalists openly by claiming that they were willing to sell sacrosanct German land and people at the price of a wheat tariff of 5.50 marks.[52] But the government weathered these attacks and responded both in plenum and in the Foreign Affairs Committee that it would address itself first to the formulation of an answer to the French note and only later to a full debate on foreign policy. To mollify the Socialists and Democrats in particular, upon whose support in foreign policy it could normally count, the cabinet agreed to lay a draft of the answering note before the Reichstag's Foreign Affairs Committee.[53]

Stresemann presented a draft to the cabinet for discussion on July 15. It evoked the immediate hostility of Frenken who, as he had in June, condemned the inclusion of specific references to the February memorandum. Indeed, the initial strife had an aura of déjà vu: Stresemann and Luther opposing the repudiation of the memorandum; Frenken and Schiele demanding it. In this meeting, however, Stresemann quickly found the broad backing that he had lacked in June. Gessler again asserted that the memorandum did in fact present the only course to a satisfactory continuation of negotiations, but he found that the draft reply, although irreproachable in content, was lacking in tone. It was too aridly juridical; there was no element of warmth in it. The tone could be softened by reemphasizing the motives that had prompted the German initiative in the first place—namely, the hope for a sound and peaceful settlement. Brauns then simultaneously bridged the gap between tone and substance and that between Stresemann and his opponents within the cabinet. Brauns asserted that a repudiation of the memorandum was out of the question for reasons of domestic as well as foreign politics, but the cabinet ought nonetheless to minimize its own difficulties by avoiding any snares that might be inherent in the memorandum or in the French interpretation of it. The draft reply did just that, but perhaps at times by interpreting the February memorandum too strictly. On this point, Brauns supported Frenken's wish that certain passages be revised. This could be accomplished most successfully by adopting Gessler's suggestion that the motives underlying the memorandum be emphasized, rather than the specific points that it had raised.[54]

Schiele quickly accepted this proposal. He remarked that he had not intended to disavow the motives that underlay the memorandum. He simply asked that the answer be worded so as to circumvent a new outbreak of domestic opposition. Frenken concurred: it had never been his wish to repudiate the memorandum formally, but only to avoid a formal reiteration of it in the present note. He found Brauns's suggestion quite acceptable. Brauns replied that a formal acknowledgment of the memorandum could hardly be avoided in actual practice. Frenken, however, raised no further objections. The cabinet then examined the draft note in detail and adopted changes that conformed to Gessler's suggestion to soften the tone.

In conjunction with these modifications, Stresemann pointed out that Germany's answer would in fact leave much unsaid. Such points, however, could be raised in the coming Reichstag debate on foreign policy. Schiele eagerly pursued this proposal, suggesting three categories of problems that the government and the parties ought to program into the debates: (1) military inspection; (2) preconditions for negotiations, such as evacuation; and (3) disarmament. If agreement could be reached on these matters, he would approve the present text of the reply note. From this point, everything proceeded smoothly. The cabinet released a communiqué announcing that it had reached a fundamental accord on the contents of the German reply. The "new stage" that Luther had proposed in early July had been reached.[55]

On July 17, Stresemann presented the note to the Reichstag's Foreign Affairs Committee. He explained, as he had to the cabinet, that the note contained three main parts. The first part covered the relationship among the proposed security pact, the Versailles Treaty, and the Rhineland statutes. The second dealt with the matter of arbitration treaties, and the third with Germany's attitude towards entry into the League of Nations. Germany's answer had been drawn up in some detail because the French note had raised considerations that, if not mentioned or, where necessary, rejected, might prejudice Germany's position in subsequent negotiations.[56]

Speaking in the ensuing discussion for the German Nationalists, Count Westarp returned to the position that he had taken in his Reichstag speech of May 19. The DNVP would not carry on any further controversy over the "prehistory" of the German proposals. He limited himself to remarks concerning the current German reply. His party found this note to be adequate as the basis for continued diplomatic discussions, and he had no objections to having the note dispatched in its existing form. The party would reserve its final judgment until the ultimate results of the negotiations could be reviewed, however. Indeed, Westarp was inclined to think that an acceptable conclusion to the current discussions concerning a pact was questionable at best. But he recognized that Germany must continue them so as not to appear the recalcitrant troublemaker in the international arena. He once again distinguished between preliminary discussions, negotiations in earnest, and the period after the conclusion of negotiations. In the first stage—in which Germany now found herself—certain points had to be clarified before one could proceed to the bargaining table. So long as the evacuation of Cologne had not been resolved, so long as the Ruhr and the sanction cities were not completely freed, Germany could not conclude a security pact. Westarp regretted that these points had not been mentioned specifically in the German note. His party would underscore them in the coming debate on foreign policy in Parliament. Furthermore, the security pact would have no rhyme or reason unless it effected a general amelioration for the occupied territories and the Saar and unless it reduced the duration of the occupation in the Rhineland. In addition, the pact ought not to diminish in any way the rights of self-determination and cultural autonomy or the protection of minority languages. These questions, Westarp concluded, would have to be resolved in the negotiations before any treaty could be concluded.

Westarp's approval, however grudging and negative its tone, sealed the new compromise and cleared the way for the German answer to be dispatched on July 18. In his instructions to Ambassador Hoesch in Paris, Stresemann pointed out that, although the German government had been obliged to contest certain points raised by France's note of June 16, it had endeavored to do so without polemics, emphasizing the rapprochement in outlook that had already taken place and the desire to continue the negotiations.[57]

And indeed, the German note, dated July 20, was mildly worded. Nonetheless, it sought effectively to disarm the unfavorable implications of the French note. It stated, for example, that the German government assumed that the path to eventual peaceful understandings concerning changed relationships remained open—an allusion to the revisionist possibilities of Article 19 of the League of Nations Charter—despite France's contention concerning the inviolability of the Treaty of Versailles. Granting that the pact would in no way affect the treaty stipulations regulating the occupation of the Rhineland, the note observed that the conclusion of a security accord would constitute such a significant step in Franco-German relations that it could hardly remain without ramifications for the situation within the occupied territories and for the entire question of occupation. The note expressed the "tremendous misgivings" that France's construction of the German arbitration treaties had occasioned, pointing out that this was a matter that demanded further clarification. Germany rejected not only the possibility that France might exercise a right of judgment and of guarantee in arbitration, but also any unilateral exercise by France of a guarantee right. The note reiterated Germany's oft-repeated stand on entering the League of Nations: obligations to apply sanctions under Article 16 would have to be tempered by a consideration of Germany's unique geographic and military circumstances. The call for universal disarmament, which prefaced the Versailles Treaty clauses governing German disarmament, was underscored. The German reply concluded that progress toward satisfactory accords had certainly been made and that any difficulties that remained could surely be overcome in a spirit of equality and reciprocity.[58]

The communication of this German note to Paris marked the end of the second phase of the conflict over the policies regarding the security accord. The climax had in fact been reached some days earlier. Since the early days of July the attitudes of the Nationalist ministers and leaders had been limited to what, by comparison to the attacks of late June and July 1, can only be called token opposition. The protestations of the more radical provincial circles were met by assurances that the DNVP was making its views so effectively felt within the cabinet that it could still stand to participate in the government. The claim was circulated that the Nationalists had shaped the German note so as to include their reservations. Rightist news reports asserted that the attack against the foreign minister had been lifted because the exigencies of coalition politics forced the DVP to unite behind Stresemann, a unity of support that allegedly belied the real sentiment within the People's Party.[59]

But these protestations barely conceal quite another development. Once again, one sees that clash between the Nationalists' sense of honor in foreign policy—with its aura of myth and its repression of reality—and their desire to wield political power and influence. The DNVP was becoming as sensitive to the exigencies of coalition politics as any admittedly parliamentary party. Just shortly before the German note of July 20 was dispatched, the government parties had reached a compromise on the tariff bill to be presented to the Reichstag.[60] It would hardly be smart politics if the DNVP were to leave the coalition before the bill became law.

The crisis of July differed, however, from the first crisis of Nationalist consciousness in March and April. This time the clash between the Nationalist world of myth and the real world of politics had broken out into the open. The attacks on Stresemann and on his politics of "renunciation," his readiness to come to terms with the enemy, and his surrender of German honor had received the temporary endorsement of the Nationalist Party's leadership. Correspondingly, the subsequent option for reality, the resuspension of the appeal to myth, and the return to the compromise of the earlier months constituted a more public act. The attacks upon Stresemann had been more heated; the opposition to the leadership's decision to renew the compromise had been commensurately more intense; the leadership's defense of its decision had been appropriately more vigorous. All this intensified the psychological climate in which the process of compromise with the realities of the postwar Weimar world took place. The DNVP had failed to force Stresemann's resignation and had failed to sabotage his response to the French note. Stresemann's foreign policy of adjustment of interests had prevailed over appeals to German honor and the glories of the past. Moreover, in public Reichstag debate, the DNVP had been obliged to confirm this by its endorsement of the German answer note.[61]

The Nationalist attacks had taken a certain toll, however. Stresemann's confident rapport with Luther had been destroyed by what the foreign minister judged to be the latter's disloyalty. Stresemann ascribed it to Luther's inability to see coalition possibilities other than on his right. Since the truce with the Nationalists was fragile and far from permanent, Stresemann feared that the greatest vigilance would be necessary if he wished to retain his office and preserve his policy of adjustment. Still, Stresemann had won the second round as well as the first. The German note was well received in France. A conference on terms that he could accept was one step nearer. A renewed struggle with the DNVP would await new diplomatic developments. The judgment rendered by Jacques Bainville, the Action française's resident pundit in Paris, aptly described the situation. Writing as the controversy between the Nationalists and Stresemann waned, he observed: "The German Nationalists fail to see that M. Stresemann, faithful disciple of Bismarck and a realist, does much better work for Germany than they do themselves."[62] Bainville was right, except that the perception within the DNVP leadership concerning the effectiveness of Stresemann's work was slowly changing.

6

THE INVITATION TO LOCARNO

In the midst of the July crisis, Count Westarp complained of doing battle with a Hydra—for every protesting head he severed, two grew in its place. His metaphor might have more accurately evoked Pandora and her box of troubles rather than one of Hercules' heroic tasks; but the phenomenon he wished to describe was undeniable: the opposition to Stresemann and to the Nationalist leadership's willingness to compromise with him had begun to organize in earnest.[1]

The DNVP's approval of the German note of July 20, 1925, marked a truce between the government and the party leaders in the struggle over Stresemann's foreign policy. But not all the Nationalists accepted the party's lead.

On July 4, 1925, the Executive Committee of the Pan-German League (Alldeutscher Verband, or ADV) had decided to concentrate its efforts at the local level to frustrate Stresemann's policy of reconciliation and to force the DNVP out of the republican government that it detested. District organizations were more susceptible to the pan-German point of view than was the DNVP's Reichstag delegation. Just a week after this decision, its impact became evident. The district organization of Bremen—a member of which had accepted at the ADV meeting the task of organizing local pressure on the leadership of the DNVP—passed and circulated a group of resolutions that were hostile to Stresemann and the security-pact negotiations and that warned the DNVP's leaders against another August 29. These constituted the first in a series of similar protests that culminated on September 1 and 2 with a public rally of representatives from about twelve district organizations of the DNVP, which opposed the security-pact negotiations and the Nationalist leaders' continued toleration of Stresemann's conduct of foreign policy.[2]

The *Deutsche Zeitung*, which was also under Pan-German influence, intensified its campaign against Stresemann with an article that indicted the DNVP's leadership for its toleration of Stresemann and that explicitly placed its hope for a truly "national" foreign policy in the party's right wing, which was led by Freytagh-Loringhoven. The article, which appeared on July 17, went on to list a score of German Nationalists in whom it still had confidence. The implication was clear: those who were not named were not trustworthy nationalists.[3]

The DNVP leaders tried to stem this maverick criticism. In early July, after it became evident that they could not unseat Stresemann, they met with ADV chairman Heinrich Class to emphasize the dangers of frontal attacks on the foreign minister, such as the ones he had been conducting through the *Deutsche Zeitung*. He was little impressed, however, with their request to trust that Minister of the Interior Schiele would protect nationalist interests in the cabinet or with their policy of opposing Stresemann's pact proposal from within the coalition. When Class allowed the publication of the July 17 article despite the DNVP leadership's request for a moratorium, the party's Reichstag delegation took more drastic action. It passed a resolution restricting members of the party from publishing by name in the *Deutsche Zeitung*, an action that Freytagh-Loringhoven felt was directed particularly at him, and it also warned the paper that continued attacks would mean that the paper's correspondent would be excluded from all confidential party meetings. This prompted Class to threaten to air in print the entire quarrel between the party and the press, so that the nationalistic public could see for itself the "presumption" of the party in trying to censor the *Deutsche Zeitung*. In the intraparty debate that Class's threatening letter touched off, Alfred Hugenberg assumed his first active part in the party's counsels. He warned against an open fight with the Pan-German League and urged reconciliation with Class and the *Deutsche Zeitung*. In meetings between Class, Westarp, and Hugenberg, the ADV leader gained the impression that Hugenberg had strengthened Westarp's resolve to repudiate Stresemann's foreign policy and had changed the mood within the Reichstag delegation. Class also tagged Hugenberg as an appropriate leader for the right wing of the party.[4]

Despite this pressure from the Right, the compromise between the Nationalist leadership and the government held for the moment. Westarp met the criticism of the party's course, which had been stirred up by the radicals, with the insistence that Germany's nationalist interests would best be served by the continued participation of the DNVP in the government.

This would prevent a leftist coalition which would not only support Strese-mann's foreign political rapprochement with France but would rob the Nationalists of their influence over policies regarding tariffs and taxes.[5]

Stresemann realized that the truce was fragile, and indeed, attacks from radical quarters never entirely ceased.[6] In spite of them, the diplomatic momentum continued to rest with the policy of reconciliation. On August 1, the British Foreign Office consulted Germany informally on the possibility of a jurists' conference to prepare a draft for a security-pact treaty. The draft could then become the subject of a later conference of foreign ministers. About the same time, Ambassador Hoesch reported that the Paris govern-ment's position with regard to the German-Polish border appeared to be flexible enough to allow for Germany's objection to any reinforcement of recognition of that border in the security pact. And on August 3, Strese-mann explored with British Ambassador Lord D'Abernon the four major questions on which he felt the German government must gain consideration in any security-pact negotiations: the questions of (1) Germany's entry into the League of Nations, (2) the arbitration treaties, (3) France's position as a guarantor to the eastern states in such treaties, and (4) the impact of the security accords on the occupation regime in the Rhineland and on the length of the occupation.[7]

The British suggestion of a conference of jurists was what carried the negotiations into their next stage. The initial German reaction was guarded but not totally negative. What the government sought was a real exchange of information and a discussion of position. Up to this point the Allies had not communicated any concrete proposals to the Germans. Privately, Strese-mann consulted Luther and, in discussions with him, agreed that the gov-ernment could hardly afford to reject a jurists' conference; but the govern-ment had to know what would be under discussion before such a conference began.[8]

Stresemann's policy of adjustment paid a dividend here; for by August 10 the German Foreign Office had received a copy of an English draft of a security pact, from which Gaus was able to prepare a careful assessment, outlining what continued to be the German negotiating position in subse-quent weeks.[9] This Allied willingness to oblige, in addition to reports that the atmosphere in London was extremely favorable to Germany and to the idea of a security pact,[10] prepared the way for the Allies' invitation to pass from written exchanges to oral exploration of the possibilities for a pact. The Allied note of August 24, 1925, suggested two possible stages: a jurists' conference, which in view of the consultations of early August promised some success, and a subsequent conference of foreign ministers to complete the critical political discussions involved in the pact.[11]

The Allied suggestions were in German hands by 5:00 P.M. on August 24. Within two hours, Chancellor Luther had assembled the political spokesmen of the major parties supporting his cabinet—Interior Minister Martin Schiele of the DNVP, Labor Minister Heinrich Brauns of the Center Party, and Stresemann of the DVP—to plan the cabinet's response to the Allied invitation. This convocation of the parties' spokesmen was in compliance with arrangements made after the struggle in July, that future decisions regarding foreign affairs would be made only on the basis of the closest consultations between the parties and the chancellor. In fact, the four ministers also formed a steering or executive committee within the cabinet, which in the coming weeks previewed important decisions before they came up for discussion among the rest of the ministers, thus smoothing the way for the final approval of those decisions.[12]

Stresemann described his interview with the representatives of France and the other Allies, sketched the proposals that had been made, and recommended that the invitation be accepted. Schiele, who did not even know about the consultations that had already taken place regarding a possible draft treaty, recognized immediately that to send the German Foreign Office's legal expert, Friedrich Gaus, to a jurists' conference would amount to Germany's approving the beginning of negotiations on a new basis. He thus announced to his cabinet colleagues that such a step was out of the question. He faced the united opposition of the other three ministers, however: Nothing in the note of August 24 presented the slightest occasion for a rejection of the invitation to a jurists' conference in London. The note, indeed, gave every indication that a satisfactory accord was possible. Schiele's resistance weakened. He did not wish to veto the Gaus mission, he remarked, but rather to insist that a strong reemphasis of Germany's earlier point of view should accompany the opening of any new stage in the negotiations. Luther took up this suggestion, and the four men finally agreed, after four and one-half hours of contention, that Gaus's departure for London should be accompanied by a cabinet communiqué which would reaffirm the German note of July 20.

By the next morning, when the full cabinet met, Schiele's agreement with the decisions of the night before had disappeared. After leaving his cabinet colleagues, he had returned home to meet with Westarp and a number of other DNVP leaders. The Nationalists decided to oppose the idea of a conference of jurists.[13] Accordingly, the Nationalists sent the party chairman's political deputy, Hans-Erdmann von Lindeiner-Wildau, and the leader of the radical wing, Alex Freiherr von Freytagh-Loringhoven, to see Luther on August 25. In their conversation, Luther outlined the situation: The Allied note was flexible in tone; the sending of Gaus to London was a practical necessity so long as Germany wished to avoid being charged by international opinion with having gratuitously ruptured the negotiations.[14] The conversation was designed to make clear that the DNVP, if it chose to withdraw its support now, would bear the responsibility for more than the breakdown of the coalition.

Count Westarp found himself once again in the uncomfortable position of having to decide between acceptance of Stresemann's foreign policy and the destruction of the rightist coalition. He recognized, as had Schiele, that the Gaus mission would be universally interpreted as the beginning of actual negotiations and therefore as the surrender of the Nationalist position. Indeed, he urged that the party oppose the jurist's trip to London. At the same time, however, he argued that the issue should not be pushed so far that there would be a cabinet crisis; and this point carried in the party's internal consultations. As a result, although Schiele raised mild objections to the Gaus mission in the meeting of the committee of four on August 25, he quickly abandoned them in the face of the united front of Luther, Stresemann, and Brauns. The meeting of the full cabinet on the next day thus ran smoothly, and the Gaus mission was approved. The cabinet further commanded the German Foreign Office to reply to the Allied note with a brief memorandum, emphasizing the German position of July 20, and to prepare for release to the press a communiqué summarizing the diplomatic situation.[15]

Westarp continued to have misgivings, however. He was fully aware of the growing pressure to have the DNVP's ministers leave the cabinet. Hugenberg had expressed it in the meeting of the party's parliamentary delegation on August 11; but numerous letters attested to the same lack of understanding among the party's rank and file with regard to the leadership's balancing act between cooperation and opposition.[16] Westarp, in a meeting with Schiele and Lindeiner-Wildau late on Thursday, August 27, reviewed the arguments once again and subsequently sent Schiele a personal note, which was accompanied by a long memorandum outlining not only his own thoughts on the problems of participation in the security-pact negotiations but also the conditions under which he felt the DNVP could ultimately approve a pact. Westarp wrote that he assumed "with 99% probability" that the party's minimum demands for the protection of German honor and interests would not be met by the Allies and, furthermore, that Gaus's mission to London would not result in any amelioration of Germany's position. He recognized that Luther and Stresemann, in their eagerness to achieve an accord, wanted to set far fewer conditions than did the party. Despite his many reservations, Westarp asked Schiele to delay any crucial decisions for as long as possible so that the party would have

106

time to hold discussions and consultation with its full Reichstag delegation.[17]

Near the end of his position paper, Westarp spoke of a division of labor between himself and Schiele, in which the latter was governed, as a result of his ministerial position, by substantive issues and by which, on the other hand, Westarp was compelled—however little he might like it—to advocate the party's point of view. The distinction is basically one between fundamental questions of national interest and questions of limited party interest, which, Westarp recognized, might lead Schiele in a direction that would be at variance with that of the party. Westarp had begun to appreciate the tensions that exist between political purity and the interaction of diverse interests in a politically plural community—the distinction, in Ralf Dahrendorff's terms, between private and public virtue.[18] Westarp's sense of this tension was by no means complete, probably not even conscious. But the decision to accept practical compromises, of which the agreement to the Gaus mission was far from the last, continued to force the issue to the fore. The "patriotic movement," which Westarp prized as an "element of recovery" in the health of the nation and which he therefore did not wish to drive from the party, had to be taken into account. But that movement's pressure on the party to reject the policy of reconciliation and to disrupt the security-pact negotiations had to be ignored, at least for the moment. All of Westarp's painstakingly outlined objections weighed less heavily than the attractions of power that the party might wield within the system, however odious that system may have been in the abstract. The DNVP leadership therefore approved the Gaus mission, although this action, the leadership admitted, marked the beginning of negotiations and, by implication, the abandonment of the DNVP's program. The Nationalists could continue to assert that they preserved their freedom to decide for or against the final treaty, that the discussions in London were still preliminary talks. But they could not insist for long, because both their assertion and their situation were equivocal.

Contrary to Westarp's hopes for an unsuccessful outcome in London, which would have removed from the DNVP any blame for having to repudiate the negotiations, Gaus registered significant gains there. As the discussions began, he was presented with a Franco-British draft treaty, which, in view of the draft he had seen in early August, contained no surprises. He at once began a forceful campaign to incorporate Germany's desires into this document, which formed the basis of the jurists' nonbinding discussions. He achieved a high degree of success. He strengthened Germany's protections against "defensive occupation," or French sanctions. He also convinced the Allied jurists to accept the German form for arbitration treaties, which distinguished between legal and political problems and which imposed no obligation to accept an arbitrated judgment in cases involving the latter. The Allies adopted his modifications of the machinery by which the guaranteeing powers would be called upon to act. But his most significant efforts covered the relationship between the proposed security pact and the right of sanction as outlined in the Versailles Treaty, on the one hand, and the problem of the guarantee by France of the arbitration treaties that were to be contracted with Germany's eastern neighbors, on the other.

Regarding the former, the Allies eventually agreed that disputes over interpretations of the meaning of all clauses in the Versailles Treaty would be subject to the arbitration procedures established by the security pact. That meant practically that in a disputed case, such as had led to the Ruhr action, France could not resort to sanctions without first going into arbitration. Regarding France's putative right to guarantee treaties with the eastern states, no satisfactory compromise was reached, but Gaus clearly spelled out the German point of view. Not a single person in Germany would believe that a French guarantee of a Polish-German treaty of arbitration would be truly impartial. A French right of guarantee was therefore politically impossible. A German-Polish treaty of arbitration, plus German membership in the League of Nations, would assure every interest that France might have in Poland's security. Germany had absolutely no intention of waging an aggressive war against Poland, and the proposed arbitration accords and Germany's membership in the league would guarantee that she could not. Anything more, such as a treaty that explicitly forbade aggressive action, would be superfluous as well as being an insupportable political burden which would threaten the entire security pact.[19]

Gaus returned from London only to set out again, to carry his report personally to the vacationing Stresemann and Luther. In the meantime, however, the DNVP leadership kept in close touch with the cabinet and with the German Foreign Office, where Gerhard Köpke, director of Department II (Western Europe), gave frequent briefings to Lindeiner-Wildau, which the latter passed on to both Schiele and Westarp.[20] During the same period, Lindeiner-Wildau also met with Bernhard von Bülow, who had accompanied Gaus to London, with General von Seeckt, with Gaus and Schubert, and with Defense Minister Gessler. In addition, Westarp and a select few of the Nationalists were given a copy of the draft treaty that Gaus had brought back from London.[21] In these conversations the Nationalists reemphasized the necessity for a careful study and consideration of the conditions they had demanded be met before they would finally approve the negotiations.

The arrival, on September 15, 1925, of an Allied invitation to a foreign ministers' conference on the security pact soon made these conditions the center of debate. Although the site had not yet been decided upon, what was to become the Locarno Conference was now clearly imminent. Hergt therefore informed Stresemann that the DNVP planned to impose a specific list of conditions for the continuation of negotiations. Count Westarp raised the same prospect. And on September 21, Stresemann received a list of what he labeled "unfulfillable demands," which Luther had been given by the DNVP. Luther's telephone call that evening, in which he told Stresemann that the list was only a "memory aid" for the DNVP's spokesman in the cabinet, was only mildly reassuring. On the next day, both the DNVP and the four-minister Executive Committee of the cabinet met. Both groups discussed guidelines for the coming negotiations. The differences between the two versions would not emerge until five weeks later.

In the September 22 meeting of the cabinet committee of four, Stresemann tried to anticipate the demands that he knew Schiele would make on behalf of the DNVP. The answer to the Allied invitation should be kept short, he advised. No written statements should accompany it, but only an oral declaration which, not at all by chance, would include the DNVP's leading demands. This ought to emphasize Germany's oft-repeated insistence upon immediate evacuation of the first Rhineland zone around Cologne and Germany's desire for a rapid settlement of the disarmament discussions; and finally, it should include a statement that Germany would not enter the League of Nations unless there were a reaffirmation of the German government's memorandum of September 1924, which denied that Germany's entry would entail any acknowledgment that she was guilty of starting the war. Stresemann also tried to emphasize the still tentative nature of the coming negotiations, pointing out that the results would be submitted for final approval to the cabinets of the governments that were involved. But Luther insisted that there be no illusions on this point. "One should not be influenced by the thought," he stated pointedly, "that the imminent conference of ministers is not the decisive and conclusive meeting. For even at this conference, more or less binding agreements will undoubtedly be made, if the final goal is ever to be reached at all."[22]

Schiele, reacting sharply to Stresemann's suggestions, declared that the verbal *démarche* that the foreign minister had proposed was totally inadequate. Especially the matter of war guilt demanded that there be a sharp, public repudiation, incorporated into a formal diplomatic note that would accompany the acceptance of the Allied invitation. The same held true for disarmament and the evacuation of the Cologne zone: these matters would have to be broached in the German response and would have to be clarified before any negotiations could be begun. Other matters would have to be incorporated into formal guidelines that the German delegates would follow

109

during the conference. These guidelines must include (1) a demand for the revision of the occupation regime in the Rhineland, (2) changes in the draft treaty which would eliminate the renunciation of German territory, (3) modification—or preferably elimination—of the proposed treaties with eastern states, and (4) reaffirmation of the conditions for Germany's entry into the League of Nations which earlier governments had laid down. To these must be added a new point: insistence upon general disarmament.

Only one of Schiele's many points really troubled Stresemann. For the most part, as he noted in his diary the next day, Schiele's demands were milder than those that had circulated in the preceding days.[23] But to the insistence upon a formal note regarding war guilt, he raised "energetic objections." Such a step could only produce negative results for Germany, not only concerning the question of war guilt itself, to which the German Foreign Office devoted constant but confidential attention, but also for Germany's entire diplomatic position. Schiele showed himself immediately ready for compromise: he was sure that there was a variety of ways in which the issue could be raised, not only the possibilities of a "formless verbal discussion" or a formal note. The matter could surely be touched upon in the reply note in a way that would circumvent an open discussion before the conference, a development that he himself held to be "undesirable." This compromise proposal won the support of the Center Party's spokesman as well, and Stresemann agreed to present a text for consideration the next day.

Schiele's other points were quickly dispatched. Stresemann agreed that the evacuation of the Cologne zone should not become the object of new negotiations at Locarno and that the evacuation must be assured before any new obligations could be contracted by Germany. He considered that it would be impossible, however, to have the actual evacuation be completed before Germany would accept any new responsibilities. Schiele agreed. Stresemann then dealt in turn with the other points, insisting that they could all be handled satisfactorily in the coming negotiations. The discussion among the four ministers ended with an agreement that they would meet the next evening to consider the German Foreign Office's drafts of guidelines to incorporate these points, as well as for the German reply to the invitation, which would include the German positions on the evacuation of Cologne and on war guilt. Thus, what had begun as a clash of mutually exclusive demands ended in compromise. For the moment, however, the compromise was only between Schiele and Stresemann. What of the DNVP?

On the same day that the four ministers met to discuss the German reply to the invitation to Locarno, the Nationalist delegation in the Reichstag met with the chairmen of the party's state committees and drew up its own guidelines for the coming negotiations. These differed significantly from the guidelines that were to emerge from the cabinet. Schiele had already abandoned certain of the party's seemingly hard-line positions in the meeting with Luther, Stresemann, and Brauns on September 22, and although on the following day, in another meeting of the four, he appeared momentarily to be more demanding, he ultimately agreed to even further compromises.

When the Foreign Office's draft of Germany's reply was laid before the four ministers on September 23, Schiele first asserted that the statement regarding war guilt was totally unsatisfactory. It merely incorporated Stresemann's suggestion of the previous day, he argued. Schiele's political friends could not support such a weak action. Moreover, they demanded that the final declaration go not only to the nations extending the invitation, as the draft envisaged, but to all the signatories of the Versailles Treaty. This demand was a direct extrapolation from the party's guidelines. Once again, Stresemann reacted sharply. The note did not simply embody his earlier suggestion, which had been for an oral procedure on war guilt. This was a precise, sharp written formulation. In the discussion that followed, a compromise was once again reached. The draft that emerged did not once mention war guilt specifically. Rather, it referred to two previous statements by the German government—one the August 29, 1924, repudiation of war guilt, which was issued by Chancellor Marx immediately after the vote on the Dawes plan, and the other a September 29, 1924, memorandum to the League of Nations Council, which reaffirmed Germany's rejection of the same charge—without repeating their more specific language. In a markedly indirect manner the German statement commented that "any declaration to be issued by the German government, on the occasion of its eventual entry into the League of Nations, concerning the fulfillment of her international obligations ought not to be understood to indicate that the assertions put forward to justify these obligations, [assertions] that contain within themselves a moral indictment of the German people, are thereby acknowledged." The note, although it in fact was written, was called "verbal" because it was to be presented orally, not as a part of the German reply to the invitation to the ministers' conference, and then was to be handed over as a separate memorandum in conjunction with that reply. In short, extreme care was to be exercised in the presentation of the note, as well as in its formulation, in order to minimize as much as possible the diplomatic anger that Stresemann expected it to arouse. Stresemann had even taken the trouble to discuss the careful wording of the note beforehand with the French and

British ambassadors, in order to explain the pressures that compelled the government to take the step and in order to plead for understanding.[24]

Once the sending of the note had been approved, Schiele returned to the question of who should receive it. Here again he compromised the Nationalist position. He admitted that sending a formal statement to all signatory powers might be going too far. He demanded, however, that the memorandum be brought to their attention at least.

In the same meeting, Stresemann presented a draft of the guidelines that should govern the German negotiators at the conference. Schiele raised no objections. The four ministers did agree, however, to propose a committee to put the guidelines into final form. This committee should consist, they decided, of the four ministers themselves.[25]

One other problem arose at these meetings: what should be the composition of the delegation to Locarno? At the beginning of the month, Luther and Stresemann had agreed that both of them should attend. The justification was that the foreign minister, or any one minister alone, would be overburdened in carrying on negotiations with a minimum of three other states. The real motive had to do more with the domestic attacks on Stresemann and his foreign policy. With the DNVP trying to divide Luther and Stresemann, every possible means of affirming their solidarity on the security-pact proposal had to be used.[26] In the meeting of September 22, Schiele had objected to having the chancellor participate in the conference on the grounds that it would imply an undesirable binding quality to the negotiations. Neither France nor England planned to send its government's leader. If domestic difficulties arose in either country concerning the final approval of the pact, neither country would face a cabinet crisis, but at most a "Briand-crisis," or a "Chamberlain-crisis." In the same way, Schiele baldly stated, the person of Chancellor Luther was too valuable to waste on this conference. Luther and Stresemann remained adamant, however, and on the next day Schiele gave way on this point as well.[27]

With the major points of conflict already resolved by the committee of four, the meeting of the full cabinet proceeded without difficulty. The memorandum on war guilt and on the occupation of Cologne produced only mild surprise but no serious resistance. Stresemann read his guidelines for Locarno and urged that the negotiating delegation be given the greatest possible tactical latitude in fulfilling them. Only one truly substantive change was suggested, and that not by Schiele but by Minister of Justice Frenken. Frenken urged that the issue of occupation be settled in the pact itself, rather than in some "more or less binding corollary document." Stresemann replied that the handling of such problems would fall within the discretion of the delegation to the conference. He could see no objection, however, to an accord over evacuation that would be separate from the main pact itself. This had been the approach in London in August 1924, and it had proved most successful. Such a procedure would also be consistent with Stresemann's efforts to bind the Allies morally to revision rather than to argue with them over their legal obligations to it.

The next day's meeting, under the chairmanship of Reichspresident Paul von Hindenburg, proceeded equally as smoothly as the cabinet meeting of September 23. Stresemann read the memorandum that was to accompany the acceptance of the invitation to the conference. He traced for Hindenburg the general guidelines, on which the four ministers, and then the cabinet, had agreed. These guidelines included as aims the modification of the preamble to the draft treaty so as to eliminate the phrase "status quo," the introduction of a clause that would allow abrogation of the security pact by prior announcement, and the formulation of specific categories—*Rückwirkungen* ("ramifications"), to use Stresemann's word—in which the conclusion of the pact ought to bring about ameliorations in the occupied territories.[28]

Reichspresident Hindenburg was both by disposition and by association inclined toward the Nationalist point of view. He knew that the DNVP was not satisfied that Germany's national honor and interests were being served by Stresemann's conduct of foreign policy. Westarp and Schiele had even visited him just before the cabinet meeting and had supplied him with the DNVP's list of demands.[29] Therefore, Stresemann's assertion that the cabinet supported his report surprised the president enough that he questioned each minister in turn. Finding no disagreement, he proceeded. He would have preferred a much more strongly worded memorandum regarding war guilt, but he accepted the factors that militated against this. He did insist upon one minor textual change, which the Nationalists claimed in private was directly attributable to proposals that they had made to him before the meeting.[30]

The meeting before the Reichspresident underscored once again the unwillingness of the DNVP's leadership to pursue its opposition, in principle, to the point of rupture, in practice. Schiele had begun sharply enough in the early consultations over the invitation to Locarno. But even given the opportunity of Hindenburg's favorable disposition, he had not insisted on the DNVP's list of guidelines, accepting instead Stresemann's milder list. Despite his earlier efforts to saddle Stresemann with sole responsibility for the conduct of the negotiations, Schiele had acquiesced to having Luther participate in the conference as well. In fact, Schiele had gained only one concession: he had forced the preparation of a written diplomatic note on war guilt. Certainly Stresemann would have avoided this step had he been able to do so. Probably he would have ignored the question entirely, or perhaps he would have broached it only informally during the conference. But even here, Schiele had approved, albeit grudgingly, a text that never once mentioned the phrase "war guilt," much less the emotional label "lie," which the Nationalists were accustomed to attaching to it. Still, Schiele's victory in forcing a note at all would raise diplomatic hackles in Paris and London.

For the most part, however, Schiele had compromised. Moreover, his compromises were not his alone. The DNVP delegation in the Reichstag met on September 25 to review its relationship to the cabinet and to discuss the form and content of the note regarding war guilt. Westarp argued that the note fulfilled the Nationalists' essential demands, whereupon members of the delegation voted to approve the acceptance of the invitation to Locarno. On the following day, Chancellor Luther consulted again with Westarp and two other members of the party's Executive Committee, Oskar Hergt and Max Wallraf. On that day, too, Westarp spoke in the meeting of the Foreign Affairs Committee about his party's conditional approval. On September 28 the party leaders met with representatives of the provincial organizations to explain their position. They insisted that the German delegates to Locarno would be bound by the Nationalist guidelines and that Luther had assured the Foreign Affairs Committee that early evacuation of the second and third zones of occupation would have to be approved before any treaty would be concluded. They made no mention of compromises. In fact, these had been extensive and had transformed the Nationalists' preconditions for a pact into general aims of the negotiations which the German delegation would strive to achieve, but would not be bound to fulfill.

For example, the early evacuation of the second and third zones had indeed come up in the September 26 meeting of the Reichstag's Foreign Affairs Committee. But it had been raised by Stresemann, not Schiele, and as a desirable ramification of a pact, not as a prerequisite. The compromises of the next few days continued this process of turning Nationalist prerequisites into desirable goals to be striven for at the discretion of the delegation to the conference.[31] General von Seeckt, who maintained close contacts with the leaders of the DNVP, labeled their conduct in these compromises "foolish beyond permitted limits." He accused them, incorrectly, of "die alte Verantwortungsscheu" ("timidity in the face of responsibility"), which they hoped to avoid by appealing to the "saving formula"—namely, that the security pact was still in a preparatory state and that a final decision could therefore be postponed.[32] More likely, the saving formula resulted from the same dilemma that the Nationalists had faced acutely since entering the

114

cabinet: could they remain both pure and in power? More and more the leadership opted for power over purity.

The web of compromise between domestic and diplomatic pressures almost came undone when the German verbal note on the issues of war guilt and the evacuation of Cologne was communicated to the Allied governments. The French and British reacted sharply to mention of the issue of war guilt. In London, Austen Chamberlain complained of typical German petulance in trying always to have the last word. In Paris, the concern was pragmatic and was directed less at the content of Germany's declaration than at her intention to publish it, which would certainly stir up the French nationalist opponents of rapprochement and would endanger the Painlevé-Briand cabinet.[33]

The crisis was complicated by the timing. Germany had delivered its note on Saturday, September 26, with the intention of publishing it the following Tuesday, the twenty-ninth. Since Briand was absent from Paris when the note was delivered, the Quai d'Orsay requested that Germany delay publication of the note. On Monday, Briand suggested a compromise: only the middle paragraphs of the German note should be published, and even those should be in indirect address. Although this procedure would eliminate nothing of the material content of the German note, it would eliminate the written forms of diplomatic politeness and thus would create the impression that the issue of war guilt had been raised only orally. Upon receiving this suggestion, Luther called an emergency cabinet meeting for late Monday evening. Now the happy composition of previous meetings of the "committee of four" became apparent by contrast. Because of the lack of notice—he had given them one hour—only four ministers attended. But among them now was Minister of Justice Joseph Frenken instead of Heinrich Brauns. Together, Frenken and Schiele blocked any compromise on Briand's suggestion. After three hours of intense discussion, Luther finally proposed a response to Briand that all four could support. At 2:00 A.M. on September 29, it was telegraphed to Paris. The German government expressed understanding for Briand's suggestion; it had considered the suggestion with care but had finally concluded that it was unfeasible in practice. Because of the constitutional requirements that the government consult with the presidents of state governments and with the parties of the Reichstag, too many people in Germany were aware that the government's démarche on war guilt had been delivered in writing. Any attempt to conceal this through the form of publication that Briand suggested would only lead to questions and to potentially embarrassing consequences for the cabinet and for Briand as well. If, under these circumstances, the French government should feel compelled to respond to the German verbal note with a note of its own, the German government would understand and would not see this per se as grounds for a cancellation of the conference. It hoped, however, that any answer would be compatible with the spirit of peaceful understanding that was the cornerstone of the proposed conference regarding a security pact.[34]

The French responded in that spirit. They still urged deemphasis, in the publication of the note, of its formal written character, suggesting that the published version include an introduction stating that the German point of view had been "communicated" along with the note accepting the invitation to Locarno. The French government's reply, for its part, was as carefully worded as had been the German note and, like it, avoided the use of the phrase "war guilt" or any similar direct mention of that sensitive issue. The British note was considerably less gentle in stating that "the question of Germany's responsibility for the war is not raised by the proposed pact, and His Majesty's Government are at a loss to know why the German Government have thought proper to raise it at this moment. His Majesty's Government are obliged to observe that the negotiation of a security pact cannot modify the Treaty of Versailles or alter their judgment of the past." Still, both governments were careful to express their "satisfaction" that Germany had accepted the invitation to the conference at Locarno.[35]

The moderation of the Allied responses left open the way to the conference. But Schiele and Westarp each made one more attempt to pressure the government into stronger action on the issue of war guilt.

Schiele's effort came in a meeting specially called at his request to discuss "whether and when" the memorandum concerning war guilt should be passed on to the rest of the signatory powers of the Versailles Treaty. Schiele argued for immediate dispatch. Stresemann, Luther, and Brauns opposed the idea, Brauns adding that the Center Party would abandon the cabinet rather than support such a move. The "appropriate time" for any additional diplomatic action on war guilt, the three agreed, would arrive with Germany's entry into the League of Nations. With his colleagues clearly moving against him, Schiele withdrew his request for immediate notification, substituting instead a proposal that the government issue a press statement directed against the British reply and announcing its intention to pursue the matter further in the negotiations at Locarno. Again Schiele met with resistance. Luther objected. Stresemann explained that nothing would be more likely to create a solid Allied front behind England than a challenge to the British note, which, as things stood, was the only one that really forcefully affirmed the old Allied position. He suggested a compromise, however: a new press communiqué might be possible. It could be directed at the German public and would avoid any mention of the British position. Once more Schiele bowed. The cabinet approved the suggestion of the communiqué, formally endorsed the idea that Germany's entry into the league represented the "appropriate time" for the notification of the remaining signatories of the Versailles Treaty, and explicitly left to the discretion of the German negotiators in Locarno any further handling of the issue of war guilt. Particularly through this last decision, Schiele had surrendered more than he had gained. The next day the cabinet unanimously approved the guidelines for the delegates to Locarno. They were a far cry from the demands that Schiele had introduced the week before.[36]

Westarp's effort came two days later, over the same issue and in a letter to Chancellor Luther, which went through at least six drafts before being sent to Locarno on October 3.[37] Westarp welcomed the press release on war guilt but labeled it inadequate as a defense of German honor and dignity. Only the immediate communication of Germany's position to the remaining signatories would give the measure the strength that it required. Moreover, Westarp "expressed the request" that the German delegation make the matter a cardinal point of the negotiation in Locarno and that it bring these efforts to public attention as well, since the question was "one of the indispensable conditions for the maintenance of Germany's equal status." Westarp concluded with the mildly threatening indication that he had called a meeting of the Executive Committee of the DNVP's Reichstag delegation for October 6 in order to review the government's measures on war guilt and that he would appreciate any news from Locarno that might contribute to this discussion.

Westarp's letter clearly represented an attempt to recoup Schiele's abandoned position of several days earlier and to placate the more radical elements within the party that were demanding stronger action in view of the "sharp replies" of the Allies to the German verbal note regarding war guilt.[38]

Luther responded immediately, but not to Westarp. Instead, he wrote Schiele concerning the evident "misunderstanding" and Westarp's apparent ignorance of the "unanimous cabinet decision" which would govern the further handling of the issue of war guilt. Luther asked that Schiele, in his capacity as the Nationalist liaison man (*Vertrauensmann*) within the cabinet, work to preserve the delegation's freedom of action at Locarno, which Luther had pointedly reaffirmed in the final cabinet meeting before Locarno.[39] Luther's obvious concern was that the convocation of a meeting of the Nationalist Executive Committee, under circumstances that were bound to accentuate the party's dissatisfaction with the government that it theoretically supported, would undermine the authority of the German negotiators. Luther had every right to be angry, too, over this effort to extort

117

what Schiele had bargained away in order to gain a press communiqué in which the government once again rejected the Allied response on war guilt.

Schiele's reply of October 5 hardly depicted a secure situation for Luther. Westarp had been fully informed of the cabinet's decisions. Despite this, he had felt compelled to urge stronger measures regarding war guilt. Schiele reminded Luther that in anticipation of just such opposition, he, Schiele, had urged a stronger cabinet stand to the very end. He accepted his obligation of loyalty to the cabinet, however, and he would defend its position before Westarp and all other critics.[40]

Schiele managed to avoid repudiating his position when the DNVP delegation met on October 6. After several hours of debate, the entire Executive Committee approved Schiele's stand within the cabinet, including his final acceptance of the cabinet's communiqué and the extension of discretion to the Locarno delegation regarding the handling of the issue of war guilt. At the same time, however, the Executive Committee also approved Westarp's letter and the requests that it contained. The party leaders had thus not repudiated the cabinet compromise; they had simply approved two positions that were almost mutually exclusive.[41]

Such contradictory positions illustrate the dilemma of the Nationalists. No matter which course they took, their position was threatened. If they satisfied their radical critics within the party, they risked destroying the coalition. If they preserved the coalition, they risked splitting the party. In the struggle over the security-pact negotiations, the leadership had gained some appreciation for the exigencies of foreign policy. This is evident not only in Westarp's instructions to Schiele of August 31 but also in the entire treatment afforded the security-pact negotiations in the party's newspaper, *Korrespondenz der Deutschnationalen Volkspartei*. Throughout the summer and the direct attacks on Stresemann, the *Korrespondenz* had made little mention of the security-pact proposals, concentrating instead on tariff and tax issues and the positive accomplishments that the party had achieved in cooperation with the government.[42] Still, cooperation with the "enemy," in addition to the admission that the German "land and peoples" were gone, went against the grain. The acceptance of political reality—which was urged by special interests within the party, perhaps even by the actual national interest, as Westarp began to recognize—demanded that the Nationalists remain in the cabinet. In contrast, injured pride, a heritage of the lost war, demanded that they reject all compromise with the enemy. Those Nationalists who were insensitive to the dilemma magnified the most insignificant slights—real or imagined—of national honor in order to arouse the fire of indignation. Those who lived with the dilemma temporized.

The Nationalists' efforts to saddle Stresemann with impossible conditions and to send him off to a conference that they hoped would fail illustrate not only their dilemma, however. They illustrate two radically different approaches to diplomacy. Both before the Dawes negotiations in London, and again before Locarno, the DNVP tried to set specific conditions to any talks, conditions that the Allies would have to fulfill in order to show their good faith. In both cases the conditions were more than an effort to overburden Stresemann and to be rid of him—although the Nationalists would not have objected if this had happened. They represented a conception of foreign policy which contended that the Allies must be compelled to recognize both their legal obligations under the Versailles settlement (evacuation and disarmament) and the absurdity of the postwar system that had reduced Germany to impotence. The Nationalists still operated with delusions of pre-1914 grandeur. They wanted to repudiate the defeat of 1918 and to refight the war through the diplomacy of confrontation in order to assert Germany's rightful place in the sun.

Stresemann's approach was the perfect contrast. He realized that German demands and resistance could never succeed and that they would never lead beyond the niggling counterdemands and hostile atmosphere by which Poincaré had justified his incursion into the Ruhr. To seek a way out of this atmosphere, Stresemann had launched a policy of adjustment of interests—first on reparations, then on security—by which, through German concessions and cooperation, the Allies could be bound *morally* to revision. The Nationalists were absolutely right: Stresemann did not receive any binding written commitments from the Allies that his expectations would be fulfilled. But Briand's care in avoiding an irritation of German sensitivities in his reply to the note on war guilt augured well. The essence of Stresemann's diplomacy, then, unlike that of the Nationalists, was his conviction that more could be gained by cooperation and adjustment than by confrontation. This involved not only a cool calculation of interests on all sides but also the consideration of those interests in all negotiations. It also involved, for Germany, an ordering of priorities. This was the real message of Stresemann's September, 1925, letter to Crown Prince Wilhelm: First things first—namely, reparations, evacuation, acceptance in the international forum of the League of Nations. Without these, no revision was thinkable; as these matters were settled, Germany would become progressively more free from the possibility of direct Allied intervention and thus would be able to act independently again.[43] These objectives could not be extorted from the Allies. Achieving them involved an element of trust, as well as the calculation of interest. Stresemann was prepared to trust because the other alternatives were so bad. The Nationalists were not. It was the old story of catching bees: the Nationalists wanted to use vinegar; Stresemann preferred to use honey.

7

LOCARNO AND THE BREAKUP
OF THE COALITION

The German delegation to the Locarno Conference left Berlin on October 2, 1925. After two weeks of earnest political infighting, both Luther and Stresemann could feel that they had booked a certain number of successes. They were both representing the German government, despite the DNVP's initial opposition to having Luther participate in the conference. The guidelines that governed their negotiations were, contrary to Nationalist claims, far more moderate than the list that the DNVP insisted it had imposed, or even than the more modest demands that Schiele had introduced into discussion on September 22. Moreover, Luther had emphasized that, without departing from the guidelines, the members of the delegation would have to make judgments and decisions independently, "responsible to our own consciences."[1]

The cabinet had given its unanimous approval to the guidelines, which had been drafted by Luther, Stresemann, Brauns, and Schiele.[2] In their final form, the guidelines were headed by the general consideration that the basis of the delegation's conduct of negotiations must remain the German government's note of July 20, 1925. Concerning the security pact and any correlative treaties, the guidelines made three points. The delegation was to try to effect changes in the preamble to the London draft of the security treaty that would negate the everlasting character of any German renunciation of former territories and populations. The guidelines did not, however, mandate that accomplishment of such changes be a condition of acceptance of the treaty. Second, treaties of arbitration with the eastern states were to be so constructed that under no circumstances could boundary questions be subjected to an obligatory legal procedure or a binding judgment but only

121

to a process of nonbinding mediation. Third, a French guarantee for the treaties of arbitration in the East was to be rejected. Concerning the League of Nations, the guidelines called for the maintenance of the German memorandum of September 1924 and mentioned specifically the reservations concerning Article 16 of the league's charter and the need to address the problem of world disarmament. Aside from these questions, which had been acknowledged by all parties to be a part of the negotiations on security, the following were included in the guidelines as general political questions: evacuation of Cologne, military control, the easing of the occupation regime in the Rhineland, and the eventual shortening of the duration of occupation.

These were the problems that had surrounded the origins of the pact proposal. They were the ramifications that Stresemann had always hoped would emerge from any negotiations concerning a security pact. But in the face of persistent efforts by France to exclude these problems from discussion and despite Nationalist pressure to the contrary, Stresemann did not want to be bound to concluding formal accords concerning them. The guidelines gave him the latitude he sought. They simply instructed that the resolution of the questions of the evacuation of Cologne, of the remaining disarmament demands, and of the end to the Allied claim to a continuing right of investigation be assured so that they would not become objects of negotiations at a later conference. Assurances—but not necessarily written commitments —of revision of the Rhineland and Saar occupation and governmental regimes were also to be secured. And the delegation was to endeavor to obtain a reduction of the term of occupation for the second and third Rhineland zones. The language of the guidelines was carefully chosen. The form that the assurances were to take remained unstipulated; and the realization of the assurances was not made a condition for the acceptance of the treaty.[3]

Upon arrival in Locarno, the German delegation set to work assiduously to conclude a pact within the guidelines set for it. In the first three days of official negotiations, the German representatives managed to raise all the points in the guidelines that were relevant to either the content of the pact and its correlative treaties or to the problem of entry into the League of Nations. During discussion of the latter point, Stresemann satisfied the cabinet's resolution regarding the issue of war guilt as discreetly as possible by simply referring to the Marx government's memorandum of September 1924, repeating its statement that Germany accepted her international obligations but not to the extent of accepting any "moral guilt" for the war.[4] In the discussion among the German delegates that had immediately preceded this exchange with the Allies, Luther had expressed concern that such a veiled reference to the issue of war guilt would not satisfy the Nationalists' demands. He abandoned his objections, however, when the minutes of the

October 1 cabinet meeting, which Schiele had approved, were read to him. The final decision of that meeting had left the timing and the form of the reiteration of the government's attitude toward responsibility for the war to the discretion of the delegation.[5]

Even the general political questions, which were outlined by the guidelines—namely, the ramifications that the German government hoped that the conclusion of the security pact would have on the status of the Cologne zone, the Rhineland, and the remaining problems of disarmament and military control—were raised in private talks between Stresemann and British Foreign Secretary Chamberlain as early as October 8, 1925, three days after the official opening of the conference. Moreover, from the first day of the conference, Stresemann discussed these points unofficially with one of the top aides of French Foreign Minister Briand, to whom he had emphasized that these were the cardinal points for German public opinion. These questions received their most serious attention, however, during the final days of the conference.[6]

But the pivotal problem for the Locarno Conference proved to be the question of Germany's entry into the League of Nations. The negotiators soon realized that some formula had to be found to allay Germany's misgivings concerning the obligation to apply sanctions under Article 16 of the league's charter. The private conversation of October 8 between Stresemann and Chamberlain, which took place in the latter's hotel room, lasted for two hours and ranged over all the related questions on which Germany hoped for some satisfaction as a result of the pact—namely, textual modifications of the preamble, arbitration treaties and France's role in them, and the like—as well as over the major points of the official negotiations. Here Stresemann suggested the procedure the eventual adoption of which resolved the German delegation's objections to Article 16. Stresemann proposed an exchange of notes between Germany, on the one hand, and the four Allied governments participating in the conference, on the other, which would clarify the manner in which Article 16 would be applied in the case of Germany. Taking up this suggestion the next day, the legal experts from the five delegations tentatively agreed upon a text for the four-power note on Article 16.

On October 10, Luther, Stresemann, Chamberlain, and Briand took a boat tour of Lake Maggiore, on which Locarno is situated, during which they again discussed Article 16 and its connection with the French guarantee in the East. The interpretation of the article that had been agreed upon the previous day by the jurists—who were also present on the boat—proved acceptable as the basis for a solution to both questions. Two days later, the proposed note was discussed for the first time in a full assembly, which included the representatives of Belgium and Italy. The note was to be addressed to Germany by the four powers, France, Great Britain, Belgium, and Italy. It stated that the four had no authority to speak for the League of Nations concerning Article 16 but that they did not hesitate to give their own interpretation of the article. Their understanding was that the obligations arising from Article 16 would bind each member of the league to work effectively for the observation of the charter and to oppose any act of aggression to the extent that each country's own military situation and geographic position would allow. The Belgian and Italian representatives accepted the note after only limited discussion.[7]

This formula, plus the assurances made by the Allies—which were extracted by Stresemann during the discussion of the note—that they considered universal disarmament a desirable practical goal, removed the German delegation's objections to entry into the league, and thereby opened the way to a compromise on the question of France's guarantee of the eastern arbitration treaties. France had earlier agreed that the League of Nations Charter indeed provided guarantees against German aggression on the eastern borders. Now that Germany would be bound by the charter, France agreed to forego any explicit guarantee in the East. She did, however, insist upon specific mention of the rights of action accorded her by the league's charter.[8]

Accords on the principal obstacles to a security pact had thus been reached. But the cabinet in Berlin had appeared restive throughout the conference. The German delegation, therefore, instructed Chancellery Secretary Franz Kempner to return to Berlin in mid conference for the purpose of informing the cabinet and the Reichspresident about the progress of negotiations. Some days earlier, one of Kempner's colleagues in the chancellery, Hermann Pünder, had urged the delegation to send a personal report from Locarno to the government. Pünder's position in Berlin made him aware that the DNVP, and even elements of the DVP, were uneasy about the course of the negotiations in Locarno. Influential Nationalists challenged the delegation's handling of the issue of war guilt, despite Schiele's efforts in the meeting of the DNVP's Executive Committee on October 6.[9]

Schiele's position within his party was in fact the subject of wildly divergent rumors. Pünder reported both extremes. On the one hand, Schiele, at a breakfast given by the British ambassador on October 7, had allegedly declared his sincere hope for a successful conclusion of the pact negotiations, and on the other, he had purportedly only narrowly avoided a direct repudiation of the cabinet in the DNVP meeting of October 6 by promising that "nothing would come of all these pact negotiations." If nothing else, the rumors were a sign of growing unrest. Pünder had discussed this unrest with acting Chancellor Heinrich Brauns and had then reported to the Locarno delegation. Brauns thought that the DNVP could be managed. For his part, Pünder suggested that a personal appearance by one of the Locarno negotiators, preferably Luther, might make this more likely. Within two days of his talk with Brauns, Pünder renewed the request urgently, adding that without such a report from Locarno, a major reversal would take place in Berlin.[10]

The atmosphere that greeted Kempner upon his return to Berlin was thus one of troubled concern. In two consultations with the cabinet, on October 13 and 14, he tried to dispel this anxiety. His initial report traced the textual modifications of the London draft treaty and presented the collective note that the Allies would issue with regard to Article 16. The delegation had been able to raise the related political questions only informally up to the time of Kempner's departure from Locarno, and it considered the results of these endeavors to be insufficient so far. Stresemann had repeated Germany's rejection of the "war-guilt lie," which had been embodied in the German memorandum of September 1924. The discussion had not been pursued by the Allies.[11]

The sharpest critic of the results that Kempner had outlined was General Seeckt. He considered the textual changes that Kempner sketched to represent an improvement in France's position, not in Germany's. They eliminated France's guarantee of the eastern settlement, but they confirmed her right, as a member of the league, to oppose aggression. Germany's position was thereby worsened, argued Seeckt, because at the moment, France enjoyed no league rights in relation to Germany. Furthermore, he denied that the collective note resolved the German objections concerning Article 16, because it spoke only of the *extent* of participation in sanctions, not of the "whether" of participation. Moreover, the interpretation given to the note in Locarno would not bind future Allied governments, since it would remain unratified by the parliaments in question. All three DNVP ministers—Schiele, Neuhaus, and Schlieben—supported Seeckt's objections. Acting Chancellor Brauns's insistence that the collective note would indeed be binding left them all unpersuaded. Schiele also demanded to know if the Allies clearly understood the German distinction between those related questions that were "conditions" as opposed to "consequences" of the security pact. The evacuation of Cologne before a pact could be concluded was not the only condition, he asserted.[12]

It is difficult to imagine that Schiele's remark would have gone unchallenged, as happened in this discussion, if Luther and Stresemann had been present; for neither in the guidelines, which had been approved unanimously by the cabinet, nor in prior cabinet discussions had a distinction been made between conditions and consequences. As for the evacuation of Cologne, Schiele himself had admitted in an earlier meeting that it could not be completed before a treaty was concluded. Brauns and Kempner both overlooked this fundamental challenge to the government's set policy. Still, the acting chancellor did try to contain the dissatisfaction with the results reported by Kempner. He pointed out that the negotiations had not yet reached a stage that would allow the cabinet to vote on their results. Thus, suggestions and expressions of opinion now were simply a means of giving Kempner an impression of the mood in Berlin. This was not the time for final judgments.

On the following day, October 14, Kempner repeated his briefing for the benefit of those ministers who had not attended the late-night meeting on the day before. With Gessler replacing Seeckt as the army spokesman in the discussions, Kempner noted a marked improvement in the atmosphere. Whereas Seeckt had voiced his evident dissatisfaction, Gessler asked for clarifications, and he suggested modifications. Although the DNVP representatives were once again present, they refrained from making the sharp attacks of the day before. As a result, the cabinet was able to discuss more thoroughly the reservations felt by various ministers. Although the enthusiasm for the resolutions concerning Article 16 and the eastern treaties was far from uniform, Kempner could report to Luther that the Berlin cabinet, including the Nationalist ministers, accepted the resolutions as being essentially satisfactory. The DNVP ministers had proposed a number of "special wishes," however. The delegation should secure a stronger assurance that the Allies would urge the Council of the League of Nations to adopt the same interpretation of Article 16 that was set forth in the collective note. In addition, Germany should formally acknowledge receipt of the collective note and, at the same time, restate her own interpretation that the note released her from all obligations under Article 16. Kempner also emphasized to Luther in Locarno that the hoped-for ramifications from the security pact in the Rhineland were of decisive significance. The delegation would have to secure meaningful results in this area; otherwise the pact would be unacceptable in Berlin.[13]

Kempner's personal report on the negotiations in Locarno had placated the cabinet for the moment. In subsequent conversations with Pünder, Schiele had even reconfirmed that the acceptance of the collective note was "essentially satisfactory."[14] But contrary to Kempner's own impression from his meeting with the Reichspresident, Hindenburg was uneasy. Seeckt's argument about the "extent" or the "whether" of participation in sanctions under Article 16 had reached Hindenburg, who laid great stress upon it. Pünder advised that an unobjectionable clarification of the official Allied interpretation of Article 16 would be essential if enormous difficulties were to be avoided in Germany.[15] In fact, by the time that Pünder wrote, Luther had already dispatched a telegram to Hindenburg, declaring that the Allied assurances gave Germany complete freedom to decide both whether and how extensively any sanctions would be applied.[16]

Kempner's report had not dispelled all dissent within the government. Outside of government circles the situation was even worse. Indeed, Schiele's acceptance of the current compromises in Locarno as being essentially satisfactory did not reflect the growing dissatisfaction within the DNVP. On October 14, 1925, Schiele and Count Westarp had prepared a letter, which the former was to address to Luther in Locarno. The letter was not sent, because it was allegedly "superseded by cabinet decision."[17] However, several important demands, made in most forceful terms in the letter, are not recorded in the cabinet discussions that supposedly superseded it. The letter states that conclusion of the treaty negotiations and Germany's entry into the league could not occur until the league's council had approved unanimously, and the General Assembly by simple majority, an interpretation of Article 16 that would be satisfactory to Germany. During the cabinet discussions, Schiele did raise most of the specific points of the interpretation that had been outlined as "satisfactory" in the letter, but the letter still goes far beyond the cabinet's decisions or the report that Kempner sent to Locarno, a report that Schiele raised no objections to when Pünder later read it to him on the fifteenth. Schiele's unsent letter, for example, mentions the DNVP's view that Stresemann's initiative concerning the question of war guilt did not fulfill the cabinet's decision of October 1 and that further action was still necessary in order to emphasize Germany's rejection of the Allied charge. Stresemann's allusion to the German memorandum of September 1924 and to the question of moral responsibility did technically satisfy the cabinet's decision. The memorandum did not, however, satisfy Westarp's interpretation of that decision. Westarp continued to contend that the Locarno delegation was still laboring under the more extensive DNVP demand that the Versailles signatories who had not yet received the German memorandum of September 26, 1925, which denied that Germany bore the sole responsibility for the war, be notified immediately and that the German denial of war guilt be made a major point of discussion at the Locarno Conference. Here was an obvious incompatibility that Schiele had not dispelled, perhaps because it was a point that Westarp could not afford to surrender.[18] The incompatibility of standpoints makes Schiele's and Westarp's position between the cabinet and the party appear suspiciously ambivalent.

The tenor of the unsent letter comes much closer than do the cabinet minutes to the rhetoric of Westarp's speech in Charlottenburg on October 15, just after Kempner's report to the cabinet. In it he warned that there was no news from Locarno that warranted optimism. Indeed nothing was yet known of the real results of the talks there. The only fixed point was the "self-evidence" of the German position, which was acknowledged by the government, by the governmental parties, and by many from the parliamentary opposition as well. This position would not be satisfied with "gentlemen's agreements" from the Allied powers regarding Article 16. It demanded "firm accords" with the entire League of Nations itself.

Westarp then began cataloging the other issues that were vital to the "German position" and about which doubts still remained. What accords had actually been reached on the rejection of a French guarantee for treaties in the East? Had assurances been secured that, before Germany's entry into the League of Nations, this body would not only have begun in earnest to come to grips with its obligations concerning universal disarmament but also have surrendered its one-sided control of Germany's demilitarization? Did anyone know whether the "preliminary questions" concerning the most recent disarmament demands on Germany—evacuation of the Cologne zone and the revision of the illegal occupation regimes in the Rhineland and Saar—had been settled to satisfaction? What had been done in Locarno to prevent the German renunciation of acts of war from assuming the character of an eternal renunciation of German territories and population? Were the Allies prepared to free the Rhine and Saar without delay? Had the German delegation pressed these "German demands"—which had the widest possible support in the nation—with energy; and above all, what results had it thereby achieved? In what form and to what effect had the recent Allied notes concerning war guilt been rejected? None of these questions, Westarp concluded, was a peripheral issue; none was a specifically German Nationalist demand; each corresponded to a particular guideline that the entire cabinet had approved. Each one must be fulfilled if the treaty were to be acceptable. The rejection of even a single one would mean that the Allies were withholding from Germany her simple claim to equal rights.[19]

Few of what Count Westarp claimed to be guidelines corresponded in either tone or content to the guidelines that had been approved unanimously by the cabinet on October 2, which Schiele had helped to draft. Westarp's rhetorical catalog even went beyond the demands that Schiele had first introduced, before the September compromises within the cabinet had robbed them of their sharpness. Westarp's assertions were certainly aimed at satisfying the radicals within his own party. But the intensely nationalistic rhetoric simply encouraged expectations that even Westarp knew were illusory. It could only bring trouble.

128

Westarp's continued assertions that the government was bound by these extreme demands, his insistence that the DNVP had imposed them in the cabinet discussions of September, is irreconcilable with the cabinet guidelines. It is equally incompatible with the understanding of those guidelines that Schiele displayed in a heated cabinet discussion the day following Westarp's Charlottenburg speech. The question before the cabinet was whether or not the delegation to Locarno ought to initial the treaties there. This would mean that the texts of the treaties could not be modified but could only be accepted or rejected as they stood. In his argument against initialing the treaties in Locarno, Schiele pointed out that according to the government guidelines, certain things had to be accomplished (*geschehen*), others had to be assured (*sichergestellt*), and still others had to be striven for (*darauf hingewirkt*). Schiele thus adopted the very verbs that had been used in the guidelines for Locarno. His understanding of the guidelines reflected a much more modest hope than did Westarp's speech.[20]

Still, Schiele argued forcefully against the German delegation's intention to fix the wording of the Locarno accords. From the information at hand, he feared that the dispositions concerning the Rhineland were unsatisfactory; and those were of the greatest concern to Germany. If the treaties were initialed now, no further negotiations would be possible on these issues. Also, the cabinet's guidelines required that the renunciation of German lands and peoples be excluded from the agreement. The inclusion of a reference to the status quo in the first article of the treaty violated this condition. Schiele's contention was supported by Minister of Justice Frenken, who mockingly asserted that any student who told him in an examination that Article 1 of the Locarno accords contained no renunciation of German land, especially in view of the evolution of the document, would fail on the spot.[21]

Brauns, as acting chancellor, tried vainly to dissuade Schiele and Frenken. But Schiele insisted that the delegation's plan compelled him to unburden his conscience by sending a personal statement of his dissenting views to Luther. To head off the possibility that Schiele could thereby later disassociate himself and the DNVP from the government's policies, Ministerial Director Hermann Pünder suggested a cabinet communiqué. Pünder proposed that the cabinet telegraph its expectation that the satisfactory conclusion of the question of ramifications would be a condition for any decision on the part of the negotiators to initial the treaties. Brauns supported Pünder's suggestion enthusiastically. Personal declarations, he insisted, were out of place. The cabinet could do no more than await the consequences of the delegation's ultimate decision. The cabinet fulfilled its responsibility if it stated once again its position on the Rhineland questions and if it pointed out that serious reservations existed with regard to the initialing.

Schiele's personal statement was thus preempted. Brauns formulated a telegram expressing the cabinet's views. It urged the German delegation to consider initialing only a final protocol summarizing the work of the conference, to which the texts of the treaties could be attached uninitialed. Significant contentions had arisen that the German chancellor's initialing would bind the government more strictly than the signatures of the Allied foreign ministers bound their governments. It was hardly necessary to label the origin of this point of view more specifically. It was the familiar Nationalist argument of a Luther crisis versus a Stresemann crisis. The telegram concluded by asserting the ministers' assumption that all prerequisites and ramifications had been assured.[22]

The telegram was sent after 6:00 P.M., October 16, and arrived in Locarno only after the final session of the conference had begun. It was therefore impossible to propose any change in the procedure that was already under way for the conclusion of the conference. Moreover, Luther realized that it was untenable that he withhold his signature and let only Stresemann sign. He thus chose to exercise the discretionary power that the delegation had been given by the cabinet before its departure. He affixed his initials to the final protocol of the conference and to the Rhineland pact. The remaining agreements of arbitration bore only Stresemann's initials.[23]

The German negotiators could leave Locarno with a sense of justifiable pride. They had conducted the negotiations of a Rhineland security pact along the general guidelines that had been established by the cabinet, gaining for Germany some concessions from the Allies with regard to league responsibilities, the nature of the eastern arbitration treaties, and the promise of future ramifications in the occupied Rhineland. Most importantly, they had managed to do this while making a positive contribution to the atmosphere of cordial cooperation which had grown up around the Locarno negotiations, an atmosphere in which Germany was accepted as an equal partner in the European concert and in which her image as a peaceful, reasonable aspirant to European reconciliation was enhanced. These gains on the diplomatic front seemed to have been matched domestically by the fact that the government that had negotiated the Locarno accords enjoyed the cooperation of Germany's strongest nationalistic party. The political maneuvering in Berlin during the preceding several months, however, particularly the continued insistence by leading Nationalists that their conditions for negotiations had been accepted by the government before the beginning of the Locarno Conference, made the allegiance of the Nationalist Party highly questionable. As had been the case the year before, after the

London Conference, the successful negotiators returned to Berlin to face a major domestic crisis.

The German delegation arrived home from Locarno at 1:20 A.M. on Sunday, October 18, 1925. They were met by Labor Minister Brauns, who had headed the cabinet in Luther's absence, by Lord D'Abernon, Margerie, and other members of the Berlin diplomatic corps. Lord D'Abernon immediately delivered the following message to Luther and Stresemann: "I have been expressly instructed by Mr. Chamberlain to congratulate you on the success of the Conference in Locarno, and to say that Mr. Chamberlain will always recall with pleasure that first meeting in Locarno and the spirit of sincerity and openness which the German delegation impressed upon the discussions. The honor will always belong to the German government for having taken the initiative which led to the Treaty of Locarno."[24]

The spirit of good will that informed Chamberlain's message even carried over into the first cabinet meeting after the return. On October 19, 1925, at 11:00 A.M., Stresemann and Luther began to make their report to the president and the cabinet. Stresemann emphasized the conformity between the cabinet's guidelines of October 2 and the final accords. The German note of July 20, 1925, had been fully realized (point 1 of the guidelines). The preamble to the security pact had been modified to exclude a guarantee of the territorial status quo in the Rhineland (point 2, sec. 1). It was true that Article 1 mentioned a guarantee of the existing Rhineland settlement, but the article also stated that this guarantee was to be observed in the manner set forth in subsequent articles of the pact, which meant, according to Article 2, a renunciation of aggression, invasion, or war. Because the treaty specifically excluded only these factors as means of revision in the Rhineland, it in effect confirmed by its silence the right to modify the territorial distribution by means of peaceful agreements.[25] Only arbitration treaties of the German model had been concluded at Locarno (point 2, sec. 2). Germany therefore obliged herself to accept arbitration settlements in questions of law but not in political disputes, particularly over boundaries.

The two main problems of the conference, Stresemann reported, had been France's demand to guarantee the eastern settlement and Germany's attitude concerning the League of Nations. In the first case, the French guarantee was completely excluded from the pact (point 2, sec. 3). France's rights and obligations concerning her eastern allies were specifically circumscribed by reference to the league's charter. Only in the event that the league made a unanimous decision charging Germany with aggression would France have the right to come to the aid of the attacked country. In addition, the guarantee clause of the pact would bind England to come to the aid of Germany if, in the event of a German-Polish involvement, France attacked from the west without the league's having designated Germany as the aggressor. Concerning Germany's entry into the league, Stresemann recounted the arguments he had used. The Allies had imposed a state of disarmament on Germany. They could not maintain it while simultaneously insisting that Germany be prepared militarily for those occasions where it would serve Allied interest (point 3 of the guidelines). Germany did not care to use the "immoral back door" of Article 16 in order to frustrate all action under the article by blocking the necessary unanimous decision in the League of Nations Council. Rather, Germany demanded that the real state of her disarmament be taken into account.

In these same discussions, Stresemann reported, he had rejected any implication of Germany's sole guilt for the war. The Allied negotiators had accepted his statement without protest. The collective note offered a satisfactory resolution of the demand for special consideration under Article 16 and, as such, had been accepted by the delegation as the full realization of German aims, the more so in that the discussions that produced it had covered universal disarmament as well as Germany's state of disarmament. The Allies offered generally satisfactory statements on general disarmament, and these were included in the conference's final protocol.[26] The last category of the guideline directives (point 4)—the eventual ramifications of the pact in the occupied territories—had been left to the end of the conference because an acceptable treaty was the natural prerequisite. When these points were finally broached, Briand had been struck by what he felt to be Stresemann's audacity, even foolhardiness, in raising so many demands. Nonetheless, Briand agreed to press for the French cabinet to take measures to ease the occupation.

A procedure for dealing with the remaining points of contention regarding Germany's disarmament had also emerged during the negotiations. Germany would address a note to France on the present state of disarmament. France would reply that, in view of the limited scope of the remaining points to be fulfilled, the evacuation of the Cologne zone would be delayed no longer; a specific date would then be set for completing the evacuation. The note would of course express the expectation that the remaining points would be taken care of soon. Stresemann recounted the results of the negotiations on military inspection and control. The Allies had also agreed that inspection and control were not permanent rights and that subsequent to the resolution of the remaining differences over disarmament, they would be exercised only through the League of Nations Council on those occasions when evidence of a specific violation by Germany was presented.

Both Stresemann and Luther were convinced that Briand would keep his promises regarding the various improvements agreed upon in Locarno. As an illustration of Briand's good will, Stresemann recounted the manner in which public mention of the Rhineland ramifications had been handled. The German delegation had considered including this in its statement during the concluding ceremonies of the conference, but Briand suggested that he himself mention the aims for the Rhineland. His domestic situation demanded that no concession made by France appear to be the result of acquiescence to German pressures. In his concluding speech, then, he emphasized France's open generosity. Both he and Chamberlain stated that they would submit requests to their cabinets to suggest decreases in troop strength in the occupied territories.[27]

After having thus covered in sequence every point in the cabinet guidelines of October 2, Stresemann turned to the final act of the conference.

The initialing of the treaties that had occurred in Locarno meant simply that the wording of the accords could not be modified. This was all to Germany's advantage. Germany would have until December 1 to decide whether or not to approve the treaties. During that time the Allies would be compelled to begin the evacuation of the Cologne zone, or at least to set a date for it. Stresemann, moreover, expressed his firm conviction that the ramifications for the Rhineland would be clearly manifest before December 1.[28]

To Stresemann's briefing, Chancellor Luther added a number of points of detail. He explained the reasons that had made it impossible to comply with the cabinet's recommendation of October 16 that the pact not be initialed. He then posed three questions for the cabinet's consideration. The first decision must be whether the cabinet approved the conduct of the Locarno delegation. The cabinet must then decide, at some later date, whether Germany should officially sign the accords in London, as provided for in the final Locarno protocol. The third decision would be the approval of the accords by the legislative bodies and the ratification of them by the government. Since the Reichstag was not scheduled to reconvene until November 20, the legislative approval and the signing in London would be clearly linked.

Luther then turned to the broader implications of the Locarno policies. He viewed the conference itself as the point of departure for a new relationship in international politics. Locarno had created a new basis on which to deal with the Allies. He and Stresemann were convinced that Germany's position was now materially improved. They were also aware, however, that the principal figures in Germany's relations, France and England, still possessed that "instrument of war," the Versailles Treaty. In both foreign lands, hostile cries would be directed at Germany's new situation. He and Stresemann were thus fully prepared to abandon their posts if hostile manifestations prevented the realization of the ramifications that had been promised. Two possible mistakes had to be avoided. The government ought not to acclaim the conference too exuberantly as the beginning of a new era. This would only encourage the Allies to believe that Germany felt so satisfied with the results of the conference that they need do very little more, and thus it would undermine the incentive to carry out the promised ramifications. On the other hand, Luther asserted, in an admonition that ought to have provoked some reflection among the German Nationalist ministers, Germany must avoid creating the impression that, while she continued to demand the ramifications promised at Locarno, she would ultimately reject the treaty itself. The government ought to declare that the accords were appropriate and binding but that there was still much to be accomplished.[29]

With surprising unanimity and enthusiasm, the cabinet welcomed the report of Luther and Stresemann regarding the Locarno Conference and its implications. DNVP spokesman Schiele prefaced his own remarks by disclaiming that approval of the delegation's conduct in Locarno could be equated with a parliamentary vote of confidence in all the particulars as well as the entire development of the accords. He nonetheless stated: "I can even now say that when it comes to the question of a general approval of the delegation's work in conformity with the guidelines of the cabinet, I will answer with a clear yes, but I cannot foresee the [party's] decision on all particulars and consequences."[30] The determinative consideration for his party's final decision, according to Schiele, would be whether the framework constructed at Locarno would be filled out by Allied concessions in the weeks to come. Schiele then raised a number of particular points of concern: Article 16, Germany's right to terminate the accords, and the shortening of the terms of occupation in the second and third Rhineland zones.

Schiele's were the only expressions of reservation to arise, however. Brauns enthusiastically described the results of Locarno as "a step forward . . . in the dismantling of the Versailles Treaty." Gessler observed that the delegation had conscientiously fulfilled its mission. Former Nationalist party member Count Kanitz, emphasizing his roots in the eastern provinces, greeted the accords as a major success, adding that the delegation had achieved far more than he had thought possible. The remaining ministers concurred. Luther proposed that a statement be released the next day indicating that the cabinet found the results of the conference satisfactory and that the final decision on the London signing would depend on the developments in the weeks to come, but that this reserve should in no way impugn the actual accomplishments of Locarno. Luther's suggestion evoked a startling testimonial from Schiele affirming the extent of the entire cabinet's

134

satisfaction with the results, which was all the more curious because it was totally gratuitous. He agreed that the cabinet must wait to see whether the expected ramifications would be implemented. But he did not feel that Luther and Stresemann would be obliged to resign if final ratification of the treaties failed because of defaults by the Allies in fulfilling these ramifications. After all, such a development would not be their failure, but the failure of the Allies to meet their obligations. Luther, however, placed his political fortunes, and therefore those of the rightist alignment that Schiele was obviously seeking to preserve, directly on the realization of the promises made at Locarno.[31]

The tenor of the cabinet meeting was clear. Reichspresident Hindenburg concluded, without encountering any objection, that the delegation's conduct in Locarno was "totally approved and gratefully acknowledged" and that the Locarno signing had the fundamental assent of the cabinet as well, a point that would cause Schiele much difficulty in the coming weeks.[32] But the euphoric flush at the delegation's success was short-lived. On the very day after the first report was delivered to the cabinet, October 20, opposition within the DNVP delegation to the results of Locarno necessitated a delay in the cabinet meeting that had been scheduled in order to complete the discussion of the press release that Luther had proposed. Schiele received instructions from his party to approve nothing until the entire Nationalist delegation had been assembled and consulted.[33] Luther was so upset by the Nationalist course of action that he could not contain himself during an interview with Westarp. Heatedly, he accused the Nationalists of courting not merely a cabinet crisis but a fundamental crisis of state as well. The German delegation had achieved 100 percent of what it had set out to gain at Locarno. Germany had never before enjoyed such a success. Germany had been looked upon as a slave nation up to now, but in Locarno she had become a state that was fully honored in the world. A wave of indignation would overwhelm the German Nationalists if they tried to destroy this work, and he, Luther, would range himself this time alongside the Nationalists' enemies. So enraged was Luther that he trembled as he spoke.[34]

Although Westarp was visibly moved by Luther's tirade, the DNVP was not. Nationalist propaganda had created a situation in which public opinion tended at best to acknowledge in passing the advantages gained in Locarno and to concentrate its dissatisfaction on the failure to fix these specific ramifications in writing.[35] If Westarp was unwilling to exploit this unrealistic dissatisfaction, the radicals in the party were not. As a result of the DNVP's delays, the government was forced to admit before the assembled provincial governors on October 21 that the cabinet had not yet reached a decision concerning approval of the Locarno delegation's conduct of the negotiations because the DNVP ministers had to await the decision of their Reichstag delegation.[36] Luther was determined to get a decision from the cabinet, however, which would permit the pursuit of both foreign and domestic policy on the basis of the Locarno accords. On October 22, just before the scheduled meeting of the Reichstag's Foreign Affairs Committee, he convened the cabinet again under the chairmanship of Reichspresident Hindenburg, and proposed a formula for such a cabinet decision. Schiele voiced certain reservations over the wording of Luther's proposal, but not over its implications. Luther replied that he was perfectly willing to change the precise formulation, since the text would not be published in any event. Brauns, Schiele, and Gessler thereupon introduced modifications until the formula read:

> The Reichscabinet has received the report of the German delegation concerning the meeting of ministers in Locarno and has decided to bring the treaty work, begun in Locarno on the basis of the German note of July 20, 1925, to a conclusion which does justice to the vital necessities of the German people. The government of the Reich acts in this matter on the firm expectation, based on the voluntary statements by the foreign ministers of England, France and Belgium, that the logical* consequences of the Locarno labor will take effect, especially in the Rhineland. [*Added in longhand.]

This cabinet decision was accepted without objection in the presence of the German Nationalist ministers.[37]

This decision gave the chancellor and the foreign minister the approval that they needed in order to represent the government before the Foreign Affairs Committee. It also strongly identified the entire cabinet, including the Nationalist ministers, with the German delegation's conduct of negotiations in Locarno.

In the meeting of the Foreign Affairs Committee on that very afternoon, Stresemann delivered substantially the same report as the cabinet had been given. Only with regard to the exchange of notes concerning disarmament and the evacuation of Cologne was he less specific. He refrained from describing in detail the procedure that had been adopted at his insistence in Locarno, saying only that the Allied ministers had "declared themselves ready" to intercede within their cabinets on behalf of an immediate evacuation of the Cologne zone. He explained, too, that the date for the final signing of the accords negotiated in Locarno had been set for December 1 at the behest of the German delegation, in order to allow sufficient time to observe to what extent the Allies would fulfill their promises regarding ramifications.[38]

In his reply to Stresemann's report, Count Westarp began with a moderation of tone and a mildness of criticism that belied the growing opposition within the DNVP. He even began by acknowledging, on behalf of the German Nationalists, that the German delegation to Locarno had advanced its goals politically and juridically with tenacity and skill. As a result, he observed, he did not want to criticize the delegation itself for the fact that the outcome fell short of what had to be attained in order to make the accords acceptable. The Reichstag's final decision on the treaties would only be called for after the results of the negotiations that were still in progress over the "so-called ramifications" became known. However, the DNVP's Reichstag delegation had already taken a position in the following resolution:

> The German Nationalist Reichstag delegation is not able to see in the results of the negotiations in Locarno the fulfillment of the demands justified by the vital necessities of the German people. The delegation also fails to find the fulfillment of the prerequisites to the conclusion of a treaty, as well as the compensations by the other participating powers commensurate with the sacrifices to be assumed by Germany. In view of these results, the [DNVP] delegation declares already that it will not approve any treaty that does not do justice to German *vital necessities* [*Lebensnotwendigkeiten*] and especially that *does not exclude any renunciation of German land and peoples.*[39]

After reading the Nationalists' decision, Westarp raised the specific aspects of the accords that were the root of his party's misgivings. He admitted, first of all, that the *wording* of Article 1 of the Locarno Treaty spoke only of a renunciation of war and force by Germany. But the assertions of the opponents, especially the French, that Germany had voluntarily renounced all claim to Alsace-Lorraine and Eupen-Malmédy necessitated that there be a specific official statement before the fear of a renunciation of German land and peoples could be allayed. The German government must place its viewpoint before world public opinion, and the Allies must acknowledge the validity of that viewpoint. If this were not possible, then the only remaining avenue of resolution would be a modification of the treaty itself. Germany's right to terminate the treaty was also an important consideration in judging the nature of the renunciation of the separated territories. The Locarno accords did not offer an effective right of termination, because they demanded that a two-thirds majority of the League of Nations Council recognize their abrogation. Westarp objected that the Allies needed only one vote other than their own in order to frustrate any German attempt at abrogation.[40]

Ironically, it was a Nationalist demand, which the delegation at Locarno sought to fulfill, that had given rise to the introduction of the two-thirds-majority clause to which Westarp objected. The London draft treaty had permitted abrogation by the petition of two contractants to the treaty, with approval by a simple majority in the League of Nations Council. But the Nationalists had insisted that the two-contractant clause was disadvantageous to Germany and had demanded that it be revised. Stresemann was at first reluctant to make the change. The diplomatic delegation had, however, pressed the revision in Locarno in an effort to meet as many Nationalist objections as possible. The Allied negotiators would only accept this modification, however, if the qualified-majority clause was introduced.[41]

Westarp continued his litany of doubts before the Foreign Affairs Committee by observing that, no matter how welcome the avoidance in Locarno of a French guarantee of the eastern treaties might seem, the statements made since the conference by the Polish foreign minister must give rise to concern that, practically speaking, such a guarantee still existed. The Locarno accords also seemed vague enough to permit the application of sanctions against Germany under the Versailles Treaty, despite the government's assertions to the contrary. Moreover, Article 16 might also still be invoked against Germany, the collective note notwithstanding. This note did not suffice to ensure Germany's interests. An additional clarification must be sought from the four main powers in question. Even this, however, would be less than the full assurance that the German point of view demanded; only a two-thirds vote of the league's assembly and a unanimous approval in its council could give that. German demands concerning general disarmament, continued Westarp, remained only a pious wish. They must be translated into discernible action prior to Germany's entry into the league. The plan for military inspection of Germany was inconsistent with the Locarno Pact and must be formally abandoned before Germany could accept the treaty. The issue of war guilt demanded still more explicit emphasis that the government stood by its renunciation note of October 2, 1925. This note must be communicated to the Versailles signatories who had not yet received it. The agreements concerning ramifications were totally unsatisfactory. The promises concerning the remaining points of contention in the disarmament controversy must be converted into binding accords. Finally, the DNVP put special stock in the realization of amelioration in the system of occupation, the reduction of the term of occupation, and improvements in the Saar.[42]

Westarp's protestations amounted to a condemnation of the treaty as being unworthy of adoption, coupled with a demand for the fulfillment of the ramifications that adoption of the treaty was supposed to occasion. Despite the length of Westarp's catalog of objections, however, his presentation had been more moderate than observers had expected given the intensely hostile pressure from provincial party organizations.[43] His intention seems to have been to place as many obstacles as possible in the path of concluding the treaties, but to preserve what bases he could for continued cooperation with Luther by avoiding a categorical repudiation of the work of the Locarno delegation.

His Charlottenburg speech notwithstanding, Westarp still wanted to maintain the DNVP's presence in the coalition as long as possible. He feared that the breakup of the existing rightist alignment at any earlier stage of the negotiations would have opened the way for the formation of a Grand Coalition with the Social Democrats. A government that was dependent on the Left would then have concluded the security accords without the limitations, reservations, and conditions that the Nationalists insisted they had been able to impose as a result of their position in the cabinet. He had not expected all the DNVP's demands to be fulfilled at Locarno. Nor did he really believe that the cabinet would reject a treaty that fell short of the Nationalist demands but that represented nonetheless a partial success for Germany. He expected the delegation, "by painting pretty pictures," to try to conceal what it had not attained.[44]

Westarp was more concerned, however, with preserving party unity than with partial success in foreign policy. Party unity, he had often stated, would necessitate a flat no to any security pact that did not meet Nationalist expectations.[45] But to him, a no could be delayed until just before the final signing of the accords in December. In the meantime, the DNVP could work within the cabinet to burden the accords with impossible conditions in the hope that they would break under the strain.

In the debate that followed Westarp's critique of the Locarno Pact, the German Foreign Office's legal expert, Friedrich Gaus, answered each of Westarp's points in detail. The explanations found ready acceptance among the representatives of the other parties, but Westarp's speech evoked demands that the government clarify the situation within the coalition by stating its own position towards the DNVP critique. Luther demurred, saying only that the government was interested in hearing from the parties in this meeting. The report Stresemann had just given was supported by a unanimous resolution of the cabinet. This, he implied, was a sufficient indication of the solidarity of the coalition. But Luther declined to respond when the question was raised as to whether the resolution included an approval by the Nationalist ministers of the results of Locarno.[46]

Luther's dodging did nothing to conceal the rift between the DNVP and the government. But Westarp's moderate tone and his acknowledgment of the skill with which the German delegation had negotiated in

Locarno made it possible for a well-placed observer to contend that perhaps the cabinet and the Nationalists might still be reconciled.[47]

The radical element within the DNVP was determined to prevent such a reconciliation, however. It now moved to put pressure on the moderate leadership through the Executive Committee of the party organization and the chairmen of the provincial party committees. A meeting of these two bodies was convened on October 23, 1925. Here, the memory of the vote on the Dawes plan, which had been alluded to in numerous provincial committee decisions of recent months, and the constant attack by the radical press against the "politics of renunciation"—carefully orchestrated largely by the Pan-German and *völkisch* elements within the party—had undermined confidence that Count Westarp and the moderate party leaders, including Schiele and Lindeiner-Wildau, would really withdraw the support of the DNVP's Reichstag delegation from the government coalition in a final showdown vote on the Locarno accords.[48]

During the morning meeting of October 23, Westarp and Schiele tried to convince the provincial delegates and the party's Executive Committee that their plan—to remain in the government until a final decision on the Locarno treaties became unavoidable—offered the greatest advantage of forcing either revision or frustration of the accords. Both of them assured the party's provincial representatives that members of the delegation would indeed oppose the government and the treaty unanimously in the Reichstag if satisfactory revisions could not be achieved. Schiele swore that he had preserved the delegation's complete freedom of decision on the accords, and he even sought to support his case by revealing the cabinet decision of the prior morning. Luther, whom Schiele contacted by telephone, was prepared to allow the Nationalist minister to use the cabinet decision if he thought it would work a calming effect, but Luther insisted that Schiele's revelation should in no way throw doubt upon the entire cabinet's conscious and positive commitment to the Locarno treaties. Schiele could indicate that no final position had been taken, but only because the complete results of the negotiations were not yet discernible.[49]

Such a limited confirmation was not enough for the radical element, however. It became apparent that they could muster a majority in this widened circle of party representatives where provincial party elements outnumbered Reichstag delegates. Still, Schiele sought some dramatic measure to turn the tide. For a second time, he contacted Chancellor Luther, explaining that the mood among the provincial Nationalists was such that the pact would be overwhelmingly rejected unless he could allay suspicions that it included a renunciation of claims to German land and peoples. After exploring numerous possibilities, Luther, who had called Schubert and Gaus from the German Foreign Office into the discussions—Stresemann was speaking in Karlsruhe that day[50]—finally agreed to provide Schiele with a statement regarding the cabinet's interpretation of the renunciation clause of the security pact. The statement read that the government could see no possibility of a misunderstanding, either legal or logical, over the Rhineland pact. The meaning and content of the first article made it clear that Germany renounced any revision of the western boundaries through aggressive war or any other application of force. It did not, in contrast, prohibit peaceful developments, in particular the right to free self-determination. The statement took cognizance of recent reports from abroad which called this interpretation into question. The government, it promised, would use the appropriate occasions to counteract any possible erroneous interpretation of the western pact. Luther assured Schiele that this statement represented his and the foreign minister's point of view and that he would act in conformity with it. On the other hand, in the absence of the foreign minister, Luther refused to extend such a statement to any foreign power, nor would he define the "appropriate occasions" referred to in the statement. Schiele promised that he would respect Luther's strictures in his use of the statement and also that he would show it only to a limited circle of his party colleagues, in whose ability to keep a secret he had the utmost confidence.[51]

Luther had tried to reach Stresemann by long-distance telephone during both of his discussions with Schiele on the twenty-third. A contact was finally made near the end of the second conversation, but before the proposed statement had been drawn up. Stresemann had expressed his energetic opposition to any diplomatic action to contact all the Locarno powers concerning Schiele's request. Some contact might be made with Chamberlain alone, but this, too, would demand Stresemann's more thorough consideration. These views were passed on to Schiele before the conclusion of his meeting with Luther.[52]

Once again Schiele's efforts to gain some formal statement from the cabinet that would strengthen his hand against the radicals had been in vain. The reservations imposed by Luther and Stresemann robbed the statement of any dramatic impact that it might have had in the meeting of the Nationalists' Executive Committee. Moreover, any effort toward compromise, especially when advanced by Schiele, was viewed with suspicion or open hostility by too many of the delegates.[53] Contrary to the obvious wishes of both Schiele and Count Westarp, the Executive Committee and the provincial party chairmen voted that "the presently existing treaty resulting from [the conference in] Locarno is unacceptable to the party." The true nature of this simple decision, which purported only to "carry forward the initiative seized by the [DNVP] Reichstag delegation," was revealed

141

only in the commentary, published simultaneously, which made it clear that while technically the Reichstag delegation could decide to remain in the coalition, the party organization expected it to withdraw its support from the government by recalling its spokesman within the cabinet.[54]

Westarp was thus left with no choice. He wanted to stay in the coalition, to continue the opposition from within. But he knew that such a course would bring an open break within the party. The DNVP's Reichstag delegation was convened on October 25, a Sunday. Some 60 of the DNVP's 105 Reichstag delegates attended. There, in an effort to avoid the sort of split that had occurred over the Dawes plan, Westarp recommended that the delegation break with the government.[55] Although a majority of the members of the DNVP delegation favored the maintenance of the coalition, even at the price of concessions on foreign policy, the delegates were aware that the provincial party structure was now decisively influenced by men who thought differently, men whose control of money and the mass media was extensive.[56] Outmaneuvered by the radicals, the moderates were forced to vote to "approve the decision of Ministers Schiele, Neuhaus, and von Schlieben to tender their resignations to the Reichschancellor."[57]

The Nationalist leaders in Berlin felt no sense of victory. On the contrary, they viewed their withdrawal from the government with a real sense of disappointment and dislocation. In taking leave of his colleagues in the cabinet the day after the delegation's vote, Schiele nearly came to tears. He had to pause as he spoke, so as to regain his composure. In his farewell remarks, he insisted that he and his colleagues had been overwhelmed by a "tidal wave" from the provinces. He was by no means convinced that ultimately an agreement between the government and the DNVP could not have been reached. He asked the cabinet to accept his assurances that the German Nationalists had no desire to assume an adamantly negative position. He urged the cabinet to avoid decisions that might exacerbate the Nationalist opposition. Westarp, too, appeared to have been unsettled by the experience.[58]

Schiele's swan song changed nothing in the party's decision, but it attests to the strength of the process of accommodation among the DNVP moderates. The Nationalist leadership had resisted the first two waves of anticoalition sentiment within the party, in March and in July. But the storm of protest against Locarno, organized and incited by the Pan-German League and increasingly by the Hugenberg press, proved to be uncontainable. The party had tried to blunt it by raising blatantly nationalistic demands with which to burden the negotiations. The leaders claimed that they could frustrate an accord that would inevitably come about if the DNVP left the government. But their efforts were consistently tempered by a desire to preserve the party's place in power. Their public statements emphasized and often exaggerated the degree to which the cabinet was bound by Nationalist conditions.

When the German delegation returned home from Locarno with a treaty in hand, the German Nationalist leaders faced a real dilemma. The treaty fulfilled virtually every condition that had been formally established by the cabinet in consultation with the DNVP's Reichstag delegation, but it was a far cry from the interpretation of these conditions that the DNVP leaders had circulated within the party. To approve the treaty was impossible. To leave the government was disadvantageous. The leaders of the Nationalists' Reichstag delegation wanted to remain in the government, in full opposition to the existing treaty, for as long as they could.

Once the party's Executive Committee, which had been broadened to include the chairmen of the provincial committees, voted to break with the government, however, the contest was over. Westarp still valued party unity over any other political consideration. Thus, he had no choice but to instruct the Reichstag delegation to comply.

Stresemann's efforts to return Germany to the first rank among nations through a policy of reconciliation seem at first glance to have been little affected by either the DNVP's presence within the cabinet or by the Nationalist opposition throughout the land. His early estimation that Nationalist participation in the government would be less dangerous than unrestrained opposition was justified in March and again in July, when the Nationalists' desire to remain in power proved stronger than their desire to disrupt foreign policy. Moreover, the security pact, which Stresemann thought of as but one of many steps towards the reestablishment of Germany's position in the world, had been approved. Thus, in spite of the Nationalists, Stresemann had preserved the essence of his foreign policy: the mutual adjustment of interests.

And yet the DNVP had exerted an influence upon the development of the policy of reconciliation, perhaps potentially the more damaging because of its very subtlety. The influence was in attitude and tone, but it eventually ran over into substance. For example, in making his original proposal, Stresemann had been quite willing to renounce Alsace and Lorraine unequivocally, because he knew that in reality he was abandoning only what Germany did not have and could never hope to acquire as things actually stood. He had even stated this in no uncertain terms before the Reichstag's Foreign Affairs Committee in March.[59] And yet, at least partly in order to accommodate Nationalist demands, Stresemann had ultimately endeavored to exclude so clear a renunciation from the final treaty. Such efforts, in addition to Germany's resultant contentions that the territorial status quo was not guaranteed, exposed Stresemann to charges of insincerity without allaying Nationalist resentment of his readiness to sacrifice "German soil."

The handling of the question of war guilt, too, was strongly marked by the Nationalist influence. It is highly probable that Stresemann never would have raised the issue if he had been free from the necessity to consider Nationalist sensitivities. It is absolutely certain that he would not have raised it in a formal diplomatic note intended for publication.

The Nationalists had affected Stresemann's position within the cabinet as well. The cooperation that had characterized the relationship between Luther and Stresemann during the cabinet's early months had almost been destroyed in the July controversy over responsibility, which was occasioned by the Nationalist attack. And in general, ever since the March compromise, Stresemann had not had the freedom of conduct in planning foreign policy that he had enjoyed prior to that time.[60] The imposition of specific guidelines, again to accommodate the Nationalists, was just the sort of restriction that Stresemann had successfully avoided in preparing the London Conference of 1924. All of these concessions to Nationalist pressure rendered the harmonious conduct of foreign affairs more difficult. None satisfied the Nationalists, who continually carped at what they saw as affronts to German honor. The more radical denounced Stresemann as a traitor and the Locarno treaties as his act of treason. The vitriolic and emotional attacks that were mounted against Stresemann and his policies blinded much of the German public to the real benefits that these policies had brought, robbing them of the impact that they might have had and of the support that they ought to have enjoyed.

The year-long struggle over foreign policy had forced the DNVP into the opposition once again. But a year of coalition partnership had confirmed sentiment within the party's Reichstag delegation in favor of participation in the government. The cooperation wing within the Reichstag had, if anything, grown stronger since the split over the Dawes plan. But the radical element's move to usurp control of the party in the provinces had also advanced. Westarp had succeeded in maintaining a façade of unity, where Hergt had failed, only by overriding the sentiment for cooperation in the delegation and in himself and by bowing to the more radical demands of the provincial party apparatus. But the DNVP's Reichstag delegation was now more than ever predisposed to take its place in the republican government. A critical question of the years 1926 to 1928 was whether this predisposition could be translated into political reality.

8

FOREIGN POLICY
VERSUS COALITION POLITICS

The DNVP's break with the Luther cabinet prevented an open intraparty rebellion, but it did not resolve the tensions that existed within the party. On the contrary, it so provoked the agrarian Reichslandbund and the commercial and industrial interests, which had profited from the DNVP's association with the government, that serious disaffection from this quarter became a real possibility.[1] At the same time, the withdrawal of the DNVP recreated the governmental problem of how to form a viable coalition. These two problems shaped German politics for several months to come.

To master its internal problems, the DNVP leadership tried to formulate a policy that would oppose both the Locarno treaties and Germany's entry into the League of Nations but in a manner that would not alienate the parties of the Middle so much that it would be impossible to reconstruct the rightist coalition eventually. The first element of this effort was that the party's central office modified its press policy in order to placate the radicals.

In the weeks prior to the Locarno Conference, the DNVP had balanced its policy between criticism and support of the Luther cabinet; the material furnished by the party's Berlin office to the nationalistic press had been remarkable in its restraint. Articles emphasized the subtleties of diplomacy, the need to trust men of "national" will, the need for patience. They consistently avoided any condemnation of Luther or Stresemann or even of the direction of the government's foreign policy, instead praising the government's strong action on war guilt, the party's one visible victory with regard to policy. The last article to appear in *Korrespondenz der Deutschnationalen Volkspartei* before the German delegation made its series of reports in Berlin even praised the accomplishments of the negotiators in terms that might have heartened Stresemann and Luther had it not been for what followed.[2]

With the rupture of the rightist coalition, this mild policy changed. The party's central office sprang to the attack on October 22, with an article in the *Korrespondenz* that denied all the advantages to the treaty that the paper had asserted that it contained just three days before. In subsequent days, the *Korrespondenz* carried the resolutions passed by the various party committees that had led to the withdrawal of the DNVP ministers, along with increasingly adamant rejections of the results of Locarno. On October 29, 1925, the DNVP leadership issued an official apologia for the party's withdrawal from the coalition. The security-pact initiative had been taken without the party's knowledge; the Locarno treaties had been initialed against its will. The party's participation in the preparatory negotiations had been motivated by a desire to limit the ill effects of a pact. Approval of a delegation's trip to Locarno had only been given because the government and the governmental parties had agreed to accept guidelines that corresponded to the Nationalist point of view. The DNVP had always maintained, the argument continued, that its final acceptance of any accord would be conditional upon the complete fulfillment of these guidelines. If the conclusion of the accords was now demanded on some basis other than these guidelines, then the violation of previous agreements within the government could not be charged to the German Nationalists.

The DNVP statement went on to assert that the guidelines had not in fact been fulfilled. None of the promises offered by the Allies represented a real concession or a real guarantee of Germany's interests. The treaty did not clearly preclude a renunciation of German land and peoples. Germany's freedom of action in the East was not ensured by sufficiently binding agreements against possible limitations under Article 16 of the League of Nations Charter. Germany's equal rights, particularly concerning armament, had not been recognized. The nonbinding assurances concerning "the so-called ramifications" gave no secure reason to believe that the Rhineland population would be less heavily burdened by foreign rule. Much less did they fulfill the "indispensable demand for binding accords" concerning the "immediate" evacuation of the second and third Rhineland zones and the Saar region. Consideration of these failures had determined the decision of the party's Executive Committee and its Reichstag delegation. The Nationalists had sacrificed "their influence as a government party in order to remain true to their fundamental principles and convictions regarding the freedom and honor of the nation."[3]

This DNVP resolution was followed on October 31, 1925, by the publication of the "DNVP guidelines for Locarno."[4] These guidelines began with the statement that the DNVP's assent to the conference could only be obtained "if an agreement over the following points can be assured by binding cabinet decisions." The points that followed were even further removed from the actual cabinet guidelines of October 2 than the insinuations made in the leadership resolution of just two days before. The inference that the government had been bound by agreement with the Nationalists on these specific points was absolutely without justification.[5]

Nonetheless, the government had no adequate answer. Only by publishing its own guidelines could it counter the DNVP's claim effectively. But publication of them would violate the accepted canons of confidentiality. Moreover, the government still hoped for more far-reaching concessions from France and England. Whatever domestic advantages the publishing of the guidelines might bring, it would undermine the diplomatic efforts to gain these concessions. The government's reply, issued on November 1, 1925, thus gratuitously asserted that the German delegation had not deviated in any respect from the guidelines that had been agreed to unanimously before Locarno; but it did not publish these guidelines in order to substantiate this assertion. Instead, the government published the cabinet's unanimous decision of October 22, with its stated intention "to bring the treaty work begun in Locarno on the basis of the German note of July 20, 1925, to a conclusion." The decision, the government argued, made it quite evident that future negotiations could not be over the text of the Locarno treaties, because they already satisfied the demands of the German note of July 20. Negotiations could only take place over those questions that had not been mentioned in the treaty draft. The cabinet's rebuttal further rejected the Nationalist interpretation of specific points of the accords. The interpretations put forward in the DNVP release of October 29 were contested by expert legal opinion regarding the treaty. The DNVP's suggestion that the treaties failed to conform to earlier cabinet decisions concerning the protection of German interests was categorically denied. The Nationalist complaint that the ramifications of Locarno were negligible was labeled as premature. The German delegation had made the importance of these ramifications perfectly clear in Locarno. They constituted the second essential part of the accords; and on this basis, the government insisted, it continued to negotiate with the Allied governments in an effort to implement them as soon as possible.[6]

The public controversy between the government and the DNVP told less than half the story of the party's attitude toward the break, however. In contrast to the position that the party's leadership promulgated in the press, it sought, behind the scenes, to limit the estrangement between the government and the party. Indeed, the majority of the DNVP's Reichstag delegates were angered by the success of the party's provincial representatives in forcing the party out of the coalition; therefore they sought to curtail the prerogatives of the broadened Executive Committee in order to prevent a repetition of the occurrence.[7] In addition, the party's leaders told the government that they would avoid all-out opposition to the Luther Cabinet. They even suggested that Neuhaus and Schlieben, who were not members of the Reichstag delegation and thus were not bound in the same way as Schiele by its decisions, might remain in the government. When the DNVP delegation's resolution of October 25 was worded so as to rule this out, Schiele made a second proposal to Luther, which enjoyed the support of Westarp, Hergt, Lindeiner-Wildau, and a number of other prominent DNVP delegates. Neuhaus and Schlieben would resign; but after a few days' delay, Reichspresident Hindenburg would reappoint them as caretaker ministers. This, the Nationalist leaders hoped, would preserve the desirable administrative continuity in the departments of economics and finance and would emphasize that the disagreement between the government and the DNVP represented only a "distancing" and not a categorical opposition. Thus, thought Schiele, the basis for continued cooperation among the nonsocialist parties could be maintained.[8]

Luther also favored such a "distancing" rather than the DNVP's outright opposition.[9] He hoped to maintain his rump cabinet at least until it had carried the work of Locarno to completion through the signing of the accords in London on December 1. The remaining ministers, and indeed most leaders of political parties, wished to avoid any dissolution of the Reichstag. It was unlikely that elections would lessen the DNVP's strength. The return of a Reichstag such as the existing one, in which a majority favored the Locarno settlement, might encourage the Allies, especially the French, to believe that Germany was satisfied with the treaties as they existed. This would then discourage them from making immediate concessions in the Rhineland. In general, then, some working arrangement with the Nationalists was preferable to open hostility.[10]

Still, the proposal to retain the German Nationalist ministers would create as many problems for the cabinet as it might solve. Schiele's proposal, if adopted, would seem to confirm his public insistence that cabinet decisions that were made before the breakup of the coalition had not included approval of the Locarno treaties as initialed. Moreover, Neuhaus and Schlieben would participate in the cabinet without assuming any responsibility for subsequent cabinet decisions.[11] In addition, the proposal to retain the German Nationalist ministers would complicate the cabinet's relations with the nongovernmental parties.

Without the DNVP votes, a Reichstag majority for the Locarno treaties would only be possible with the support of the Social Democrats. Neither they nor the German Democrats, who still stood apart from Luther's cabinet, were inclined to "save the chestnuts from the fire" for the governmental parties in this foreign-policy matter without any assurance that they would be brought to power themselves. Within both these parties, which had remained outside Luther's government, hostility towards the German Nationalists and the influence that they had gained on government programs was high. But both the DDP and the SPD realized that the nation had a great stake in the Locarno accords. The government hoped that they would therefore support the final vote on the treaties. Discreet soundings revealed, however, that an essential condition of such support would be the filling of the vacated portfolios by men other than those Nationalists who had resigned.[12] In the light of this information, the cabinet decided to appoint Luther, Gessler, and DVP Minister Rudolf Krohne to assume the vacated positions in addition to the ministerial portfolios that they already held. The real business of the three ministries would be conducted by the state secretaries in each department.[13] This procedure won ready approval from President Hindenburg.

In spite of the exclusion of the DNVP ministers, many delegates—especially in the SPD and DDP but even in the Center Party—had developed a mistrust toward Luther. They felt that he was too concerned with preserving whatever rightist support he could.[14] Luther was therefore closely questioned when he met with the various party leaders during the afternoon of October 26. He expressly refused to answer questions relating to the cabinet's plans after December 1, the scheduled date for the signing of the Locarno accords in London. He neither confirmed nor denied that he planned either to resign after that date or to dissolve the Reichstag. He reiterated his personal position that if the expected ramifications were not realized, he would have to withdraw. But he assured the parties that the cabinet intended to pursue the Locarno accords to a successful conclusion, undeterred by the resignation of its Nationalist members.[15]

The cabinet added emphasis to the statements that Luther made before the party leaders by releasing a press communiqué on the evening of October 26. The communiqué publicly affirmed the cabinet's intention to seek approval of the Locarno treaties in the Reichstag before December 1. In the light of this responsibility, the cabinet declined to resign.[16]

Luther's refusal to chart his course for the period after December 1, however, only increased reluctance among the delegates of the SPD and the DDP to give their support to the existing, still potentially rightist cabinet. Moreover, Luther's reaffirmation of his position that the ramifications would have to be fulfilled to his satisfaction had heightened suspicion that he planned to use this issue ultimately as an occasion for rejecting the accords and regaining the DNVP's support. Stresemann, to whom these fears were expressed, tried to convince the doubters that their suspicions were ground-less and that, in any case, a move against Luther would endanger the whole Locarno project. Stresemann, moreover, could not see anyone to replace Luther who possessed the same energy and competence. With the growing suspicion of the Left in mind, therefore, Stresemann proposed to Luther that the speech that the chancellor was scheduled to give in Essen on October 28 be carefully prepared in order to allay these fears. He advised Luther that he should attend to the Left rather than attempt to win those twenty or thirty Nationalist delegates who still might be influenced to vote with the government.[17] Indeed, for the Left, it was not simply the Nation-alists' withdrawal from the cabinet that rankled. It was, rather, that the Nationalists were seeking to repudiate all responsibility for their participa-tion up to the time of that withdrawal. The *Hamburg Fremdenblatt* fairly expressed the sentiment of many when it argued that it must be "continually hammered into the German public that the German Nationalists, even with their objections and inhibitions . . . , participated and share responsibility in the negotiations" leading to Locarno and that it was a misrepresentation to argue otherwise.[18]

The possibility of immediate reconciliation with the DNVP was finally eliminated by the decision of the remaining government parties to issue a joint statement confirming their support of the measures taken by the Luther Cabinet in the face of the DNVP withdrawal. On November 4, 1925, in a public release, they expressed their complete agreement that the German Nationalists had disqualified themselves from participation in the government by their precipitate behavior.[19]

Such adverse reaction to the conduct of the DNVP's Executive Com-mittee and to the delegation's decision to withdraw from the government was not confined to the Nationalists' political competitors. Opposition within the DNVP itself ran so deep that certain moderate elements and economic interest groups, especially members of the Reichslandbund, con-sidered leaving the party.[20] Others, while wishing to remain loyal to the party, judged that the withdrawal from the cabinet was severely detrimental to the interests of both the nation and the party.[21] Many such Nationalists, like Westarp himself, were by no means satisfied with the Locarno accords. But the possibility of exerting a moderating influence existed, in their opin-ion, only as long as the party remained in the cabinet. Moreover, to sur-render the positions of influence on tariff, financial, and economic policy that the party had controlled within the cabinet seemed foolish indeed, especially since the Locarno treaty had not yet been irrevocably approved.

150

Even after the formal signature of the treaty in London, it would not take effect until Germany entered the League of Nations. The delay would have allowed even greater opportunity for frustrating the treaty and also for attributing its failure to the Allies rather than to Germany.[22]

The DNVP's withdrawal did not prevent the Nationalist point of view from being represented within the government, however. Reichspresident Hindenburg's political outlook was highly sympathetic to the Nationalist Party and movement; and although he objected to the DNVP's break with the cabinet, which to his military mind was tantamount to insubordination, he was still predisposed to an immediate reconciliation with the Nationalists.

Just one week after the split, Hindenburg intervened in the cabinet's conduct of the continuing foreign negotiations by means of a memorandum which he labeled "Notes for the Preparation of the [December 1] London Conference." The memorandum repeated virtually every objection that the Nationalists had raised against the Locarno settlement and urged that these points be pressed to a satisfactory resolution in London, "in order that the government of the Reich can be reestablished on the *hitherto existent* broad basis."[23]

The reply to Hindenburg's demands repeated the refutations of specific objections concerning Article 16, of the renunciation of German lands, and the like, which the cabinet had been using in dealing with Nationalist objections since its return from Locarno, all of which Hindenburg had heard before. The cabinet's reply ignored the problem of a reestablishment of the rightist coalition and rejected the suggestion that further demands be made in London, arguing that the clarification of the ramifications must come prior to the London conference and must be complete and visible. Failing this, the government could not sign the treaties.[24]

Neither this intervention by Hindenburg nor continuing pressure from the DNVP disrupted the cabinet's pursuit of its foreign-policy goal: namely, fulfillment of the promised ramifications and ratification of the Locarno treaties. The Allied answer to the German disarmament note of October 23, 1925, was the first visible result of the government's policy. Following the outline that Stresemann had suggested at Locarno, the Allied note of November 6, 1925, observed with pleasure the efforts that Germany had made to conform to the disarmament demands made in the Allied note of June 4, 1925. The new note expressed the hope that enough progress would be made on the few remaining points of dispute so that evacuation of the Cologne zone could begin on December 1. This suggestion of so proximate a withdrawal would have been a more meaningful victory for the cabinet's Locarno policy if the Allied comments on Germany's remaining obligations had not been so sharply worded.

For some weeks, Stresemann had been aware of the possibility of Allied, especially French, recalcitrance in relation to the promises of ramifications. On October 23, Ambassador Hoesch had reported from Paris that Briand was reluctant to confirm the troop reductions that Stresemann hoped for. On the other hand, both Briand and his general secretary in the French Foreign Office, Philippe Berthelot, seemed to be satisfied with Germany's note on disarmament and had agreed that no conditions would be set to evacuations, which would begin because of the "expectations" that Germany would fulfill her remaining obligations. Berthelot did warn, however, that the French military, which had not been in on the Locarno deal regulating the exchange of notes on disarmament, would try to stiffen the tone of the Allied response.[25]

Shortly thereafter, one of Briand's confidants, Oswald Hesnard, requested that Luther's scheduled speech in Essen carefully avoid any suggestion that the ramifications that Germany expected had in any way constituted a quid pro quo for Germany's signature of the Locarno treaties. Luther should also avoid making any reference to "formal promises," although Hesnard admitted freely that Germany justifiably entertained "certain expectations." In general, Hesnard's tone was very discouraging.[26]

Stresemann had tried to counteract these negative signs by arguing that his own situation would become "insupportable" in the face of Nationalist criticism if the ramifications did not materialize. He believed that his pleas had had some success.[27] But the Allied note of November 6 was much stronger in its delineation of the specific measures that Germany was to undertake in order to complete disarmament than Stresemann had anticipated. Briand's domestic problems were similar to Stresemann's own, and the military had to be mollified.

Stresemann viewed the Allied conditions with great disappointment. His negative reaction was dispelled somewhat when Briand informed him, through an emissary, that the evacuation of the Cologne zone would begin in any case on December 1. The French representative further outlined the concessions that Briand was prepared to make regarding the specific issues of dispute among the military experts. Nonetheless, the diplomatic communiqué had a decidedly unfavorable impact on the government's Locarno policy, seemingly justifying the loudly voiced DNVP skepticism of the Allies' good will.[28]

In formulating Germany's reply, Stresemann tried to regain the lost ground in both the domestic and international arena by making full use of Briand's conciliatory attitude. This answer, dated November 11, expressed a willingness to satisfy Allied demands; but in each specific case, the note justified Germany's desires for accommodation by raising extenuating circumstances. The Allies accepted the German pledge of good faith, and they responded through the Conference of Ambassadors with a note and an oral declaration of November 14, plus a second note on November 16. The first note referred to the spirit of confidence, faith, and good will that had animated the Locarno Conference, and the note asserted that, in this same spirit, the Allied governments had decided to introduce into the Rhineland territories "all alleviations that are compatible with the Treaty of Versailles." The note mentioned specifically the appointment of a German Rhineland commissioner, the possibilities of reciprocal amnesties, the reduction of troops, and the facilitation of German administration of the occupied territories. Moreover, the Allied ordinances that were already in force would be revised "in the same spirit of conciliation and appeasement."[29]

The Allied verbal declaration to Hoesch confirmed that the date for the beginning of the Cologne evacuation would be December 1. This was reiterated in the note of November 16, which stated further that the evacuation could begin before the actual satisfaction of all the remaining points of the disarmament issue, because complete agreement had been reached on them. The evacuation would be completed by the end of January 1926, if possible; in any event, before February 20. The military control commission would be withdrawn as soon as it had confirmed the completion of the few remaining points, and there would immediately be a substantial reduction in its size.[30]

Stresemann's gambit thus proved to be eminently successful with the Allies. But this success did seemingly little to dispel Reichspresident Hindenburg's negative attitude. The pessimism evinced in Hindenburg's opening rebuff during the cabinet's November 16 discussion of the first Allied note was evident: "Melancholy observations about how the prenegotiations in Locarno became negotiations are pointless. . . . We must see what benefits we can extract from the situation and how we can get out of it"; it indicated his continued sympathy with the general Nationalist refusal to admit that any gains could be attributed to Locarno.[31]

In defending his foreign policy before the old field marshal, Stresemann emphasized that the Allied note meant a reduction of perhaps fifty thousand men in the troop contingents for the Rhineland, the abrogation of all but thirty or forty of the more than three hundred special ordinances introduced by the occupation regimes, and the end of the system of Allied bureaucratic delegates that paralleled and paralyzed the German administrative structure in the area. Luther insisted that he, too, saw a positive amelioration of Germany's political situation as a result of the Locarno accords, although he was less optimistic about the extent of troop reductions, a reserve that was fully justified by future developments. The treaties represented a tremendous stride toward the undermining of the Versailles settlement. This had been the most fundamental wish in Germany since the war. The immediate ramifications of the Locarno negotiations were not all that one could desire, but they represented the limits of the possible in Luther's judgment. The political statement embodied in the Allied note of November 14 formed a reliable basis for the eventual satisfaction of German interests.[32]

Minister of Defense Gessler contributed by far the most colorful language to the cabinet's efforts to dispel Hindenburg's sympathy for the Nationalist criticism of the Locarno accords. For Gessler, Locarno represented a German renunciation "of nothing, absolutely nothing." He did not see any German sacrifices but tremendous gains, in that France had abandoned her hostile policy toward Germany. The charge that Germany had surrendered a degree of her sovereignty by renouncing war was unrealistic. Germany was in the position of a man who had lost both his legs and was lying in his hospital bed saying, "I refuse to dance at carnival this year."[33]

Despite these and other statements in support of the accords, Hindenburg remained skeptical. He found that the agreements were based on what he called a fundamental inequality: the Allies were armed, and Germany was not. Obviously influenced by the public stance of the Nationalists and by actual contacts with his close friends on the Right, he objected that Germany was obliged to maintain a neutral zone on the Rhine, whereas the neutralization of Alsace-Lorraine was not offered as a counterbalance.[34] The early evacuation of the second and third Rhineland zones should have been formally secured. The conditions for the termination of the treaties were unsatisfactory. France's guarantee of Poland would have to be ended. Any prejudice of the Russo-German alliance through obligations contracted under Article 16 would have to be excluded. The catalog of objections was familiar, but Luther was forced to answer it once again.[35]

Confronted with the second Allied note of November 16 and with Luther's accurate assessment that German demands had been met to such an extent that any response other than to accept the treaties was impossible, Hindenburg admitted that Germany was the "weaker side" and had to accept the negotiated path, "even though it is particularly hard for me personally." One was left with no recourse other than to ask God's blessing upon the solution.[36] He requested, however, that the public be informed very carefully, so as to contribute to the reestablishment of domestic calm. Luther replied, in words that applied to Hindenburg as much as to anyone, that domestic calm was virtually impossible to achieve when the official explanations by the government were ignored and when the DNVP propagated the slogan "Endless battle against Locarno."[37] Hindenburg's acquiescence, however, permitted Luther to gain the government's unanimous approval to submit to the Reichstag a motion endorsing the Locarno accords and German entry into the League of Nations and empowering the cabinet to send a delegation to London to sign the treaties.[38]

The cabinet's motion progressed through the Reichstag without serious mishap. By agreement between the cabinet and the parties that were favorably disposed to the treaties, the vote was to be free of the implication of confidence in Luther's rump cabinet. In this way, the SPD and the DDP could vote for the treaties without perpetuating the Luther government, which had expressed its intention to resign after the signing of the treaties in London.[39]

But the Nationalists had by no means abandoned their efforts to frustrate the Locarno accords. They tried now to block passage of the government's resolution by demanding a two-thirds vote on the Locarno treaties and on Germany's entry into the league. The government denied that the treaty necessitated a change in the constitution.[40] The DNVP's final attempt to block acceptance of the Locarno accords was made indirectly, through Hindenburg, as well as directly on the Reichstag floor. The DNVP's Reichstag delegation submitted an amendment to the government motion, which demanded that the approval of the Locarno treaties and the authorization to enter the league be considered as two separate bills. Simultaneously, prompted by the urgings of German Nationalist leaders, Hindenburg addressed a letter to Luther, recommending that the cabinet give serious consideration to separating the two parts of the government motion.[41] Since the Locarno treaties were to come into effect only upon Germany's entry into the league, such a move would mean that even though the motion for approval passed, Germany would not simultaneously have accepted the accords.

Hindenburg's letter, written on November 27, reached the chancellor in the Reichstag building, where deliberations on the final reading of the motion on the Locarno agreements were in progress. Luther hurriedly called a meeting of the cabinet to present Hindenburg's request. Stresemann categorically rejected the idea of separating the two parts of the motion. Such an action would be a direct affront to the Locarno powers, who had made their declaration concerning Article 16 an integral part of the Locarno settlement only because of Germany's insistence. If Germany now showed any hesitation about entering the league, this could easily occasion the withdrawal of the invitation to London. The cabinet supported Stresemann's judgment and informed Hindenburg that a separate handling of a motion to authorize Germany's entry into the league was out of the question.[42] Once again, Stresemann had preserved his policy from being disoriented by the Nationalists.

The failure of this last effort to upset the Locarno accords opened the way for passage of the government's motion. Supported by the remaining coalition parties, the DVP, the Center, and the BVP, as well as by the SPD and the DDP, the Locarno accords and the authorization for entry into the League of Nations passed by a comfortable 291 votes against 174, the Nationalists voting solidly against.[43]

The immediate crisis concerning foreign policy was thus over. The domestic crisis that it had provoked remained. The loss of the DNVP's support over the issue of the Locarno treaties left the governmental coalition without a dependable majority in the Reichstag. The SPD vote in favor of the Locarno treaties had not been a vote of confidence in the Luther Cabinet. Much to the contrary, it had been accorded only grudgingly and after repeated assurances that Luther would resign once the treaties had been ratified. In keeping with these assurances, the cabinet submitted its resignation to Reichspresident Hindenburg on December 5, 1925, following the return of Stresemann and Luther from the signing of the Locarno Pact in London.[44]

Since the DNVP had virtually excluded itself from any coalition in the foreseeable future, only two possibilities remained: either a Grand Coalition from the SPD to the DVP or a minority coalition of the Middle, such as Marx had led throughout 1924. The Center Party and the German Democratic Party both favored a Grand Coalition; but even under the best of circumstances, agreement between the opposite wings of such an alignment would have been difficult. In this case it was further impeded by Hindenburg's preference for the second solution.

Hindenburg had little enthusiasm for Socialists in government; he much preferred a cabinet of the Middle under Luther. He felt that such a minority cabinet of the Middle could survive without further alienating the Nationalists. And although he realized with regret that there was no possibility of admitting the Nationalists to the new government for the time being, a minority cabinet under Luther would preserve the possibility of future cooperation with the DNVP. Early in the cabinet negotiations, Hindenburg consulted Count Westarp about these views, hoping to persuade the Nationalist leader not to force the resignation of such a minority government but to give tacit Nationalist consent to it. Westarp's reply was ambiguous enough to make such a solution seem feasible. He first emphatically promised that there would be sharp Nationalist opposition to any government that included Social Democrats. A minority cabinet of the Middle, however, would be quite another matter; Westarp stated that his party would reserve judgment about this possibility. He pointed out that while his party was unalterably opposed to Germany's entry into the league and while it would continue to oppose the Reichstag's resolution favoring entry, it could support efforts by any government to win further concessions from the Allies in relation to the league. But he insisted that a definitive attitude toward a particular minority cabinet would have to await the actual developments.[45]

The DNVP welcomed Hindenburg's plan for maintaining its connections with the government and for preserving its possible avenues of reentry into power. Martin Schiele let the government know that the Nationalists might be willing to form a silent partnership with a nonsocialist government under Luther's chancellorship. The condition of such tacit support, however, would be the removal of Stresemann as foreign minister. Schiele noted that "politics is influenced not only by substantive [*sachliche*] considerations, but in a most essential manner by moods as well." The mood within the DNVP against Stresemann, which had continued to increase in intensity, was responsible for the party's break with the government.[46] Schiele's reservation represented fundamentally the same attitude that Westarp had expressed to Hindenburg. For with Stresemann gone from the German Foreign Office, the whole program of reconciliation, not simply entry into the league, would become vulnerable.

For his part, Hindenburg pursued a plan for the cabinet negotiations that would frustrate the plan for a Grand Coalition and would produce the desired minority cabinet, open to the Right, under Luther. First he called upon the parties that were interested in a Grand Coalition to work out a basis for a common program within three days. The SPD submitted a ten-point program, which incorporated its demands and expectations. Hindenburg presented these to the DVP leaders, who rejected them. The latter, however, whom Hindenburg informed of his true intentions, offered to negotiate, fully expecting that they would never be called upon to fulfill any concessions that they might make. They demanded that any negotiations be conducted by a candidate for the chancellorship rather than by the president himself. Hindenburg turned to the leader of the DDP, Erich Koch-Weser, but rather than giving him a free hand to form any government that Koch-Weser might choose, Hindenburg commissioned him to form a Grand Coalition, thus cutting Koch-Weser's chances of success at least in half by excluding the most promising coalition arrangement, that of a minority government of the Middle parties. Koch-Weser took up the task on December 14. He formulated several sets of cabinet guidelines in an effort to accommodate both the DVP and the SPD, but to no avail. The DVP showed considerable tactical flexibility. The SPD showed none. On December 17 the Socialists issued a statement that while Koch-Weser's own "republican and democratic trustworthiness [was] beyond doubt," his efforts to form a truly solid republican government had foundered on a "lack of readiness to compromise" on the part of the DVP, especially on social and economic measures that the SPD held to be essential.[47]

The first act was over. Koch-Weser, who reported the failure of his effort to form a Grand Coalition and returned the mandate to Hindenburg, was convinced that the SPD had been responsible for his failure and only vaguely suspected that his efforts had been surreptitiously opposed by the President's Office and possibly by the Chancellor's Office as well.[48] The public impression of the intransigent SPD fit the president's plan perfectly, for it helped to convince both the Center Party and the DDP that a government of the Middle was the only coalition that would be possible. Hindenburg suspended the official negotiations over the Christmas holidays. On January 11, 1926, he gave the DDP and the Center Party one last chance to reach agreement with the SPD on a program for a Grand Coalition, again imposing a three-day limit to negotiations and justifying his deadline by insisting that the country could not endure a prolongation of the crisis that was now more than a month old. On January 12, 1926, the SPD reiterated its insistence that a coalition was impossible because the DVP was not willing to make the necessary concessions. The Center Party and the DDP were thus forced to abandon their efforts to form a Grand Coalition. Hindenburg was now free to commission Luther to seek a "neutral government of the Middle." Unlike Koch-Weser, Luther was given the latitude to form a coalition without first having the parties agree on a program. Hindenburg thus removed what had been the most difficult obstacle to the formation of a coalition with the SPD.[49]

Luther found that even this was not an easy task. After four days of interparty negotiations, Hindenburg called in the representatives of the four parties concerned—the DDP, the Center Party, the Bavarian Peoples Party (BVP), and the DVP—and urged them to set aside their remaining reservations and to establish a government so that the six-weeks' crisis could be resolved. Luther then gave the parties until 10:00 that evening, January 19, 1926, to accept or reject his nominations for the people to fill cabinet posts. The parties agreed to support a Luther cabinet, but only if Luther would make a change in one of his appointments, a change that would conform to the DNVP's objections.[50]

The Nationalists had viewed Luther's preliminary list of nominees with some alarm. Although they were not actively involved in the negotiations, they were anxious to keep open the possibility of eventually returning to government circles. They feared that Luther's original choice for the Ministry of the Interior, Erich Koch-Weser, would destroy the gains that the Nationalists had made by controlling that portfolio during 1925. Schiele protested Koch's nomination to Luther, observing that such a choice would have a most unfortunate impact on his party and that it would hinder any eventual reconciliation between the DNVP and the government. Schiele, who admitted that Luther was obliged to build a bridge to the Left, said that he would regret it very much if the Ministry of the Interior were used for this purpose.[51]

The Nationalists' attempt to exert a negative control over the key Ministry of the Interior was abetted, perhaps inadvertently, by the Bavarian People's Party. When Luther submitted his list of ministerial appointments, with the ultimatum that they be accepted or rejected by the Middle parties before 10:00 P.M. on January 19, Koch-Weser's name still figured on it. The BVP, however, objected that Koch-Weser was too typically Democratic in his outlook and, as such, too inclined towards administrative centralization. The party therefore made its support of a Luther cabinet conditional upon the replacement of Koch-Weser. Luther accepted the BVP's demand, and Koch-Weser was dropped from the list of ministers.[52]

Luther had always considered that the support of the BVP was politically indispensable to any new cabinet.[53] His compliance with the BVP's demand was therefore consistent. It must be noted, however, that the BVP and the DNVP were coalition partners in the Bavarian state government, a fact that might have promoted a stronger community of interest in blocking Koch-Weser's appointment than protection of the BVP's particularist interests might have dictated. In any event, the Nationalists feared turning the Ministry of the Interior, which they had controlled, over to the "leftist" Koch-Weser as much as the BVP feared his inclination towards centralization.

The security-pact negotiations, which had begun in January 1925 and which were concluded formally with the signing of the Locarno Pact in London on December 1, 1925, undeniably worked an improvement in Germany's international situation. The most evident gain was the evacuation of the Cologne zone, which was begun on November 30, 1925, and was completed by February 1, 1926. Less visible but no less important were the elimination of the delegate apparatus in the remaining occupied areas, which took place on December 1, 1925, and the simultaneous easing of the whole regime of occupation. In addition, the question of disarmament had been successfully nudged from a place of prominence in Germany's relations with the Allies to an inferior level of diplomatic activity and concern. The Military Control Commission was drastically reduced. Civil aviation in Germany was freed from most of the restrictions placed upon it by the Versailles Treaty.[54]

More important, however, than the specific gains that Germany had made in freeing herself from foreign control and the restrictions of the Versailles Treaty was the tremendous improvement in international prestige that the conclusion of the security pact garnered for her. Perhaps the best witness to this phenomenon was Professor Otto Hoetzsch. Even as a moderate Nationalist, Hoetzsch had never been enthusiastic about the security-pact negotiations, but he was a devoted student of foreign policy and was sensitive to the role that international mood could play for Germany. In a private letter to Count Westarp, written shortly after the signing of the accords, he talked of the change in attitude towards Germany that he had observed in recent visits to foreign capitals. So forceful was it that he could virtually "grasp the change in hand." In his estimation, it opened possibilities for Germany to carry on foreign political activity of significant proportions. He continued:

> This in no way affects our stance on Locarno; it was well founded and was directed against specific fundamental points, over which we were and are in agreement. But that the situation is different today from that of one, two, or three years ago—that can be felt unmistakably by anyone such as I, who is so continually occupied by foreign-policy matters and who comes into contact and conversation with people whose concern is foreign policy.[55]

Hoetzsch had recognized an important point, which was discounted by most Nationalists and has been minimized by many historians since: the most significant gains that Stresemann had won in Locarno were intangible but no less real. The specific Nationalist criticism that "ramifications" had not been fixed in binding written commitments from the Allies was correct. Stresemann had accepted instead moral commitments from the men who were currently conducting French and British diplomacy. But written commitments were not only beyond Stresemann's—or anyone's—power to compel; they were also beyond the capacity of any Western statesman to give. Had Stresemann, then, gained nothing? Quite the contrary. Aside from the measurable ameliorations in the Rhineland—on disarmament, inspection, and occupation—he had transformed the atmosphere that had prevailed in January 1925, or even in August 1923. Germany's pursuit of her goals in the international arena—even of peaceful revision—had been accepted.[56] Evacuation had begun. The Western powers had acknowledged the anomaly of the persistence, in an atmosphere of cooperation, of military occupation and control. The immediate international impact of the "spirit of Locarno" was indisputably to Germany's advantage.[57]

But the domestic impact of the long negotiations was more complex. They had become the dominant divisive element in relations between the DNVP and the government in March 1925, when Stresemann's February initiative had first been revealed to the public. The initial response from the extreme right wing of the Nationalist camp had been to brand Stresemann as a traitor and to brand his efforts to reach an accommodation on the Rhine as his treason. But the leaders of the DNVP's Reichstag delegation, who were interested in exploiting their recently acquired position of influence within the government, had moved with more moderation and had accepted a compromise resolution which stated that the party's objections to Stresemann's foreign-policy initiative were procedural only. They successfully resisted the first wave of anticoalition agitation, but they did not overcome it.

The anticoalition forces within the party were thus able to prepare a second attack upon the security-pact negotiations throughout the spring of 1925. Faced with mounting criticism, the Nationalist leadership temporarily adopted this attempt to saddle Stresemann with sole responsibility for the security-pact policy, pressing its attack with insistence in late June and early July. They hoped to dump Stresemann but to retain the Luther Cabinet and the Nationalist influence within it. For a fleeting moment, it looked as though the move might succeed. But, forced into a choice between accepting Stresemann or destroying the coalition, the leaders of the DNVP chose again to try to silence radical criticism in the interest of preserving the party's position in the government.

The party leaders knew, however, that sentiment within the DNVP was dangerously divided and that in order to preserve party unity, they would indeed have to disassociate the DNVP from the proposed security pact. In the final phase of the struggle they therefore tried to block the preparations for a conference between Germany and the Allies. They hoped to claim that they had frustrated an accord that would inevitably have been concluded if the DNVP had not been in the cabinet to fight against it. And while their efforts to cripple the policies of reconciliation were always tempered by a desire to preserve their place in power, their public statements emphasized, often even exaggerated, the degree to which the cabinet was bound by Nationalist conditions.

Once the governmental tie was broken, the DNVP's public opposition to the Locarno treaties became even more strident. Free from the restraint that he had observed in order to preserve the coalition, Westarp went so far as to state that the DNVP would refuse to recognize the legally binding nature of the Locarno treaties, because they required, but had not won, a two-thirds vote of approval in the Reichstag.[58] Westarp's extreme statement provoked renewed thought among various members of the DNVP's Reichstag delegation concerning an open split with the party. They received encouragement from Stresemann, but their revolt never materialized.[59] Westarp's statement so alienated the Middle parties, however, that open acknowledgment of the binding nature of the Locarno accords became the *sine qua non* of the DNVP's reentry into the government.

Still, the party's public stance did not end the process that had been developing throughout the year. The leaders publicly claimed that they had sacrificed their influence in order to preserve their ideals. In fact, they never ceased their efforts to restore that influence. They had learned that access to power provided a range of operation for their ideals and interests, which ideological purity did not, and that absence from power was no guarantee of party unity in any event. For a time their rhetoric against Locarno and against Germany's entry into the League of Nations excluded them from exercising any direct influence. But more and more the party's leaders tended toward pragmatic compromises that would permit them to reenter the cabinet.

In this they were actively aided and abetted by Reichspresident Hindenburg, who manipulated the negotiations for a new cabinet so as to produce the government that would be most congenial to an opening to the Right. The Locarno Pact had thus impinged indirectly upon German domestic politics so as to contrive the earliest form of a "presidential" cabinet.[60]

The coalition that emerged under Luther enjoyed thus a negative binding force: it was seemingly the only grouping that was possible. The SPD, with help, had disqualified itself in the eyes of the parties that were most sympathetic to it. The Locarno Pact and the issue of Germany's entry into the League of Nations had excluded a rightist coalition, towards which much of the Middle still inclined.[61] Luther's remark to the Reichstag described the situation aptly, if poignantly: "After all, Germany must eventually have some sort of government."[62]

9

OVERCOMING IDEOLOGY

Between 1926 and 1928 the League of Nations became a central arena for German diplomatic activity. The Locarno negotiations had made Germany's entry into the Geneva-based organization a condition for concluding the security pact. In addition to this, Stresemann saw the league as a positive means in his struggle to restore Germany's prestige, influence, and power in international affairs. It could be used as a forum in which Germany could press her remaining grievances over the settlement of the war and could demand full rights. Germany's presence in Geneva, if properly exploited, could become a permanent moral reproach against the punitive nature of the Treaty of Versailles. As an integral part of Stresemann's policy of reconciliation, Germany's policy with regard to the league was bound to affect the relationship between the government and the DNVP.

To the DNVP, the League of Nations had always been anathema—the enemy's private club, the instrument for the execution of the hated Versailles settlement. The Nationalist attack upon the Locarno treaties had put special emphasis upon the contention that Germany's entry into the league would limit German sovereignty and thus required a two-thirds vote in the Reichstag. This contention committed the party to an opposition course as long as entry into the league remained an open issue.

The DNVP was once again caught in the dilemma of the conflict between foreign policy and domestic aspirations to power. Its October defection and the potent sentiment behind it made it mandatory for the DNVP to oppose, for the time being, the Locarno accords and the issue of Germany's entry into the league. Yet many party leaders were still not convinced that the Nationalists' continued exclusion from power was to their advantage; for them, the desire to participate in the government continued to be strong. The dilemma, then, was to conduct an opposition that to some degree would mollify the radicals, but in a manner that would preserve the possibility of again participating in the government. In this situation, what could lend greater respectability to the party's demands regarding foreign policy than to have them taken up by the president of the republic? Even before the formation of Luther's second cabinet in January 1926, the DNVP had begun to use this avenue of influence for the purpose of trying to modify the government's policy. Early in December, after the Reichstag had approved the Locarno Pact and after it had been formally signed in London, the DNVP had sought to impose on the government, through Reichspresident Hindenburg, a list of objections and conditions concerning the future conduct of foreign policy. The latter had accepted from Martin Schiele a list of conditions for Germany's entry into the league. On December 4, 1925, Hindenburg had addressed a letter to Chancellor Luther in which the DNVP's demands appeared as though they were his own. He urged Luther to pursue them with vigor. He observed that the Reichstag's resolution on Locarno empowered, but did not require, the government to seek entry into the league.[1]

Once the Luther Cabinet had been re-formed, Hindenburg's efforts were supplemented by an open drive to bind the minority cabinet to the DNVP program. Anticipating a reaffirmation of the Locarno policies by the cabinet in its program presentation to the Reichstag in late January 1926, the DNVP prepared and introduced a resolution "through which the *preconditions* for Germany's entry into the League of Nations would be regulated."[2] At the same time, it prepared a motion for a vote of no confidence. The "preconditions" paralleled the demands that Hindenburg had incorporated in his December 4 letter to Luther. The Nationalist attack provoked a sharp response from Luther. Not only did he reject the Nationalist conditions for entry into the league, he countered their motion for a vote of no confidence by demanding, on advice from Stresemann, that the Reichstag give a positive vote of confidence in his new cabinet, rather than simply granting approval of his program.[3]

Surprised by the audacity of Luther's demand for a positive vote of confidence and dismayed at the rejection of their own program, the Nationalists turned again to Hindenburg, who called in Luther to discuss with Westarp and Schiele the issue of entry into the league, in an effort to win Nationalist neutrality at least as an alternative to a DNVP vote of no confidence. The conversation was conducted amicably, but it only served to emphasize the contradiction between the government's policies and the Nationalists' desire. Luther insisted that he foresaw no possible incident that would be of enough importance to delay Germany's request for admission to the league. Westarp contended that the Nationalist Party and the government were separated by two fundamental differences of opinion. Whereas Luther believed that Germany was no longer politically free to change her own mind about her entry into the league or to make her entry conditional upon demands heretofore not explicitly expressed, the DNVP believed the contrary. The second irreconcilable difference was that Luther believed Germany's long-range interests would be better served from within the league; the Nationalists were of exactly the opposite opinion. As a result, Westarp was obliged, despite Hindenburg's pleas, to confirm his party's intention of actively opposing the Luther cabinet.[4]

The Nationalist maneuver in the Reichstag failed, however. Luther's forthright admission, in response to the Nationalists' challenge that he favored immediate entry into the league without the imposition of additional conditions, made a sharp impression in the Reichstag, especially upon the Social Democrats.[5] The government, in fact, only won its vote of confidence by the grace of the SPD, which abstained from voting. The minority cabinet won a vote of confidence with 160 votes in favor out of 440 potential ballots. Voting against the motion were 150 Nationalists, Communists, and members of fringe parties.[6]

Having received the Reichstag's approval, the Luther Cabinet moved toward execution of its foreign policy. Its position was uncomfortable, however, and the DNVP's pressure was constant. Reports on the progress of the ramifications in the occupied territories admitted of rather meager improvements. The size of the occupation force, which was still around 80,000 in late January 1926, with the first zone almost cleared, had not approached the number of 40,000 to 45,000 men that Stresemann had overoptimistically cited before the cabinet in November (see chap. 8). The Nationalists seldom neglected to mention this discrepancy. Hope for the early evacuation of the second and third zones of occupation grew constantly dimmer. Confidentially, the Nationalists raised the question of the rumored negotiations for the return of Eupen-Malmédy and urged that, if Germany hoped for any success in these, they be completed before Germany's application for entry into the league.[7]

The government had little with which to counter the Nationalist charges that the Locarno policy was bankrupt. The Eupen-Malmédy negotiations could not be hurried. Negotiations over the improvements in the occupied territories had been stalled during the cabinet crisis. Aside from resuming the negotiations, the government could do little more than insist again upon its expectations and trust that Briand's good will would overcome the resistance of both the French military and the occupation regime.[8]

In the meantime, the DNVP's challenge to Germany's entry into the League of Nations had to be faced in the Reichstag. The Nationalist motion to impose preconditions on entry into the league had been referred to the Reichstag's Foreign Affairs Committee, which met on February 3, 1926, to deal with it. There, by a vote of eighteen to eight, the committee rejected the DNVP's demands.[9] But they were raised once again, that same day, by Reichspresident Hindenburg, who addressed still another plea to Luther to delay Germany's formal petition for membership in the league until after the Allies had made further concessions. Hindenburg urged Luther to "devote [his] constant attention" to the conditions mentioned in Hindenburg's letter of December 4, 1925. Finally, he declined to sign the formal petition to the league from the German government, requesting that Germany be admitted. Hindenburg kept Count Westarp fully informed of his efforts to influence the cabinet, by sending the Nationalist leader copies of all his correspondence with Luther over the issues of the League of Nations and the Locarno Pact.[10]

The Reichspresident's letter of February 3 provoked a lengthy discussion within the cabinet. A number of ministers interpreted Hindenburg's intervention as an indication that he did not have complete confidence in his ministers. They viewed his refusal to endorse the cabinet's petition to enter the league as an attempt to divorce himself from the responsibility for the cabinet's foreign policy. Some urged that Hindenburg be asked to withdraw the letter. Others urged that Hindenburg be drawn into accepting full mutual responsibility for the cabinet's policy regarding the league, so as to avoid the development of any "legend concerning differences of opinion between the Reichspresident and the government." Ranged against these ministers were those, including Luther, who disapproved of Hindenburg's persistent refusal to accept the cabinet's judgment that the Allied concessions satisfied all of Germany's demands and interests adequately but who were reluctant to involve the venerable field marshal in an open political debate. They argued that a distinction should be made between Hindenburg's expressions of personal opinion—such as the letter in question—and his official statements. They agreed that disastrous domestic and foreign consequences would follow if the letter became public knowledge. They argued, therefore, that the situation ought to be resolved in confidence between the cabinet and the Reichspresident.[11]

State Secretary Meissner, speaking for Hindenburg, denied that the Reichspresident's letter and his absence from the cabinet meeting concerning entry into the league, which he was supposed to have conducted, were in any way intended as disavowals of the cabinet's policies. Meissner asserted that Hindenburg fully supported the cabinet's strategic approach, that his reservations were only over tactics. Hindenburg felt that his presence at the cabinet meeting and his signature on the eventual petition for entry were unnecessary, since the cabinet had been fully empowered by the Reichstag to seek Germany's admission to the league. The Reichspresident had no intention of divulging his letter. He had naturally kept a copy of the letter for his own files, observed Meissner, tactfully neglecting to mention that a copy had also gone to Westarp. One thing was certain, Meissner insisted: Hindenburg would not retract the letter. It might be possible to clarify the situation, however, by means of a further exchange of correspondence between the chancellor and the Reichspresident.[12]

Luther seized upon this compromise suggestion in the hope of ending what had become a dangerously divisive problem. With some difficulty, he brought the cabinet to agree that its decision to make an immediate petition for admission to the League of Nations would be presented to the Reichspresident for his approval in a memorandum from the chancellor. The memorandum would not demand that the president sign the German petition; it would simply point out that the formal petition specifically mentioned the interpretation given to Article 16 by the Locarno contractants. If no objections were raised in the league to the German petition, the Reichspresident could not only set aside his current reservations concerning Germany's entry but could also contribute his full constitutional authority and assent to the cabinet's course of action.[13] The Reichspresident agreed to the compromise. He affirmed that Germany's application for entry was so worded that acceptance of it by the league would dispel all his doubts concerning Article 16.[14]

The Nationalists' attempt to block Germany's entry into the league had failed. The German petition for admission was communicated to the secretary general of the league on February 10, 1926. Two days later, a special session of the League Assembly was scheduled for March 8, to consider Germany's entry.[15] The government continued to pursue its foreign policy in the "spirit of Locarno."

In spite of this, the fate of Germany's request for membership in the League of Nations dealt a sharp blow to the government's policies of reconciliation. The prolonged cabinet crisis had prevented Germany from taking quick advantage of the first flush of excitement over the Locarno Pact. Delay had allowed this advantageous glow to dissipate. On the day that the decision to request entry was made, Stresemann had warned the cabinet that the situation in Geneva was no longer as favorable as it had been initially. Rumors were prevalent that certain countries might raise demands of their own for admission to the League Council.[16] Luther had passed the warning on to Reichspresident Hindenburg, insisting that any attempt to broaden the council concurrently with Germany's assumption of a seat on it would place the government before a radically changed political situation, thus requiring the German government to review its petition for admission.[17]

By February 11, 1926, it was apparent that at least Spain and Poland planned to seek permament seats on the League Council. Germany could not countenance the elevation of Poland to a position that would be comparable to the one that she herself was about to assume. Such a procedure would excite a domestic protest of major proportions. Germany could not voice her real objections to Poland before international opinion, however. Therefore, she would have to base her opposition on principle and would have to demand that Germany alone be admitted before any further petitions would be considered.[18]

The government outlined this position to the secretary general of the league when he visited Berlin on February 15 and before the Foreign Affairs Committee of the Reichstag on February 19.[19] Stresemann's report to the party representatives on the Foreign Affairs Committee was discouraging. Brazil had added its name to the list of those seeking permanent seats. Of the Locarno powers, France was definitely inclined to support Poland's claim. Briand would try to win over Chamberlain, but England's position on the whole was unclear. Public opinion in Great Britain and in the dominions was increasingly in favor of rejecting all petitions other than Germany's for a seat on the council. The cabinet in London had expressed no opinion, however. Italy was apt to favor the additional requests. Belgium's position was ambiguous. In fact, Stresemann could report only one definitive position. Sweden would oppose all applications other than Germany's; and because of Sweden's position as a temporary member of the council, her veto would be enough to cause them to be rejected.[20]

Stresemann emphasized that the government had left no doubts in informing the Locarno powers of its keen disappointment over the turn of events. Germany considered that the present situation represented a breach of loyalty. The developments in Geneva undermined the very basis of the Locarno accords, Stresemann continued; and if events in Geneva ran counter to her interests, Germany would be obliged to review her commitment to those accords. Stresemann informed the Foreign Affairs Committee of his intention to recommend that the cabinet secure guarantees from the Allies that no nation other than Germany would be admitted to the council at the coming special session. Germany could justify such a demand on the grounds that she deserved to find the council that she would actually enter the same as the council that she had been requested to enter during the Locarno negotiations.[21]

The parties accepted the government's policy with only minor reservations. Stresemann wanted to obtain unanimous approval of a resolution passed by the Foreign Affairs Committee, which urged that Germany's entry into the league be made conditional upon the acquisition of a permanent seat in an unmodified council. The SPD refused to approve such a resolution, however. The Nationalists, on the other hand, wanted to bind the government to vetoing any future application by Poland for a seat on the council. Here Stresemann refused.

The Nationalists, however, were not the ones who demanded that Germany withdraw her application for entry into the league because of this latest rebuff; the Communists were. And although the Nationalists felt obliged to vote in favor of the foredoomed Communist motion, they were also able to support the committee's final resolution. This stated the committee's opinion that the German application for entry into the league was made under the supposition that Germany would be awarded a permanent seat on the council without any further modification of the council. The resolution was milder than Stresemann's original demand but was more advantageous to the government in that the SPD was willing to support it.[22] Moreover, the fact that the Nationalists also supported it amounted to a tacit acceptance on their part of the cabinet's application for admission to the league. It was a sign of their growing pragmatism in the face of the exigencies of foreign policy.

Stresemann reviewed the situation for the cabinet just a few days later. Germany's position in Geneva had not improved. Moreover, the procedural handling of Germany's application presented a new danger. The council would first vote on Germany's request for membership in the league and only then would it vote on her request for a permanent seat on the council. Stresemann therefore proposed that Germany seek gentlemen's agreements with the ten current members of the council in order to ensure that Germany would immediately receive a seat on the council and that no other power would receive a permanent seat at this special session. Such agreements would have to be concluded in Geneva before the beginning of the official session of the assembly. Stresemann pointed out that such diplomatic action would have to be discreet. A written proposal for such gentlemen's agreements or a demand for a written promise would only embarrass France and lessen the chances for successfully concluding the agreements. The move could be justified by pointing out that Germany had to exclude any possibility that her admission to the league would be approved while her application for a seat on the council would be denied. Luther suggested that Germany should adopt a policy of absolute opposition to awarding Poland a permanent seat on the council at any future date. This was a demand that the Nationalists had raised in the meeting of the Foreign Affairs Committee. But Stresemann counseled the cabinet against such a rigid stance. Any attitude that might adversely affect Germany's own case, as Luther's proposal might, ought to be avoided for the time being, Stresemann argued. Germany ought to contend simply that any broadening of the council that would take place at the same time as her own inclusion in that body would be inadmissible. Germany could perhaps oppose Poland's claim to a permanent seat on the substantive grounds that such seats were reserved for great powers and that Poland could not lay claim to this status either by virtue of her size or of her history. He voiced his strongest reservations about another suggestion, that of promising Spain that Germany would support her claim to a permanent seat if only she would postpone it. Such a promise could not be kept secret, he pointed out. And once it had become known, it would undermine Germany's fundamental argument: namely, that she could not accept *any* concurrent broadening of the council.[23]

Stresemann's suggestions were unanimously approved by the cabinet and then were transmitted to the Reichspresident. Hindenburg wholeheartedly approved of making Germany's entry conditional upon the preservation of the existing composition of the League Council. He advised Luther, however, against accepting any compromise in Geneva. Echoing the demand that the Nationalists had made before the Reichstag's Foreign Affairs Committee, he warned that he would consider it intolerable to have Poland simultaneously awarded a council seat of any kind. Moreover, any agreement that would bind Germany to accepting Poland at some future date was out of the question. Any such compromise would constitute for him "the most serious obstacle to the domestic realization of the policies pursued through the Locarno Pact and entry into the League of Nations. . . . I consider it an obligation of conscience to give you this clear and written expression of my personal point of view."[24]

Hindenburg's "obligation of conscience" constituted an attempt to impose the sort of Nationalist restrictions upon Germany's freedom of action in Geneva that Stresemann had resisted before the London and Locarno conferences. The effort, moreover, involved more serious machinations than the letter alone indicates. An earlier draft of the letter had threatened Luther with dismissal if he made any concessions in Geneva. It was modified when Luther let State Secretary Meissner know that if such a threat were made, he would immediately resign. But coupled with rumors that the president was planning to install and support a dictatorship under Article 48 of the constitution, the letter gave Stresemann and Luther pause.[25]

Talk of a dictatorship was indeed current on the Right. One name mentioned within the DNVP was that of Minister of Defense Otto Gessler, who enjoyed the president's confidence and who inspired some hope among the Nationalists because of his consistent defense of the Reichswehr.[26]

On the far Right, however, Alfred Hugenberg was being touted as the man who could save Germany from perdition and democracy. His chief drummer since the previous summer had been the chairman of the Pan-German League, Heinrich Class, who had kept a steady stream of friendly visitors going to see Reichspresident Hindenburg since December, all of whom were instructed to suggest that Hugenberg be appointed as chancellor and dictator. Class even explored the matter with Oskar Hindenburg, also urging him to work on his father. The immediate results disappointed Class and his friends in the Pan-German League. But the suggestion that Hindenburg could influence policy from his office certainly took root, and Stresemann and Luther had reason for concern.[27]

Since Hindenburg had already assumed a position of some detachment from the cabinet's policy with regard to the league by refusing to sign the German petition for admission, Luther was virtually obliged to take the president's warnings into serious account. Any further defection on the part of the president could bring the cabinet down. Luther therefore replied to Hindenburg's expression of his "obligation of conscience" in a letter dated March 4, one day before the German delegation was to depart for Geneva. In his letter, Luther took note of Hindenburg's misgivings but neatly avoided accepting his conditions. Rather, he simply reaffirmed a cabinet decision of February 24, 1926, by which the ministers had unanimously approved the procedure of seeking informal guarantees—gentlemen's agreements—from the Locarno powers, to the effect that Germany would be the only country to gain a new permanent seat on the League Council at the special session. Luther pointedly reminded Hindenburg that the latter had already given his assent to this decision. The chancellor insisted that the German delegation in Geneva would adhere to this plan and that the rumors of a change in tactics, which had prompted Hindenburg's letter, were unfounded.[28] Having thus disarmed the Reichspresident by invoking his earlier approval of the cabinet's plan of action, Luther left with Stresemann for Geneva.

Events there awarded the Nationalists one final chance to bring down the Luther Cabinet over the issue of Germany's entry into the league. For in the first few days of the league's special March session to consider Germany's entry, compromise with regard to broadening the League Council beyond the inclusion of Germany seemed to be impossible. Spain, Brazil, and Poland maintained their demands for permanent places. Just as stubbornly, Sweden insisted that she would veto any appointment to the council other than Germany's. In conferences between the Locarno powers, Briand

and Chamberlain tried to exonerate themselves from the charge of disloyal maneuvering. But public opinion in Geneva was, at the outset, almost universally sympathetic to Germany's point of view that the extending of seats on the council to anyone other than herself would be a diplomatic affront. Briand and Chamberlain were held responsible for the crisis, because they had encouraged the claims of Poland and Spain, respectively. As a result, they came under tremendous pressure to effect a compromise. They finally convinced Poland and Spain to postpone their demands for permanent seats, on the condition that Germany agree, even before her entry, not to block any action during the special session to create a new nonpermanent seat for Poland.[29]

At first, Stresemann and Luther rejected the compromise; but their action caused a rapid change in the climate of opinion. Whereas Briand and Chamberlain had been held accountable for the impasse up to this point, Germany now began to suffer from the accusation that she was obstructing a solution. Sweden, too, was exposed to tremendous diplomatic and public pressure to modify her stand.[30]

On the morning of March 14 the Swedish delegation visited Luther and German Foreign Office Secretary Schubert. The Swedes indicated that they were planning to seek new instructions from their government, which would allow them to resign their own temporary seat—which they planned to give up at the end of the year anyway—so that at the current session, Poland could be elected to the council in Sweden's place. They assured the German chancellor that they contemplated this move only because their negotiations with Briand had revealed that he would not break his promise to acquire for Poland a position on the council. The German representatives raised "energetic objections," but the Swedes insisted that it was the only solution they could find. Moreover, it was a solution that they thought would really work to Germany's advantage by underscoring the fundamental merit of Germany's case.[31]

The German delegation was forced by this turn of events to reconsider its position. The representatives were well aware of the accuracy of the Swedes' assessment of Briand's attitude. They were also conscious of the unfavorable turn of public and journalistic opinion since their last refusal to compromise. But they decided that German public opinion would never accept the replacement of Sweden, essentially a friendly neutral, by Poland. The Germans therefore informed the Swedish delegation that its proposal would not resolve the situation for Germany.[32] Schubert then visited the British delegation. Here the proposal arose that Sweden not be the only country to relinquish a seat, but perhaps that also Czechoslovakia do so, these two countries being replaced by Poland and the more clearly neutral

Holland. The Germans favored the idea. The exchange of Poland for Czechoslovakia would not increase the weight of French influence, since both were allies of France. The exchange of Holland for Sweden would also leave the balance of the council unaltered. In conversations with Briand that evening, Stresemann advanced the idea. Briand expressed sympathy for the plan. Upon leaving Stresemann, he indicated that he intended to propose the matter to the Czech foreign minister.[33]

Meanwhile, the German delegation telegraphed the plan to Berlin. The rump cabinet in Berlin was divided on the issue, but State Secretary Meissner, speaking for Hindenburg, gave a qualified endorsement to the plan. Hindenburg definitely favored completely excluding Poland from the council, Meissner reported. But if this were impossible, as the reports from Geneva seemed to indicate, he was prepared to accept the substitution of Holland and Poland for Sweden and Czechoslovakia on the council. The Reichspresident's decision to submit to political necessity was immediately communicated to Geneva.[34] The German delegation never really had a chance to act upon it, however; for on the same day, the Brazilian delegate announced that he had received renewed instructions from his government to veto the admission of Germany to the council unless Brazil's temporary seat were converted to a permanent seat.[35]

The European nations had finally found a satisfactory compromise, but Brazil's unyielding position ended all possibility of Germany's being admitted at the March session. There was a sharp sense of personal disappointment among the men who had worked to maintain the spirit of Locarno at having come so close only to see success vanish. The Locarno signatories tried to salvage what they could by issuing a joint communiqué, which announced that they, at least, had arrived at an agreement that would overcome all the difficulties that had arisen between them. They noted with satisfaction that "the work for peace which they had realized at Locarno . . . remains intact. They remain attached to it to-day as yesterday and are firmly resolved to work together to maintain and develop it."[36] In the closing assembly of the special session, Briand declared even more forcefully:

> We have solved the difficulties and the serious misunderstandings between ourselves and Germany through that spirit of reconciliation and compromise which the German representatives have also shown in so commendable a fashion. Now we stand before the necessity of having to adjourn without having realized our goal. This is a cruel irony of fate for us all. . . . We do not want to part, however, without at least declaring the implicit moral admission of Germany [to the league].[37]

Briand's words could have been but small consolation to Luther and Stresemann as they returned to Berlin to face the cabinet and the Reichstag.

173

Upon returning, Luther and Stresemann represented the Geneva fiasco as a moral vindication of Germany's cause. The reaction within the cabinet was one of disappointment, tempered by a realization that the final outcome had been out of Germany's hands. The ministers who had remained in Berlin rehearsed for Luther and Stresemann the criticisms to be expected in the Reichstag: the delegation had been insufficiently prepared for the situation that it had faced; it had contracted new obligations by approving the communiqué reaffirming the Locarno treaties; it had failed to secure additional accords to extend the ramifications that had been promised in Locarno.

Luther responded that Germany's international position had improved because of the difficulties she had encountered and because of the bearing of the delegation. The communiqué was to Germany's advantage: the politics of the Locarno Pact bound her to no specific action, but it did bind the Allies. Although concrete extensions of the ramifications such as the Nationalists demanded had been impossible, all essential points had been discussed. The public statement made by the Locarno powers at the end of the session could be viewed with confidence as being more than just words. The cabinet guidelines for negotiations in Geneva had not been violated. Germany could not dictate institutional procedure to the league. The disposition of a vacant temporary seat on the council was the prerogative of the League Assembly.

The cabinet accepted Luther's rationalizations and agreed that a positive public statement was indispensable if the opposition in the Reichstag were to be overcome. Moreover, the statement ought to emphasize the reaffirmation by all powers concerned of the politics of Locarno.[38]

Events in Geneva thus extended the DNVP's opportunity to oppose Germany's entry into the league. Presenting to the Reichstag a Nationalist motion for the withdrawal of Germany's application to join the league, Count Westarp condemned the betrayal of Germany by France and Britain and the failure of the personal policies of Luther and Stresemann. He denounced the two ministers for having abandoned Germany's opposition to a council seat for Poland. Germany, he insisted, had suffered a defeat and a humiliation in Geneva, which nothing, especially not the communiqué of the Locarno powers, could obscure. In view of the "catastrophe of Geneva," Stresemann and Luther were admonished by Westarp to consider whether they were "the appropriate agents for the further negotiations of the summer."[39]

The basic issue in the Reichstag was not so much Geneva, however, as Locarno. The failure in Geneva merely provided the confirmation of the Nationalists' insistence since January that Germany's foreign policy needed to be reappraised.[40] Admiral von Tirpitz raised the question in the Reichstag: "Ought the policies of the present government to be pursued further in the same manner in spite of the breakdown at Geneva?" The Nationalist answer was clear in Tirpitz's remarks. The policies had not brought the awaited result. No matter how one turned the events in Geneva, they represented a setback for Germany's political methods, a setback that, in Tirpitz's view, was all the more significant because it was the first time since the autumn of 1918 that Germany had come forward with a positive policy.[41]

With the Social Democrats supporting the government's entry into the league, the Nationalist motion to withdraw Germany's application had no chance of success, however. In fact, for all their protestations of opposition to entering the league, the Nationalists must have been as disappointed as anyone that the German mission to Geneva had been unsuccessful. Return to the government was now a basic goal of the DNVP's policy.[42] The greatest obstacle to that goal was still Locarno. If the Nationalists entered a coalition before the Locarno treaties became operative due to Germany's entry into the league, they faced the potential embarrassment of cooperating in the final confirmation of the treaties because of which they had originally left the government. Thus, the leader of the DNVP in Bavaria, Hans Hilpert, felt compelled to denounce the league before the provincial convention of party regulars, suggesting that the Locarno accords were abrogated by the Geneva fiasco and claiming that the DNVP could never enter the cabinet under the obligations that the government had contracted.[43]

With Germany's failure to gain entry to the league in March, however, the significance of the party's inflexibility took on new proportions. The next opportunity for Germany to enter would be at the league's regular session in September. Until then, the Nationalists' rigid stance on foreign policy stood in the way of their participation in the government, just as it had throughout the summer of 1924. They were unable, as a result, to take advantage of the situation when Luther's cabinet finally did fall over the issue of the national flag in May 1926. Early in the month, Luther had countersigned a document that had been issued by Hindenburg, which decreed that all German embassies, legations, and consulates outside Europe, in addition to designated ones within Europe, were to fly the colors of the old empire in addition to the republican flag. In the resulting furor that broke out among the old partners of the Weimar coalition at this insult to the republican standard, Luther's cabinet fell. It was, in fact, the Nationalists who ensured the passage of the resolution to disapprove of Luther. They first offered him their support in exchange for his promise to reestablish the rightist coalition of the previous year. When he refused to offer any guarantee, they abstained in the Reichstag vote on the flag issue, thus allowing his critics (the SPD, the KPD, and the DDP) to win, 176 to 146.[44]

In the ensuing negotiations to form a new cabinet, Hindenburg displayed his continuing anxiousness to reestablish a rightist coalition. He sought to manipulate the governmental crisis in such a way as to return the Nationalists to power. Ernst Scholz, chairman of the Reichstag delegation of the German People's Party, who was on particularly good terms with Hindenburg, became the political broker in an effort to re-create the coalition between the middle parties and the DNVP. The Nationalists were willing enough to enter the government. But the Center and the DDP opposed including them until they accepted Stresemann's foreign policy. Stresemann, too, rejected a widening to the Right, objecting that the timing would be catastrophic from the viewpoint of foreign policy. Pressure from the Reichspresident only consolidated the minority coalition. The expressed condition for the formation of a new government became the recognition of the "legally binding nature of existing international agreements" and the "continuation of the existing foreign policy." The only issue from the crisis seemed to be the return of the previous cabinet, but with Marx rather than Luther as chancellor.[45]

The Nationalists' stubborn resistance to the government's foreign policy continued to block a widening of the cabinet to the Right. Even the good offices of Hindenburg and DVP Chairman Scholz could not overcome this impediment. A widening of the minority coalition to the Left, however, proved equally impossible because of the SPD's public attitude towards a settlement of the claims for compensation of the nobility, whose property had been confiscated since the 1918 revolution. The SPD favored moderate compensation for the previous owners. The Socialists were forced, however, by the astute political maneuvering of the Communist Party, to join in a referendum which rejected absolutely all claims to indemnification. The referendum's complete disregard for the rights of private property alienated the parties of the Middle and created a certain negative community of interest between them and the DNVP on this domestic issue. The Nationalists were able to exploit this situation to block any coalition of the Left and the Middle and to increase the pressure within the German People's Party for including the DNVP in the cabinet.[46]

Throughout May and June of 1926, concurrently with the controversy over indemnification, Westarp continued to hold consultations with Hindenburg and Scholz, which were aimed at the formation of a rightist coalition as soon as possible.[47] Westarp recognized that the DNVP's self-imposed banishment from power threatened the unity of the party. Increasingly, influential groups within the Nationalist camp—namely, the agrarians and the industrialists—demanded that the DNVP accept the *fait accompli* of the Locarno treaties and clear the way for a return to power.[48] By mid summer, Westarp was willing to admit to Hindenburg—not without embarrassment, according to Stresemann—that the DNVP was prepared to accept the foreign minister and his policies and would stand ready if the government sought to reorganize.[49] Hindenburg, in turn, urged the Marx government to consider a widening to the Right in the autumn.[50] But Marx was unenthusiastic.[51]

Westarp gave further evidence of the modification of the Nationalist position as the September session of the League of Nations approached. In a letter to Chancellor Marx, Westarp acknowledged that "a secure [Reichstag] majority stands behind the policy of the Reich government not to make the [German] entry into the League of Nations dependent on the conditions that we feel are indispensable." Westarp's unyielding opposition of the winter and spring and his demand that the government retract its petition for membership in the league had now become "serious reservations" and a warning against "unconditional" entry. Moreover, Westarp expressed his inclination to desist, for the moment at least, from any public discussion of the matter, "in view of the [present] state of negotiations." This sensitivity attests once more to the process of accommodation that was at work within the DNVP, which increasingly influenced its relationship to the Weimar system. After months of public railing, Westarp now merely, in the most polite terms, "requested a briefing" on those measures "corresponding to our wishes" that the government had already taken, or planned to take, to ensure Germany's interests.[52]

The Nationalists' decision to eschew agitation over entry into the league and about foreign policy in general in the interests of an early formation of a rightist coalition did not mean that the DNVP was prepared to endorse the Locarno policies.[53] The party proposed, rather, a somewhat noncommittal neutrality which would allow the Locarno policies to continue as long as they bore fruit.[54]

In this change of tactics, Stresemann saw an opportunity to test the extent of the DNVP's willingness to cooperate. On August 16 the foreign minister invited the Nationalist leaders to send Professor Otto Hoetzsch, a relatively moderate but influential DNVP expert on foreign policy, to Geneva as a member of the German delegation to the league. Hoetzsch himself favored accepting the invitation. He realized the danger: his presence in Geneva would appear to associate the DNVP with Germany's entry into the league. He thought that the party therefore ought to make clear that his participation would be a sign of approval *only* insofar as the German Nationalists' conditions for entry were met. He, as well as one of Westarp's top aides, Gottfried Treviranus, considered the invitation to be one more step towards a rightist coalition.[55] Others within the DNVP's Reichstag delegation, however, viewed the invitation to the moderate Hoetzsch, who was known to consider Germany's entrance into the league as inevitable, a "ticklish affair" and a master stroke by Stresemann to embarrass the party.[56]

The party leaders met on August 25 to take a position on Stresemann's invitation. All agreed that the criticism of past policies had to be maintained but that, at the same time, the DNVP had to attest to its new willingness to cooperate on the basis of "accomplished facts," the euphemism that the DNVP leaders had adopted in order to disguise their growing acceptance of the imperatives of foreign policy. The leaders feared, however, that the logical distinction between approval of Germany's entry—which would be accomplished even before the German delegation arrived—and Hoetzsch's participation in the delegation's work subsequent to entry would be too hard for the public mind to draw. Moreover, they suspected that Stresemann would try not only to obscure the distinction but also to publicize Hoetzsch's presence as a DNVP endorsement of the government's foreign policy. And finally, it appeared that the entire delegation would be more or less bound by the instructions of the government. The assuming, by any DNVP representative, of responsibility for the government's policy with regard to the league was still unacceptable to the majority of the Nationalist leaders. Stresemann's invitation was therefore declined.[57]

The Nationalist leaders continued to demonstrate their restraint, however, by virtually ignoring the Eupen-Malmédy incident, a sharp setback that Stresemann's policy suffered in late August 1926. Unofficial talks among politicians, industrialists, and financiers concerning the return of the areas to Germany in return for enough credit to stabilize the Belgian currency had been under way since early 1925.[58] Both the German and the Belgian governments had been aware of the discussions but had only become involved in them in any official capacity in early 1926.[59] A satisfactory exchange had been worked out between the two governments by July. A plebiscite would be held in the two counties, which were certain to choose Germany. In consideration of this concession by the Belgian government, the Reichsbank and the Rhineland would put a credit of about 250 million marks at Belgium's disposal.[60] In August, however, the Belgian government broke off the negotiations, under pressure both from a systematic French and British press campaign and from Poincaré, who had recently returned to the French government as premier.[61]

The DNVP's leadership could have exploited the incident to Stresemann's acute embarrassment. Throughout the long debate on the Locarno Pact, the foreign minister had explicitly insisted that the return of Eupen-

Malmédy through a peaceful agreement between Germany and Belgium was not prohibited by the terms of the treaty. In the very early stages of the Locarno negotiations, he had mentioned to the French ambassador Germany's desire to reacquire Eupen-Malmédy through a peaceful agreement. At the Locarno Conference itself, he had repeatedly insisted, with Briand's expressed agreement, that peaceful modification of frontiers through mutual accords was not forbidden by the security pact. He had even informed Briand, early in August 1926, of the impending settlement between Germany and Belgium, adding that he hoped the agreement could be signed at the coming session of the league in order to add emphasis to the fact that this accord bore the sign of the spirit of peace that was characteristic of the Locarno policies and of the league.[62]

Now, events contradicted Stresemann's fundamental interpretation of the security pact. Briand himself sent an emissary to Stresemann to protest that the return of Eupen-Malmédy would run counter to the Locarno accords. Stresemann reacted sharply to Briand's contention. He insisted that the Locarno Pact did not include an eternal general guarantee of existing borders, but that it was a renunciation of aggression or coercion as a means of modifying them. He argued against what he called the absurdity of interpreting a peace treaty—which he considered Locarno to be—as precluding peaceful cooperation between neighboring states. He asserted that if Briand's contention corresponded, in fact, with the interpretation of all the Locarno powers, he would feel obliged to inform the cabinet that Germany had concluded the Locarno Pact on the basis of false assumptions.[63] If, in fact, the Nationalists had pressed the issue, Stresemann might even have been compelled to live up to this threat, a course of events that would have left him little choice but to resign. The Nationalist leaders were, however, more interested in removing obstacles to their return to the government than in carrying on their vendetta against Stresemann. They listened in the Foreign Affairs Committee as he tried to explain away the setback, and they never once murmured a word about the "everlasting renunciation" of German land and peoples that the incident seemed to confirm. Indeed, Westarp found nothing stronger to say than that the incident attested to the "lack of clarity" in the Locarno accords concerning revision of borders.[64]

The DNVP had been out of power for nearly a full year. In that time, the party leaders had come a long way toward accepting the political realities of the moment. They were willing to acknowledge the "accomplished fact" of German entry into the league even before it had become official. They were willing to forego nationalistic bombast over the Eupen-Malmédy incident. They were becoming, in fact, *Vernunftspolitiker* ("reasonable politicians") of a most pragmatic bent.

10

THE FRUITS OF PRAGMATISM

Over the summer of 1926 the deadlock concerning the expansion of the League Council was resolved so that only Germany would receive a permanent seat, while three other aspirants would be offered temporary seats. With the way thus cleared, Germany entered the League of Nations on September 10, 1926, amid great fanfare and jubilation, captured in Aristide Briand's dramatic words, "Away with the rifles. . . . Make way for peace!" At nearly the same moment, another speech signaled a new phase in German domestic policy as well. The occasion was the DNVP's convention in Cologne; the speaker was Hans Schlange-Schöningen, a vice-chairman of the party. His words: "Forward into the State with all men of good will." Thus the Nationalists publicly confirmed their new course.[1]

The pragmatism that the leadership of the DNVP had adopted proved to be immediately valuable in that party's quest for a return to power, because the most significant diplomatic developments of 1926, which constituted a continuing theme of German diplomacy throughout 1927, were the expectations raised by the conversations held at Thoiry and the paucity of the actual results. And yet, even as the spirit of Locarno waned, acceptance of Stresemann's foreign policy of reconciliation and adjustment, for better or for worse, remained the basic condition of the DNVP's reentry into the government.

The meeting at Thoiry between Briand and Stresemann, which came after Germany's entry into the league and after the approval of the Locarno Pact, was surrounded by an atmosphere of romantic melodrama. The two men arranged the meeting in the French village because of its proximity to Geneva and because of its seclusion from the world of the press. The idyllic and secretive aspects of the conversations were much ballyhooed once the meeting came to public attention. But the conversations at Thoiry were no spur-of-the-moment affair. Since Locarno, Stresemann had been anxious to review with Briand the entire range of difficulties that he hoped could be resolved in the new spirit of reconciliation. Neither the signing of the Locarno Pact in London nor the unfortunate league session of March 1926 had provided enough opportunity for such a general discussion. Both men had looked to the September session of the league as the next logical occasion for the meeting, which they hoped could be conducted free from the pressures of publicity.[2]

With the return of Poincaré to the French premiership in the summer of 1926—he was called upon to try to solve France's then chronic monetary crisis—Stresemann felt an increasing need for such a discussion. The German government was aware that Poincaré still advocated a much harder line towards Germany than had been characteristic of Briand. Briand's emissaries to Berlin tried to reassure the German government that Poincaré would be forced to support Briand's policies because any radical reorientation would in itself threaten confidence in the franc.[3] But in the weeks just prior to Germany's entry into the league, Poincaré's increasing influence upon foreign policy seemed evident. The Conference of Ambassadors renewed its stern tone in notes concerning Germany's disarmament and the activity of the Interallied Military Control Commission. The return of Eupen-Malmédy was blocked. Moreover, Poincaré's financial policies and his initial successes in restoring confidence in the franc threatened to remove the very basis for a quid pro quo arrangement such as Briand and Stresemann had been discussing throughout the summer of 1926. The plan under discussion was to involve the mobilization of German capital resources to support and stabilize the franc, in return for which the Rhineland occupation would be terminated, the Saar mines would be returned, and plebiscites would be permitted in the Saar and in Eupen-Malmédy.[4]

The potential political harvest for both Stresemann and Briand from such a dramatic, far-reaching settlement was enormous. Neither foreign minister seems to have been falsely optimistic about the possible success of such a venture, but both seem to have been prepared to explore what they realized might be a fading opportunity.[5]

Well before his departure for the meeting of the League of Nations in Geneva, Stresemann informed the cabinet about the proposed discussion with Briand and invited his colleagues to express their opinions about the possibility of mobilizing 1.5 billion marks for France by means of railroad bonds in return for sufficiently far-reaching counterconcessions. When the minister of finance and a spokesman from the Ministry of Economics objected to any mobilization of these obligations, Stresemann observed that he was not thinking in terms of any binding promises in Geneva, but that he did want to conduct cautious exploratory conversations with Briand. He took note of the "veto of the Reichsminister of Finance," which he promised to keep in mind throughout his negotiations. He even voiced his doubts that such a far-reaching rapprochement could be accomplished under Poincaré. Despite the objections of the Ministry of Finance and the Ministry of Economics, the cabinet approved Stresemann's plans to try to negotiate a general settlement in the coming talks with Briand. If this proved impossible, the cabinet agreed that the specific problems, especially with regard to the occupation and German disarmament, ought to be pressed little by little.[6]

Throughout the September session of the league, as a result, German diplomats negotiated for concessions on disarmament, on troop reductions, and on other alleviations in the occupied Rhineland. But the entire German delegation in Geneva was aware that the best chance for marked improvement would be the scheduled meeting between Briand and Stresemann.

On the morning of September 17, 1926, just hours before the proposed meeting in Thoiry, the German delegation to the league assembled in order to review the problems that Stresemann planned to raise with Briand. The delegation agreed that a broad general settlement ought to be pursued, if it appeared to be at all possible, and that only if this proved beyond reach should Stresemann return to the specific difficulties, such as an amelioration of the regime of occupation in the Rhineland. The general settlement ought to include the immediate concession to Germany of the right to repurchase the Saar mines; the immediate return of political control of the Saar to Germany, preferably without a plebiscite; and the simultaneous termination of the occupation of the second and third Rhineland zones. The delegation agreed that a mobilization of perhaps as high as 1.5 billion marks in railroad bonds was possible as Germany's share of the bargain. This would only be tolerable, however, if France agreed to an immediate and final withdrawal from the Rhine and not simply to a shortening of the term of occupation. Moreover, Stresemann was urged to raise the demand that France retract her objections to the Eupen-Malmédy accord that Germany and Belgium had negotiated. The Polish question, on the other hand, was to be avoided, as well as any mention of the Dawes plan. Any German demands regarding the former would place too great a burden on Briand in asking the French cabinet to approve the settlement. Any discussion of the latter issue would only embarrass Germany by emphasizing the contradiction between her claims that the Dawes-plan obligations were unacceptably high and her readiness to mortgage so large a portion of her national capital in order to free the Rhineland.[7]

After extensive precautions to avoid attracting the press, Briand and Stresemann arrived in Thoiry about 1:00 P.M. on September 17, 1926, each accompanied by a single aide. Over a leisurely luncheon, they entered upon a four and one-half hour discussion. The two foreign ministers agreed at the outset that they would talk in terms of a global settlement of French-German differences.[8]

In discussing the financial compensation that France was to receive from Germany as her share of the exchange, Stresemann made no secret of the opposition that the mobilization of the railroad obligations faced among his cabinet colleagues, as well as in political and commercial circles outside the cabinet. There was considerable concern that mobilization of railroad bonds would weaken Germany's credit collateral to a dangerous extent; many people also felt that in order to preserve Germany's financial soundness, political concessions ought to be foregone.[9] Stresemann indicated that in order to overcome this opposition, he would have to present guarantees for all his demands for concessions. Briand assured Stresemann that complete fulfillment of Germany's demands was not out of the question. France's foreign minister was confident that his country would more readily accept a total solution than a long series of concessions to Germany's many specific demands. Moreover, a plan that would restore the stability of the franc would be irresistible in France. Stresemann presented the terms that Germany would set for such a settlement: return of the Saar and repurchase of the Saar mines, evacuation of the second and third Rhineland zones of occupation, abolition of the Interallied Military Control Commission, and the return of Eupen-Malmédy. Briand acknowledged that these points would be legitimate expectations in the event of a general settlement. He indicated that, in his opinion, it would not be necessary to hold a plebiscite in the Saar region. He acknowledged that evacuation of the Rhineland would have to begin immediately after the conclusion of a Franco-German accord and would have to be completed as rapidly as would be technically possible. Briand agreed that the Military Control Commission could be withdrawn shortly, but he complained to Stresemann about the paramilitary organizations that were active in Germany. Briand noted that his own policies of rapprochement would meet with far less resistance if such organizations did not exist. He accepted Stresemann's explanation, however, that these organizations were militarily insignificant and that they enjoyed no official support or favor. Concerning the final point, Briand assured Stresemann that France would raise no more objections to a German-Belgian accord on the return of Eupen-Malmédy.[10]

The two foreign ministers concluded their discussion by reminding one another that neither government was in any way bound by the proposals made at Thoiry. They then formulated a press communiqué which indicated that they had reached personal agreement concerning a general solution of problems existing between France and Germany; if their governments approved the compromises reached in Thoiry, the discussions would be continued.[11]

The general reaction in Geneva to the Thoiry talks was one of excited optimism. The very fact that France and Germany were discussing a global solution of their outstanding differences connoted bright new vistas in European affairs. State Secretary Pünder carried this rose-tinted outlook from Geneva back to Berlin, where, on September 20, he reported to the cabinet over the activities of the league and the talks at Thoiry. His lengthy and detailed account of the discussions moved Marx to express his sense of the historical importance of the talks for the political development of Germany in Europe. But the chancellor also observed that Pünder's report seemed almost too good to be true. He accepted, however, the premise that Briand had offered at Thoiry—namely, that Poincaré could not oppose a general settlement without endangering the franc and his own political position. It appeared, Marx admitted, as though the political development of the two countries were dependent upon their economic fortunes. His view of the likelihood of a meaningful general settlement was obviously less optimistic than Pünder's, however.[12]

Minister of Economics Curtius added a note of caution. The proposed mobilization of credit would pose an exceptionally difficult economic question about which he would have to reserve his final judgment for a later date. On the other hand, he would be opposed to discarding the plan for a general settlement, the political consequences of which would certainly be enormous, simply because it entailed economic difficulties. Despite his caution, Curtius denied that he had ever vetoed the idea of mobilizing Germany's credit in order to stabilize the franc, and he did not wish to do so at this point.[13]

Four days later, after Stresemann had returned from Geneva and given his own account of the Thoiry talks to the cabinet, Curtius was more specific and somewhat less encouraging. He agreed that the greatest economic burdens would be justified if they would win freedom for the Rhineland and a general settlement of Franco-German difficulties. But he had serious reservations concerning the specific financial measures that had been proposed in Thoiry. He failed to see where the capital for purchasing an issue of railroad bonds could possibly be secured. If the bond issue were added to all of Germany's credit needs, the sum total would amount to 2.4 billion marks, all of which would have to be found before the turn of the year. This would be a prodigious mobilization of capital under any circumstances. In a period in which German demands would be competing with growing needs for capital in other countries, it would be even more difficult.[14]

Stresemann agreed that these difficulties ought to be spelled out in the German press in order to discourage too optimistic a view of the possibilities for a broad settlement. The immediate outcome of the cabinet's discussion was thus a press release, which noted that the cabinet had "unanimously approved" Stresemann's exploratory talks with Briand. It also announced that a cabinet committee had been formed to pursue the matter further.[15]

The optimism within certain government circles persisted, encouraged by what seemed to be an acceptance by the French cabinet of Briand's report on the plans for a general settlement.[16] State Secretary Pünder expressed to Berlin politicians his distinct impression that the Thoiry talks and, in fact, the entire experience at Geneva represented such a dramatic success in foreign policy that the government felt little necessity to broaden the coalition at the time, and especially not to the Right.[17]

The reaction of the DNVP's leadership to Germany's entry into the league and to the talks at Thoiry gave renewed evidence of the increased willingness of the party's leaders to subordinate issues of foreign policy to their desire to return to power. Despite outbursts in the radical press against Germany's entry into the league, the party's leaders pursued a moderate course.[18] At a DNVP assembly in Bavaria, Oskar Hergt spoke of the party's new view that, in the light of the "now accomplished fact" of her entry into the League of Nations, Germany's foreign policy would only be carried out "within the framework of this organization." To be sure, Hergt criticized the failure of the German delegation in Geneva to make any concrete political gains. Nonetheless, he expressed his party's readiness to accept the idea of having Germany cooperate within the league. The spokesman for the Bavarian DNVP, Hilpert, followed Hergt by urging that the party be included in the government.[19] The new pragmatism displayed by these official party spokesmen was in sharp contrast to views that they had expressed in a similar setting after the league session in March, when denunciation of the league, the Locarno Pact, and the government had been categorical.[20]

As chairman of both the party and the Reichstag delegation, Count Westarp officially voiced the DNVP's new policy. In a series of speeches, beginning in Cologne, he announced that the DNVP was prepared to cooperate with the government, that it was willing to close the curtain on the past.[21] Moreover, in a series of circulars, he specifically instructed the Nationalist provincial organizations to refrain from making any personal attacks upon Stresemann, to confine their criticism of foreign policy to issues such as the policies of the League of Nations rather than those of the German government, and to submit to the party leaders, for review, all political decisions that were destined for publication.[22]

The new course was so firmly set that even the opportunity to embarrass the government over the fading promise of Thoiry was resisted. Early in October, doubts began to grow about France's willingness to accept the general solution proposed by Stresemann and Briand. Despite this atmosphere of doubt, which could have been used to justify a thorough skepticism, Westarp reaffirmed before the Foreign Affairs Committee of the Reichstag —which was convened on October 7 to discuss rumors of the waning prospects for Thoiry—that his party was thoroughly prepared to support a new foreign political adjustment aimed at gaining for Germany the fulfillment of her unresolved demands. The DNVP, he announced, agreed with the government that a general settlement ought to be sought for the Rhineland. Such a solution ought not to prejudice, however, the continued pursuit of those specific ameliorations, such as a reduction in the number of occupation forces, which had thus far characterized Germany's policy. He counseled, moreover, against banking too heavily on France's good will and against paying too high a price for the withdrawal of French troops, especially since it still appeared possible that France would be compelled to evacuate because of her financial situation. The modesty of the remarks testified strongly to the DNVP's overriding concern to accept the "accomplished facts of Geneva and not to pursue barren opposition," a change of attitude that was not lost on contemporary observers.[23]

By early November it had become clear that American financial and political pressure would block any Franco-German financial arrangement that did not guarantee the full recognition of the war debts that France owed to the United States.[24] Moreover, Poincaré's own efforts to stabilize the franc had progressed so well that France's need for substantial foreign funding had become less acute.[25]

The position of the Marx Cabinet was thus decidedly weaker with regard to the policy of reconciliation than it had been in September. Nonetheless, the DNVP leadership held the line, even in the face of mounting objections from provincial committees and the opposition of the Hugenberg press, where vitriolic attacks upon Stresemann and his *"Illusionspolitik"* continued to appear. The provincial leaders protested to Westarp that the new line of policy set by the national leadership amounted to a surrender by the DNVP of its distinctive "national" character and threatened the unity of the party.[26] But Westarp and the DNVP's national leadership remained undeterred. They continued to practice a limited criticism (*sachliche Kritik*) of specific aspects of Stresemann's conduct of foreign policy, as Westarp had done in the meeting of the Foreign Affairs Committee on October 7. But they refused to repudiate the means that Stresemann had chosen to use in his conduct of foreign policy: namely, an understanding with France. In fact, they were now admitting that rapprochement was acceptable as long as it produced the proper concessions from the Allies. DNVP opposition to the existing Marx Cabinet, the leadership argued, was less against the government's conception and conduct of foreign policy than against the fact that the cabinet represented only a minority of the political opinion in the Reichstag. The strongest observation that the Nationalist leaders chose to make concerning foreign policy was the quite accurate statement that the results of the most recent public manifestation of that policy, Thoiry, were indeed meager.[27]

The admission, in such explicit terms, that the DNVP was prepared to accommodate itself to the Stresemann policies of rapprochement was a direct result of the realization among the Nationalist leaders that the coalition between the Middle parties and the SPD, which inevitably had formed to support foreign policy and which had protected minority cabinets against repeated Nationalist attacks since Locarno, was threatening to take more formal political shape. In this situation, personal attacks against Stresemann or his policies would only push his party, perhaps against its will, toward such a Grand Coalition. But even if the prevention of this new alignment should prove impossible, Westarp and his closest advisors were now convinced that they stood to gain more by maintaining a policy that would leave open the possibility of forming a coalition with the DNVP as a practicable alternative to an opening to the Left.[28]

The DNVP leaders decided to put their new position to a test. The failure to realize the expectations that Thoiry had aroused might provide the occasion for their entry into a new government. The leaders therefore informed Marx that they would take every parliamentary opportunity to bring down his minority government, taking care, however, to emphasize that their attitude was determined by a desire to clear the way for a new rightist majority government.[29]

The initial effects of the new DNVP maneuver were counterproductive. The Marx Cabinet decided to open negotiations with the SPD in an effort to implement a Grand Coalition. The Socialists proved receptive, and before long, Marx had reached a working arrangement with the SPD on a number of specific legislative problems that the SPD looked upon as being of critical importance, such as the dire situation that was facing labor as winter approached and certain modifications of the Reichswehr. For the time being, however, both the cabinet and the SPD were content to postpone the actual reorganization of the cabinet which their working arrangement presaged.

Despite the fact that the DNVP's action had stimulated activity toward the Left, it proved successful in the long run, because it revitalized the strong desire within the DVP to bring the DNVP back into the government. During Marx's negotiations with the SPD, the DVP's chairman, Ernst Scholz, had raised objections, contending that the possibility of a coalition with the Nationalists ought to be explored at the same time. When Marx indicated that he considered a coalition with the DNVP to be possible only in the event that exceptional circumstances arose, Scholz set out to create just such circumstances.[30]

Scholz's protest against a Grand Coalition represented a strong feeling within the DVP which had remained quiescent for some time after the breakup of the government of 1925. Throughout the summer of 1926, as the Nationalist position had become increasingly more reasonable, the sentiment had reasserted itself. It had been held in check by Stresemann, but now that the DNVP had made it perfectly evident that it was willing to live with the foreign minister's diplomatic policies, the disposition within the DVP to align itself with the Right became too great to contain. On December 5, 1926—while Stresemann was attending a session of the League Council in Geneva—Scholz publicly expressed the mood of the DVP's right wing in a speech in which he intimated that a coalition with the DNVP, rather than with the SPD, ought to be his party's aim.[31]

The Socialists angrily protested that this speech by the chairman of one of the coalition parties amounted to a repudiation of the agreements that Marx had contracted with them. They had demanded an immediate clarification of the situation, when, from Geneva, Stresemann advised against reorganizing the cabinet before he had completed the delicate negotiations that he was then conducting with regard to terminating the activities of the Interallied Military Control Commission in Germany.[32]

The SPD, however, had grown tired of its role as the external support of the cabinet, a position that denied the party the advantage either of power or of a clearly defined policy of opposition.[33] Still, it appeared at first that the Socialist leaders were prepared to delay any reorganization of the cabinet on the government's promise that it would welcome negotiations for a Grand Coalition on the basis of the agreements reached between Marx and the SPD. But the party's left wing won a majority in a caucus of the delegation, approving a completely new and more radical set of demands on which Socialist participation in the cabinet would depend. Marx rejected the new program. The Socialist leaders, bowing to the majority decision of their delegation, decided to introduce in the Reichstag a motion of no confidence. To give their motion the proper justification, they directed former Chancellor Philipp Scheidemann to raise the question of the Reichswehr's clandestine military activities in Russia, activities that violated disarmament clauses in the Versailles Treaty.[34]

The government leaders reacted sharply to Scheidemann's speech. The matters that he raised had been the subject of conversations between the SPD and the government since early December, at which time the cabinet representatives had given assurances that the Socialist complaints against the Reichswehr's activity would be properly handled.[35] Not only did Scheidemann's speech violate the settlement that the government thought it had reached with the SPD concerning these affairs; the public exposure that the speech lent them was extremely ill-timed. Only a few days earlier, Stresemann had convinced the Allies to announce that they had agreed to withdraw the Interallied Military Control Commission from Germany. The revelation that the Reichswehr was cooperating with the Russian army, in violation of the Versailles Treaty, would endanger this newly promised liberation of Germany. In the Reichstag, Marx replied by trying to minimize the significance of Scheidemann's remarks. But the SPD's effort to prepare the ground for its motion of no confidence was highly successful. Communists and Nationalists alike, eager to topple the government, supported the motion; the Marx Cabinet was placed in the minority. On December 17, 1926, the cabinet resigned.

In the negotiations about forming a new cabinet, Reichspresident Hindenburg favored having the DNVP return to the government, and thus he turned first to the DVP as the most appropriate agent for forming such a combination, standing as it did between the Center Party and the DNVP. But Schloz, who was chairman of the DVP delegation, declined the mandate to form a government on the grounds that he was a *persona non grata* to the Center Party, whose cooperation was essential to any majority combination. His party colleague, Minister of Economics Curtius, was therefore entrusted with the task. Curtius's efforts were frustrated, however, by a Center Party resolution, which not only voiced doubts that had been raised by the party's left wing concerning the advisability of having the DNVP participate in any government but also suggested that a government of the Middle seemed to offer the greatest advantage in the existing crisis.[36]

Hindenburg next commissioned Marx to form a government. Marx pursued his party's suggested course. But neither the SPD nor the DNVP was willing to tolerate a minority cabinet; and the DVP continued to emphasize its interest in a rightist coalition.[37]

Stresemann, whose advice both Curtius and Marx had sought throughout the negotiations, had favored a coalition of the Middle as being most desirable from the point of view of foreign policy.[38] He realized, however, that as a result of the SPD's intemperance, the domestic situation tended toward the Right. Even before Marx's tactics had opened the way for negotiations with the DNVP, Stresemann had written the chancellor a letter in which he outlined the conditions under which the DNVP's participation in the government would be acceptable to him as foreign minister. The Nationalists would have to give their unconditional support to the pursuit of the policies of reconciliation and to Germany's participation in the League of Nations. They would have to both recognize the Locarno treaties and accept responsibility for the policies growing out of them, especially for any concessions that might eventually become necessary in order to secure the evacuation of the Rhineland. The Nationalists would have to guarantee, moreover, that attacks from the more radical elements within the party would be officially discouraged and publicly disavowed if they did occur.[39]

Behind the scenes, Hindenburg and his circle of advisors manipulated constantly to produce the rightist coalition that they desired.[40] Curtius's commission to form a cabinet had been circumscribed by conditions that were designed to make it more difficult for him to succeed, as had been the case a year earlier with Koch-Weser's attempt. Now that the time was right, Hindenburg prepared his public intervention so as to produce a success for Marx. On State Secretary Meissner's initiative and with the concurrence of Marx, Hindenburg readied a letter that would constitute an emphatic appeal to all parties to lay aside their differences in the interest of the state. On January 20, Marx officially informed Hindenburg that it had proved to be impossible to form a minority government of the Middle. Hindenburg thereupon sent Marx the letter that he and his advisors had formulated. Its delivery was timed so that it would reach Marx during a meeting with the Center Party's Reichstag delegation. The letter had the desired effect. The Center Party announced its readiness to enter a government with the DNVP.[41] It then prepared and published a manifest, which was to constitute the party's "minimum program" in the cabinet negotiations. The manifest was not to be the basis for negotiations, however. For these, secret guidelines had been formulated, which Marx had adopted in his discussions with the DNVP. The guidelines incorporated Stresemann's demands that the DNVP accept his foreign policy. In addition, they called for the defense of the Republic against defamation or attack and demanded that republican symbols be accepted by all parties supporting a new cabinet.[42]

Guidelines that were remotely suggestive of these demands would have been out of the question a year earlier. Now, however, the DNVP was eager to return to the government. Since July the party leaders had been working for just such an occasion, making an attempt especially to contain within more moderate limits the party's criticism of foreign policy, since such criticism had cost them their influence in the cabinet. On January 24,

25, and 26, 1927, Westarp and several other DNVP leaders met with Marx and Stresemann for the purpose of discussing the guidelines. They accepted the program almost without change. A passage in the guidelines concerning the "unqualified recognition of the Republic" was modified to assure "the recognition of the legally binding nature of the constitution." But the policies of reconciliation with the Allied governments were accepted unchallenged, and in a secret supplement to the guidelines, the DNVP leaders agreed that "the recognition of the legally binding force of the Treaties of Locarno will not be questioned [from the standpoint of] either international or national law."[43]

Within a few days of the DNVP's acceptance of the guidelines, Marx was able to present to Hindenburg a list of ministers for appointment. The new majority government appeared before the Reichstag on February 3, 1927; it was supported by the Center Party, the DVP, the BVP, and the DNVP.

The DNVP had traveled a long road since it had last participated in the government. The opposition course, on which the breakup of the 1925 coalition had set it, had been followed vigorously while the Locarno treaties were still being debated in the Reichstag. But by the end of the year 1925, Westarp and the moderate leaders had already decided that return to the government had to be the aim of the party's policy. Long before the autumn 1926 session of the league, Westarp had admitted privately to Reichspresident Hindenburg that his party was prepared to accept both Stresemann and his policies if this were to be the price of its reentry into the government. And immediately after that session, at which Germany was formally admitted to the League of Nations, the leaders of the DNVP publicly expressed their realization that the "accomplished fact" of Germany's membership in the league necessitated that she pursue her foreign policy within the framework of that organization. Continuing attacks on the government from the vocal radical Right—the Pan-German League and the Hugenberg press— were now opposed by the DNVP's leaders as being inconsistent with their aims. Westarp, as chairman both of the national party organization and of its delegation in the Reichstag, worked hard to silence the radicals and to keep the party in line.[44]

Finally, in January 1927, the restraint shown by the party leaders during the preceding six months paid off. Admittedly, a number of factors, for which the DNVP could claim little credit, converged to permit a rightist coalition. By allowing ideology to obscure interest, the Social Democrats had destroyed any possibility of a Left-oriented government. Reichspresident Hindenburg's personal inclination toward including the DNVP had played its part. Ernst Scholz, who had so effectively voiced the right-wing sentiment of the DVP, had added impetus to the shift to the Right. But most of these elements had been present and active throughout 1926. The decisive change was that the DNVP leaders, recognizing the limits of the possible, translated into action their willingness to accept these limits, especially as they applied to foreign affairs. In the Reichstag debate over the ratification of the Locarno treaties in November 1925, Westarp had proclaimed that "for the sake of the future of the fatherland, we stand free of the responsibility for these treaties; we cannot recognize [their] legally binding force." On February 3, 1927, in justifying his party's entry into the new government, he asserted that "the treaties realized in Locarno, and Germany's related entry into the League of Nations, have become the legal and political foundation of German policy." A year of futile exile from power, in addition to pressure put on him by political moderates and economic interests within the DNVP, had convinced Westarp that access to the centers of power and influence was worth the trouble of trying to contain the Nationalists' reflex rebellion against the exigencies of foreign policy and the republican system.[45]

The decision of the leaders did not, to be sure, go unopposed. The Pan-German League mobilized against the moderate direction and began to create cells of "loyal" *völkisch*-racist and nationalistic leaders in all localities, an effort that progressed "with great secrecy."[46] Class himself, who held direct talks with Westarp during the cabinet negotiations of December 1926 and January 1927, argued vociferously against the DNVP's entry into the government.[47] He arranged for men of military rank who were sympathetic to the Pan-German point of view to visit Hindenburg and Meissner.[48] But Class's most energetic effort was to convince Hugenberg that he should assume leadership of the dissident elements within the DNVP. Although Hugenberg had been reluctant at first to assume this role, the DNVP's entry into the cabinet in January 1927 convinced him to do so.[49] During the negotiations regarding the formation of a new cabinet, he informed Westarp that he would consider the party's entry into the government "a new misfortune for our poor country . . . , a tragic turn in the evolution to the Right which has taken place since the revolution."[50] He opposed the DNVP's final decision to enter the cabinet in a speech before the party's Executive Committee late in January 1927.[51] And finally, he organized a committee, the "Schutzverein für die geistigen Güter Deutschlands," as a cover for collecting money to finance the eventual assumption by the radicals of control within the party.[52]

The tide of opinion within the party ran strongly against the radicals, however; and their discouragement is occasionally palpable. Reports from the provinces that reached the Pan-Germanists' Central Committee indicated that "60–80– even 90%" of the party's supporters favored its entry into the government.[53] Hugenberg faced criticism from industrial circles, and he found only marginal support within the DNVP's Reichstag delegation. A mere twelve delegates voted with him in the party's Central Committee against its entry into the cabinet.[54]

The final stage of the cabinet negotiations of January 1927 did furnish the radicals with one small victory. They managed to block the appointment of Hans-Erdmann von Lindeiner-Wildau as minister of the interior and party spokesman in the cabinet. The radicals judged Lindeiner-Wildau to be "incontestably exceptionally gifted, intelligent, facile at repartee, quickminded, a clever debater, well above average as a speaker," but they mistrusted him "as an innovator friendly to the Republic."[55] But the radicals failed to prevent the formation of the new coalition. The party's leadership held firmly to the new course.

Perhaps fortunately for the new coalition, diplomatic activity during the year after the DNVP's return to the government never reached the level of significance for Germany that had been characteristic of the preceding three years. A number of events occurred around Germany, especially in the league, but nothing that rivaled in significance the events of the past several years—the Dawes plan, the security pact, Germany's entry into the league, or even the proposed general settlement of Thoiry—happened *to* Germany, involving her in the same fundamental way that these diplomatic milestones had.[56]

One of the reasons for this was the very presence of the DNVP in the government. The policy of rapprochement between Germany and the Western powers was based primarily on France's willingness to grant concessions to Germany. This policy was espoused by the political Left-Center in the face of considerable opposition from France's own nationalistic groups. These elements, however, were most reluctant to grant the concessions that would be necessary for an active policy of reconciliation to a government that appeared to be as antidemocratic as did the new German coalition. Before the formation of the new Right-oriented cabinet, Germany's ambassador in Paris had predicted that a government in which the DNVP was represented would stand little chance of attaining the immediate goal of full evacuation of the Rhineland.[57]

The reluctance on the part of Left-Center elements in France to strengthen the position of the German Nationalists by granting concessions to a government in which they participated was not the only factor militating against an active policy of rapprochement, however. Another was the fact that the entire political position of the French Left had been seriously weakened by its failure to solve France's financial problems. Poincaré, who again became the dominant figure in French politics, had displaced Briand's preponderance of influence and had limited the latter's freedom of action in the sphere of foreign politics. The withdrawal of the Military Control Commission from Germany in January 1927, which Briand had conceded to Stresemann in December 1926, had provoked a sharply critical reaction in France. Briand was a canny enough politician not to want to push his luck by urging France to make further concessions that she no longer seemed to be politically prepared to grant.[58]

Despite this recognition of the less conciliatory mood that had taken root in France, Stresemann was determined to press for the ameliorations that Briand had promised. If a general settlement was out of the question, step-by-step progress toward the goals that the Allies had accepted as legitimate German expectations was not. The German foreign minister thus pursued his policies through the League of Nations and in private consultations with the statesmen at Locarno, which the Geneva sessions allowed.

Stresemann chaired the League Council in its first meeting subsequent to the DNVP's entry into the government. The session produced only meager benefits for Stresemann's policies of understanding and cooperation. It dealt primarily with the relatively insignificant questions regarding protection of German cultural and economic rights in Poland. On these matters, Germany's interests were satisfactorily acquitted. The session also handled a question concerning the evacuation of French troops from the Saar, with the exception of a limited number who would remain as a railroad security force. On this question, Stresemann chose to make a practical compromise, which he thought would ensure the immediate evacuation of the majority of the French troops, rather than rigidly to maintain Germany's legal position, which might have delayed evacuation until the conflict of legal views could have been arbitrated.

Although the question of the evacuation of the Rhineland was not on the agenda of the League Council, Stresemann did raise it privately with Briand and Chamberlain. The conversations revealed that complete evacuation could not be gained through the individual efforts of the Allied foreign ministers. Briand, especially, was clearly not in a position to grant major concessions to Germany. He averred, however, that he would not protest if Germany were to raise formal demands for the early evacuation of the Rhineland on the basis of Article 431 of the Versailles Treaty, which provided for early evacuation in the event that Germany gave evidence of having satisfactorily complied with the treaty. Reporting these developments to the cabinet, Stresemann recommended that Germany press her claim to satisfaction under Article 431, but only after the few remaining disagreements concerning Germany's production of armaments and her defensive fortifications in the East—which Poincaré might be able to use for the purpose of undermining Germany's case—had been cleared up.[59]

Chancellor Marx's reaction to Stresemann's report reflected the reaction of the entire cabinet. Very little had been accomplished in Geneva, he observed. But all things considered, he had no reason to criticize the conduct of the delegation, and therefore he felt justified in recommending that the cabinet give its approval to the results of the Geneva consultations and to Stresemann's conduct there.

Vice-Chancellor Hergt—one of the four DNVP ministers in the cabinet—reacted only slightly more critically, attesting, by his moderation, to the DNVP's resolve to keep matters of foreign policy from disrupting the new coalition. He objected to Stresemann's decision to accept a practical compromise on the Saar question rather than to defend a legal principle. He regretted that the cabinet had not been informed of the issue in time to take a position on it before the decision was reached in Geneva. But he complimented Stresemann on his bearing as chairman of the council session, which, he asserted, had constituted a success for Germany. And neither he nor the other DNVP ministers raised objections to the cabinet communiqué confirming the government's approval of the activities in Geneva.[60] The DNVP's criticism in the meeting of the Reichstag's Foreign Affairs Committee on March 17, 1927, followed the same moderate course.[61] The DNVP leaders raised no objections concerning the general orientation of foreign policy. They only questioned the tactical decisions and pointedly mentioned the paucity of results. Even under gentle chiding by the Social Democratic spokesman, however, the Nationalists maintained their front with the government.

On the issue that occupied European foreign relations from spring to summer 1927—namely, the deterioration of relations between England and Russia—the DNVP gave virtually unfaltering support to the foreign minister. The party was in full agreement with Stresemann's resolve to avoid any diplomatic action that might infer a choice between the West and the East. German policy was determined, on the one hand, by the Locarno treaties with the Western powers and, on the other hand, by the 1926 Berlin Treaty with Russia. That treaty had been negotiated largely in order to allay Russian fears that the Locarno accords meant that Germany had moved into an anti-Soviet camp but also to keep open Germany's diplomatic flexibility. The treaty, which was the product of long negotiations that ran roughly contemporaneously with those leading to the Rhineland security pact, was initialed by Germany and the Soviet Union in Berlin on April 24, 1926. It provided for an extension of the friendly political and economic ties between the two countries, which were based on the Rapallo Pact of

1922, and it included mutual declarations of neutrality in case hostile action were undertaken against one of the contracting parties by a third power. Although the initial reaction outside Germany was sharply negative because of fears that the Russo-German agreement might conflict with Germany's proposed obligations under the League of Nations to participate in sanctions against a declared aggressor (Article 16), this reaction was short-lived. France and Great Britain rather quickly accepted Germany's explanation that the Berlin Treaty was complementary to the Locarno accords, rather than being in conflict with them. The domestic reaction was almost uniformly favorable: the treaty was approved by the Reichstag in late June 1926, with only three negative votes. The Russo-German agreement meant, in practice, that when the relations between England and Russia soured in 1927, Germany stood on good terms with both parties. Stresemann could assure the Soviets that no situation could induce Germany to join an anti-Bolshevik front. Quite the contrary, Germany was anxious to do what she could to resolve difficulties between the two disputing countries.[62] The Nationalists reacted positively to this line of policy. Otto Hoetzsch, who was frequently a spokesman for the DNVP in the Foreign Affairs Committee, labeled Stresemann's policy statements "faultless." Westarp, too, in letters to his party colleagues, supported Stresemann's neutral stance. Within the cabinet, the DNVP ministers endorsed Stresemann's policy without objection.[63]

Stresemann's scrupulous observance of neutrality in the conflict between Germany's two allies by separate treaties enhanced his country's international prestige. Both parties to the dispute turned to Germany to represent their interests. In May, Russia asked Stresemann to present her views in London. In June, Chamberlain suggested, during the meeting of the league in Geneva, that Stresemann use his good offices so as to reassure Russia that Great Britain had no bellicose designs in the dispute.[64]

The fact that both sides appealed to Stresemann to act as the "honest broker" was a testimony to the effectiveness of his foreign policy in re-establishing Germany's role in European affairs, which was all the more welcome due to the lack of any recent tangible benefits from his policy of rapprochement. In March 1927, Stresemann had intimated that evacuation of the Rhineland would not come soon, but he had promised that Germany would mount a "moral offensive" to achieve it. He had told the cabinet, however, that this moral offensive could only be pressed after the Allies had confirmed that Germany had satisfactorily disposed of her eastern fortifications. In May, moreover, he responded to a question in the cabinet from DNVP representative Martin Schiele, now minister of food and agriculture, that the appeal for early total evacuation could not be made before August or September. Although the DNVP representatives endorsed the delay, the situation was a constant embarrassment to Stresemann.[65]

In the absence of assurances regarding total evacuation, Stresemann continued to demand that the Allies reduce the number of troops in the Rhineland to conform with promises made after the signing of the Locarno accords. On May 4, 1927, in a formal diplomatic démarche, the German representative in Paris reminded Briand of those promised reductions.[66] Stresemann confronted the Western Allies with the issue at Geneva in June. During a meeting between delegates from Germany and from the countries that were represented at the Allied Conference of Ambassadors, he received the unequivocal admission from Chamberlain that the German reproaches of the Allies were fully justified. The Allies had not fulfilled their promises. France was in fact the recalcitrant power. Briand tried to excuse her failings, but Chamberlain insisted that measures be taken to satisfy Germany.[67]

Stresemann returned to Berlin without having gained anything more than assurances regarding troop reductions and a communiqué, issued in Geneva by the Locarno powers, reaffirming the Locarno policies that had, in the words of the statement, already contributed important results in the interests of peace and would continue to do so. In the altered domestic setting, this renewal of broken promises was enough to keep the Nationalist leaders content; in the cabinet and in the Reichstag they reaffirmed their support of Stresemann's conduct of foreign policy.[68]

Stresemann was not happy, nor were the Nationalists, over the recent results of the policy of rapprochement with France. Moreover, Stresemann was forced to undertake the unwelcome task of explaining to the cabinet in August 1927 that prospects for significant progress in the reconciliation were indeed bleak. The political stalemate in France between Briand and Poincaré was the real cause of the difficulties which had arisen between France and Germany. This stalemate could not be resolved before France's parliamentary elections, which were scheduled for May 1928. Despite the likelihood that German aspirations would remain unfulfilled until after these elections, Stresemann counseled against any change in German policy.[69]

The DNVP spokesman in the cabinet, Vice-Chancellor Hergt, agreed that although the present policy offered little immediate promise, no alternative was open to Germany that would be more advantageous. The specific questions that would be apt to arise at the September session of the full League Assembly, Hergt asserted, were of little consequence. Even the matter of the Rhineland occupation force—in which a reduction of ten thousand men was likely—received short shrift from Hergt, who designated it a secondary consideration (*Nebenfrage*). Moreover, he advised against making any official petition in Geneva for total evacuation of the Rhineland, since such a petition would certainly miscarry. He proposed, however, that a change of nuance in Germany's conduct and attitude might be possible and profitable. If France refused to meet German demands for evacuation of the Rhineland, Germany could underscore France's bad faith and assert Germany's own right to seek the evacuation even in the face of resistance from France.

Stresemann discouraged Hergt's suggestion. It would be unwise, he argued, to undermine cooperation with France by publicly pointing out her recalcitrance. Tactically, it would be more advantageous to give France the impression that her elections would determine Germany's position: that if the elections confirmed France's unwillingness to pursue the policy of rapprochement, then Germany would draw the appropriate conclusions.[70]

Hergt's admission that the policy being followed by Stresemann was the best alternative available to Germany and his relegation to a level of secondary importance of the question of reducing the Rhineland occupation forces illustrate how far removed the DNVP's official policy line was from the days in October 1925 when Count Westarp had declared that none of his demands were *Nebenfragen*. Despite its support for Stresemann's present conduct of foreign affairs, the DNVP could not pass up the opportunity that France was creating to point out "with appropriate calmness," as Otto Hoetzsch phrased it, that "both of the German plenipotentiaries in Locarno [Stresemann and Luther] had let themselves be deceived."[71] Accordingly, in the cabinet meeting that immediately preceded Stresemann's departure for the September session in Geneva, the DNVP minister of food and agriculture, Schiele, undertook a carefully prepared critique of Stresemann's foreign policy.[72] He noted that disappointment over the fruits of the Locarno policies ran high throughout Germany. If a public expression of this disappointment were made in Geneva, it would therefore meet with wide approval.

Stresemann protested that the written promises that the Allies had made in conjunction with Locarno had been fulfilled faithfully, with the sole exception of the unsatisfactory reduction of occupying forces. Furthermore, the oral promises concerning military inspection and control of the German aviation industry had also been observed. Any expression of German disappointment, Stresemann argued, could only be based upon France's departure from the "inner sense" of Locarno. Stresemann could not help but be aware, however, that Schiele's remarks were well founded. He parried the criticism that was implicit in them by asserting that he had intended in Geneva, in a speech on world disarmament, to voice his specific disappointment.[73]

Schiele pressed his advantage further. He quoted Stresemann's statement, which had been made long before in a discussion of the promised reduction in Rhineland occupation forces, that the "normal force" for the area could be reckoned at 45,000 to 50,000 men, to which number the Allies had formally agreed to reduce their troops. Schiele demanded that, on the basis of this figure, Germany publicly declare that the reduction of the Rhineland forces from 70,000 to 60,000, which the Allies were about to grant, left 10,000 more men in the area than could be justified by the Allied commitment in the note from the Conference of Ambassadors of November 16, 1925. Stresemann was obliged, most unwillingly, to accept Schiele's proposed declaration.[74]

Finally, Schiele extorted a promise that Stresemann would not prejudice the cabinet's freedom of decision concerning the handling of Germany's demand for total evacuation by coupling it with German concessions regarding an "eastern Locarno," an Anschluss between Germany and Austria, Allied demands for security guarantees, or reparations.[75]

Stresemann's weakened position, due to the paucity of results in the past several months from his policy of reconciliation, left him little choice but to capitulate to these restrictions upon his freedom of action in the conduct of foreign policy, restrictions the likes of which he had resisted so energetically in earlier years. The DNVP made its demands in a more effective manner than had ever characterized its approach to foreign policy before. They were well prepared, well founded, and well timed. They took account of what diplomatic practice would bear. The two public remarks, for example, were distinctive among DNVP demands by virtue of their understatement.

Stresemann executed the cabinet's instructions imposed by the DNVP in a nearly irreproachable manner during the session of the league. He protested the slow pace of German-French understanding in his private conversations with both Chamberlain and Briand. He upbraided France's military establishment for having stingily granted concessions that failed, because of their very niggardliness, to fulfill Germany's legitimate expectations. He reserved the right of the German cabinet to demand complete evacuation of the Rhineland, on the basis of Article 431 of the Versailles Treaty and free from any restrictions of a quid pro quo. And in his speech to the General Assembly he reproached the Allies with the assertion that the full flowering of the policies of reconciliation would never be realized within any country "as long as it is still exposed to foreign might."[76]

Both Briand and Chamberlain acknowledged the validity of Stresemann's complaints. Both assured him that they were still personally committed to the policy of understanding. Both, however, counseled patience. Nothing could be accomplished, they argued, and much harm might be done, by making even the most legitimate demands just as preparations for elections were getting under way in France and in England.[77]

Stresemann's report to the cabinet concerning the activities in Geneva was once again accepted as a matter of course. DNVP representative Hergt averred that this session had, in fact, provided greater positive impetus for Germany's foreign political reemergence than any previous Geneva meeting. He considered that the outcome of the conversations that Stresemann had held with the Locarno powers represented an improvement of Germany's position with regard to complete evacuation. He regretted, of course, that the troop reduction in the Rhineland was so small. He suggested that Stresemann's speech before the League Assembly might have more strongly expressed German disappointment (*Enttäuschung*—the word that Schiele had suggested and that Stresemann had avoided using) over the Allied failure to observe the spirit of the Locarno accords. He refrained from making any formal reproach, however; and his general reaction was decidedly positive.[78]

The policy of moderate, limited criticism accompanied by an acknowledgment of both the difficulties and the gains in foreign affairs, which the DNVP leadership had chosen to follow with consistency, met resistance within the party. From the very beginning of the coalition, the party's right wing had attacked the decision to enter the government, which had been made by the leaders of the delegation. The DNVP's Racist Committee (Völkischer Reichsausschuss), which was chaired by Axel von Freytagh-Loringhoven, one of the chief spokesmen of the radical Right, and which since 1922 had been a vehicle for the promotion of the ambitions of the Pan-Germans in the DNVP, had early informed Westarp that "from the national [*völkischen*] standpoint, it must be most deeply regretted that the Weimar constitution and the so-called Locarno policy have been paid recognition" by the party.[79] The committee's resolution continued by stating that those who believed in what the resolution represented had always looked to the DNVP as the standard-bearer of the patriotic (*vaterländischer*) movement, as the only party that was free from the taint of parliamentarianism and the policies of fulfillment, free from responsibility for the disaster of the Republic and ready to assume the leadership of the country when the parliamentary system and the policies of cooperation with the former enemy had crumbled.[80]

Reinhold Quaatz reproached Westarp, too, for the support that the DNVP delegation seemed to be giving to Stresemann's policies. He warned against being forced into a "false foreign political orientation, which is by the nature of things . . . more compromising for us than for the other coalition partners." The policy would one day be used against the DNVP,

Quaatz predicted. The democratic parties would charge that the German Nationalists had conducted *schlimmere Erfüllungspolitik*—that is, a more compromising policy of fulfillment—than had the Left.[81] The nationalist press—which belonged in large part to Alfred Hugenberg, who more and more came to see himself as the leader of the truly "national" opposition— also continued to make public attacks on Stresemann and his policies.[82]

But Quaatz and Freytagh-Loringhoven no longer exerted the influence on DNVP policy that they had brought so successfully to bear in the party's flight from responsibility for the security-pact negotiations in the spring and summer of 1925. Westarp paid more heed at this time to moderates, such as Otto Hoetzsch, who pointed out that attacks on Stresemann's foreign policy would weld a front of support for Stresemann from the DVP to the SPD. Westarp had given Hoetzsch a copy of an important speech on for- eign affairs and had asked him to make comments and suggestions. When Hoetzsch returned it, he wrote: "I hope with all my heart that you succeed in holding [the party] to the letter of *your* comments, which say all that is necessary from our viewpoint and [which] endanger or destroy nothing."[83]

The measured response of the moderate faction prevailed even in the face of Stresemann's admission that progress on the issue of the Polish- German border was unlikely. In December 1927 he acknowledged before the Reichstag's Foreign Affairs Committee that there was no real chance that Poland would collapse, and thus there was little likelihood of any betterment of Germany's eastern border. When he was asked how, then, Germany could hope to improve its eastern boundaries, Stresemann replied: Through friendly relations with the Western powers. Germans could gain nothing at all "if we stand alone in sharp opposition to Poland." The Ger- man Nationalists, who had railed against the "renunciation of German land and peoples" in Locarno just two years earlier, now said nothing.[84]

The Nationalist leadership's careful policy on foreign affairs hardly provided grounds for complaint from either Stresemann or the Western Allies. But the very presence of the Nationalists within the government offered Briand an excuse for not granting Germany the concessions that Stresemann was seeking. Briand had observed, at the September session of the league, that he could do nothing concerning the complete evacuation of the Rhineland until after the French elections in 1928. But even if the elections had not intervened, Briand had asserted, he would refuse to act on the matter. A concession such as evacuation could only be granted to a Grand Coalition government, Briand insisted, not to one that included German Nationalists. Strengthening the DNVP would be inimical to France's own political interests.[85]

Briand returned to the idea in conversations with Stresemann during the December meeting of the League Council. Subsequently, Stresemann broached the topic—in far subtler form—in his report to the cabinet on league affairs. Briand expected a victory of the Left in the coming French elections, Stresemann recounted. Such a victory would open the way for evacuation of the Rhine, because the policy of reconciliation, in general, and the Rhineland evacuation, in particular, had become specific parts of the Left's political program. The new French government would, of course, want to deal with a German government that had full political authority, not one that would be of questionable stability or authority because it faced imminent parliamentary elections. Stresemann's implication was clearly that the German elections—which had to be held before the end of 1928 because of the constitutional requirement to renew the Reichstag—should be advanced to the spring, so that a new cabinet could take up negotiations with France. DNVP spokesman Hergt replied to Stresemann by objecting to Briand's attempt to set the date for Germany's elections. He did not express his concern that, to the exclusion of the DNVP, Stresemann would work for the coalition that would be most advantageous to his foreign policy. Hergt only protested that the present government would certainly have to be considered perfectly capable of conducting negotiations for the evacuation of the Rhineland, since in June 1928 it would still be six months before elections would become mandatory.[86]

The necessity to test Hergt's contention or Briand's willingness to deal with a coalition that included the DNVP never arose. The coalition was already coming apart over domestic issues. By February 1928 the coalition had effectively ceased to exist. The ministers stayed on under Marx until the Reichstag was dissolved and new elections were held in May 1928. The elections confirmed a movement to the Left. The SPD emerged with 152 seats, still the strongest party in the Reichstag. The Communists made significant gains. The Middle parties suffered noticeable losses. But the most sizeable change came in the ranks of the DNVP; of the 110 seats it had controlled after December 1924, it retained only 78.[87] The coalition of 1928 to 1930 would be dominated by the Social Democrats.

By the summer of 1928 the Nationalist Party stood at the threshold of a period of self-examination which would throw into question the whole experience of the four years since 1924. But the increasing pragmatism that the party had shown, especially since early 1926, had awakened hope among the politicians of the Middle. In a letter to his cabinet colleague Otto Gessler, Labor Minister Heinrich Brauns had commented on the DNVP's predicament. The party needed "very clever leadership" to maintain its course and to overcome its internal tensions. The best development for Germany, Brauns thought, would be a split of the DNVP that would exclude

202

the radical Right. As Brauns wrote, in the summer of 1926, such a split might have served his country well, allowing the moderate Nationalists time to find their proper place in the Weimar system. The split came, not in 1926, but between 1928 and 1930. The radicals, under Alfred Hugenberg, and not the moderates, retained control of the party. Indeed, before the moderates had even completed their self-examination, time had passed them by.[88]

11

THE CONJUNCTION
OF FORCES ON BALANCE

Since May 1924 the German National People's Party had vied for center stage in German politics. After the elections of May 1928, new forces commanded the role that the DNVP had enjoyed: its most substantial, potentially constructive hour upon the stage had passed. What can one conclude?

First, certain patterns of behavior emerge which offer insight into two important facets of the history of Weimar Germany: namely, the conduct of politics by Stresemann and the evolution of the German National People's Party itself. Throughout the four years the Nationalists consistently approached foreign policy by demanding that the Allies meet certain preconditions before Germany would negotiate. The DNVP thus sought to exact prior evidence of Allied good will as the price for German cooperation in the disposition of its own fate. The attitude was basically one of petulance: if you won't play by my rules, I just won't play at all.

Stresemann, on the other hand, fought consistently and successfully for a policy of reconciliation that would be based on an adjustment of interests and a measure of trust. He sought to avoid preconditions for negotiations such as the Nationalists wished to set, but he pressed the logic of reconciliation with tenacity: the German accommodation to Allied interests could only continue—confrontation and chronic instability could only be avoided—so long as Germans received evidence that their interests were being fulfilled through the policy of reconciliation. The concessions that Stresemann insisted upon in applying this logic often corresponded to the Nationalists' demands, but the method was radically different. Stresemann's choice of means distinguishes him in the evolution of Germany's foreign policy.

In his compromises with the Nationalists in domestic politics, we also see at work the same principle that he applied to his foreign policy, the principle of mutual adjustment of interests—government, in other words, by controlled and regulated conflict. Stresemann accepted the Nationalists' desire for power as legitimate and their pressure to realize certain political objectives on behalf of their constituencies as proper. Concessions to these interests were a part of the rules of politics as he saw them. Thus, he accepted the divergence of political interests, their clash and adjustment through political activity, and their emergence in some mutually acceptable policy in which compromises had been reached but which was supportable by all concerned to the extent that their essential interests had been advanced. Such regulated conflict is a necessary component in a functional parliamentary order, and a desirable feature of an ordered international system.[1] Stresemann clearly saw such regulated conflict as a means whereby the wishes and desires of German society could be reshaped into more internationally acceptable ambitions. This willingness to struggle to reeducate his own society again distinguishes Stresemann from both his predecessors and his immediate successor.[2]

That Stresemann accepted regulated political conflict and the need for a reeducation of German society is less surprising than the degree to which he succeeded in drawing the leaders of the DNVP along with him. Indeed, the DNVP's response to Stresemann's conduct of Germany's foreign policy reveals more than a clash of approaches; for the clash forced certain accommodations from both sides. In this process, the Nationalists, as a party, adapted themselves considerably more to Stresemann's conception of foreign policy than he did to theirs. The Nationalists continued to try to set prior guidelines for negotiations, it is true, but the manner in which they did so changed significantly. In 1924, from outside the government, they loudly demanded that their seven conditions be met before Germany should accept the Dawes plan. In 1925, from within the government, they sought to impose their guidelines for Locarno. They made much in public of their insistence upon prior commitments from the Allies, although in the cabinet they had failed to impose them as preconditions to negotiations. In 1926 their tactics began to change markedly. Initially, they continued to oppose Stresemann's foreign policy, but they sought to influence it less through their public posture than through the existing institutions of government, notably the office of the president. When this failed, they began to speak of adjusting to "accomplished facts." By mid summer they let President Hindenburg know that they could accept a policy of reconciliation, and even could tolerate Stresemann himself, if that were the price of their reentry into the government. By October, after Germany had been admitted to the League of Nations, they announced publicly and quasi-officially that the party's opposition was not directed against "the aims, nor is it directed fundamentally against the path taken: Security Pact, League of Nations, Thoiry. Our negation is directed exclusively against the method applied"—that of paying numerous times for each small concession.[3]

This new, moderate position, which represented the majority opinion of the politically engaged Nationalists, characterized DNVP policy from 1926 through the summer of 1928. It was continually reaffirmed, despite internal party opposition, at party conventions and meetings of the Executive Committee. In this sense, the party's break with the Luther government over Locarno in October 1925, which has so often been depicted because of the inherent drama of the situation, must be seen as the exception rather than the rule of behavior of the German National People's Party. Between 1925 and 1928—to be sure, not without exceptions and opposition—the normal pattern of the DNVP's behavior was that of an increasing acceptance of the realities of the post-1918 international system.

This does not mean that Stresemann's foreign policy remained uninfluenced by the opposition of the DNVP. Quite the contrary, in the clash between the party and the government over foreign policy, Stresemann's freedom of action was increasingly circumscribed by the progressively more limited, pragmatic nature of the DNVP's opposition. In 1924 he managed to avoid the restrictions of the DNVP's "seven minimum demands" for the Dawes plan, while he still won domestic approval for the plan and for his foreign policy. A year later, he managed to preserve the security pact and to emasculate the DNVP's guidelines within the cabinet so that he retained his freedom of action at Locarno. But this now entailed sacrifice. The Nationalists insisted upon a reintroduction of the question of war guilt, a move that Stresemann opposed for reasons of foreign policy, but on which he finally compromised for reasons of domestic policy. Nationalist attacks upon Stresemann's alleged "renunciation of German land and peoples" and Stresemann's denials that such a renunciation existed undermined confidence in the Locarno settlement in other countries. Stresemann's original renunciation of Alsace-Lorraine had been quite straightforward. For his own diplomatic reasons he would have retained the legal phrase guaranteeeing, not the "status quo," but the current territorial distribution on the Rhine; this would have allowed peaceful reacquisition of Eupen-Malmédy with Belgian consent. But he would not have been compelled, had it not been for Nationalist opposition, to veil this initial abandonment of all claims to Alsace-Lorraine with denials that he was renouncing the land and its people.

His repeated insistence that Alsace was not worth a war and that self-determination held no hope of reunification did not compensate for the seeming equivocation on the guarantee for the Franco-German boundary.

In addition, for many Germans, Nationalist opposition obscured the real ameliorative results of Stresemann's Locarno policies, which were lost in the controversy over "preconditions" and "ramifications"—that is, over the guidelines for Locarno. This controversy, by publicizing the DNVP's guidelines, which the cabinet had never adopted, created a domestic situation in which Allied concessions, when they came, were automatically discounted. Moreover, the government abetted this situation by failing to publish the actual guidelines and by its sense of the necessity to appear to be as demanding in the national interest as was the DNVP.

Stresemann recognized the government's error retrospectively. He noted that the negotiations in Locarno had netted "one hundred percent" of what the government had expected out of the treaty, but that the cabinet's decision to try to win domestic support on the basis of the ramifications to come had been a psychological mistake. Not knowing what ramifications had been negotiated, the German people entertained false expectations, stimulated by the Nationalists' inflated "guidelines." When the promised ramifications began to take effect, the government compounded its psychological blunder by instructing the press, ostensibly to ensure against Allied complacency, but also to protect itself against Nationalist vilification, that the German government was disappointed with the results. In Stresemann's judgment, however, the ramifications "had been realized to a greater extent than any one of us had been able to imagine." The public-relations contest with the Nationalists thus helped to create an atmosphere of disappointment, which was deepened by the government's own mistaken tactics. In this inauspicious atmosphere there unfolded the most potentially significant foreign-policy victory that Germany had won since the war. "We did not have to praise our own successes," Stresemann observed, "but we ought not to have disparaged our achievements."[4]

The Nationalists did not completely surrender their influence on foreign policy when they withdrew from the cabinet in October 1925. Although their absence limited their direct intervention to halter Stresemann, their opposition gained voice in the government throughout 1926 by means of the constant interventions of Reichspresident Hindenburg. Their insistence that Germany's rejection of any implication of war guilt be communicated to the remaining signatories of the Versailles Treaty, which had been accepted by the first Luther Cabinet prior to Locarno, cropped up again in the German note of application to the League of Nations. Luther insisted that his second cabinet honor that commitment.[5] Stresemann raised the question in an unofficial and very mild form just after Germany's entry into the league, in his "Gambrinus" speech of September 21, 1926, before the German colony in Geneva. By that time, however, the gesture was unnecessary, given the DNVP's new pragmatism and its overriding desire to reenter the government.[6]

It is finally in the cabinet of 1927 that one sees the extent to which the DNVP's new pragmatism limited Stresemann's freedom of action. Martin Schiele's insistence upon guidelines for Stresemann's conduct at the Geneva session of the league in September 1927 represents a success such as the Nationalists had never won before. The slow pace of Franco-German understanding and the failure of the promise of Thoiry combined with the Nationalists' more realistic, limited criticism to make the foreign minister's position far less independent. The encounter may partially explain Stresemann's willingness to see the rightist coalition end in 1928 and his use of the otherwise flimsy argument that Briand would be unwilling to deal with a cabinet that would be incapacitated by the impending necessity for elections.

Although forced at times to give ground, Stresemann did resist Nationalist efforts to influence foreign policy. The confrontation sets his attitudes toward the politics of reconciliation in relief. He was unwilling to sacrifice cooperation with France, or even to burden it unnecessarily with nationalistic rhetoric. This conduct is revealing in the light of the controversy over Stresemann's place in German history. Those who criticize Stresemann for suspected duplicity have argued that there is an irreconcilable incompatibility between his beautiful, moving words and his public statements on peace and cooperation in Europe, on the one hand, and, on the other hand, his "hidden" words on the "cease-fire" of the Dawes plan and of Locarno, on "*finassieren,*" or the necessity to seek by subtlety and cleverness what the lack of raw power made unattainable in any other way.[7] In addition to Stresemann's words, of course, we have his actions by which to measure him. In his clashes with the Nationalists over matters of substance, such as the challenge to the entire direction of the security-pact policy during June and July 1925, these actions show that he accepted the risk of bringing down the government in order to preserve his policy. In matters of form, he accepted the burden of compromise, as over the German note on war guilt in October 1925 and on the informal guidelines of September 1927. But even in these two instances, he sought to limit the negative impact of the Nationalists' influence by softening the language of the diplomatic exchanges, in the one instance by excluding any direct mention of war guilt, in the other by voicing the reality—while avoiding the word—in expressing Germany's "disappointment" over the results of Franco-German cooperation. However one may interpret his words, these actions, when projected against the background of DNVP opposition, testify to a commitment to a foreign policy of reconciliation and adjustment.

If one concludes, then, that the Nationalists exercised no influence on the aims of German foreign policy, that they exercised only a limited influence on its rhetoric and an increasing influence in Marx's cabinet of 1927 on Stresemann's freedom of action, what can one conclude about the converse: the influence of foreign policy upon the Nationalists? Here lies the major significance of the relationship between Nationalist politics and the government's foreign policy in the period from 1924 to 1928. Clashes over foreign policy confronted the DNVP with a clear choice between ideology and practicality, between myth and reality, in a matter—namely, the image of the state's might in foreign politics—that involved the essence of the German conservative political conception in a way that grain tariffs and taxes did not. Walther Graef-Anklam acknowledged this in his essay "Der Werdegang der Deutschnationalen Volkspartei, 1918–1928" ("The course of the German National People's Party, 1918–1928") when he wrote that "in matters of foreign policy, compromise at the cost of its particular position is much less supportable for the party than it is in questions of domestic politics."[8]

After the loss of the war, the Nationalists had refused to accept the obvious fact that Germany's powerlessness in foreign affairs made cooperation and the mobilization of world moral opinion to Germany's side the only basis for her relations with the stronger Allied powers. The Nationalists insisted upon a policy of stubborn and belligerent recalcitrance in Germany's dealings with the former enemy. They rejected the policy that Stresemann pursued, a policy that evinced a readiness to meet the obligations of the Versailles Treaty in order to cooperate in revising that treaty.

When the DNVP emerged from the elections of May 1924 as the strongest party in the Reichstag and as the apparently logical cornerstone for a majority coalition, the party's leaders were convinced that their commanding position permitted them to insist upon a complete reorientation of foreign policy. They woefully overestimated their own position and completely ignored the pressure of necessity in the field of foreign affairs, which the parties of the political Center and Left felt. The parties of the Middle supported the policy of reconciliation with the Allies out of this sense of necessity. Their rejection of the Nationalist demands concerning foreign policy on the grounds that they were inimical to Germany's real interests prevented the rightist alignment to which the Nationalists aspired.

The DNVP's failure to gain access to the government during the cabinet negotiations of May and June 1924 left it with two choices. Either it could continue to oppose the conciliatory foreign policy and its immediate corollary, the Dawes plan, or it could seek some compromise that would induce the parties of the Middle to broaden the government to the Right. Through a failure of decisive leadership, the DNVP attempted to do both. It continued to denounce the Dawes plan and the cabinet's entire orientation in foreign policy as a betrayal of German honor. Simultaneously, certain of its members tried to negotiate entry into the government on the basis of some compromise over foreign policy. Left without effective direction, the more moderate members of the party and special interest groups, who were already eager to gain access to governmental power, were exposed to tremendous pressure, which was skillfully exploited by the cabinet, to accept the necessary relationship between the passage of the Dawes plan and the achievement of economic stability. This stability was the fundamental condition for the eventual reassertion of Germany's place in Europe and the world. Ultimately, nearly half of the DNVP's Reichstag delegation, rebelling against the lack of political realism that the party leaders had displayed, voted for the Dawes plan.

The split over the Dawes-plan vote in August 1924 laid bare the fundamental divergence between those Nationalists who were willing to come to terms with the political realities of the moment and those who were not. The former hoped to advance the cause of German nationalism by joining the government and modifying it to match their ideals or to satisfy their interests. The latter were determined to destroy the government and the Republic, even if doing so would mean leaving the DNVP or destroying it by purging it of its "weaker" elements. In the innerparty struggle that immediately followed the vote on the Dawes plan, the moderates emerged as the dominant element. They urged the party to accept the *fait accompli* of the Dawes plan and to work to shape execution of it so that it would conform with Nationalist interests. Finally, in January 1925, they led the party into the government.

But in 1925, as in 1924, the demands imposed by foreign policy proved more than the DNVP could bear. When Stresemann's initiative concerning a Rhineland security pact first became known, the DNVP leaders, who were then headed by Count Westarp, tried to minimize the significance of the initiative. Interested in maintaining and exploiting the influence that the party then enjoyed over domestic economic and tariff policy, the leadership groups—both in the party's national structure and in the Reichstag delegation—strung along with the government in its negotiations with France, Great Britain, and Belgium, hoping all the while that they would be saved from assuming full responsibility for the policies by their ultimate failure. The leadership of the party muted its criticism in the Foreign Affairs Committee. It accepted a formula for compromise within the cabinet. It even tried to curb the personal attacks on Stresemann in the radical-right-wing press.

To the radicals, however, the slightest hint that the party shared responsibility for policies of rapprochement was unacceptable. Starting in local DNVP committees and the provincial press, they began a campaign to undermine confidence in Stresemann. They intimated that he had never fully informed the cabinet of his proposals for a Rhineland security pact. They insinuated that the Nationalist members of the cabinet, not having been informed, could not be held responsible.

This attempt to excuse the DNVP of any complicity in the policies regarding a security pact was not immediately adopted by the DNVP leaders. When in June, however, the French government showed signs of real interest in the security-pact proposals, the DNVP's leaders in the Reichstag found it expedient to espouse this argument. They claimed that Stresemann's memorandum had drastically forfeited German interests and that Stresemann alone was answerable. Outmaneuvered by the politically dexterous foreign minister, however, who forced them to choose between accepting the responsibility for the security-pact policies or for the breakup of the coalition, the DNVP leaders trimmed their sails. They endorsed Stresemann's reply to the French note, claiming that their efforts had regained for Germany the vital interests that Stresemann had been prepared to bargain away. The reply, they rationalized, created a new basis for negotiations concerning Rhineland security.

The DNVP leaders had reached a critical stage of political development. They accepted the desirability of preserving the coalition with the republican government, but they still hoped to avoid paying the price. Westarp, as chairman of the DNVP's Reichstag delegation and de facto leader of the nationwide party organization as well, personified the dilemma. In 1924 he had been cool to the idea of entering a government coalition. The Middle parties, he then argued, would never be willing to accord the Nationalists the influence that was commensurate with their ambitions. By mid 1925 he was convinced enough of the value of participation to urge his party's spokesman in the cabinet, Martin Schiele, to preserve the arrangement as long as possible. Yet he refused to take the obvious step that would be necessary in order to secure the Nationalist position within the coalition. He refused to bow to the imperatives of foreign policy. He steadfastly refused to divorce the party from the radical nationalistic element that mounted almost continuous attacks on Stresemann, because he saw, in this "patriotic [*vaterländischer*] movement, healing elements that ought not to be destroyed."[9]

Westarp's practical conduct of Nationalist policy amounted to a decision

211

all the same, a decision to tolerate reconciliation in order to preserve Nationalist influence within the government. Throughout August and September 1925, therefore, the Nationalist leaders raised diplomatically impossible demands and conditions within the cabinet, but they never pushed them to the breaking point. In the cabinet they compromised, but throughout the land they proclaimed that their demands and conditions had been accepted by the government, that Nationalist guidelines circumscribed Germany's position in the negotiations, and that if these guidelines were not fully satisfied, the DNVP would refuse to support the security pact.

When, despite the obstacles that the Nationalists had raised, Stresemann succeeded in negotiating a security pact, the situation became critical once again for the DNVP's leaders. The accord did not come anywhere near meeting the expectations that they had falsely created among their constituents. On the other hand, it fulfilled nearly all of the cabinet's official but secret guidelines. The DNVP leaders thus stood between the party, to which they had promised too much, and the government, which had delivered too much. Any decision would betray one side or the other. Westarp and his closest advisors in the DNVP's Reichstag delegation therefore proposed to postpone any decision at all. They would reject the Locarno treaties *as negotiated*, but remain in the coalition until the treaties came before the Reichstag. To their coalition partners they thus implied that they might accept the treaties if they were renegotiated so as to meet the Nationalists' objections. Before the party they insisted that they could best hope to modify the treaties by exerting influence from within the government and that if their influence did not effect the changes that they demanded, they would lead the party to the unanimous rejection of the accords in the Reichstag.

Once again, this amounted to a practical decision in favor of the government—continued toleration for continued influence. The radicals recognized the implications of this conduct, and they abhorred them. Since they were opposed to the coalition in any event, they saw no justification for remaining in it after it had failed to satisfy their injured national pride. By playing upon the memory of the leadership fiasco surrounding the vote on the Dawes plan, they undermined any feeling of confidence that the DNVP leaders could hold the Reichstag delegation solidly together on a showdown vote over the Locarno accords. Working through the party's local committees, over which they had built considerable influence during the previous year, they induced the party's Executive Committee to demand that the DNVP Reichstag delegation break with the government immediately. To preserve some semblance of Nationalist unity, Westarp withdrew the delegation from the coalition, and the DNVP ministers left the cabinet.

The Locarno treaties, like the Dawes plan, had exposed the DNVP's internal disarray. Although a majority of the members of the DNVP's Reichstag delegation favored compromise on foreign policy in order to maintain their influence in the government, Westarp could not bring himself to tear the fabric of the party irrevocably. To placate the radicals, in the Reichstag debates he adopted a policy of absolute opposition to the Locarno accords.

But party unity could no more be preserved by strident opposition than it could have been by acceptance of the Locarno treaties. One or the other of the party's opposing factions would be dissatisfied in either case. The experience of 1925 had made it clear to the DNVP's leaders, moreover, that Nationalist influence was more effectively wielded to the advantage of a broader range of interests when the DNVP was in the government than when it was in opposition. Westarp became convinced that coalition politics had to take precedence if the party ever hoped to modify the government's orientation. The stand that the party had taken on Locarno and the immediate consequence, Germany's entry into the League of Nations, precluded any immediate return to the coalition. However, once she had entered the league and once the Locarno treaties had become "accomplished facts" of German foreign policy, the party would be able to accept them with less embarrassment, and the way to coalition would be open.

The failure of the League of Nations to admit Germany in March 1926 pushed Westarp and the party's leadership one step further. Unable to argue that entry into the league was an accomplished fact, they finally adopted the most politically pragmatic approach of all: the majority that supported entry into the league was secure; this made the government's policy regarding the league a foregone conclusion. Therefore, the DNVP would bow to the inevitable. For the first time, the party began to display an element of realism in its reaction to foreign policy. It refrained from attacking Stresemann for the Eupen-Malmédy disappointment in August 1926, because it was more concerned with reentering the government than with calling Stresemann to account. It tried to level only well-founded criticism at the Thoiry proposals, and it even attempted to control the natural urge to say, "I told you so," when the settlement that was discussed there failed to materialize.

Finally, through a combination of fortuitous events and its own new pragmatism, the DNVP reentered the government in January 1927. It pledged its acceptance of the treaties of Locarno and the foreign policy of reconciliation and understanding that they represented. It is undeniably clear that the diplomatic events of 1927 never challenged this resolve in the way in which the Dawes plan or the Locarno accords would have. Nonetheless, the commitment was maintained throughout a year in which the policy of rapprochement brought practically no tangible ameliorations for

Germany, a situation in which the acceptance of the policy was continually attacked by the radical element within the party. But by 1927 the Nationalist leaders seemed to have come to the realization that opposition to the policy of rapprochement was politically futile. The only way to bring Nationalist influence to bear on that or any other policy was by participating in its formulation and execution.

Thus, in each confrontation since early 1925 over the foreign policy of reconciliation with the former "enemy," the leaders of the DNVP chose to compromise their opposition in principle in order to retain or regain political influence. In view of the disappointments that Germany had suffered in foreign policy—the London ultimatum, the disposition of Upper Silesia, the Ruhr incursion, the nonevacuation of the Cologne zone of occupation—it is no great wonder that men who valued might as the essence of the state were slow to convert to the new attitude. Given their conservative backgrounds and the psychological distances that they had to cover, the surprising feature is that they were able to come as far as they did. By the summer of 1926 the party had developed a theory of responsible opposition that was fully consonant with a parliamentary system. Its task consisted, not in fighting government policy tooth and nail, but rather, in "proceeding from the established facts to indicate a direction, to advance in that direction, and thereby to bring government foreign policy around to this direction. . . . The opposition accepts as unquestionable that the government desires the best" for the country. The party further perceived that the European balance could not be restored by military might, "but rather, by placing our economic power as producers and consumers in the scales. But for that we must be free! Free not only from the Dawes obligations and from the occupation," but from all of the restrictions of the Versailles Treaty.[10] Here, indeed, is a conception of the role of Germany's economic potential and a pragmatism in foreign policy that sounds more characteristic of Stresemann than of the *Korrespondenz der Deutschnationalen Volkspartei*, where it actually appeared.[11]

At a minimum, then, one can conclude from this series of incidents that Stresemann had won converts in the DNVP to his conception of limited revision of the Versailles settlement based on conciliation and adjustment of interests. This conclusion is all the more significant in view of the criticism that has so often been leveled against the Weimar system—namely, that its failures were a "direct consequence of the nature of German political parties, their unwillingness to form coalitions and to compromise, their rigid ideological stance, their preoccupation with prestige, and their authoritarian tradition."[12] Although the movement was halting, weak, and ultimately unsuccessful, there is clear evidence that the men who led the DNVP in the middle years of the Republic were drawing away from this traditional pattern. A parliamentary consensus on foreign policy was emerging, one that was based on adjustable interest rather than on prestige or ideology, one that included the DNVP. The series of encounters with the government over foreign policy forced the Nationalist Party's leadership to modify its political conduct and to face more directly Germany's postwar situation.

As the Nationalist leaders began to demythologize their treatment of foreign policy and to move from questions of honor to questions of advantage, they began to discover that the state and the system—and even the conduct of foreign policy by Stresemann—were compatible with their nationalist aims. Power, however, to influence the state, the system, and foreign policy existed only for those who came to terms with the "established facts." The Nationalists never abandoned their desire to permeate the state with their conservative ideology, to reform what Schlange-Schöningen still called "this impossible system," against which he had plotted only two years earlier. More and more, however, they abandoned any idea of violent change. Plans for a *Putsch*, Schlange declared in the same speech in which he called the system impossible—which was delivered in May 1926, at a moment when the Pan-Germanists were actively considering a coup d'état— would be "madness, a crime." Reform had to take place within the system itself, through "a gradual transformation to a reasonable foundation."[13]

Westarp, too, who had supported the Kapp *Putsch* in 1920, now rejected the overthrow of the existing system. When Heinrich Class urged him in early 1927 to "go the limit"—that is, to establish himself as chancellor and to "save Germany"—Westarp replied that the current situation allowed no "grand designs" and that one must be content to govern in peace and respectability, to prevent attacks upon the Reichswehr, to improve the lot of civil servants, and to "purify" the administration of justice.[14] In later, more critical times, he added: "The thought that things must get worse, indeed very bad, before they get better may be a hard and bitter recognition of fact. As a maxim of political conduct, the thought must be rejected. . . . For the hope that the Phoenix will rise up from the ashes is groundless."[15]

In light of this evolution, one ought not to speak of *lernunfähigen* ("incorrigible") Nationalists without pointing out that the label applies only to a part of the DNVP, and not even to the dominant part during the middle years of the republic. Further, when one criticizes Stresemann for trying to win Nationalists to the support of a foreign policy that they allegedly neither could nor would tolerate, one overlooks Stresemann's success in winning a good measure of support or toleration from the Nationalists, even in spite of themselves. It is equally inaccurate—or at best misleading—to say that the more reasonable German foreign policy became, the greater the cleft between it and the obdurate and rigorously expressed opinion of the Nationalists. None of these statements has been taken from a study that has the Nationalists as its focus of attention; still, they illustrate the prevalent but inaccurate judgment that the Nationalist position remained static; they ignore the fundamental ferment that was in progress on the political Right.[16]

A convincing argument that such a fundamental ferment was in progress cannot be constructed exclusively on such statements as those made by Schlange-Schöningen and Westarp. Confirmation lies not in words alone but in actions, in this case in the series of actions that constitutes the relationship between the government and the German National People's Party during the middle years of the Weimar Republic. The years from 1924 to 1928 were not a "period of stagnation" if one looks at the political decisions of the German Nationalist leadership rather than at the ideological development of "young conservatism."[17] For these decisions trace an increasingly pragmatic, tolerant approach to both foreign policy and the Weimar Republic. As within the Reichswehr, the question became progressively less one of republic versus monarchy, but one of whose republic and what sort of republic.[18] Whose republic? Not Liebknecht's or even Scheidemann's, but "ours." What sort? Not socialistic, but capitalistic and authoritarian, one with which, but for accidents of time and place, the Charles de Gaulle of 1958 might have been contented. Such may not be the republic that the historian would have wished for Germany. But such a preference ought not to obscure the practical political development that the DNVP experienced. It is, after all, one thing to regret a development that does not fulfill our hopes; it is quite another thing to explain it. Only by ignoring the middle years and the decisions that were made during them can one describe German Nationalist behavior during the Weimar Republic as a "flight into myth."[19] It may be true that Stresemann's policies encouraged some Germans to persist in having dangerous illusions concerning revision.[20] On balance, however, evidence for the opposite is stronger, that Stresemann's policies and his defense of them in domestic politics promoted an abandonment of dangerous illusions.

Flight into myth was, of course, still possible. As the party leadership had deemotionalized its myths by practical compromise, it had neglected to fill the void thus created and to educate its rank and file to the necessity of the change. Many followers were thus left with outmoded concepts in the form of campaign slogans that no longer conformed to the positions that the party had adopted in practice. The moderate leadership thus failed to translate its own growing pragmatism and retreat from myth into a rank-and-file movement. It failed to understand the imperatives of party organization and operation. But this lack of perception is hardly unique to the DNVP moderates. The understanding of mass party politics was in its infancy everywhere in the 1920s and 1930s.[21] In this regard, Hugenberg proved to be little better equipped than Westarp, as the ultimate fortunes of the DNVP in the face of National Socialism demonstrate.

Indicative of both the extent of the evolution that the DNVP's policy had undergone and of the inner contradictions that this development accentuated within the party is an exchange of letters between Count Westarp and a provincial party officer, Professor Dr. Eduard Engel, who was a literary historian, author, and stylistic reformer. In January 1928 Engel wrote to protest, by his resignation from the party, the DNVP's complicity in the government's foreign policy, "which consists of withdrawing from any manly deed and submitting endlessly to the disgrace of the occupation of German soil." In order to stop the erosion of support for the party in the land, which its cooperation in the government had provoked, Engel proposed dramatic action. The party must demand that Germany boycott the League of Nations as long as the occupation endured; such an act, "after a year of nonaction," might still save the situation. Westarp, in a polite reply, rejected Engel's plan of action: "The radical means of boycotting the League of Nations until the Rhineland is evacuated, which you suggested, would find no majority in the Reichstag, and without such a majority, politics cannot be conducted under the existing system. Our duty must be to turn the policies of the foreign minister as far as possible in the direction that you and I desire, of manly insistence upon Germany's rights."

Westarp's letter gives an unguarded indication of the extent to which he was willing to accept the political realities of the Weimar system. It evoked an impassioned denunciation from Engel: "Germany's misfortune has long been the belief that in the life of the nation, prudence is the greatest source of strength. It is useful, to be sure, but there are two more powerful forces—a sense of honor and courage. There have been more prudent men than Bismarck—but no one more courageous or more sensitive to honor. With 'honor at stake,' there must prudence be silent about any lack of a Reichstag majority for the absolutely essential measures that honor demands. If our ministers feel that it is against the honor of Germany and the dignity of man to sit down at table—for negotiations or for dinner—with the slaveholders of our people, then the participation in negotiations in Geneva *must* cease."[22]

This exchange between Westarp and Engel illustrates how far the party had come since the dilemma that the elections of May 1924 had posed. The two questions related to that dilemma were: Can the DNVP work for and within a state that it formally rejects? and How far can it go in making concessions to potential partners? The answer to the first had been given: Yes, it can work within the state; indeed, it must. The opposition to the state had been rhetorically maintained but practically abandoned. The second practical response was: The party can go very far indeed, to the point of sublimating ideological aversion in exchange for practical influence; for only in this course lay even the possibility of modifying the state so that it would approach the desires of German nationalism. Not all the consequences of these answers had been worked out, but the direction, at least, had been set.

That direction did not hold, of course; for others were prepared to speak to Engel's desires in a way that Westarp no longer could. In the summer of 1928 such forces coalesced around Hugenberg and prepared to wrest control of the party from the moderates. The Hugenberg circle had given much time to organizing its attack. An article by Walter Lambach gave them the perfect pretext. In the article, Lambach suggested that monarchism's appeal was limited and fading and that republican conservatives ought to be welcomed openly into the DNVP. This article meant that the attack could be launched against Lambach and the repudiation of monarchism rather than directly against Westarp and his leadership of the party. But even with its organization and this excellent pretext, the victory of the radicals was by no means certain. It came only because of the lassitude of Count Westarp—perhaps the psychological costs of cutting the last ties with that antebellum world which the radicals invoked were too great —and because of the mishandling of the situation by his lieutenants. Moreover, it surprised Hugenberg's supporters. Hugenberg's election to the chairmanship of the party in October 1928 came, not because of any ground swell of support for his position, but because a small, dedicated group of organizers worked hard for it with a single-mindedness that the moderates lacked. Even then, Hugenberg won only because Westarp refused to stand against him for the party chairmanship. Although he was the only candidate, Hugenberg won by only the slightest of margins.[23] The victory stirred more doubts than enthusiasm among the newspapers that were independent of Hugenberg's control but were generally sympathetic to the DNVP.[24] Most western German industrialists had opposed Hugenberg's election and continued to oppose his actions as chairman of the party.[25]

Finally, Hugenberg's victory did not represent any wave of the future. He was no more successful as a leader of a mass party than Westarp had been. Indeed, he led the party, as his critics and opponents within it feared and predicted, "durch Reinheit zur Kleinheit" (through purity to insignificance). Over half of the seventy-eight delegates who remained after the elections of May 1928 left the party over the next two years. Rather than uniting into an effective political force, which they might have become had they retained control of the DNVP apparatus, they fragmented into a variety of competing and ill-organized groups whose story is one of tragic ineffectiveness.[26] Under Hugenberg the DNVP continued to decline, ending its days as a minor support to the Nazi Juggernaut.

Certainly, the moderate domination of the DNVP in the middle years of the republic was only an interlude, but for that matter, so was all of Weimar.[27] In a more important sense, it was an opportunity, not fulfilled in its own time, but an important sign in Germany's past of a possible future divergent from the one that we know she took in 1933. If, in the short run, the radical fanatics of the Hugenberg wing proved more politically "relevant,"[28] in the longer short run of fifty, rather than five, years, the DNVP's moderate phase becomes more relevant to the emergence, in the post-1945 political life, of three political blocks within the Bonn Republic's parliamentary system: the SPD (in a much modified form), a "liberal" Middle (periodically and prematurely described as "dying"), and a pragmatic, nondenominational, Christian national party, in which moderate conservatives and former German Nationalists have found a home since its organization. In this context, the "episode" of moderate leadership may be more than an isolated phenomenon and may instead form part of a continuity that bears further exploration. Bonn is not Weimar, to be sure. But perhaps it owes more to Weimar and to the experience of German conservatism in the Weimar years than has thus far been acknowledged.

This study proposed, not to resolve the riddle of the dissolution of the DNVP, but to examine the relationship between that party and the government over the policy of reconciliation during the middle years of the Weimar Republic. In so doing, however, the conclusion becomes inescapable that, if there is a causal line to be found from Versailles to Hitler, it passes only tangentially through the Deutschnationale Volkspartei and the men who led it from 1924 to 1928. They had tried at first to reorient German foreign policy, but they failed. They had then tried to limit Gustav Stresemann's freedom of action, and in this they succeeded a little. They affected the rhetoric but seldom the substance of foreign policy. And ultimately they accepted it. In so doing, they also came to terms with the existing state and recognized the necessity of working for their goals within the framework of the Weimar system.

No historian ignores the divisions that plagued the German Left before and during the Weimar Republic, or minimizes their significance in explaining what did and did not happen after the war. The distinctions on the Right are equally important: like so many socialists before them, the men who led the DNVP during the middle years of the republic had become gradualists, as apt to support the republic as to oppose it—a fact that is worth recognizing in the tortuous history of German democracy. The causes of the demise of the Weimar system are to be found less among these men than around them; they had come a long way, if still not far enough to save their country from disaster.

Yet, even if the causal line touches them only tangentially, the German Nationalists of the middle years cannot escape entirely from responsibility for what followed. Their dilemma illustrates the fragility of democracy in its Weimar setting. These moderate conservatives *might* have become a stabilizing force in a conservative republic—but they did not. Westarp *might* have defeated Hugenberg for the party chairmanship—but he did not. In fact, he did not even stand! This collective and individual failure to accept and implement the logical extension of the practices that had dominated the few years before 1928—this failure, in effect, to develop a workable strategy for participation in existing institutions, a strategy that was compatible with the values of the conservative tradition, as well as adaptable to the changes of the day—closed off one possibility for a brighter future. This indecisiveness in the face of change proved most profoundly unconservative. Moreover, this indecisiveness and political ineptitude, which was shown by the moderate conservatives in the face of the challenge of the radical Hugenberg wing, offers a depressing preview of the ultimate ineffectiveness of the Hugenberg-Papen-Hindenburg combination in their competition with Hitler. If only by their indecisiveness, then, the moderate Nationalists contributed to the early drift toward fascism. Among those who were responsible, Count Westarp's role—which reaffirms the significance of individual decisions in history—bears closer examination than this study can afford it.

Foresight, Hajo Holborn has written, is one of the main qualities that distinguish the statesman from the mere political professional. But a statesman, however gifted, cannot foresee the future and the trends that will dominate it; thus, 'his foresight of future developments can often express itself only by cautious attempts at keeping the way open for an evolution of new forces."[29] Early in his career as foreign minister, Stresemann had recognized the irreconcilable contradictions within the DNVP. He had hoped that those "führende Köpfe," those leading men among the Nationalists, who, he felt, thought and acted as true statesmen do, could be won to the support of his foreign policy, to the support of the republic, providing it ultimately with a respectable conservative political force. His assessment of both the contradictions and the possibilities proved correct; his ability to exploit them to the republic's advantage, far more limited. Still, he sought to keep the way open for a more positive evolution of forces.

Unfortunately, it took Westarp much longer to recognize the irreconcilability of the conflicts within his own party. From 1925 to 1928, certainly, the competing wings of the German National People's Party had nothing in common but a name. Westarp was perhaps psychologically incapable of exerting the leadership that would have been necessary in order to dissolve even that tenuous tie. Party unity remained his principal concern, and he succeeded in preserving a semblance of it—at least until it cost him his position of leadership. If he was slow to learn that one could be respectable and conservative within the republican system, he was even slower to admit the obvious irreconcilability of his position with that of his successor, Hugenberg. By the time he did, the party was no longer the party he had led, and any chance to contribute constructively to the maintenance of the Republic had passed. By 1930, when Westarp finally resigned from the DNVP, too many options had been closed off. Time was running out—for the DNVP, for the Weimar Republic, and for Germany.

APPENDIX: DNVP LEADERSHIP

DNVP *Fraktionsvorstand*, June 1924

Source: *Korrespondenz der Deutschnationalen Volkspartei*, no. 87 (June 30, 1924).

As *Vorsitzende*:
   Hergt, Oskar
   Tirpitz, Alfred von
As *Stellvertretende Vorsitzende*:
   Westarp, Kuno Graf von
   Schultz-Bromberg, Georg
   Behrens, Franz
As *Geschäftsführer*:
   Lambach, Walther
   Budjuhn, Gustav
   Hensel, Paul
Members:
   Behm, Margarete
   Biener, Franz Hermann
   Bruhn, Wilhelm
   Goldacker, Hans von
   Hugenberg, Alfred
   Lind, Heinrich
   Malkewitz, Gustav
   Mumm, Reinhard
   Schiele, Martin
   Weilnböck, Luitpold

Ex officio, as president of the Reichstag:
    Wallraf, Max
Ex officio, as *Schriftenführer* in the Reichstag:
    Laverrenz, Wilhelm
    Philipp, Albrecht
    Schulze-Frankfurt/Oder, Paul

DNVP *Parteileitung*, elected February 21, 1925

Source: *Korrespondenz der Deutschnationalen Volkspartei*, no. 46 (February 24, 1925).

As *Vorsitzender*:
    Winckler, Johann Friedrich
As *Stellvertretende Vorsitzende*:
    Wallraf, Max
    Dietrich, Hermann
    Kries, Wolfgang von
As *Mitglieder*:
    Meyer-Magdeburg, ———
    Westarp, Kuno Graf von
    Graef-Anklam, Walther
    Hilpert-München, Hans
    Hergt, Oskar
    Tirpitz, Alfred von
    Gürtner-München, Franz
    Behrens, Franz
    Hugenberg, Alfred
    Baecker, Paul
    Behm, Margarete
    Behr-Behrenhoff, Graf Carl
    Graef-Thüringen, Walter
    Beisswänger, Gustav
    Rippel, Otto
    Lehmann, Annagrete

DNVP *Parteileitung*, 1926

Source: Forschungsstelle für die Geschichte des Nationalsozialismus in Hamburg, Nachlass Diller, 11/D9.

As *Vorsitzender*:

Westarp, Kuno Graf von
As *Ehrenvorsitzender*:
Tirpitz, Alfred von
As *Stellvertretende Vorsitzende*:
Wallraf, Max
Schlange-Schöningen, Hans
As *Geschäftsführendes Vorstandsmitglied*:
Jacobi, ———
As *Schatzmeister*:
Widenmann, Wilhelm
As *Politischer Bevollmächtigter*:
Treviranus, Gottfried Reinhold
As *Hauptgeschäftsführer*:
Weiss, Max
As *Vorsitzender der Preussischen Landtagsfraktion*:
Winckler, Johann Friedrich
As *Vorsitzender der Reichstagsfraktion*:
Schultz-Bromberg, Georg [*sic*]
As *Vorsitzender der Bayrischen Landtagsfraktion*:
Hilpert, Hans
As *Vorsitzender der Sächsischen Landtagsfraktion*:
Hofmann, ———
As *Staatsrat*:
Gayl, Wilhelm Freiherr von
Elected members:
Baecker, Paul
Behm, Margarete
Behrens, Franz
Behr-Behrenhoff, Graf Carl
Beisswänger, Gustav
Gürtner, Franz
Graef-Anklam, Walther
Graef-Thüringen, Walter
Hergt, Oskar
Hugenberg, Alfred
Lehmann, Annagrete
Rippel, Otto
Dietrich, Hermann
Kries, Wolfgang von
Koch, Wilhelm
Schiele, Martin
Goldacker, Hans von

NOTES

Some Abbreviations Used in the Notes

AA	Auswärtiges Amt, Bonn
BA	Bundesarchiv, Koblenz
FS	Sicherheitsfrage
FS-Hamburg	Forschungsstelle für die Geschichte des Nazional-sozialismus in Hamburg
GStA, München, MA	Bavaria, Geheimes Staatsarchiv, München, Akten des Ministeriums des Äusserns
KDnVP	*Korrespondenz der Deutschnationalen Volkspartei*
NL Luther	Hans Luther's Papers
NL Maltzan	Ago von Maltzan's Papers
NL Seeckt	Hans von Seeckt's Papers
NL Stresemann	Gustav Stresemann's Papers
NL Westarp	Count Kuno von Westarp's Papers
NsäStA	Niedersächsisches Staatsarchiv
RM	Büro des Reichsministers
StS	Büro des Staatssekretärs
VM	Stresemann's *Vermächtnis*
ZStA	Zentrales Staatsarchiv, formerly Deutsches Zentral-archiv

Chapter 1

1. The description is from Louis P. Lochner, *Always the Unexpected: A Book*

227

of Reminiscences (New York: Macmillan, 1956), pp. 135–36, as quoted in Otto Friedrich, *Before the Deluge: A Portrait of Berlin in the 1920's* (New York: Avon Books, 1973), pp. 324–25. For a description of the format of the conferences see Julius Curtius, *Sechs Jahre Minister der deutschen Republik* (Heidelberg: Carl Winter Universitätsverlag, 1948), pp. 149–50.

2. In connection with the current debate over continuity and discontinuity in German foreign policy, the question of whether Stresemann aimed at world power or at a more limited European great-power status becomes significant. For a brief excursion into this question see Robert P. Grathwol, "Stresemann Revisited," *European Studies Review* 7 (1977): 341–52. More generally on Stresemann's foreign policy of reconciliation see my "Gustav Stresemann: Reflections on His Foreign Policy," *Journal of Modern History* 45 (1973): 52–70.

3. Werner Weidenfeld, *Die Englandpolitik Gustav Stresemanns* (Mainz: von Hase & Koehler, 1972), p. 111; Michael-Olaf Maxelon, *Stresemann und Frankreich: Deutsche Politik der Ost-West-Balance* (Düsseldorf: Droste Verlag, 1972), pp. 88–89.

4. Maxelon, *Stresemann*, p. 26 and passim for subsequent paragraphs.

5. Ibid., p. 50.

6. Ibid., p. 102.

7. Ibid., pp. 85–90.

8. Ibid., pp. 88–89.

9. Grathwol, "Gustav Stresemann," *JMH* 45: 52–70; Martin Walsdorff, *Westorientierung und Ostpolitik: Stresemanns Russlandpolitik in der Locarno-Ära* (Bremen: Schünemann Universitätsverlag, 1971), pp. 22–23.

10. This is a very free paraphrase; nevertheless, it captures the sense of a passage from Stresemann's letter to Prince Wilhelm of September 7, 1925. The letter, which is most easily accessible in Gustav Stresemann, *Vermächtnis: Der Nachlass in drei Bänden*, ed. Henry Bernhard, 3 vols. (Berlin: Im Verlag Ullstein, 1932–33), 1:390 (hereafter cited as *VM*, with volume and page numbers), and the controversy that has surrounded it are discussed in detail in Grathwol, "Gustav Stresemann," *JMH* 45:54–61.

11. Weidenfeld, *Englandpolitik*, pp. 145–49; Walsdorff, *Westorientierung*, pp. 42–48; Edgar Vincent, First Viscount D'Abernon, *An Ambassador of Peace*, 3 vols. (London: Hodder & Stoughton, 1929–30), 2:141–42, 234, 3:27–28. The American edition, *The Diary of an Ambassador*, has different pagination.

12. Erich Kordt, *Nicht aus den Akten* (Stuttgart: Union Deutsche Verlagsgesellschaft, 1950), p. 32. On Gaus, see Walsdorff, *Westorientierung*, pp. 47–48.

13. Auswärtiges Amt, Bonn, Politisches Archiv (hereafter referred to as AA), Büro des Staatssekretärs (hereafter StS), FS (Sicherheitsfrage), vol. 1, E124815–21, Gaus [?] to Bülow, January 12, 1925, with Anlage. I am indebted to Professor Peter Krüger, University of Marburg, for calling this

228

reference to my attention. See also F. G. Stambrook, "'Das Kind'—Lord D'Abernon and the Origins of the Locarno Pact," *Central European History* 1 (1968): 254. Subsequent citations of the documents of the German Foreign Office will be abbreviated; thus the citation above would appear as: AA StS FS/2, E124815–21. For the archival designation Büro des Reichsministers the abbreviation RM will be used.

14. Hajo Holborn, "Diplomats and Diplomacy in the Early Weimar Republic," in *The Diplomats, 1919–1939*, ed. Gordon Craig and Felix Gilbert (Princeton, N.J.: Princeton University Press, 1953), p. 151; Ludwig Zimmermann, *Deutsche Aussenpolitik in der Ära der Weimarer Republik* (Göttingen: Musterschmidt-Verlag, 1958), pp. 37–38; Ernst Geigenmüller, "Botschafter von Hoesch und die Räumungsfrage," *Historische Zeitschrift* 200 (1965): 606–20.

15. Weidenfeld, *Englandpolitik*, pp. 150–52, 154; Holborn, "Diplomats," p. 152.

16. Hans Luther, *Politiker ohne Partei* (Stuttgart: Deutsche Verlags-Anstalt, 1960), pp. 345–46.

17. Peter Haungs, *Reichspräsident und parlamentarische Kabinettsregierung: Eine Studie zum Regierungssystem der Weimarer Republik in den Jahren 1924 bis 1929* (Cologne and Opladen: Westdeutscher Verlag, 1968), pp. 267–70 and passim.

18. Ibid., pp. 270–71; Michael Stürmer, *Koalition und Opposition in der Weimarer Republik, 1924–1928* (Düsseldorf: Droste Verlag, 1967), pp. 135 ff., 149 ff.

19. Annelise Thimme, *Flucht in den Mythos: Die Deutschnationale Volkspartei und die Niederlage von 1918* (Göttingen: Vandenhoeck & Ruprecht, 1969), p. 76, for the quotation, and passim for a stimulating exploration of the Nationalist world of myth which is sketched briefly in the following paragraphs.

20. "Revolution" is perhaps as misleading a word in this context as "stability," but for two studies that portray the ferment of the middle years of the Weimar Republic see Charles S. Maier, *Recasting Bourgeois Europe: Stabilization in France, Germany and Italy in the Decade after World War I* (Princeton, N.J.: Princeton University Press, 1975), pp. 421 ff., and Gian Enrico Rusconi, *La crisi di Weimar: Crisi di sistema e sconfitta operaia* (Turin: Einaudi, 1977), passim, but esp. pp. 37–70, in which he shows that the incidence of conflict between workers and employers remained high even after economic stabilization, because the owners tried to regain through lockouts what had been conceded in earlier confrontations.

21. The social composition of the party is described in Wolfgang Ruge, "Deutschnationale Volkspartei (DNVP), 1918–1933" (hereafter cited as "DNVP"), in *Die bürgerlichen Parteien in Deutschland*, ed. Dieter Fricke, 2 vols. (Berlin: Verlag Enzyklopädie Leipzig, 1968), 1:721–22; but see also Werner Liebe, *Die Deutschnationale Volkspartei, 1918–1924* (Düsseldorf: Droste Verlag, 1956), pp. 15–18; and Attila Chanady, "The Disintegration

of the German National Peoples' Party, 1924–1930," *Journal of Modern History* 39 (1967): 66–69.

22. Ruge, "DNVP," p. 721.

23. Generally, see Chanady, "Disintegration," *JMH* 39:67–68; for a list of the RLB members from the DNVP Reichstag delegation see *Die Organisation des Reichslandbundes* (Berlin: Reichs-Landbund-Verlag, 1927), pp. 271–74.

24. Quoted in Liebe, *Deutschnationale Volkspartei*, p. 51.

25. Lewis Hertzman, *DNVP: Right-Wing Opposition in the Weimar Republic, 1918–1924* (Lincoln: University of Nebraska Press, 1963), pp. 113–14, 180–81.

26. No study of the DNVP to date explores the organization and dynamics of its decision-making. This sketch is based on my work in the Count Kuno von Westarp Papers (hereafter cited as NL Westarp), for use of which I am indebted to Dr. Friedrich Freiherr Hiller von Gaertringen, and upon the other studies of the party mentioned in this chapter. See also Max Weiss, "Organisation," in *Der nationale Wille, 1918–1928*, ed. Max Weiss (Berlin: Wilhelm Andermann Verlag, 1928), p. 367; and Bundesarchiv, Koblenz (hereafter referred to as BA), Kleine Erwerbung no. 293, letters from Prof. Dr. Axel Frhr. von Freytagh-Loringhoven to Amtsgerichtsrat Dr. Otto von Sethe, p. 202. The letters, written in 1942, contain autobiographical reflections that fill 263 pages. In his article, Weiss notes that the provision for a committee of six was eventually dropped but doesn't say when; it seems to have been in effect in 1924 and 1925. See *Korrespondenz der Deutschnationalen Volkspartei* (hereafter cited as *KDnVp*), no. 87, June 30, 1924, for a list of the new *Fraktionsvorstand* (of twenty-two persons), and no. 46, February 24, 1925, for a list of the *Parteileitung* (of twenty-one persons), which are also reproduced in the Appendix (see pp. 223–24 above).

27. Manfred Dörr, "Die Deutschnationale Volkspartei, 1925 bis 1928" (Dissertation, Marburg, published by its author, 1964), p. 466 n.1. Westarp's succession to Hergt as *Fraktion* chairman was not immediate, Martin Schiele having held the office briefly in December/January 1924/25.

28. Hertzman, *DNVP*, pp. 115, 234; Ruge, "DNVP," pp. 724–25, 729; Liebe, *Deutschnationale Volkspartei*, pp. 52-61; *Politischer Almanach, 1925: Jahrbuch des öffentlichen Lebens, der Wirtschaft und der Organisationen . . .* , ed. Maximilian Müller-Jabusch (Berlin: Verlag K. F. Koehler, 1925), p. 638, lists Westarp, as late as 1925, as being a member of the party's right wing.

29. BA, NL Leo Wegener, no. 65, p. 485, Hugenberg to Wegener, January 15, 1927, and p. 445, Wegener to Hugenberg, April 22, 1927.

30. *Politischer Almanach, 1925*, p. 627; BA, NL Alfred Hugenberg, no. 28, Schlange to Hugenberg, May 19, 1924, with accompanying *Denkschrift*, and May 25, 1924, in which Schlange describes himself as a proponent of Hugenberg's "entschlossenere Richtung." The *Denkschrift* has been printed in Dörr, "Deutschnationale Volkspartei," pp. 490–93.

31. Weiss, "Organisation," p. 363.

32. For an account of some of these see Weiss's essay "Organisation," pp. 362–90. Newsletters, circulars, and political-information outlines are available, although with lacunae, in the Niedersächsische Staatsarchive (hereafter referred to as NsäStA) of Osnabrück and Aurich, Bundesrepublik Deutschland, both of which have collections on local chapters of the DNVP; and in the DNVP and the Reichslandbund holdings of the Zentrales Staatsarchiv (hereafter referred to as ZStA; formerly Deutsches Zentralarchiv) in Potsdam. For answering questions about the central organization within the DNVP, the Potsdam archives are disappointing.

33. Maier, *Recasting Bourgeois Europe*, pp. 36–39, offers an interesting discussion to the effect that German bourgeois consciousness represented "little more than rampant anti-Marxism" (p. 36).

34. Liebe, *Deutschnationale Volkspartei*, p. 11; Chanady, "Disintegration," p. 66.

35. Liebe, *Deutschnationale Volkspartei*, pp. 51 ff.

36. Erasmus Jonas, *Die Volkskonservativen, 1928–1933* (Düsseldorf: Droste Verlag, 1965), p. 26; Hertzman, *DNVP*, p. 189.

37. Hertzman, *DNVP*, pp. 168, 190; Friedrich Stampfer, *Die vierzehn Jahre der ersten deutschen Republik* (Karlsbad: Graphia, 1936), p. 321; Jonas, *Volkskonservativen*, p. 27.

38. Stampfer, *Vierzehn Jahre*, pp. 324–25; Hertzman, *DNVP*, pp. 187–90, 197–201.

39. Stampfer, *Vierzehn Jahre*, p. 355; Hertzman, *DNVP*, pp. 189–90, 199–201; Liebe, *Deutschnationale Volkspartei*, p. 74; ZStA, Potsdam, 06.01 (Präsidialkanzlei), no. 41, p. 263, Hergt to Reichspresident Ebert, November 29, 1923, and 60 Vo 2 (DNVP), no. 9, pp. 59–63, "Darstellung der Mitwirkung der Deutschnationalen Volkspartei bei den Verhandlungen zur Neubildung der Reichsregierung in der Woche von 23.–30. November 1923," circulated to the party by the Central Committee in Berlin.

40. *Schulthess Europäischer Geschichtskalender*, vol. 65 (1924), ed. Ulrich Thürauf (Munich: C. H. Beck'sche Verlagsbuchhandlung, 1927), pp. 24–25; cited hereafter as *Schulthess*, with appropriate year and page numbers.

41. The figures given in many standard sources for election results, e.g., *Statistisches Jahrbuch für das Deutsche Reich*, do not take into account various combinations arising during the organization of the Reichstag, such as that between the Reichslandbund and the DNVP. Generally, my figures reflect seats controlled on the floor rather than seats won directly, and are frequently taken from *Schulthess*.

42. An excellent brief account of this action is given in Arnold J. Toynbee's *Survey of International Affairs, 1924* (London: Oxford University Press, 1926), pp. 268–93. Volumes from this series will be referred to hereafter as *Survey*, with the appropriate year and page designations.

43. D'Abernon, *Ambassador*, 2:275, 290. This phase of Franco-German relations is explored at length in K. Paul Jones, "Stresemann and the Diplomacy of the Ruhr Crisis, 1923–1924" (Ph.D. diss., University of Wisconsin, 1970).

44. *Survey*, 1924, pp. 270, 288–90.
45. Stampfer, *Vierzehn Jahre*, pp. 360–62, gives a lucid outline of the Dawes Committee's recommendations.
46. The issue was discussed in a host of cabinet meetings before the committee's report was published. See BA, "Akten der Reichskanzlei," R43I, "Akten betr. Kabinettsprotokolle," vols. 1391–94, hereafter cited with volume number and microfilm frame numbers, where they exist, to designate the pages. Since my research in Koblenz was completed, the Bundesarchiv has published *Die Kabinette Marx I und II*, ed. Günter Abramowski, 2 vols. (Boppard: Harald Boldt Verlag, 1973), and *Die Kabinette Luther I und II*, ed. Karl-Heinz Minuth, 2 vols. (Boppard: Harald Boldt Verlag, 1977), which contain many of the cabinet meetings cited in this study. Since the meetings are easily located by date in the published volumes and since the published volumes cover only a part of the period studied here, I have chosen to retain my original form of archival citation throughout.
47. Stampfer, *Vierzehn Jahre*, p. 363.
48. Bavaria, Geheimes Staatsarchiv München, "Berichte der bayerischen Gesandtschaft in Berlin," Abgabe 1935, politische Akten 1924, vol. 104, report of February 19, 1924, on a meeting of the Reichstag's Foreign Affairs Committee. These Bavarian state documents will hereafter be cited as bay. Ges. Berlin, pol. Akten, with designation of year, volume number, and the date of the report.
49. Ibid., report of April 11, 1924 (on conversations with State Secretary Bracht concerning the report of the Dawes Committee).
50. Ibid.
51. Hertzman, *DNVP*, p. 76, quoting a 1919 speech by Count Kuno von Westarp.
52. BA, R43I/1020, Akten betreffend Besprechungen mit den Parlamentariern und Fraktionsführern des Reichstags, meeting with DNVP representatives, April 14, 1924.
53. *Schulthess*, 1924, p. 29; *VM*, 1:390.
54. *VM*, 1:254; *Schulthess*, 1924, pp. 30–31.
55. *Schulthess*, 1924, pp. 30–31.

Chapter 2

1. Chanady, "Disintegration," *JMH* 39:71.
2. *Schulthess*, 1924, pp. 33, 37.
3. Ibid., pp. 30, 36, 65.
4. NL Westarp, Westarp to Hergt, July 11 and 15, 1924; Liebe, *Deutschnationale Volkspartei*, pp. 80 and 165 n.380; Chanady, "Disintegration," *JMH* 39:65–91.

5. Stampfer, *Vierzehn Jahre*, p. 372.
6. Ibid.; Henry A. Turner, *Stresemann and the Politics of the Weimar Republic* (Princeton, N.J.: Princeton University Press, 1963), pp. 154–60, 166.
7. *VM*, 1:322–26, 254, 287, 374, 395.
8. Ibid., p. 374.
9. Ibid., p. 406.
10. *Schulthess*, 1924, p. 37.
11. Liebe, *Deutschnationale Volkspartei*, pp. 78–79.
12. Cabinet meeting, May 15, 1924, 6:00 P.M., BA, R43I/1394, D760650; Werner Link, *Die amerikanische Stabilisierungspolitik in Deutschland, 1921–1932* (Düsseldorf: Droste Verlag, 1970), pp. 272 ff.
13. Cabinet meeting, May 15, 1924, BA, R43I/1394, D760751.
14. Ibid.
15. The cabinet could count on the support of the SPD, the DDP, the Center Party, the DVP, and the BVP in its pursuit of the Dawes negotiations. See *Schulthess*, 1924, p. 38; Stampfer, *Vierzehn Jahre*, p. 374.
16. Text in *Schulthess*, 1924, pp. 38–39. See also cabinet meeting, May 24, 1924, BA, R43I/1394, D760868 ff.
17. Cabinet meeting, May 24, 1924, BA, R43I/1394, D760868 ff.; *Schulthess*, 1924, p. 39.
18. Cabinet meeting, May 24, 1924, BA, R43I/1394, D760869.
19. Ibid.
20. Ibid.
21. NL Westarp, Ausschuss der Vaterländischen Verbände to Westarp, May 24, 1924.
22. *Schulthess*, 1924, p. 39.
23. Ibid.
24. These events are reviewed in the cabinet meeting of May 21, 1924, BA, R43I/1394, D760916–19, from which the following account is drawn.
25. ZStA, Potsdam, 06.01 (Präsidialkanzlei), no. 41, pp. 324–25, "Bericht [Radlauer] vom 26. Mai 1924 über eine DNVP Fraktionssitzung."
26. The quoted passages are from ZStA, Potsdam, 60 Vo 2 (DNVP), no. 9, pp. 4–5, Hergt to Scholz, June 2, 1924. See also cabinet meeting, May 31, 1924, BA, R43I/1394, D760916–19.
27. *VM*, 1:412, diary notes. Also Turner, *Stresemann*, pp. 168–69; and Stampfer, *Vierzehn Jahre*, p. 376.
28. *Schulthess*, 1924, pp. 41, 46; Otto Gessler, *Reichswehrpolitik in der Weimarer Zeit* (Stuttgart: Deutsche-Verlags-Anstalt, 1958), p. 363.
29. AA, RM, 67/2 (Innere Lage), D685640–43, telegram, June 4, 1924; *VM*, 1:415.
30. AA, RM, 67/2, E136986–89, memorandum, marked in longhand, "Entwurf (Gaus) . . . 17/5/24"; bay. Ges. Berlin, pol. Akten of 1924, vol. 104, report of April 11, 1924; cabinet meeting, May 3, 1924, BA R43I/1394, D760638–40.

31. See, for example, Link, *Amerikanische Stabilisierungspolitik*, p. 310 n.210.
32. *Schulthess*, 1924, pp. 43–44.
33. AA, RM, 67/2, D685644–45, Maltzan to Washington, June 6, 1924, and AA, StS I/2, Maltzan to diplomatic missions, June 4, 1924. Stresemann had raised these same points earlier in conversations with the United States ambassador, Alanson B. Houghton, and James Logan, a United States representative to the reparations commission: *VM*, 1:415 ff.
34. *Schulthess*, 1924, p. 44.
35. Ibid., pp. 44–45; *VM*, 1:426, 435–36.
36. Bay. Ges. Berlin, pol. Akten of 1924, vol. 104, report of June 18, 1924, on the meeting of the Reichstag's Foreign Affairs Committee.
37. Cabinet meeting, June 11, 1924, BA, R43I/1394, D761003; Stürmer, *Koalition*, pp. 48–49.
38. Stürmer, *Koalition*, pp. 49–52.
39. NL Westarp, Westarp to Hergt, July 11, 1924: "In den Kreisen v. L[indeiner?] . . . und v. Schl[eicher?] wird der Gedanke ventiliert, Regierung mit dn. Kanzler, Stresemann schlucken, Preussen." See also *VM*, 1:462, for Stresemann's diary notes of July 18, 1924; and Stürmer, *Koalition*, p. 46.
40. For a more sophisticated view of Poincaré's policies see Stephen A. Schuker, *The End of French Predominance in Europe* (Chapel Hill: University of North Carolina Press, 1976).
41. Cabinet meeting, June 11, 1924, BA, R43I/1394, D761002–3.
42. *Survey*, 1925, 2:172–93. See also *Schulthess*, 1924, pp. 399–402, 410–15, 418; and Michael Salewski, *Entwaffnung und Militärkontrolle in Deutschland, 1919–1927* (Munich: R. Oldenbourg Verlag, 1966), pp. 240–57.
43. Cabinet meeting, June 25, 1924, BA, R43I/1394, D761150–57; AA, RM, 67/2, D685649, telegram no. 125, to Brussels, June 4, 1924; *VM*, 1:441.
44. AA, RM, 67/2, D685640–43, telegram no. 125, to Brussels, June 4, 1924. Seeckt may still have been involved in efforts aimed at including the DNVP in the government. See also NL Westarp, Westarp to Hergt, July 11, 1924.
45. *Survey*, 1925, 2:177.
46. Cabinet meeting, June 25, 1924, BA, R43I/1394, D761550–57.
47. *Survey*, 1925, 2:178; *Schulthess*, 1924, p. 418.
48. NL Westarp, "Entwurf für Presseveröffentlichung," inscribed with the marginal note "nicht veröff[entlicht]." Undated, but written sometime after June 24, 1924, probably before Germany's reply note of June 30.
49. NL Westarp, DNVP Reichstagsfraktion to Dr. Stresemann, July 12, 1924.
50. NL Westarp, Westarp to Hergt, July 15 and 11, 1924. Westarp's letters refer to "v. L[indeiner?]" and "v. Sch[leicher?]" as being engaged in negotiations for a possible DNVP entry into the cabinet. Westarp misspelled the names of the state secretary of the German Foreign Office, Ago von Maltzan, and of the director of Department 2, Western Europe, Gerhard Köpke.

51. *VM*, 1:449, 456; *Survey*, 1924, p. 369 n.4; NL Westarp, Westarp to Hergt, July 11, and Schultz-Bromberg to Westarp, July 9, 1924.
52. Cabinet meeting, July 9, 1924, BA, R43I/1395, D761309–14.
53. Cabinet meetings, June 30 and July 9, 1924, BA, R43I/1394, 1395, D761222–29, D761309–14.
54. Cabinet meetings, June 30, July 9 and 15, 1924, BA, R43I/1394, 1395, D761222–29, D761309–14, D761444; NL Westarp, Westarp to Schultz-Bromberg, July 7, and to Hergt, July 11, 1924.
55. Meeting with party leaders, July 22, 1924, 5:00 P.M., BA, R43I/1395, D761578.
56. See above, p. 36, and cabinet meeting, June 30, 1924, BA, R43I/1394, D761222 ff.
57. Cabinet meeting, July 15, 1924, BA, R43I/1395, D761447.
58. Liebe, *Deutschnationale Volkspartei*, pp. 80, 165–66 n.382; bay. Ges. Berlin, pol. Akten of 1924, vol. 104, report of July 23, 1924, gives July 23 as the date of publication. Liebe quotes the *Nationale Rundschau* of July 24, 1924. On the parenthetical note to point 4, see *VM*, 1:461.
59. Bay. Ges. Berlin, pol. Akten of 1924, vol. 104, report of July 23, 1924.
60. Cabinet meeting, July 21, 1924, BA, R43I/1395, D761568.
61. Cabinet meetings, July 15 and 17, 1924, BA, R43I/1395, D761444, D761458.
62. Bay. Ges. Berlin, pol. Akten of 1924, vol. 104, July 23, 1924.
63. See cabinet meeting, July 15, 1924, BA, R43I/1395, D761445.
64. Bay. Ges. Berlin, pol. Akten of 1924, vol. 104, report of July 23, 1924.
65. Ibid.
66. Cabinet meetings, July 23 and 24, 1924, BA, R43I/1395, D761586 ff.
67. Germany, Büro des Reichstags, *Verhandlungen des Reichstags, 18. Sitzung,* Friday, July 25, 1924, vol. 381, p. 661 (hereafter cited as *Verhandlungen*).
68. Ibid., pp. 736–44.
69. Cabinet meeting, May 3, 1924, BA, R43I/1394, D760638–40.
70. Cabinet meeting, June 11, 1924, BA, R43I/1395, D761003; Stürmer, *Koalition*, p. 48.
71. Bay. Ges. Berlin, pol. Akten of 1924, vol. 104, report of June 18, 1924, on the meeting of the Reichstag's Foreign Affairs Committee; *VM*, 1:433 ff. This appears to be Stresemann's report before the committee.
72. Cabinet meeting, July 11, 1924, BA, R43I/1395, D761003.
73. Cabinet meeting, July 21, 1924, BA, R43I/1395, D761554.

Chapter 3

1. *VM*, 1:468; Zimmermann, *Deutsche Aussenpolitik*, p. 238; *Survey*, 1924, p. 374. The particulars of the London Conference are set out in *VM*, 1:466–501; also in Hans Luther's Papers (hereafter NL Luther), BA, vol. 287,

"Tagebuch über die Londoner-Konferenz, 5.–18. August 1924." This diary and some of the related documents have now been printed in *Kabinette Marx*, vol. 2, appendices 1–11, pp. 1283–1342. A good summary discussion is presented in *Survey*, 1924, pp. 359–84. See also Zimmermann, *Deutsche Aussenpolitik*, pp. 238–44.

2. Cabinet meeting, August 2, 1924, "Richtlinien . . . zur Londoner Konferenz," *Kabinette Marx*, 2:937.

3. *VM*, 1:469, 474.

4. Ibid., pp. 476–77; AA, RM, 7/4, telegram no. 653 to Paris, August 9, 1924. This French suggestion, repeatedly aired during the London Conference, bears striking similarities to the security pact of 1925.

5. Jacques Chastenet, *Histoire de la Troisième République*, vol. 5: *Les années d'illusions, 1918–1931* (Paris: Librairie Hachette, 1960), pp. 124 and 328 n.4; AA, RM, 7/4, D502216–18, August 11, 1924.

6. AA, Ago von Maltzan Papers (hereafter NL Maltzan), Londoner-Konferenz, H121789–91, telegram no. 470, to Paris, August 11, 1924 (also filed in AA, RM, 7/4, D502216–18), and telegram no. 472, to Paris, August 11, 1924.

7. AA, RM, 7/4, D502210–11, telegram no. 653, to Paris, August 9, 1924.

8. Italics added. BA, NL Luther, Tagebuch London, Anlage 7, "Notes on discussions between the German, French, and Belgian delegates . . . on August 13, 1924," 10:30 A.M. This particular discussion lasted about three and one-half hours.

9. Ibid., Anlagen 7–11. Each "Anlage" is a report on a confidential conference.

10. Cabinet meeting, August 15, 1924 (7:30 A.M.), BA, R43I/1395, D761796–802.

11. BA, NL Luther, Tagebuch London, Anlage 12, August 14, 1924, 2:30 P.M.

12. AA, NL Maltzan, Londoner-Konferenz (a separate volume, not microfilmed), telegram, London, August 15, 1924 (no. 68).

13. BA, NL Luther, Tagebuch London, Anlage 13, August 14, 1924, 4:30 P.M.

14. Cabinet meeting, August 15, 1924, 8:00 A.M., BA, R43I/1395, D761809–14.

15. BA, NL Luther, Tagebuch London and Anlage 17. MacDonald's reply, urging that the matter be dropped, is printed in excerpts in *Kabinette Marx*, 2:1341 n.4.

16. *VM*, 1:463.

17. See cabinet meeting, July 9, 1924, BA, R43I/1395, D761313.

18. AA, NL Maltzan, Londoner-Konferenz, H121952, telegram, August 6, 1924. Maltzan's contacts with Hoetzsch seem to have been quite regular throughout the summer. See also a copy of a memo dated Berlin, July 22, 1924, in NL Maltzan, Londoner-Konferenz vom Juni 1924 bis August 1924, H121482–89.

19. AA, NL Maltzan, Londoner-Konferenz, H121893 and H121770, telegrams, August 8 and 12, 1924, respectively.

20. AA, NL Maltzan, Londoner-Konferenz (a separate volume, not micro-

filmed), telegram, no date ("14/8," i.e., August 14, written in the margin).
21. Ibid., August 15, 1924.
22. Ibid., telegram, August 16, 1924, and "Zur vertraulichen Information" (sent to twelve German embassies).
23. Ibid. The two Nationalists are unidentified. See also *Kabinette Marx*, 2:968 n.8
24. NL Westarp, Bismarck (Külz) to Westarp, August 1, 1924, and numerous letters from local party organizations demanded total rejection. But some influential party members, among them Hoetzsch and Bazille, DNVP minister-president of Württemberg, favored adoption. See Hertzman, *DNVP*, p. 215.
25. NL Westarp, Tirpitz to Westarp, August 18, 1924.
26. *Schulthess*, 1924, pp. 60–61.
27. NL Westarp, Westarp to his wife, August 20, 1924 (evening).
28. Ibid., August 20 (evening), 21, and 23, 1924.
29. Cabinet meeting, August 21, 1924, BA, R43I/1395, D761857 ff.
30. NL Westarp, Westarp to his wife, August 23 (morning), 23 (evening), and 26, 1924.
31. *VM*, 1:503, 523–24; NL Westarp, Westarp to his wife, August 26, 1924; cabinet meeting, August 21, 1924, BA, R43I/1395, D761857–61.
32. NL Westarp, "Stellungnahme des Präsidiums des Reichs-Landbundes zur gegenwärtigen politischen Lage" (copy), n.d., but given to Westarp on August 23, 1924; Hertzman, *DNVP*, p. 216; cabinet meeting, August 21, 1924, BA, R43I/1395, D761857–61.
33. Liebe, *Deutschnationale Volkspartei*, pp. 82–83; Stürmer, *Koalition*, pp. 49–51 and 64–70 nn.77 and 78. Note, however, that not all these members earned their living primarily through agriculture.
34. Hans von Seeckt Papers (hereafter cited as NL Seeckt), Institute für Zeitgeschichte, roll 28, Seeckt to his wife, August 26 and 29, 1924.
35. *Verhandlungen*, vol. 381, pp. 794–807, esp. 796; Liebe, *Deutschnationale Volkspartei*, pp. 83–84.
36. *Verhandlungen*, vol. 381, pp. 794–807; NL Westarp, Westarp to his wife, August 26, 1924; Liebe, *Deutschnationale Volkspartei*, pp. 84 and 167 n.403.
37. Ibid., p. 84; Hertzman, *DNVP*, p. 220, citing NL Westarp, Hergt to Landesverband Ostpreussen, September 9, 1924, in which Hergt tried to justify his actions during the crisis. The text of this letter is printed in Liebe, *Deutschnationale Volkspartei*, pp. 173–78 n.449. Westarp was still confident of rejection when he wrote his wife early on August 27.
38. NL Westarp, letter to his wife, August 27, 1924.
39. Ibid., Hergt to Landesverband Ostpreussen, September 9, 1924, cited in Liebe, *Deutschnationale Volkspartei*, p. 175.
40. *Schulthess*, 1924, pp. 75–76; ZStA, Potsdam, 60 Vo 2 (DNVP), no. 10, pp. 114, 115, von Guérard to Hergt, August 29, and Zapf to Hergt, August 28, 1924.

41. E.g., NL Westarp, DNVP Landesverband Hannover-Ost to Parteileitung, August 28, 1924.
42. Liebe, *Deutschnationale Volkspartei*, pp. 175–76, quoting Hergt to Landesverband Ostpreussen, September 9, 1924; ZStA, Potsdam, 60 Vo 2 (DNVP), no. 10, pp. 117–18, Hergt's reply to an invitation to join the government, with the DNVP's conditions, August 29, 1924.
43. Liebe, *Deutschnationale Volkspartei*, p. 176.
44. NL Seeckt, roll 28, Seeckt to his wife, August 29, 1924: "Gestern abend ist von uns noch Stresemann mobil gemacht. Hauptverdienst hat Schleicher."
45. Compare Hergt's letter in Liebe, *Deutschnationale Volkspartei*, pp. 173 ff., with the cabinet meeting of August 28, 1924, 7:15 P.M., BA, R43I/1395, D761981.
46. See *Kabinette Marx*, 2:1004–5 n.4, 1006–7.
47. Hertzman, *DNVP*, pp. 222–23; Liebe, *Deutschnationale Volkspartei*, pp. 85–86.
48. *Vossische Zeitung*, no. 412 (August 30, 1924), cited by Liebe, *Deutschnationale Volkspartei*, p. 86. The following presentation of the scene in the Reichstag follows very closely Liebe's account, pp. 86–88, which was drawn from the *Vossische Zeitung*.
49. This had been evident in the prevote caucus as well. See Liebe, *Deutschnationale Volkspartei*, p. 177, quoting Hergt to Landesverband Ostpreussen.
50. *Vossische Zeitung*, as quoted in Liebe, *Deutschnationale Volkspartei*, pp. 86–88.
51. Liebe, *Deutschnationale Volkspartei*, p. 175, quoting Hergt.
52. AA, NL Maltzan, Londoner Konferenz, telegram, August 27, 1924. The step failed to produce the desired concessions from France. See *VM*, 1:565.
53. See above, p. 51.
54. See above, p. 46.
55. This sketch is based upon the summary of events surrounding the "Notification of the Statement by the Reich Government on the War Guilt Question," which was prepared for the cabinet by the German Foreign Office and was dated in longhand by Maltzan, August 10, 1924, printed in *Kabinette Marx*, 2:1026–31. War guilt was rejected in the German memorandum concerning entry into the League of Nations that was issued some weeks later (see ibid., p. 1062 n.2) and in the days just before the Locarno Conference (see *VM*, 1:561–70, and below, chap. 6).
56. See, for example, NL Westarp, Steinicker to Westarp, August 29, 1924.
57. Stürmer, *Koalition*, pp. 72–73.
58. NL Westarp, Lindeiner-Wildau to Westarp, September 22, 1924. The letter is quoted in part in Hertzman, *DNVP*, p. 229. See also Lindeiner to Goldacker, September 13, 1924, printed in Stürmer, *Koalition*, p. 287; ZStA, Potsdam, 60 Vo 2 (DNVP), no. 10, pp. 93–94, Hergt to Lindeiner, September 20, 1924.
59. NL Westarp, Büro Westarp to Sonnenschein, September 3, 1924.

60. ZStA, Potsdam, 60 Vo 2 (DNVP), no. 10, p. 90, [Lindeiner] to Graf [Westarp], September 22, 1924.
61. Ibid., Westarp to Hergt, September 18, 1924; Westarp to Lindeiner-Wildau, September 25, 1924. See also ZStA, Potsdam, 60 Vo 2 (DNVP), no. 10, pp. 72 f., Hergt to Negenborn, n.d. (ca. September 30, 1924), in which Hergt comments on Westarp's "inner aversion" to the party's attempt to enter the government.
62. Liebe, *Deutschnationale Volkspartei*, p. 96; *Schulthess*, 1924, p. 92.
63. *Schulthess*, 1924, p. 92; Hertzman, *DNVP*, p. 230.
64. *VM*, 1:559.
65. Ibid., p. 560; Liebe, *Deutschnationale Volkspartei*, pp. 76, 179 n.470; cabinet meetings, October 1 and 6, 1924, BA, R43I/1396, D762196, D762240.
66. *Schulthess*, 1924, pp. 91–95; cabinet meetings, October 1, 1924, D762194–96, October 3, 1924, D762207–10, October 6, 1924, D762238–41, October 9, 1924, D762249–52, BA, R43I/1396; "Meetings with party leaders," October 2, 3, 9, and 10, 1924, BA, R43I/1020.
67. Cabinet meeting, October 15, 1924, BA, R43I/1396, D762230. See also ZStA, Potsdam, 60 Vo 2 (DNVP), no. 10, pp. 51 f., Dryander to Hergt, October 6, 1924, on tendencies within the Center Party.
68. Cabinet meeting, October 16, 1924, BA, R43I/1396, D762369.
69. *Schulthess*, 1924, pp. 95–97; cabinet meetings, October 15, 1924, D762318–22, October 16, 1924, D762368–74, October 18, 1924 (1:00 P.M.), D762399–401, October 20, 1924, D762403–6, BA, R43I/1396; also "Meetings with party leaders," October 15, 1924, BA, R43I/1020.
70. *Schulthess*, 1924, pp. 97–98.
71. Cabinet meeting, December 10, 1924, BA, R43I/1397, D762845; *Schulthess*, 1924, p. 108.

Chapter 4

1. BA, Military Archives, Nachlass Kurt von Schleicher H 08 42/32, pp. 28–45, October 28 and 24 and November 1 and 5, 1924 (the latter three being telegrams from Hoesch to the German Foreign Office); BA, NL Luther, vol. 287, "Tagebuch über die Londoner-Konferenz," app. 6, notes on a conversation with MacDonald, August 12, 1924; Gustav Stresemann Papers (hereafter referred to as NL Stresemann), reel 3120, serial 7178, vol. 17, H158558–70, Hoesch to Stresemann, November 6, 1924. The papers are available either on film from the National Archives, Washington, D.C., as part of the captured German documents series T 120, or in the original from the Politisches Archiv of the German Foreign Office, Bonn. My citations follow the National Archives form, except that I have chosen to include the German Foreign Office's volume numbers for easy cross reference. Accord-

ing to this plan, the citation above reads: 3120/7178/vol. 17, H157558–70.

2. Bay. Ges. Berlin, pol. Akten of 1924, vol. 104, report of February 19, 1924, on a meeting of the Reichstag's Foreign Affairs Committee; BA, NL Luther, vol. 287, "Tagebuch Londoner Konferenz," app. 6.

3. BA, R43I/1395, D761626, cabinet meeting, July 29, 1924, and D761849–50, meeting with "Staats- und Ministerpräsidenten," August 19, 1924; bay Ges. Berlin, pol. Akten of 1924, vol. 104, report of January 11, 1925, on meetings of the Foreign Affairs committees of the Reichstag and Reichsrat on January 9 and 10, 1925. The party spokesmen who offered the ideas that are paraphrased in the last lines of this paragraph were Breitscheid for the SPD and Bernsdorff for the Democrats.

4. Bay. Ges. Berlin, pol. Akten of 1924, vol. 104, report of January 11, 1925.

5. BA, R43I/1020, meeting with the DVP leaders, December 13, 1924, and BA, R43I/1397, D762846, cabinet meeting of December 10, 1924.

6. *VM*, 1:604–8, article in *Hamburger Fremdenblatt*, December 25, 1924; BA, R43I/1020, Parteiführerbesprechung, December 13, 1924; *KDnVp*, no. 227, December 18, 1924.

7. Dörr, "Deutschnationale Volkspartei," pp. 83–84, 89–93.

8. On negotiations between the parties see Haungs, *Reichspräsident*, pp. 82–94; Stürmer, *Koalition*, pp. 78–89; *Schulthess*, 1925, pp. 6–7; cabinet meeting, December 19, 1924, printed in Gessler, *Reichswehrpolitik*, pp. 498 ff.

9. AA, StS, I/2, E136892–94, telegram, January 16, 1925, Stresemann to twelve diplomatic missions.

10. Bay. Ges. Berlin, pol. Akten of 1925, vol. 106, report of January 11, 1925.

11. AA, telegrams of December 17 and 19, 1924, filed in BA, R43I/1397, D762887–93 and D762894–95; cabinet meeting, December 20, 1924, in ibid., D762880–83; *VM*, 2:25, letter to Adenauer, January 7, 1925. The German note in reply is printed in *Schulthess*, 1925, pp. 399–401. See also *Survey*, 1925, 2:182.

12. Zimmermann, *Deutsche Aussenpolitik*, pp. 255–56; D'Abernon, *Ambassador*, 3:121, 151.

13. NL Stresemann, 3114/7135/vol. 277, H148917–22, "Die Vorgeschichte der Überreichung des deutschen Memorandums vom 9. Februar" [Schubert], dated in longhand, February 28, 1925; AA, StS, I/2, E136886–87, dated in longhand, January 18, 1925, notes concerning the pending Reichstag debate on Luther's cabinet program, including a reference to the security problem; Luther, *Politiker*, pp. 356–57; D'Abernon, *Ambassador*, 3:121, 123. See also F. G. Stambrook, " 'Das Kind,' " *CEH* 1:233–63.

14. The German text of the note is in NL Stresemann, 3166/7309/vol. 20, H158121–23, printed in Harald Schinkel, "Die Entstehung und Zerfall der Regierung Luther" (diss., Berlin, published by the author, 1959), pp. 185–86; an English translation appears in D'Abernon, *Ambassador*, 3:276–77; on the phrase "gegenwärtigen Besitzstand" see Robert P. Grathwol, "Germany

and the Eupen-Malmédy Affair, 1924–26," *Central European History* 8 (1975): 226–32.

15. *Survey*, 1925, 2:18.
16. AA, RM, 15-1/1, D642129, telegram, Paris, January 29, 1925.
17. *KDnVp*, no. 19, January 23, 1925, by-line of Werner v. Heimburg.
18. AA, RM, 15-1/1, D642141–43, Sthamer to Schubert.
19. *Survey*, 1925, 2:18, quoting the Paris *Temps* of January 25, 1925.
20. Ibid., p. 15.
21. Ibid., p. 19, quoting Luther from the *Deutsche Allgemeine Zeitung*, January 31, 1925; *Schulthess*, 1925, pp. 20–24, for extensive citation of the speech; Luther, *Politiker*, p. 361.
22. AA, RM, 15-1/1, D642175–85. The presentation was not made by Hoesch on February 9, because he had been injured in an automobile accident. This also accounts for the delay. The memorandum is printed in *VM*, 2:62–63. It differs slightly from the memorandum sent to London, in that it eliminates mention of the relationship among disarmament, evacuation, and security.
23. AA, RM, 15-1/1, D642258–62, February 9, 1925, telegram no. 94 from Paris, for this and the preceding paragraph.
24. AA, Botschaft London, Geheim, packet 412, K566896 f., telegram, February 19, 1925; Zimmermann, *Deutsche Aussenpolitik*, p. 256.
25. NsäStA, Osnabrück, C1/19, "Schwarz-Weiss-Rot," January 27, 1925, no. 2; *KDnVp*, no. 34, February 10, 1925.
26. See the press clippings in AA, RM, 15-1/1, near the end of the volume, and 15-1/2, near the beginning, none of which appears on the films of these documents. They include *Neue Zürcher Zeitung*, no. 314, February 27, 1925, which mentions the discussion in the French press; *Wolff's Telegraphisches Büro*, no. 374, March 2, no. 388, March 4, no. 394, March 5, 1925; *Deutsche Allgemeine Zeitung*, no. 105, March 3, 1925; *Le Petit Parisien*, March 4, 1925. See also Archives générales du Royaume, Brussels, Hymans Papers, dossier 466, Gaiffier to Hymans, Paris, February 25, 1925, no. 2432/1183/P.B., "Le pacte de garantie et la presse" which mentions articles in *Matin, Figaro, Débats, Echo de Paris, Temps,* and *Éclair,* as well as Herriot's consultations and the "trial balloons" launched by the Paris press. On Chamberlain's comments in the House of Commons see Great Britain, Parliament, *Debates* (House of Commons), vol. 181 (March 2 to 20, 1925), cols. 707–8, 713–14.
27. AA, RM, 15-1/2, D642498, March 5, 1925, telegram to Paris.
28. AA, RM, 15-1/1, D642184, February 5, 1925. Stresemann's remarks to the press are in *VM*, 2:64–73, and NL Stresemann, 3166/7310/vol. 21, H158405–15, which form the basis of the account in the preceding and subsequent paragraphs here.
29. Bay. Ges. Berlin, pol. Akten of 1925, vol. 106, report of March 10, 1925;

VM, 2:74–81; NL Stresemann, 3114/7135/vol. 277, H148981 ff., March 11, 1925.

30. Bay. Ges. Berlin, pol. Akten of 1925, vol. 106, report of March 10, 1925. The observer was Konrad von Preger.
31. Ibid., report of March 11, 1925.
32. Ibid.
33. NL Westarp, answer by Hergt, March 13, 1925, to an inquiry from the political office of Count Westarp concerning a letter, Traub to D. Winckler, March 7, 1925. The remark reappears in answers to inquiries concerning the security-pact proposals sent out by Westarp's office: e.g., Büro Graf Westarp to Hempel, March 25, 1925, and Büro Graf Westarp to ?, April 8, 1925.
34. BA, R43I/424, L280321–23, March 17, 1925, 5:00 P.M., meeting between Luther, Kempner, Schubert, and Stresemann. For protests to the DNVP leadership see NL Westarp.
35. NL Stresemann, 3114/7135/vol. 277, H149013 ff., meeting of March 17, 1925, 6:45 P.M.; Luther, *Politiker*, p. 363.
36. NL Westarp, notes from March 23, 1925, on conversations and meetings from March 19 and 20 (authorship unclear); ZStA, Potsdam, 61 Ve 1 (ADV), no. 142, pp. 73–101, Sitzung des Geschäftsführenden Ausschusses des Alldeutschen Verbandes, Dresden, March 21, 1925.
37. NL Westarp, notes from March 23, 1925. For the text of the DNVP letter see BA, R7VI/615a, and NL Stresemann, 3166/7311/vol. 22, H158590–92.
38. BA, R43I/1020, pp. 189–97, March 22, 1925, meeting between Luther and leaders of the DNVP.
39. BA, R45II/58, Luther to Schultz-Bromberg, March 23, 1925. Copy also in NL Westarp and in NL Stresemann, 3114/7135/vol. 277, H149018 f.
40. BA, R43I/1020, April 2, 1925, meeting with German Nationalist delegates in the Reichstag. Chamberlain's speech appears in Parliament, *Debates* (Commons), vol. 182, cols. 318–21 (March 24, 1925). Delayed publication of the memorandum was to become a matter of controversy, but even at this point, Stresemann had made the text available to the Bavarian government in which the DNVP was represented. See Bavaria, Geheimes Staatsarchiv, München, Akten des Ministeriums des Äusserns (hereafter cited as GStA, München, MA, with register number and date of the document), MA 103063, report by Konrad von Preger, March 16, 1925, which includes a copy of the February 9 memorandum.
41. BA, Nachlass Hermann Pünder, vol. 26, Pünder to Luther, March 26, 1925; *Schulthess*, 1925, p. 49; ZStA, Potsdam, 61 Ve 1 (ADV), no. 142, pp. 73–102, Sitzung . . . , March 21, 1925; *KDnVp*, for all of March, but esp. no. 72, March 26, 1925, "Aussenpolitische Aktivität," by Werner v. Heimburg; NsäStA, Osnabrück, Erw. C1. As with the *Korrespondenz*, the impression of reserve in the Osnabrück holdings is created by the *absence* of material on the security-pact revelations in the entire file of DNVP documents;

but for one of the few mentions of it see C1/17-II, p. 43, DNVP Hauptgeschäftsstelle, Rundschreiben, no. 37, March 12, 1925. On the silence of the Nationalist press, in addition to Pünder, above, see NL Westarp, Graf Eulenburg-Wicken to Westarp, April 7, 1925, and Dr. Quaatz to D. Winckler [April 15, 1925]. That the press's reserve represented a conscious political decision on the part of the party's leadership is evident from instructions from the party's business office to the Landesverband chairman in Osnabrück, NsäStA, Onsabrück, C1/18, p. 40, April 17, 1925.

42. For such a contention see Walsdorff, *Westorientierung*, pp. 87 f., 106, 146.
43. D'Abernon, *Ambassador*, 3:136–37; Schinkel, "Enstehung," p. 77; Archives générales, Brussels, Hymans Papers, dossier 466-II, "Notes pour Monsieur le Ministre" (December 12, 1924), and 466-III, "Suggestions Allemandes Relatives au problème de la Securité" (March 8, 1925).
44. See Dörr, "Deutschnationale Volkspartei," pp. 91, 98.
45. On the Nationalist world of myth see the highly provocative study by Annelise Thimme, *Flucht in den Mythos: Die Deutschnationale Volkspartei und die Niederlage von 1918.*

Chapter 5

1. NL Westarp, mimeographed summary of DNVP negotiations and activities, March 20 to April 8, 1925; Turner, *Stresemann*, pp. 191–200; NL Westarp, Traub to D. Winckler, March 7, 1925—all on the elections. On pending trade-treaty negotiations see NL Westarp, Westarp to Gürtner, February 9, 1925; Stürmer, *Koalition*, pp. 98 ff.
2. NL Westarp, Traub to D. Winckler, March 7, 1925, with notes for an answer from Hergt; Wildgrube to D. Winckler, March 9, 1925; Hempel to Westarp, March 17, 1925, with answer, from which the quotation above is taken; Ausschuss der Vaterländischen Verbänden to Westarp, March 17, 1925, with answer.
3. NL Westarp, Bismarckjugend der DNVP to Westarp, March 28, 1925; Graf Eulenburg-Wicken to Westarp, March 31 and April 7, 1925; DNVP Kreisverband Vogtland, April 6, 1925; Dr. Lienau to Westarp, May 27, 1925; Bismarck to Westarp, Külz, April 5, 1925.
4. NL Westarp, Quaatz to Westarp, April 29, 1925; Quaatz to DNVP Annaberg, April 15, 1925; Quaatz to Schwabe (Plauen), April 8, 1925; and Quaatz to D. Winckler (April 15, 1925).
5. No. 84, April 9, 1925.
6. NsäStA, Osnabrück, C1/18, p. 40, Weiss to DNVP Landesverband Osnabrück, April 17, 1925.
7. Stresemann, instructions to Hoesch, February 5, 1925, printed in Democratic Republic of Germany, *Locarno-Konferenz 1925: Eine Dokumentensamm-*

lung, compiled by the Foreign Ministry (Berlin: Rütten and Leoning, 1962), pp. 55–60, esp. p. 59, point 7.

8. See notes on conversations with the French ambassador, March 16, 1925, BA, R43I/424, L280317–20, and *VM,* 2:83–85; AA, RM, 15-1/2, D642715–16 and D642789–94, telegrams, March 17 and 21, 1925, D642841–43 and D642845, telegrams, March 25 and 26, 1925, E125590–91, D642874–75, memoranda (3) from March 27, 1925.

9. Schubert to Sthamer, January 19, 1925, printed in *Locarno-Konferenz,* pp. 47–51.

10. AA, StS, FS/2 (Sicherheitsfrage), E124924–26, Ow to Schubert, February 23, 1925, with Schubert's marginal comment, "Luther will Eupen-Malmedy herauslassen." I am indebted to Prof. Peter Krüger, Marburg, for calling Schubert's marginal note to my attention. See also NL Stresemann, 3114/7135/vol. 277, H149020, Luther to Stresemann, March 24, 1925. For a more extensive discussion of this issue, see Grathwol, "Germany and the Eupen-Malmédy Affair," *CEH* 8:221–50.

11. AA, RM, 15-1/3, D642965–68, April 3, 1925.

12. Negotiations concerning Germany's entry into the league are traced in Jürgen Spenz, *Die diplomatische Vorgeschichte des Beitritts Deutschlands zum Völkerbund: 1924–1926* (Göttingen: Musterschmidt-Verlag, 1966). The points made above can be found on p. 25.

13. AA, RM, 15-1/1, D642142, telegram, January 30, 1925, and 15-1/3, D643134 f., telegram, April 29, 1925; Spenz, *Diplomatische Vorgeschichte,* passim.

14. Salewski, *Entwaffnung,* pp. 288–302.

15. *Survey,* 1925, 2:31; Archives générales, Brussels, Hymans Papers, dossier 466-V, Paris, April 20, 1925, no. 4636/2157/P.B., Gaiffier to Hymans; Grathwol, "Germany and the Eupen-Malmédy Affair."

16. AA, RM, 15-1/3, D642924, conversation with Margerie, March 31, 1925.

17. *VM,* 2:142; NL Westarp, Westarp to Deutschnationalen Volksverein Plauen, January 30, 1926.

18. *VM,* 2:142; this account from Stresemann's "Herringsdorfer Niederschrift" of July 5, 1925, is confirmed by NL Westarp, Westarp to Deutschnationalen Volksverein Plauen, January 30, 1926, in a review of the situation for use in a possible court case. State Secretary Schubert had long since made the text of the memorandum available to the Bavarian government, in which the DNVP was represented. See GStA, München, MA 103063, March 16, 1925, report from von Preger.

19. BA, R43I/424, L280383–85, notes from May 20, 1925, on a conversation of May 18 with Berg-Markienen and Graf zu Eulenburg.

20. *Verhandlungen,* vol. 385, pp. 1894–1900.

21. Dörr, "Deutschnationale Volkspartei," p. 135; and Walsdorff, *Westorientierung,* p. 106, miss this point.

22. Walsdorff, *Westorientierung,* p. 106.

23. No. 115, May 19, 1925.

24. No. 116, May 20, 1925.
25. No. 124, May 30, 1925.
26. NL Westarp, Freytagh-Loringhoven to Westarp, May 28, 1925. The response outlined in this letter, which bears handwritten notations by Westarp, was incorporated into numerous answers to letters of inquiry and protest in late May and early June. For protests from the Right see NL Westarp, LV Bremen to Westarp, May 27, 1925, and Dr. Lienau to Westarp, May 27, 1925; Dörr, "Deutschnationale Volkspartei," p. 136; and *Schulthess*, 1925, p. 96.
27. NsäStA, Osnabrück, C1/17-II, p. 117, DNVP Rundschreiben no. 108, May 28, 1925.
28. Ibid., C1/19, "Schwarz-Weiss-Rot," no. 6, June 12, 1925, is the source from which all quotations in the preceding paragraph were drawn. As an internal party organ circulated by the central office in Berlin, "Schwarz-Weiss-Rot" reflected the policy of the Central Committee. In this case, comments on the disarmament note closely follow the policy laid down by the cabinet in its meeting of June 5, BA, R43I/1403, D764856–63. The public reaction of the DNVP appears in *KDnVp*, no. 128, June 6, and no. 129, June 8, 1925.
29. NL Westarp, "Protokoll der Fraktionssitzung am 9. Juni 1925"; Dörr, "Deutschnationale Volkspartei," p. 137. Stresemann got hold of one of the DNVP's innerparty circulars when it was delivered by mistake to the DVP's Dr. Rudolph Schneider-Dresden rather than to DNVP radical Bruno Schneider-Thüringen. It says nothing that is very different from what the DNVP leaders had been saying all along. See NL Stresemann, 3161/7401/ vol. 94, H172814–15.
30. *VM*, 2:103.
31. *Survey*, 1925, 2:25–39; Turner, *Stresemann*, pp. 202–3.
32. AA, RM, 15-1/4, D643536–41, original French text of the note.
33. Zimmerman, *Deutsche Aussenpolitik*, p. 264.
34. *VM*, 2:103–8; AA, RM, 15-1/4, D643610–16, June 22, 1925, to Sthamer, and D643588–90, June 21, 1925, to Hoesch.
35. See above and *VM*, 2:142. For the cabinet meeting see BA R43I/1403, D765044–68, which forms the basis of the account presented here and in subsequent paragraphs.
36. *VM*, 2:128; NL Stresemann, 3113/7129/vol. 272, H147889–91, notes, June 26, 1925; cabinet meetings, June 24, 25, and 26, 1925, BA, R43I/1403, D765044, D765092, and D765109.
37. BA, R43I/1403, D765103–4; *VM*, 2:110–11.
38. Dörr, "Deutschnationale Volkspartei," pp. 139–40; *VM*, 2:130–31. The *Landesverbände* were Hamburg, Hannover-Ost, Osnabrück, Oldenburg, Ostfriesen, and Bremen.
39. *KDnVp*, no. 147, June 29, 1925; Dörr, "Deutschnationale Volkspartei," pp. 140–41.
40. *KDnVp*, no. 147, June 29, 1925; NL Westarp, *Deutsche Zeitung* to Westarp,

June 27, 1925, in which Westarp received the copy of the article for verification; *Berliner Tageblatt*, June 30, 1925 (morning); *VM*, 2:130–31.

41. For Westarp's article see *KDnVp*, no. 140, June 20, 1925; for the resolution made by the fifty-one DNVP delegates see NL Westarp.

42. Bay. Ges. Berlin, pol. Akten of 1925, vol. 106, report of July 1, 1925, on the meeting of the Reichstag's Foreign Affairs Committee. Subsequent paragraphs depend on this same source.

43. *VM*, 2:141.

44. Ibid., p. 110; the phrase is not in the minutes of the cabinet meeting, BA, R43I/1403, D765044 ff.

45. *VM*, 2:132.

46. In his memoirs, Luther denies that he had any intention of forcing Stresemann out of the cabinet. See his *Politiker*, p. 364; but see NL Stresemann, 3113/7129/vol. 272, H147918–19, notes, July 19, 1925. There is no concrete evidence to suggest collusion between Luther and the Nationalists in this attack on Stresemann; thus the tentative language in the text. Still, in the absence of collusion, the episode makes little sense. The putative lapse of memory on Luther's part seems unlikely, especially in view of his conduct in earlier, similar crises.

47. *VM*, 2:136; BA, R43I/1403, D765165 ff., for this and the following paragraphs. The minutes of this cabinet meeting are dated in longhand July 2, but they were filed in the Reichskanzlei acts only on December 7, 1925. Stresemann, *VM*, 2:136–37, gives the date of the meeting as July 3. The text of the minutes speaks more for the earlier date. On Westarp see NL Stresemann, 3113/7129/vol. 272, H147903.

48. *VM*, 2:138.

49. BA, R43I/1403, D765175–76, cabinet meeting, July 2, 1925.

50. *VM*, 2:143.

51. NL Seeckt, roll 28, July 2, 1925; also Friedrich von Rabenau, ed., *Seeckt: Aus Seinem Leben, 1918–1936* (Leipzig: Hase & Koehler, [1940]), p. 418. The DNVP kept in constant contact with Seeckt throughout this period. See Stürmer, *Koalition*, p. 114.

52. *Verhandlungen*, vol. 386, pp. 2803 ff., 2811 ff.

53. *Schulthess*, 1925, pp. 121–22; bay. Ges. Berlin, pol. Akten of 1925, vol. 106, report of July 8, 1925, on a meeting of the Reichstag's Foreign Affairs Committee.

54. BA, R43I/1403, D765345–50, meeting of July 15, 1925.

55. Ibid., D765350–55.

56. Bay. Ges. Berlin, pol. Akten of 1925, vol. 106, report of July 17, 1925, on a meeting of the Reichstag's Foreign Affairs Committee. The reference applies to subsequent paragraphs as well.

57. AA, RM, 15-1/5, D643961 ff., telegram, July 18, 1925.

58. Text of the note in *Schulthess*, 1925, pp. 424–27, and in *Locarno-Konferenz* doc. no. 16.

59. NL Westarp, answer to *Nationale Rundschau*, July 22, 1925; NL Stresemann, 3113/7129/vol. 272, H147917 ff., notes, July 19, 1925, in which Stresemann denies that the DNVP shaped Germany's reply.
60. *VM*, 2:152; *KDnVp*, no. 154, July 7, 1925.
61. See Westarp's speech, *Verhandlungen*, vol. 387, pp. 3399–3404.
62. *Liberté*, July 15, 1925, quoted by Hoesch in a telegram of July 16, 1925, AA, RM, 67/2, D685651. For Stresemann's comments see *VM*, 2:152–53, and NL Stresemann, 3113/7129/vol. 272, H147936–38, notes, August 2, 1925.

Chapter 6

1. Westarp's remark is recorded, at second hand, by Stresemann, *VM*, 2:145.
2. See Stürmer, *Koalition*, p. 118–19; ZStA, Potsdam, 61 Ve 1 (ADV), no. 143, pp. 40–64, Sitzung des Geschäftsführenden Ausschusses des ADV in Berlin, July 4 and 5, 1925; NL Westarp, *Nationale Rundschau* (Bremen) to Westarp, July 14, 1925; NsäStA, Osnabrück, C1/6, DNVP Landesverband Osnabrück to Hauptgeschäftsstelle, August 3, 1925.
3. *Deutsche Zeitung*, July 17, 1925, morning: the men named were Oberfohren, Quaatz, Lohmann, Gok, Goldacker, Stubbendorff, Dewitz, Logemann, Wormit, Wolf-Stettin, Giese, Domprediger Martin, Schneider-Thüringen, Everling, Haedenkamp, Brekelbaum-Hamburg, Mentzel-Pommern, Philipp-Sachsen, Jandrey, Schulze-Frankfurt, Graf Schulenburg, Graf Eulenburg, and Treviranus.
4. The quarrel between Class and the DNVP in July 1925 is sketched in NL Westarp, Freytagh-Loringhoven to Westarp, July 26, 1925, Westarp to Freytagh-Loringhoven, July 27, 1925, and Freytagh-Loringhoven to Westarp, July 28, 1925, as well as in ZStA, Potsdam, 61 Ve 1 (ADV), no. 144, pp. 6–44, Sitzung . . . ADV, September 4, 1925. See also Dörr, "Deutschnationale Volkspartei," p. 142.
5. NL Westarp, Westarp to Goeze, July 30, 1925, and ZStA, Potsdam, 61 Ve 1 (ADV), no. 143, pp. 40–64, Sitzung . . . , July 4 and 5, 1925. The Westarp Nachlass is replete with protests against the party's decision to tolerate the German reply note of July 20. It would be an exhausting but perhaps rewarding task for a historian of the party to trace the connections between the protests from individual local organizations and the influence in those organizations of members of the ADV. The replies to these protests run close to that which Westarp offers Goeze in the letter cited above. On DNVP tactics regarding tariff and taxes see Stürmer, *Koalition*, pp. 102 ff.
6. See *VM*, 2:162–63; *Deutsche Zeitung*, August 6, 1925, morning.
7. AA, RM, 15-1/6, August 4, 1925, D644153–54, Stresemann to Paris, no. 952, in which Sthamer's report of August 1 is repeated; ibid., 31/3, D682142–43, Hoesch to Berlin, on conversations with Berthelot, on which see also GStA,

München, MA 103063, report by the Bavarian emissary Konrad von Preger on a conversation with Stresemann, August 10, 1925; ibid., 31/3, D682131 ff., August 3, 1925, Stresemann's notes on a conversation with D'Abernon, also filed in ibid., 15-1/6, D644145 ff.

8. Ibid., 15-1/6, D644157–58, August 4, 1925, Stresemann to Sthamer; and Stresemann to Hoesch, August 3, 1925, ibid., D644145 ff. On consultations with Luther see BA, R43I/424, L280561–62, August 4, 1925, meeting of Luther, Kempner, Stresemann, and Schubert.

9. AA, RM, 15-1/6, D644195–204, "Bemerkungen zu dem englischen Entwurf eines Sicherheitspaktes."

10. BA, R43I/424, L280567–70, report from London, also filed in AA, RM, 15-1/6, D644262–65, August 17, 1925.

11. Ibid., D644321–26, Stresemann's notes on a meeting with Margerie, August 24, 1925, and the French text of the note that Margerie delivered, D644327–32. A sketchy summary of the note appears in *VM*, 2:168–69.

12. *VM*, 2:162–63; BA, R43I/1404, D765763–69, meeting of August 24, 1925, 7:00 P.M.

13. NL Westarp, Westarp to his wife, August 24, 1925. The other Nationalists present were Hoetzsch, Lindeiner-Wildau, Leopold, and Keudell. Westarp's letter should be dated August 25.

14. Ibid., Aufzeichnung von Frhr. v. Freytagh und v. Lindeiner, August 25, 1925.

15. Ibid., Westarp's longhand comments on the report from Freytagh-Loringhoven and Lindeiner-Wildau, August 25, 1925, and Freytagh to Westarp, August 31, 1925; for the government's meetings of August 25 and 26 see BA, R43I/1404, D765772–75 and D765791–94. The German reply to the invitation and the press communiqué are in AA, RM, 15-1/6, D644354–56 and D644357–62.

16. NL Westarp, among other examples see Goldacker to Westarp, August 19, 1925; DNVP Landesverband Potsdam-I to Westarp, August 7, 1925.

17. Ibid., Westarp to Schiele, with memorandum, August 31, 1925.

18. Ralf Dahrendorf, *Society and Democracy in Germany* (Garden City, N.Y.: Anchor Doubleday, 1967), pp. 285–362.

19. BA, NL Luther, vol. 362, "Bericht über die Londoner Juristen Besprechungen," September 18, 1925. See also Sir Cecil Hurst's semiofficial account of the discussions, filed with Gaus's report in AA, RM, 15-1/7, following D644592.

20. NL Westarp, Lindeiner to Westarp, September 4, 1925, and to Schiele, September 11, 1925.

21. *KDnVp*, no. 235, October 29, 1925.

22. BA, R43I/1404, D765921–37, cabinet meeting, September 22, 1925, for this and for subsequent paragraphs.

23. *VM*, 2:179–80.

24. Ibid., pp. 177–78; Stresemann mentions his consultation with the French

ambassador on this point in his report of their later meeting on September 27, 1925, AA, RM, 15-1/7, D644742. I have not found a direct report of the earlier meeting in which the note was discussed before it was sent. For the cabinet meeting and a draft of the verbal note see BA, R43I/1404, D765938–42.

25. Stresemann's draft of the guidelines appears in AA, RM, 15-1/7, D644819–21, without a date, and in *VM*, 2:181–82, dated September 23, 1925, but without Stresemann's longhand notes which indicate that three paragraphs were to be added, "8) Garantie 9) Kündigungsfrage 10) Saargebiet." The DNVP's guidelines appear in Dörr, "Deutschnationale Volkspartei," pp. 522–23, as the party published them—five weeks after their origin—on October 30, 1925. See also BA, R43I/431, pp. 179 ff., "DNVP Richtlinien." The final version of the cabinet's guidelines, to be discussed again below, is in ibid., 1405, D766131–32. Only one point from Stresemann's draft does not appear in the cabinet guidelines: "Kündigungsfrage." The DNVP version, on the other hand, diverges substantially from the official version.

26. BA, R43I/424, L280561–62, August 5, 1925, notes on a meeting of Luther Kempner, Stresemann, and Schubert.

27. Ibid., 1404, cabinet meeting, September 23, 1925. Inexplicably, these minutes of the meeting of the full cabinet that followed the meeting of the four ministers seem not to have been filmed. The page numbers within the *Reichskanzlei* volume are 182–85, constituting eight typewritten pages.

28. BA, R43I/1404, D765953–57, September 24, 1925.

29. NL Westarp, Westarp to his wife, September 24, 1925. Schiele's and Hindenburg's residences shared abutting gardens, thus allowing the Nationalists an unobtrusive access to the president "through the garden door," as Westarp observed.

30. Ibid., Frl. v. Watter to Prof. Otto, September 25, 1925. Frl. v. Watter was a close personal and political associate of Count Westarp's at the time. See also *Die Kabinette Luther*, 1:570 and n. 16.

31. NL Westarp, minutes of Fraktionssitzung, September 25, 1925; BA, R43I/425, L280692, meeting between Luther, Westarp, Hergt, and Wallraf, September 26, 1925; bay. Ges. Berlin, pol. Akten of 1925, vol. 106, report of September 27, 1925, of the preceding day's meeting of the Foreign Affairs Committee; NL Westarp, Frl. v. Watter to Prof. Otto, September 26, 1925. Dörr (see his "Deutschnationale Volkspartei," pp. 145 ff., esp. p. 171) fails to take the compromises into account in his discussion of the DNVP guidelines, which he treats as synonymous with the cabinet guidelines. He even says (p. 157 n.142) that Stresemann's proposals (*VM*, 2:180–82) "incorporated in essence the German Nationalist demands, which the Nationalists [however] designated, not as goals of the negotiations, but as conditions for the conclusion of a treaty," without seemingly recognizing that this constituted an essential difference. He ignores the cabinet guidelines entirely.

32. NL Seeckt, Seeckt to his wife, September 24, 1925, roll 28.

33. AA, RM, 15-1/7, September 26, 1925, D644673–76, on Chamberlain's reaction, D644693–96, on the French reaction.
34. BA, R43I/1404, D765971–78, cabinet meeting, September 28, 1925; AA, RM, 15-1/7, D644753–54, September 29, 1925, Stresemann to Hoesch.
35. AA, RM, 15-1/7, D644762 f., September 29, 1925, Schubert to London, Brussels, Rome; ibid., D644809 and D644828, for the British and French notes in the language of origin. Briand's suggestion contained not only the proposed procedure for the publication of the German note but also the approximate text of the British and French answers, without the evidence of Chamberlain's pique over German petulance which the British note displays.
36. BA, R43I/1405, D765989–97 and D766129–32, cabinet meetings, October 1 and 2, 1925. See also Robert P. Grathwol, "DNVP, Stresemann und die Einladung nach Locarno," in *Tradition und Neubeginn: Internationale Forschungen zur deutschen Geschichte im 20. Jahrhundert*, ed. Joachim Hütter, Reinhard Meyer, and Dietrich Papenfuss (Cologne, Berlin, Bonn, Munich: Carl Heymanns Verlag, 1975), pp. 89–99.
37. For the six drafts see NL Westarp, October 2 and 3, 1925. The original, as Luther received it, is in BA, R43I/429, L280114–15.
38. See, for example, NsäStA, Osnabrück, C1/58, "Entschliessung" Deustchnationaler Landesverband Lübeck, September 30, 1925, "Nicht zur Veröffentlichung bestimmt"; and the numerous protests in NL Westarp, e.g. Deutscher Wehrverein to Westarp, October 1, 1925.
39. Luther emphasizes this point in his memoirs, *Politiker*, p. 366.
40. BA, R43I/429, L280127–28.
41. Schiele to Luther, October 6, 1925, ibid., L280132; and Pünder to Kempner, ibid., 426, L279154–56.
42. For an example of the latter see an article reviewing the party's year in government in *KDnVp*, no. 188, August 18, 1925.
43. See Kronprinzenbrief; and Grathwol, "Gustav Stresemann," *JMH* 45:52–70.

Chapter 7

1. BA, R43I/1405, D766130; and Luther's quotation of this passage in his *Politiker*, p. 366.
2. See cabinet meetings, September 22–24 and October 2, 1925, BA, R43I/1404 and 1405, D765921 ff., D765938 ff., pp. 189–99, and D766119–30.
3. See "Richtlinien für die Ministerzusammenkunft in Locarno," BA, R43I/1405, D766131–32, for this and the preceding paragraph.
4. *VM*, 2:195, BA, NL Pünder, vol. 65, pp. 73–89, "Locarno Tagebuch," prepared by Franz Kempner on October 25, 1925, from daily notes taken in Locarno. During the conference itself, Kempner was not convinced that Stresemann had satisfied the cabinet decision of October 1. See ZStA, Pots-

dam, 06.01 (Präsi), no. 687/1, p. 104, letter Kempner to Pünder, Locarno, October 7, 1925.

5. *VM*, 2:188; cabinet meeting, October 1, 1925, BA, R43I/1405, D765997.

6. *VM*, 2:194–202; BA, NL Pünder, vol. 65, pp. 73–89, "Locarno Tagebuch."

7. The text is given in *Locarno-Konferenz*, pp. 182–83. This collection of documents also reproduces the minutes of the full sessions of the Locarno Conference. The Locarno journal by Kempner gives brief but useful summaries of the jurists' meetings and of private conversations as well. The volume AA, RM, 15-1/—"Aufzeichnungen und Sitzungsprotokolle von Locarno, v. 4.–17. Oktober 1925," contains minutes from the plenary sessions and all relevant meetings between German and Allied negotiators as well as from consultations among German delegates. See also NL Stresemann 3169/7319 and 7320/vols. 30 and 30a, which cover the period of the conference, as well as *VM*, 2:186–204.

8. *Locarno-Konferenz*, pp. 183–88.

9. BA, NL Pünder, vol. 26, pp. 81–83, Pünder to Kempner, October 8, 1925.

10. Pünder to Kempner, October 9, 10, and 12, 1925, BA, R43I/426, L279181–84, L279189–92, L279195.

11. BA, R43I/1405, D766280 ff., cabinet meeting, October 13, 1925, which is also relevant to the following paragraphs.

12. Ibid., D766283–85.

13. Ibid., D766286–97, cabinet meeting, October 14, 1925, and ibid., 429, L280136, Kempner to Luther, October 14, 1925.

14. BA, NL Pünder, vol. 26, pp. 112–16, Pünder to Staatssekretär [Kempner], October 15, 1925.

15. Kempner's report to Luther, BA, R43I/429, L280136 ff., and BA, NL Pünder, vol. 26, pp. 112–16.

16. AA, RM 15-1/—, D644997, October 14, 1925 (from Locarno).

17. NL Westarp, "Briefentwurf Schiele an Luther," October 14, 1925, "nicht abgegangen, weil durch Kabinettsbeschluss überholt." This phrase and substantive pencil corrections are in Westarp's hand. Schiele's letter refers to a cabinet decision of October 2 on the issue of war guilt (see the discussion in the text following this note). The minutes of the cabinet meeting of October 1 reveal such a discussion, but not for October 2. For this reason, I have changed the reference in the text below to read October 1 rather than, as in the original letter, October 2.

18. Ibid., Westarp to Deutscher Wehrverein, to Traub, both October 12, 1925.

19. Ibid., Count Westarp in Charlottenburg, October 15, 1925.

20. Compare Schiele's remarks in the cabinet meeting of October 16, 1925, BA, R43I/1405, D766303, with the Richtlinien, ibid., D766131–32.

21. Cabinet meeting, October 16, 1925, ibid., D766301–6.

22. Ibid., D766307–9.

23. See BA, NL Pünder, vol. 65, pp. 73–89, Kempner's "Locarno Tagebuch,"

p. 18; cabinet meeting, October 19, 1925, BA, R43I/1405, D766332; *Locarno-Konferenz*, pp. 198, 202, 208, 214.

24. *VM*, 2:205, translated from the German version.
25. For the texts of the articles in question see *Locarno-Konferenz*, p. 199. This and the next several pages are based on BA, R43I/1405, D766324–47, cabinet meeting, October 19, 1925.
26. Cabinet meeting, October 19, 1925, ibid., D766324–28.
27. Ibid., D766328–30.
28. Ibid., D766330.
29. Ibid., D766330–33.
30. Ibid., D766334. Dörr, "Deutschnationale Volkspartei," p. 168, is thus wrong in saying that Schiele voiced no personal approval of the treaty but correct in stating that he reserved final judgment; although see Hindenburg's conclusion of the meeting below. Stresemann's assertion, *VM*, 2:205, that Schiele's objections were only because the texts of the treaties were not at hand is also inaccurate.
31. BA, R43I/1405, D766334–39.
32. Ibid., D766340, and note 30 of this chapter, above, on Schiele.
33. *VM*, 2:205–6.
34. Ibid., p. 206.
35. GStA, München, MA 103069, report of October 20, 1925.
36. Bay. Ges. Berlin, pol. Akten of 1925, vol. 106, report of October 23, 1925.
37. Cabinet meeting, October 22, 1925, BA, R43I/1405, D766345–47. Stürmer, *Koalition*, p. 124, perhaps following Stresemann, *VM*, 2:206, or Luther, *Politiker*, p. 388, says incorrectly that the Nationalist ministers were not present, suggesting thus that they had already withdrawn from the cabinet's deliberations. In fact, Schiele not only approved the statement but also helped to formulate it.
38. Bay. Ges. Berlin, pol. Akten of 1925, vol. 106, report of October 23, 1925.
39. NL Westarp, dated October 22, 1925; emphasis in the original.
40. Bay. Ges. Berlin, pol. Akten of 1925, vol. 106, October 23, 1925.
41. BA, NL Pünder, vol. 65, p. 75, in Kempner's "Locarno Tagebuch," dated October 25, 1925, also BA, R43I/429, Schulz to Locarno delegation, October 5, 1925.
42. Bay. Ges. Berlin, pol. Akten of 1925, vol. 106, October 23, 1925.
43. Especially the Bavarian representative in Berlin. See ibid. and *VM*, 2:206.
44. NL Westarp, Westarp to Traub, October 12, 1925.
45. Ibid., Westarp to Schiele, August 31, 1925, Westarp to Traub, Westarp to DNVP Landesverband, Bremen, and Westarp to Deutschen Wehrverein—all on October 12, 1925.
46. Bay. Ges. Berlin, pol. Akten of 1925, vol. 106, report of October 23, 1925.
47. The Bavarian representative in Berlin, Preger; see ibid.
48. NL Westarp, Deutscher Wehrverein to Westarp, October 1, 1925, and the

answer, October 12, 1925; also Dörr, "Deutschnationale Volkspartei," pp. 172–73.

49. *Vermerk*, Luther, October 23, 1925, BA, R43I/429, L280150–57; see also Dörr, "Deutschnationale Volkspartei," pp. 172–74.

50. *VM*, 2:206.

51. Notes by Kempner, October 23, 1925, BA, R43I/429, L280159–61.

52. Ibid.; see also *VM*, 2:206.

53. Dörr, "Deutschnationale Volkspartei," p. 174.

54. Ibid., pp. 175–76; see also NL Westarp, Sahl to Westarp, October 24, 1925, BA, R43I/429, p. 41.

55. Dörr, "Deutschnationale Volkspartei," p. 178.

56. Stürmer, *Koalition*, p. 102; Alfred Kruck, *Geschichte des Alldeutschen Verbandes, 1890–1939* (Wiesbaden: Franz Steiner Verlag, 1954), pp. 168–69; notes initialed by Wachsmann, October 25, 1925, BA, R43I/429, L280175.

57. BA, R43I/429, L280174. The text of the delegation's decision, without the words "noch heute," which appear in the WTB release of October 25, 1925, is recorded in this memorandum by Stockhausen.

58. Cabinet meeting, October 26, 1925, BA, R43I/1405, D766381–82; *VM*, 2:207.

59. Bay. Ges. Berlin, pol. Akten of 1925, vol 106, report from March 10, 1925.

60. NL Stresemann, 3113/7129/vol. 272, H147936–38, and 3114/7133/vol. 276, H148549–51, Luther to Stresemann, July 14, and Stresemann, notes, August 2, 1925.

Chapter 8

1. NL Westarp, Frl. v. Watter to Prof. Otto, December 3, 1925; Dörr, "Deutschnationale Volkspartei," pp. 185–88; *VM*, 2:248.

2. See *KDnVp* for October 1925, but esp. no. 211, October 1, and no. 226, October 19. The general tone contrasts sharply with the publication *Der Ostmärker*, no. 3, September 22, 1925, put out by the "Ostmarken-Ausschuss der Deutschnationalen Volkspartei." See also NsäStA, Osnabrück, C1/15, pp. 64–78, "Leitsätze zu politischen Vorträgen," early October 1925, for a negative but moderate and issue-oriented critique of the Locarno negotiations.

3. NL Westarp, "Resolution der Parteileitung vom 29. Oktober 1925." See also BA, R43I/429, L280188–90 for articles from *Deutsche Tageszeitung* and *Kreuzzeitung* in a similar vein.

4. Published in *KDnVp*, no. 237 (October 31, 1925), and reprinted in Dörr, "Deutschnationale Volkspartei," pp. 522–23.

5. See *KDnVp*, app. no. 237, October 31, 1925, "Locarno: Grundsätzliches—Nationale Forderung," by Graf Westarp.

6. *Schulthess*, 1925, pp. 157–59.

7. Memos by Wachsmann, both October 26, 1925, BA, R43I/429, L280172, L280175.

8. Notes by Wachsmann, ibid., L280175, and by Luther, ibid., L280168–70, from October 26 and 25, 1925, respectively.
9. Haungs, *Reichspräsident*, p. 313 n.76, quotes Koch-Weser's report that Gessler and Brauns had difficulty in convincing Luther that he should reject Schiele's suggestion that Neuhaus and Schlieben be reappointed.
10. Notes by Pünder, October 26, 1925, BA, R43I/429, L280176–78.
11. Notes by Luther, and Kempner to Stresemann, both October 25, 1925, ibid., L280168–70 and L280166–67.
12. Notes by Pünder, October 26, 1925, ibid., L280176–78.
13. Cabinet meeting, October 26, 1925 (12:00 noon), ibid., 1405, D766383 ff.
14. *VM*, 2:209.
15. Cabinet meeting, October 26, 1925 (6:00 P.M.), BA, R43I/1405, D766386–88.
16. Ibid., D766388–89.
17. Notes on a telephone conversation between Stresemann and the Reichschancellery, October 28, 1925, ibid., R43I/429, p. 63; *VM*, 2:209.
18. Forschungsstelle für die Geschichte des Nationalsozialismus in Hamburg (hereafter cited as FS-Hamburg), 7533/DNVP/III, from November 17, 1925.
19. *Schulthess*, 1925, p. 160.
20. *VM*, 2:206, 380; NL Stresemann, 3169/7322/vol. 32, H160526–31, Alvensleben to Stresemann, November 14 and December 2, 1925, and 3113/7131/vol. 274, H148333–34, November 11, 1925.
21. NL Westarp, Sahl to Westarp, October 24, 1925.
22. Letter to the Executive Committee of the DNVP from party members in Breslau, with numerous signatures, November 3, 1925, copy in BA, R7VI/615a; BA, NL Luther, vol. 290, Batocki to Luther, October 29, 1925, and Keyserlingk to Tramm, November 20, 1925, copy sent to Luther by Tramm.
23. Dated November 2, 1925, BA, R43I/429, L280228. Emphasis as in the original. The heading and signature are in Hindenburg's own hand.
24. Ibid., L280238.
25. AA, RM 15-1/8, D645289, telegram from Paris, October 23, 1925.
26. BA, R43I/425, L280962–69, report from October 28 of a conversation on October 27, 1925.
27. AA, RM 15-1/8, D645294 and D645353–59, October 24, 1925, to Paris, and October 28, 1925, from Paris.
28. NL Stresemann, 3113/7129/vol. 272, H148026 ff., November 8, 1925.
29. *Survey*, 1925, 2:191–92.
30. Ibid., p. 192
31. Cabinet meeting, November 16, 1925, BA, R43I/1406, D766571.
32. Ibid., D766572 ff.
33. Ibid., D766579.
34. ZStA, Potsdam, 61 Ve 1 (ADV), no. 145, pp. 20–39, Sitzung des Geschäftsführenden Ausschusses des ADV in Berlin, December 12, 1925.

35. BA, R43I/1406, D766583–86.
36. Cabinet meeting, November 17, 1925, ibid., D766595–601.
37. Ibid., D766601.
38. Ibid., D766601–3.
39. Ibid., D766604; cabinet meeting, November 19, 1925, ibid., D766675–77; Luther's Reichstag speech, *Verhandlungen*, vol. 388, p. 4475.
40. Bay. Ges. Berlin, pol. Akten of 1925, vol. 106, report from November 25, 1925, on a meeting of the Reichstag's Foreign Affairs Committee. See also AA, RM 15-1/8, D645514. This November 21, 1925, memo from the Departments of Justice and the Interior contends that no constitutional necessity for a two-thirds majority existed. The decision predated the memo, however. See cabinet meeting, November 17, 1925, BA, R43I/1406, D766603.
41. Hindenburg to Luther, November 27, 1925, printed in Walter Hubatsch, *Hindenburg und der Staat* (Göttingen: Musterschmidt-Verlag, 1966), p. 220, document 37(a). The German Nationalist leaders who were involved in the talks with Hindenburg that preceded the letter were probably Westarp and Hergt. See NL Westarp, Frl. v. Watter to Prof. Otto, December 3, 1925: "Aus mehreren Verhandlungen unseres Freundes W[estarp]. und des Ex[cellenz Hergt]. mit ihm [Hindenburg] hat sich . . . gezeigt, wie beeinflussbar er doch sein kann."
42. Cabinet meeting, November 27, 1925, R43I/1406, D766700–702; Hubatsch, *Hindenburg*, p. 221, document 37(b).
43. *Schulthess*, 1925, p. 181; *Verhandlungen*, vol. 388, p. 4654. On December 1, 1925, Luther and Stresemann signed the Locarno accords in London.
44. Cabinet meeting, December 5, 1925, BA, R43I/1407, D766841–44.
45. NL Westarp, notes on a meeting with the Reichspresident, December 7, 1925.
46. BA, NL Pünder, vol. 26, pp. 144–45, December 14, 1925, notes on a conversation between Pünder and Schiele.
47. *Schulthess*, 1925, p. 192; on the cabinet negotiations in general see Stürmer, *Koalition*, pp. 134–43, and Haungs, *Reichspräsident*, pp. 94–108. The memorandum in which the plan that Hindenburg followed was proposed by State Secretary Meissner is printed in Stürmer, *Koalition*, pp. 288 ff. Other relevant memoranda are in BA, R43I/1307.
48. Haungs, *Reichspräsident*, p. 105, citing BA, NL Koch-Weser, no. 32, notes from December 15, 1925.
49. Andreas Dorpalen, *Hindenburg and the Weimar Republic* (Princeton, N.J.: Princeton University Press, 1964), p. 100.
50. *Schulthess*, 1926, pp. 5–8.
51. BA, NL Pünder, vol. 27, p. 124, January 14, 1925, notes on a telephone conversation between Pünder and Schiele.
52. *Schulthess*, 1926, p. 7; Erich Eyck, *A History of the Weimar Republic*, trans. Harlan P. Hanson and Robert G. L. Waite, 2 vols. (Cambridge, Mass.: Harvard University Press, 1962–63), 2:74. The DDP, insulted by this slight

to its chairman, very nearly extended the crisis by refusing to support the Luther Cabinet. The final acceptance of the minority solution passed in the party by only one vote, which Koch-Weser himself cast in order to break the deadlock and permit the formation of a government. The ministry was, however, given to another DDP politician.

53. Cabinet meeting, December 5, 1925, BA, R43I/1407, D766843–44.

54. Cuno Horkenbach, *Das Deutsche Reich von 1918 bis Heute*, 2 vols. (Berlin: Verlag für Presse, Wirtschaft und Politik, 1930–31), 1:218, 221; Hans W. Gatzke, *Stresemann and the Rearmament of Germany* (Baltimore, Md.: Johns Hopkins University Press, 1954), pp. 44–45.

55. NL Westarp, Hoetzsch to Westarp, December 29, 1925.

56. Grathwol, "Gustav Stresemann," *JMH* 45:52–70; AA, RM 15-1/Beiheft, D645144 and D645155–62, conversations at Locarno with Belgian Foreign Minister Vandervelde on October 7 and 9, 1925, respectively.

57. For one of the most recent denials of the advantages of Locarno, see Walsdorff, *Westorientierung*, pp. 146 ff. For an example of Nationalist criticism in its restrained, official form, see *KDnVp*, no. 239, November 3, 1925.

58. *Verhandlungen*, vol. 388, p. 4654.

59. *VM*, 2:210, 246, 248, 380.

60. The characterization of the second Luther Cabinet as "presidential" comes from Curtius, *Sechs Jahre Minister*, p. 13.

61. *VM*, 2:248.

62. Eyck, *History of the Weimar Republic*, 2:76.

Chapter 9

1. NL Westarp, Frl. v. Watter to Prof. Otto, December 3, 1925; ibid., notes on a conversation, December 7, 1925, with the Reichspresident; and Hindenburg to Luther, December 4, 1925, printed in Hubatsch, *Hindenburg*, pp. 221–23, document 37(c). Hindenburg sent copies of a series of letters, including this one, to Westarp.

2. *Verhandlungen*, vol. 388, p. 5149, the emphasis is mine; NsäStA, Osnabrück, C1/20, p. 1, Politischer Brief no. 1, January 24, 1926.

3. *Verhandlungen*, vol. 388, p. 5173; *VM*, 2:386, diary entry from January 28, 1926; BA, NL Luther, vol. 362, January 28, 1926.

4. BA, NL Luther, vol. 362, January 28, 1926.

5. *VM*, 2:387.

6. The SPD's 130 abstentions highlighted the anomalousness of the negotiations regarding a coalition. The SPD could have established a majority coalition under the Left-oriented Democratic leader, Erich Koch-Weser. Instead, they saved a minority coalition under the Right-oriented Luther.

7. *KDnVp*, Parlamentarische Beilage, January 25, 1926; bay. Ges. Berlin, pol.

Akten of 1926, vol. 108, reports on meetings of the Reichstag's Foreign Affairs Committee from January 14 and 15, 1926.

8. BA, NL Luther, vol. 362, January 26, 1926, conversation with Margerie; BA, R43I/1409, D767407–37, material on the negotiations with the Rhineland Commission.

9. Bay. Ges. Berlin, pol. Akten of 1926, vol. 108, report from February 4, 1926.

10. NL Westarp contains all the documents printed as 37(a) through (p) in Hubatsch, *Hindenburg*, pp. 220–31.

11. Cabinet meeting, February 8, 1926, BA, R43I/1409, D767547–48; printed in *Akten zur deutschen auswärtigen Politik, 1918–1945* (hereafter cited as *ADAP*), ser. B, 1925–33 (Göttingen: Vandenhoeck & Ruprecht, 1966), vol. 1, pt. 1, pp. 209–18.

12. BA, R43I/1409, D767547–48.

13. Ibid., D767547–48 and D767551–61.

14. Ibid., D767561; Hubatsch, *Hindenburg*, pp. 224–26, documents 37(f)–(h).

15. Horkenbach, *Das Deutsche Reich*, 1:222–23.

16. Cabinet meeting, February 8, 1926, BA, R43I/1409, D767551–52.

17. Luther to Hindenburg, February 10, 1926, in Hubatsch, *Hindenburg*, pp. 226–28, document 37(l); also in *Locarno-Konferenz*, pp. 235–37.

18. Cabinet meeting, February 11, 1926, BA, R43I/1409, D767632–33.

19. Zimmermann, *Deutsche Aussenpolitik*, p. 307; bay. Ges. Berlin, pol. Akten of 1926, vol. 108, report from February 19, 1926.

20. Bay. Ges. Berlin, pol. Akten of 1926, vol. 108, report from February 19, 1926.

21. Ibid.

22. Ibid.

23. Cabinet meeting, February 24, 1926, BA, R43I/1409, D767851–55.

24. Hindenburg to Luther, February 27, 1926, printed in Hubatsch, *Hindenburg*, pp. 229–30, document 37(n); and in *ADAP*, ser. B, vol. 1, pt. 1, pp. 311–12.

25. *ADAP*, ser. B., vol. 1, pt. 1, p. 312 n.4.

26. Ibid.; NsäStA, Osnabrück, C1/18, p. 67, back, handwritten notes [by the chairman of the DNVP Landesverband Osnabrück, Hagen, made during Westarp's presentation to the Parteivertretertagung in Berlin, March 24, 1926], C1/27-I, pt. 1, pp. 184 f., Hagen to Bürgermeister Buff of Bremen, March 29, 1926, and C1/27-II, pt. 1, p. 277, Hagen to Winckler, March 15, 1926.

27. Class's efforts are evident from the documents of the FS-Hamburg, 11/C3 and 412/ADV, which are titillating in their revelations. The campaign is more extensively discussed in Brewster S. Chamberlin's "The Enemy on the Right: The *Alldeutschen Verband* in the Weimar Republic 1918–1926" (Ph.D. diss., University of Maryland, 1972). See also BA, NL Leo Wegener, no. 11, "Zeitungsausschnitte und Schriftwechsel (mit und betreffend) Alfred Hugenberg, 1926–1928," in general, but esp. pp. 260 ff., Hayessen to Traub, January 9, 1926, and p. 252, Hayessen to Wegener, February 25,

1926, in which Oldenburg-Januschau's efforts on Hugenberg's behalf are mentioned. See also A. Thimme, *Flucht*, p. 53.

28. Luther to Hindenburg, March 4, 1926, in Hubatsch, *Hindenburg*, pp. 230–31, document 37(o); also in *ADAP*, ser. B, vol. 1, pt. 1, pp. 333–34.

29. See Paul Schmidt, *Statist auf diplomatischer Bühne* (Bonn: Athenäum-Verlag, 1949), pp. 96–105; *Survey*, 1926, pp. 1–40; Spenz, *Diplomatische Vorgeschichte*, pp. 126 ff.; *ADAP*, ser. B, vol. 1, pt. 1, see under "Völkerbund" in the table of contents for the numerous documents relating to Germany's diplomatic efforts on the problems surrounding her entry into the league.

30. Schmidt, *Statist*, pp. 105–6.

31. Telegram from Geneva, March 14, 1926 (no. 30), BA, R43I/1410, D768083–85, published in part in *ADAP*, ser. B, vol. 1, pt. 1, p. 389 n.4.

32. BA, R43I/1410, D768085–87; *ADAP*, ser. B, vol. 1, pt. 1, p. 392 n.5.

33. Telegram from Geneva, March 15, 1926, BA, R43I/1410, D768088–89.

34. Cabinet meeting, March 15, 1926, ibid., D768063–64; Eyck, *History of the Weimar Republic*, 2:81–82, erroneously implies that Germany was completely unwilling to compromise. The two telegrams cited above and the cabinet meeting of March 15 indicate that this was not the case.

35. *Survey*, 1926, pp. 44–46; Schmidt, *Statist*, pp. 107–8; also *ADAP*, ser. B, vol. 1, pt. 1, for related documents.

36. Quoted in *Survey*, 1926, p. 46.

37. Quoted in Schmidt, *Statist*, p. 109.

38. Cabinet meeting, March 18, 1926, BA, R43I/1410, D768090–95, printed in *ADAP*, ser. B, vol. 1, pt. 1, pp. 412–14.

39. *Verhandlungen*, vol. 389, pp. 6453–60.

40. See *KDnVp*, January to March, 1926, esp. no. 9, January 22; no. 18, February 13; no. 25, March 2; nos. 32–34, March 18, 20, and 23.

41. *Verhandlungen,* vol. 389, pp. 6510–12.

42. NL Westarp, Hoetzsch to Westarp, December 31, 1925; Westarp to Schrader, January 18, 1926; *Berliner Lokalanzeiger*, quoting Westarp, April 26, 1926 (evening edition), "Gegen Stresemanns Aussenpolitik," in AA, StS, I (Innere)/5; NsäStA, Osnabrück, C1/20, pp. 16–20, Politischer Brief no. 7, May 5, 1926.

43. BA, R43I/2654, p. 143, government report from Munich, no. 140, March 22, 1926.

44. S. William Halperin, *Germany Tried Democracy: A Political History of the Reich from 1918 to 1933* (New York: W. W. Norton & Co., 1965), p. 350; Dorpalen, *Hindenburg*, pp. 104–7; Haungs, *Reichspräsident*, pp. 109–16. BA, NL Karl Jarres, no. 37, Luther to von Richthofen, July 3, 1926, provides an extensive discussion of DNVP contacts with Luther, which were aimed at readmitting the party to the cabinet.

45. Stürmer, *Koalition*, pp. 148–62; *Schulthess*, 1926, pp. 100–101; Haungs,

Reichspräsident, pp. 109–16; cabinet meeting, May 10, 1926, BA, R43I/1412, D768784–90.

46. Dorpalen, *Hindenburg*, pp. 107–9; NL Westarp, Westarp to Seidlitz, July 7, 1926.
47. NL Westarp, Westarp to Gossler, June 21, 1926.
48. Dorpalen, *Hindenburg*, pp. 114–15.
49. *VM*, 2:407.
50. Hindenburg to Reichskanzlei, July 23, 1926, BA, NL Pünder, vol. 27, pp. 77–79.
51. NL Westarp, Treviranus to Hoetzsch, August 18, 1926.
52. Ibid., Westarp to Marx, August 5, 1926. Reichspresident Hindenburg reiterated his earlier objections to unconditional entry in a letter that echoed several of the reservations that Westarp had mentioned. Hindenburg to Marx, August 9, 1926, BA, R43I/486, D803460–63.
53. See also NL Westarp, comment by Hergt, June 16, 1926, on a letter, Arbeitsausschuss Deutschnationaler Industrieller to Westarp, June 3, 1926; Hoetzsch to Westarp, August 10, 1926.
54. BA, NL Pünder, vol. 27, pp. 78–79, letter to Reichskanzler, July 23, 1926.
55. NL Westarp, Westarp to Hoetzsch, August 18, 1926, Treviranus to Hoetzsch, and Hoetzsch to Westarp, both August 21, 1926.
56. Ibid., Wallraf to Westarp, August 21, 1926.
57. Ibid., Westarp to Hoetzsch, and Westarp to Stresemann, both August 26, 1926.
58. AA, RM 9/1, D555018–23, telegram, April 1, 1925; ibid., 15-1/3, D642965–68, telegram, April 3, 1925; ibid., 88/1, telegram no. 236, from Paris, April 4, 1925 (not filmed). See Grathwol, "Germany and the Eupen-Malmédy Affair," *CEH* 8:221–50, for more detail on this entire episode.
59. Cabinet meeting, March 31, 1926, BA, R43I/1410, D768375–76.
60. *Vermerk*, July 3, 1926, ibid., 1413, D769038; BA, NL Pünder, vol. 27, p. 85, letter to the Reichskanzler, July 25, 1926.
61. Horkenbach, *Das Deutsche Reich*, 1:229; *Schulthess*, 1926, pp. 136–37; GStA, München, MA 103542, report from August 26, 1926, on a meeting of the Reichstag's Foreign Affairs Committee; Grathwol, "Germany and the Eupen-Malmédy Affair," *CEH* 8:241–50.
62. AA, RM 88/1, notes on a conversation between Hesnard and Stresemann, August 5, 1926, printed in *ADAP*, ser. B, vol. 1, pt. 2, pp. 15–19.
63. AA, RM 88/1, *Aufzeichnung*, August 22, 1926, printed in *ADAP*, ser. B, vol. 1, pt. 2, pp. 109–16.
64. ZStA, Potsdam, 06.01 (Präsi), no. 695, pp. 178–88, "Aufzeichung über die Sitzung des Auswärtigen Ausschusses" (August 26, 1926); for another account of the same meeting see GStA, München, MA 103542, report of August 26, 1926. The DNVP was very well informed on the Eupen-Malmédy negotiations, as its Politischer Brief no. 12 shows. See NsäStA, Osnabrück, C1/20, pp. 30 ff., August 27, 1926.

Chapter 10

1. On the *Parteitag*, see Dörr, "Deutschnationale Volkspartei," pp. 251–52.
2. Zimmermann, *Deutsche Aussenpolitik*, p. 314; Jon Jacobson and John T. Walker, "The Impulse for a Franco-German Entente: The Origins of the Thoiry Conference, 1926," *Journal of Contemporary History* 10 (1975): 157–81.
3. BA, NL Pünder, vol. 27, pp. 81–96, Pünder to Marx, July 23 and 28, 1926.
4. AA, RM 88/1, August 5, 1926, conversation between Stresemann and Hesnard; ibid., August 22, 1926, conversation between Stresemann and Laboulaye, particularly pp. 8 and 9, both printed in *ADAP*, ser. B, vol. 1, pt. 2, pp. 15 ff. and 109 ff.; cabinet meeting, September 2, 1926, BA, R43I/1415, D769979; for the German Foreign Office's assessment of Poincaré's financial policies and successes, see AA, RM 69/4, D690033–39, August 13, 1926, report by Hoesch.
5. AA, RM 88/1, August 22, 1926, conversation between Stresemann and Laboulaye.
6. Cabinet meeting, September 2, 1926, BA, R43I/1415, D767976–80.
7. Ibid., September 20, 1926, D770045–74. The foregoing is based on this fifty-five page stenographically recorded report that Pünder delivered to the cabinet.
8. On the presence of Stresemann's aide see *ADAP*, ser. B, vol. 1, pt. 2, p. 663, Stresemann's appointment calendar, and Jacobson and Walker, "Impulse," *JCH* 10:176 n.1.
9. Cabinet meetings, September 24, 1926, BA, R43I/1415, D770116–24, and September 20, 1926, D769976–770100; Stresemann's notes on the Thoiry talks, September 20, 1926, ibid., D770125–30; *ADAP*, ser. B, vol. 1, pt. 2, pp. 210–33 and 202–10.
10. Cabinet meetings, September 20, 1926, BA, R43I/1415, D770075–81, and September 24, 1926, D770116–18; Stresemann's notes on the Thoiry meeting, ibid., D770125–39.
11. Text of communiqué in Pünder's report, cabinet meeting, September 20, 1926, ibid., D770075.
12. Ibid., D770086–88.
13. Ibid., D770096–97.
14. Ibid., September 24, 1926, D770120–21.
15. Ibid., D770122.
16. Ibid., appendix, D770124.
17. GStA, München, MA 103217, report from September 21, 1926; BA, NL Pünder, vol. 27, pp. 131–33, letter of September 27, 1926.
18. GStA, München, MA 103217, report from September 21, 1926.
19. BA, R43I/2654, p. 143, government report from Munich, no. 506, September 27, 1926.
20. Ibid., p. 140, no. 153, March 22, 1926; see also above, chap. 9 at n.43.

21. NL Westarp, Dr. Rademacher to Dr. Philipp, October 7, 1926.
22. NsäStA, Osnabrück, C1/17-III, pp. 80, 85, 86, 103; NsäStA, Aurich, dept. 51/2, Landesverband Ostfriesland an Kreisvereine, October 12, 1926; Dörr, "Deutschnationale Volkspartei," pp. 252–53.
23. Bay. Ges. Berlin, pol. Akten of 1926, vol. 108, report of October 7, 1926.
24. See NL Westarp, Hoetzsch to Westarp, September 26, 1926; cabinet meeting, October 13, 1926, BA, R43I/1415, D770221–23; bay. Ges. Berlin, pol. Akten of 1926, vol. 108, reports of October 13, 1926, on a meeting of the Reichsrat's Foreign Affairs Committee, and of October 7 and November 4, 1926, on meetings of the Reichstag's Foreign Affairs Committee; GStA, München, MA 103217, report of September 27, 1926.
25. AA, RM 69/5, D690091–98, report by Hoesch on Poincaré's financial measures, October 5, 1926.
26. NL Westarp, e.g., DNVP Landesverband Thüringen to Westarp, December 2, 1926.
27. Bay. Ges. Berlin, pol. Akten of 1926, vol. 108, reports of November 4, 1926; NL Westarp, Hoetzsch to Westarp, November 15, 1926; ibid., DNVP Landesverband Thüringen to Westarp, December 2, 1926.
28. Ibid., Westarp to Dr. Rademacher, October 20, 1926, and Westarp to DNVP Landesverband Thüringen, December 9, 1926.
29. Cabinet meeting, December 13, 1926, BA, R43I/1417, D771252; NL Westarp, Hoetzsch to Westarp, November 15, 1926; Stürmer, *Koalition*, pp. 165–67.
30. Cabinet meeting, December 13, 1926, BA R43I/1417, D771252–53; Turner, *Stresemann*, pp. 224–26.
31. Turner, *Stresemann*, pp. 224–26; Stürmer, *Koalition*, pp. 171 ff.; Haungs, *Reichspräsident*, pp. 117–23.
32. Haungs, *Reichspräsident*, p. 119 and n. 166; Stürmer, *Koalition*, pp. 175–76.
33. Stampfer, *Vierzehn Jahre*, p. 453; Eyck, *History of the Weimar Republic*, 2:126; and esp. Dorpalen, *Hindenburg*, pp. 118–22.
34. Cabinet meetings, December 15 and 16, 1926, BA, R43I/1417, D771311–13, D771314–16; Turner, *Stresemann*, p. 227; Dorpalen, *Hindenburg*, pp. 122–23.
35. Meeting between representatives of the SPD and the cabinet on December 1, 1926, in Otto-Ernst Schüddekopf, *Heer und Republik: Quellen zur Politik der Reichswehrführung, 1918 bis 1933* (Hanover: Norddeutsche Verlagsanstalt O. Goedel, 1955), pp. 214–17.
36. Horkenbach, *Das Deutsche Reich*, 1:234; *VM*, 3:94, 98; Haungs, *Reichspräsident*, pp. 117–38, covers the entire crisis in detail.
37. *VM*, 3:99; Horkenbach, *Das Deutsche Reich*, 1:234.
38. *VM*, 3:91–107.
39. Ibid., pp. 94, 97.
40. See, for examples of this, ZStA, Potsdam, 06.01 (Präsi), no. 44; one of these documents, Aktennotiz, December 17, 1926 [Meissner], bears the notation in

Meissner's hand, "Abg. Westarp hat *vertraulich* Abschrift dieses erhalten." For additional evidence of extensive contacts between the President's Office and the DNVP leadership, see Class's account of the cabinet negotiations in ibid., 61 Ve 1 (ADV), no. 149, pp. 35–82, Sitzung des Geschäftsführenden Ausschusses des Alldeutschen Verbands in Berlin, February 12 and 13, 1927.

41. *VM*, 3:101; Dorpalen, *Hindenburg*, pp. 125–26; Haungs, *Reichspräsident*, pp. 123–28 and 134 n.222; Stürmer, *Koalition*, pp. 186–88 and 302–3.
42. Horkenbach, *Das Deutsche Reich*, 1:234–35.
43. Ibid., p. 235; BA, NL Pünder, vol. 33, pp. 40–44.
44. See Dörr, "Deutschnationale Volkspartei," pp. 256–60.
45. See, for example, ZStA, Potsdam, 61 Re 1 (Reichslandbund), no. 144, pp. 162–70, "Bericht über die Sitzung des Bundesvorstandes am 13. Januar 1927," and the comments critical of this pressure in the ADV meetings of September and December 1926 and February 1927, ibid., 61 Ve 1 (ADV), no. 147, pp. 83–102; no. 148, pp. 20–47; no. 149, pp. 35–82.
46. ZStA, Potsdam, 61 Re 1 (Reichslandbund), no. 146, p. 88, Sitzung . . . , April 10, 1926, and no. 212, pp. 265–67, 269, Brockhusen to Westarp, May 9, 1926, with covering letter and copy to ADV.
47. ZStA, Potsdam, no. 149, pp. 35–82, Sitzung . . . , February 12 and 13, 1927.
48. FS-Hamburg, 11/C3 (ADV), pp. 843–900; ZStA, Potsdam, 06.01 (Präsi), no. 0/3/10, p. 237, Generalleutnant von Cramon to Meissner, January 1, 1927.
49. Chamberlin, "Enemy on the Right," pp. 344–46; BA, NL Wegener, no. 11, pp. 260, 252, Hayessen to Traub, January 9, 1926, and to Wegener, February 25, 1926; also Wegener's reply to Hayessen, March 4, 1926.
50. NL Westarp, Hugenberg to Westarp, January 15, 1927.
51. BA, NL Hugenberg, no. 113, notes for a speech before the Executive Committee, January 1927.
52. ZStA, Potsdam, 61 Ve 1 (ADV), no. 149, pp. 27–28. The document is an early copy of Class's survey of the cabinet negotiations of late 1926 to early 1927, most of which was eventually incorporated into the minutes of the ADV's meeting of February 12 and 13, 1927. Class himself, however, cut the mention of the "Schutzverein" from the final copy of the minutes.
53. Ibid.; and for similar statements see the ADV meetings of September and December 1926, no. 147, p. 89, and no. 148, pp. 23–26.
54. BA, NL Hugenberg, no. 65, pp. 503, 475, Hugenberg to Wegener, November 12, 1926, and January 31, 1927, respectively; NL Westarp, June 23, 1925 (mentioned in chap. 5, n. 41 above), and March 18, 1927, Ellenbeck et al. to Westarp. By 1927 the DNVP's Central Committee included about 120 members. Attendance at meetings during the summer of 1927 seems to have run only about 50 to 60 percent of this, however. Under the circumstances, attendance by Hugenberg's supporters was probably higher than average attendance. For some rather spotty information on membership in the Central Committee, see FS-Hamburg, NL Diller, 11/D9.

55. Gottfried Treviranus, *Das Ende von Weimar: Heinrich Brüning und seine Zeit* (Düsseldorf and Vienna: Econ-Verlag, 1968), pp. 99 and 405 n.34, quoting Freytagh-Loringhoven. The four ministers finally appointed from the DNVP were Hergt, Schiele, Wilhelm Koch-Eberfeld, and Walther von Keudell. See Dörr, "Deutschnationale Volkspartei," pp. 270–89.

56. As an exception to this statement, one might list the Franco-German trade agreements, a topic that is still largely unexplored.

57. AA, RM 67/2, D685671–75, telegram no. 31, from Paris, January 8, 1927.

58. Ibid.; Zimmermann, *Deutsche Aussenpolitik*, pp. 324–25, cabinet meeting, March 15, 1927, BA, R43I/1419, D772064. See also for subsequent paragraphs.

59. Cabinet meeting, March 15, 1927, BA, R43I/1419, D772060–68, for this and preceding paragraphs.

60. Ibid., D772070 ff.

61. Bay. Ges. Berlin, pol. Akten of 1927, vol. 110, report of March 17, 1927.

62. On the Berlin Treaty see Walsdorff, *Westorientierung*, pp. 157–89, and the relevant documents in the series from the German Foreign Office and the Reichskanzlei in *Akten zur Deutschen Auswärtigen Politik*, ser. B, vol. 1, pt. 1, and in *Die Kabinette Luther*. For the situation in 1927 see Horkenbach, *Das Deutsche Reich*, 1:237; bay. Ges. Berlin, pol. Akten of 1927, vol. 110, reports of April 21 and May 27, 1927; cabinet meeting, May 30, 1927, BA, R43I/1420, D772586–91.

63. NL Westarp, Hoetzsch to Westarp, March 19, 1927, and Westarp to Sieveking, March 27, 1927; cabinet meeting, May 30, 1927, BA, R43I/1420, D772588; cabinet meeting, June 9, 1927, ibid., 1421, D772716–17.

64. Cabinet meeting, May 30, 1927, BA, R43I/1420, D772587; NL Westarp, Westarp to Wallraf, May 25, 1927; *VM*, 3:152.

65. Cabinet meeting, May 30, 1927, BA, R43I/1420, D772591, and June 9, 1927, ibid., 1421, D772718.

66. Horkenbach, *Das Deutsche Reich*, 1:238.

67. *VM*, 3:156–57, 161.

68. Horkenbach, *Das Deutsche Reich*, 1:240; cabinet meeting, June 20, 1927, BA, R43I/1421, D772866–87; *Verhandlungen*, vol. 393, p. 11003.

69. Cabinet meeting, August 10, 1927, BA, R43I/1423, D773601–10. See also for subsequent paragraphs.

70. Ibid.

71. NL Westarp, Hoetzsch to Westarp, August 5, 1927, "Anliegende Denk-schrift II," vol. 2.

72. Ibid., Westarp to Hoetzsch, September 2, 1927.

73. Cabinet meeting, August 30, 1927, BA, R43I/1423, D773649–53.

74. NL Westarp, Westarp to Hoetzsch, September 1, 1927.

75. Cabinet meeting, August 30, 1927, BA, R43I/1423, D773649–53.

76. *VM*, 3:186.

77. BA, NL Pünder, vol. 66, reports from Geneva, September 1927, pp. 3–21, 34–49.
78. Cabinet meeting, October 8, 1927, BA, R43I/1424, D774115–24.
79. Hertzman, *DNVP*, p. 161.
80. NL Westarp, Freytagh-Loringhoven to Westarp, February 9, 1927; Dörr, "Deutschnationale Volkspartei," pp. 289–92.
81. NL Westarp, Quaatz to Westarp, October 18, 1927.
82. Dörr, "Deutschnationale Volkspartei," pp. 313–19; Jonas, *Volkskonservativen*, pp. 30–32.
83. NL Westarp, Hoetzsch to Westarp, September 16, 1927; italics in original.
84. Bay. Ges. Berlin, pol. Akten of 1927, vol. 110, report of December 19, 1927.
85. BA, NL Pünder, vol. 66, pp. 3–4.
86. Cabinet meeting, December 20, 1927, BA, R43I/1426, D775116–17.
87. See Turner, *Stresemann*, p. 237.
88. Brauns's letter is in BA, NL Otto Gessler, vol. 9, June 27, 1926.

Chapter 11

1. On the issue of conflict and the regulation of it in Germany see Ralf Dahrendorf, *Society and Democracy in Germany*, chaps. 9 and 10, esp. pp. 137–38.
2. See Klaus Hildebrand, *The Foreign Policy of the Third Reich* (Berkeley: University of California Press, 1972), p. 81, for the suggestion that Hitler's foreign policy was "an expression of the sum of demands and wishes of that [German] society" and for a sketch of the connections linking Bülow and Tirpitz with Hitler. Stresemann stands apart from this "continuity," both because of the means he chose in foreign policy and because of his willingness to struggle to reshape those "demands and wishes" of German society that Hitler exploited so successfully.
3. The quotation is from *KDnVp*, no. 114, October 12, 1926; but the progressiveness of the change is only evident if the paper is read from January on. For a selection that traces the evolution see nos. 9, 18, 25, 44, 75, 88, 89. The same evolution can be seen by reading the DNVP circulars in NsäStA, Osnabrück.
4. All quotations in this paragraph are from *VM*, 2:246–48, journal notes from December 1925.
5. Cabinet meeting, February 8, 1926, BA, R43I/1409, D767564–65, now printed in *ADAP*, ser. B, vol. 1, pt. 1, pp. 209–18.
6. For Stresemann's speech, see *ADAP*, ser. B, vol. 1, pt. 2, pp. 665–69; and *VM*, 3:26–30, where it is incomplete.
7. See Annelise Thimme, "Gustav Stresemann: Legende und Wirklichkeit," *Historische Zeitschrift* 181 (1956): 332–33; and for a more extensive rejoinder than is offered here, see Grathwol, "Gustav Stresemann: Reflections on His Foreign Policy," *JMH* 45:52–70.

8. "Der Werdegang der Deutschnationalen Volkspartei, 1918–1928," in *Der nationale Wille*, ed. Max Weiss (Leipzig: Vaterländischer Buchvertrieb Th. Rudolph, 1928), p. 52.

9. NL Westarp, Westarp to Schiele, August 31, 1925.

10. *KDnVp*, no. 75, July 16, 1926, and no. 44, April 27, 1926.

11. On Stresemann's perception of economics and its role in foreign policy see Michael-Olaf Maxelon, *Stresemann und Frankreich*.

12. Karl Dietrich Bracher, *The German Dictatorship: The Origins, Structure, and Effects of National Socialism* (New York: Praeger, 1970), p. 78.

13. *KDnVp*, supplement to no. 60, June 14, 1926, citing a speech by Schlange-Schöningen from May. For Schlange-Schöningen's thoughts on the overthrow of the system see his memorandum dated May 19, 1924, to Hugenberg, printed in Dörr, "Deutschnationale Volkspartei," pp. 490–93.

14. The exchange is cited by Wolfgang Ruge, "Deutschnationale Volkspartei," p. 738, from the documents of the Deutsches Zentralarchiv (now Zentrales Staatsarchiv), Potsdam, ADV, no. 149, pp. 46 f. (perhaps through a typographical error Ruge incorrectly cited no. 146). Class mentions the exchange, which took place during the cabinet negotiations of late 1926 and early 1927, in his report to the ADV's Executive Committee, February 12 and 13, 1927.

15. Jonas, *Volkskonservativen*, pp. 61–62, quoting an article by Westarp from February 1930.

16. The statements are taken, in order, from Maxelon, *Stresemann und Frankreich*, pp. 89, 282; Walsdorff, *Westorientierung*, p. 106; and Peter Krüger, "Friedenssicherung und deutsche Revisionspolitik, die deutsche Aussenpolitik und die Verhandlungen über den Kellogg-Pakt," *Vierteljahrshefte für Zeitgeschichte* 22 (1974): 236.

17. Jonas, *Volkskonservativen*, p. 10.

18. See Gaines Post, *The Civil-Military Fabric of the Weimar Republic* (Princeton, N.J.: Princeton University Press, 1974), p. 92, for Kurt von Schleicher's comment on the Reichswehr's dilemma.

19. This weakness applies to Annelise Thimme's otherwise highly stimulating study *Flucht in den Mythos*, in which the period 1924-28 goes practically unmentioned.

20. Maxelon, *Stresemann und Frankreich*, p. 298.

21. See Geoffrey Barraclough's comments on mass democracy in *An Introduction to Contemporary History* (Baltimore, Md.: Penguin Books, 1964), chap. 5, esp. pp. 130–33.

22. The exchange quoted in this and the preceding paragraph comes from NL Westarp, letters dated January 31 (Engel), February 4 (Westarp), and February 8, 1928 (Engel). Engel's fervent nationalism, which was tragically ironic, did not compensate for his Jewish blood; he died at the hands of the Gestapo in November 1938.

23. Writing in 1968, Gottfried Treviranus claimed, on the basis of information

given to him by Schultz-Bromberg, who had counted the votes, that Hugenberg won only a minority of the votes cast: *Das Ende von Weimar*, p. 100.
Jonas, *Volkskonservativen*, p. 39, mentions majorities of one—referring to a
1964 article by Treviranus—and of five. For the surprise of Hugenberg's
victory see BA, NL Wegener, no. 23, p. 98, Class to Wegener, October 22,
1928; and ZStA, Potsdam, 61 Ve 1 (ADV), no. 156, pp. 48–64, Sitzung . . . ,
December 1 and 2, 1928. On the Lambach affair and the struggle for party
leadership see Jonas, *Volkskonservativen*, pp. 33–42; and Dörr, "Deutschnationale Volkspartei," pp. 391–465. Neither account is really satisfactory,
and many questions remain unresolved.

24. Ruge, "Deutschnationale Volkspartei," p. 741.
25. Klaus-Peter Hoepke, "Alfred Hugenberg als Vermittler zwischen gros-
    sindustriellen Interessen und Deutschnationale Volkspartei," in *Industrielles
    System und politische Entwicklung in der Weimarer Republik*, ed. Hans
    Mommsen, Dietmar Petzina, Bernd Weisbrod (Düsseldorf: Droste Verlag,
    1974), pp. 907–19.
26. For that story in greater detail see Jonas, *Volkskonservativen*, passim.
27. This assertion is made by Stürmer, *Koalition*, p. 254.
28. The judgment is expressed in Reinhard Behrens, "Die Deutschnationalen in
    Hamburg, 1918–1933" (diss., University of Hamburg, 1973), p. 343.
29. Hajo Holborn, *The Political Collapse of Europe* (New York: Alfred A.
    Knopf, 1951), pp. 27–28.

BIBLIOGRAPHY

Part 1
Unpublished and Primary Archival Materials, by Country and City

In special instances, the holdings of archives have been cited at considerable length as a service to others who are interested in the material. In other instances, where the collections are well known, much less detailed bibliographic citations seemed to be in order.

Belgium
    Brussels
        Archives générales du Royaume Belge
            Personal Papers of Paul Hymans
Bundesrepublik Deutschland
    Aurich
        Niedersächsisches Staatsarchiv
            Registry entry Dep. 51 (Deutschnationale Volkspartei), by volume number and title:
                1. Schriftverkehr des Landesverbandes Ostfriesland der DNVP, 1919–20
                2. Schriftverkehr des Kreisverbandes [sic] Aurich, 1919–33
                3. Propaganda- und Wahlschriften, Zeitungen, Zeitungsausschnitte, Aufrufe, 1921–33
                4. Rundschreiben und Mitteilungen der Parteizentrale in Berlin, 1928–33
                5. DNVP Kreisverband [sic] Aurich, 1931–32
    Bonn
        Auswärtiges Amt, Politisches Archiv. This is a voluminous collection,

which is conveniently indexed in George O. Kent's four-volume work (listed in part 2 of this bibliography). The following list includes only the files that are cited in the notes.

Büro des Reichsministers, by registry number and title:

   3b   Kabinett-Protokolle

   7   Frankreich

   9   Russland

   15-1 Verhandlungen mit den Alliierten über einen Sicherheitspakt

   67   Aufzeichnungen über die innere Lage

   69   Informatorische Aufzeichnungen

   88   Politische Parteien, ihre Verbände und ihre Propaganda

Büro des Staatssekretärs

   FS Sicherheitsfrage

   I   Innere Politik

Botschaft London, Geheim

Handakten Gaus

Nachlass Ago van Maltzan

Nachlass Gustav Stressmann

Gärtringen

    Nachlass Graf Kuno von Westarp. In the private possession of Dr. Friedrich Freiherr Hiller von Gaertringen.

Hamburg

    Forschungsstelle für die Geschichte des Nationalsozialismus in Hamburg. This collection is much richer than the title of the archives suggests.

Koblenz

    Bundesarchiv. Again, because of the accessibility of George Kent's guides, the volumes listed below represent only those entries that I have cited from this vast and very rich source.

    R43I   Alte Reichskanzlei, by registry number and title:

        424 Sicherheitsfrage

        425 Sicherheitsfrage

        429 Handakten betr. die Konferenz in Locarno

        431 Handakten zur Sicherheitsfrage

        486 Völkerbund

        1020 Akten betreffend Besprechungen mit den Parlamentariern und Fraktionsführern des Reichstags

        1391–1428 Akten betr. Kabinettsprotokolle, 1924–28

        2654 DNVP, 1919–31

    R45II (Deutsche Volkspartei)

    R7VI Reichswirtschaftsministerium

        615a Handakten des Reichswirtschaftsministers betr. Locarno

    Kleine Erwerbung Nr. 293, Briefe Prof. Dr. Axel Frhr. von Frey-

tagh-Loringhoven an Amtsgerichtsrat Dr. Otto von Sethe
Nachlässe (private papers):
  NL Otto Gessler
  NL Alfred Hugenberg
  NL Karl Jarres
  NL Erich Koch-Weser
  NL Hans-Erdmann von Lindeiner-Wildau
  NL Hans Luther
  NL Hans Schlange-Schöningen
  NL Leo Wegener
Military Archives:
  NL Kurt von Schleicher
Munich
  Bayerisches Geheimes Staatsarchiv:
    Akten des Ministeriums des Äusserns, Abgabe 1943
    Berichte der bayerischen Gesandtschaft in Berlin, Abgabe 1935
    (Both of these sources contain material from the Bavarian repre-
    sentative to the federal government in Berlin, Konrad von Preger.
    Of special interest are his reports on the secret meetings of the For-
    eign Affairs committees of the Reichstag and the Reichsrat, which
    he attended regularly.)
  Institut für Zeitgeschichte
    Nachlass Hans von Seeckt (on film)
Osnabrück
  Niedersächsisches Staatsarchiv
    Erwerbung C1 (DNVP Landesverband-Osnabrück). This is a very
      rich source, containing over one hundred volumes. Summary
      of holdings:
      1. Vorstand
          a. Schriftwechsel
          b. Umdrucke
      2. Büro
      3. Kasse
      4. Presse, Propaganda, Rundfunk
      5. Landesverbände, Kreisverbände, Ortsgruppen
      6. Berufständige und pp. Ausschüsse
      7. Wahlen
    Volumes consulted:
      1. Vorstand, (a) Schriftwechsel, by volume number and title:
          1. Vorstandsakten Hagen, 1925–27
          5. Schriftwechsel mit dem Parteivorstand
          6. Politischer Beauftragter, 1925 (Juli) 1927 (Aug.)
          7. Hauptgeschäftsstelle, Schriftwechsel mit der, 1922–25
          8. Hauptgeschäftsstelle, Schriftwechsel mit der, 1925–27

1. Vorstand, (b) Umdrucke:
    13. Landesverband-Vorstand (Sitzungsprotokolle Entschliessungen, Satzungen usw. 1922–26)
    14. Parteivorstand, Parteileitung, Politischer Beauftragter, 1925–27
    15. Informationen über Fragen verschiedener Inhalt, doch meist vertraulicher Art, 1925–28
    16. Fall Lambach 1928 July–Sept.
    17. Hauptgeschäftsstelle "Rundschreiben," 3 vols., 1922–28
    18. Hauptgeschäftsstelle. Umdrucke betr. Organisation, 1922–27
    19. "Schwarz-Weiss-Rot" (Vertraulich, nur zur Information), 1925
    20. "Politische Briefe," 1926
2. Büro:
    27. Allg. Korrespondenz, A–Z, 2 vols., 1922–25
    29. Korrespondenz mit den Propaganda-Rednern, 1924–25
    30. Niedersächische Telefon Gesellschaft, 1925–26
    32. Geschäftsanzeigen, Angebote, Briefwechsel mit Firmen, 1928–33
3. Kasse:
    36. Kassenbelege, 1923–26
    37–39. Kassenbelege, 1925
    40. Kassenbelege, 1926
    41. Nachweisungsbuch über gezahlte Vergütungen, 1928
    42. Belege, 1928
    44. Osnabrücker Bank, 1921–26
    45. Sonderkonto Hagen, 1927
    46. Schriftverkehr mit der *Niederdeutschen Zeitung*, Hannover, 1923–25
    47. Osnabrück *Allgemeine Zeitung*, Schriftwechsel betr. 1925–26
    50. Der Nationale Wille, 1932
    51. Deutschnationale Schriftenvertriebs-Stelle, 1924–28
    54. Zeitungsausschnitte, März–Apr. 1928
    55. Flugblätter—Texte
5. Landesverbände, Kreisverbände, Ortsgruppen: volume nos. 57–80
6. Berufsständische u. pp. Ausschüsse:
    84. Deutschnationaler Arbeiterbund, Ortsgruppe Osnabrück, 1923–28
    85. Bund der Deutschnationalen Parteibeamten, 1923–26
    87. Reichsausschuss Deutschnationaler Beamtenschaft, 1926–27

88. Deutschnationaler Lehrerbund, 1924–33
90. Hypotheken- Gläubiger- u. Sparer-Schutzverband, 1924–26
91. Deutschnationale Industrielle, 1925–27
92. Reichsmittelstandbund, 1923–25
94. Schutzverband für Handel u. Gewerbe
96. Volkische Reichsausschuss der DNVP, 1923–26
98. Reichskatholikenausschuss der DNVP, 1923–26
7. Wahlen:
    102. Landtagswahl, 24.IV.1924
    103. Kostenbelege der Reichstagwahlen u. Vorabstimmung für Hannover, 1924
    104. Reichstags- u. Landtagswahlen, 7.XII.1924
    105. Reichstagswahl, 7.XII.1924 (Auswahl der Kandidaten)
    106. Landtagswahl, 7.XII.1924 (Auswahl der Kandidaten)
    107. Reichspräsidentenwahl
See also the following registry entries:
Dep. 29^b 1. Stadt Lingen:
    XII. Polizeisachen/K, Politische Polizei (Geheimakten), 1924–28
Rep. 430. Dez. 201–15. Regierung Osnabrück ab 1912/acc. 11/57I, die an das Staatsarchiv Osnabrück abgegebenen Sachakten ... der ehem. Schutzpolizei in Osnabrück
Rep. 430I/1—acc. 5/66, by volume number and title:
    1. Politische Berichte, 1921–28
    4. Zeitungsausschnitte, 1926–28
    5. Rechtsorganisationen, 1925–28
    6. Politische u.a. wichtige Berichte (insbesondere verbotene Organisationen)
    8. Arbeits- und Wirtschaftslage
    21. Einwanderung verfassungsfeindlicher Personen u. regierungsfeindliche Bestrebungen überhaupt, 1921–31
    23. Durchführung der Verordnung zum Schutze der Republik
Rep. 430 Dez. 101 Regierung Osnabrück, ab 1912:
    1235. Politische Wochenberichte, ab 1923–31
Dep. 3b XVI. Freund'sche Zeitungsausschnitte—Sammlung
Dep. 3b XVII. Stadt Osnabrück, Zeitungen
Erw. C3. Flugblätter, Maueranschläge und Broschuren der Parteien in Osnabrück
Deutsche Demokratische Republik
    Potsdam
        Zentrales Staatsarchiv (formerly Deutsches Zentralarchiv)
        60 Vo 2 DNVP, by volume number and title:

Bibliography

1. Organisation, 1919–20
2. Geheim-Akten Hergt, 1919–24
3. Strömungen in der Partei (Akten Hergt-Lindeiner, 1919–22)
4. Geheimberichte, 1920–26
5. Der 13. März 1920
6. Verhandlungsberichte, 13. März 1920 (Exc. Hergt)
7. Putschgerüchte und eventuelle Folgen, 1920–23
8. Geheimbesprechungen, 1920–27
9. Regierungsbildung (Akten Hergt), 1920–24
10. Regierungsumbildung, 1924 (Akten Hergt)
11. Krisen in der Partei, 1926–33
12. Landesverband Berlin, 1927
13. Polemiken, 1928
14. Dolchstoss
15. Entschliessungen, 1928–29
16. Verschiedene Aufsätze u. Materialien
17. Deutschnationaler Arbeiterbund: Eingegangene Erklärungen, 1930
18. Rundschreiben Nr. 39/7, 7.11.1930
21. Verfassungsausschuss, 1923–24
22. Flaggenfrage. Schwarz-Weiss-Rot, 1925–26
23. Flaggenfrage, 1922–23
24. Verwaltungs- u. Verfassungsreform, 1927–28
25. Neugliederung des Reiches
26. Bayerische Mittelpartei, 1920–26 (Akten Hergt-Lindeiner)
27. Bayern u. das Reich, 1919–26 (Akten Hergt-Lindeiner) Geheim
28. Braunschweig
29. Aufwertungsfrage: Finanzpolitik
30. Aufwertungsfrage: Finanzpolitik
35. Hugenberg
36. Agrarpolitik, 1930–31 (Roggenstützungsaktion)
37. Roggenstützungsaktion, 1931
38. Kommunal-Politik, 1926
39. Rede Leopolds
40. Beamtenfragen, 1927
41. Engerer Reichsausschuss der Deutschnationale Beamtenschaft, 1929–30
42. Schulgesetz, 1927–28
43. Stellungnahmen von individuellen Professoren zur Keudellschen Entwurf
50. Fall v. Dewitz (DNVP)—Fenner, 1925
51. Freytagh-Loringhoven

52. Anordnungen für Partei-Zentrale, 1930–31
53. 2. Parteitag in Hannover (Okt. 1920)
54. Parteitag-Kassel-I
55. Parteitag Kassel-II
58. Schulungswoche, März 1928
59. Schulungswoche, März 1928
62. Wahlreform, 1927
63. Wahlrechtsvorlage, 1931
64. Zusammenstellung über die Wahlen zum Nationalversammlung, 1919
65. Materialien z. Reichstagswahl, 1924
66. Materialien z. Reichstagswahl, 1928
67. Hamburger Bürgerschaftswahl, Feb. 1928
68. Wahlmaterial, 1928
69. Sachsenwahlen, 1929–30
70. Statistisches . . . Reichstagswahlen, 1930
71. Volksentscheid, 1926
72. Volksbegehren, 1929
73. Volksbegehren, 1929
74. Statistik Volksbegehren, 1929
75. Volksbegehren Übergriffe, 1929
76. Stellung Beamten zum Volksbegehren, 1929
77. Volksbegehren, 1929—Presse
78. Deutschvölkische Freiheitspartei, 1926–28
79. Wirtschaftspartei
90. Verschiedenes Material, 1925–30
91. Verschiedenes, 1929–30
108. Briefe an Herrn Gustav Lücke; Cosel, Schlesien
180. Arbeiterbund: Kreisvereine u. Ortsgruppen, Orte S, 1922–29
187. Arbeiterbund: Allgemeine Korrespondenz, Orte mit B, Namen K–M, 1923–29
204. Arbeiterbund: Allgemeine Korrespondenz, Orte M, Namen A–Z, I, 1922–28
204-Beiheft. Arbeiterbund: 1928/IV, Kandidatenaufstellung, Magdeburg, Verbandssekretär Friedrich Mesenholl
210. Arbeiterbund: Allgemeine Korrespondenz, Orte S, St, Sch, Namen A–Q, 1929–I
235. Akten Rüffer, Arbeitssekretariat, 1919–28
248. Rundschreiben
249. Rundschreiben
250. Rundschreiben
251. Rundschreiben der Parteizentrale

252. Hilfskasse des Deutschnationalen Arbeiterbundes, 1927–30, A–Q
323. Deutschnationale Studentenschaft, Briefwechsel, 1924–25
327. Gedrucke Berichte u. Rundschreiben, 1919–22
406. Kandidatenfragen u. Wahlangelegenheiten
408. Besatzungsstärke
409. Material zum Etat des Reichsvermögensverwaltung, 1926–27
410. Besatzungsleistungsgesetz, 1926–27
411. Reichsministerium für die besetzten Gebiete u. Anträge des 19. Auschschusses, 1929–30
412. Vertrauensmännersammlungen
413. Presse
414. Presse
415. Wirtschaftsfragen der Besetzten Gebiete, 1923–27
416. Wirtschaftsfragen (Allgemein), 1.1.28–31.12.28
418. Betr. Verteilung des 30 Millionen Fonds, 1925–27
419. Material über Landwirtschaft, 1929
420. Verkehrsfragen im besetzten Gebiet, 1927–30
421. Brückenbauten im besetzten Gebiete
422. Kultur, 1927–29
423. Kultur
424. Deutschnationaler Arbeiterbund Landesverbandsgruppe Nordrhein
425. Arbeiterfragen, besetztes Gebiet & Saar, Arbeiterbeihilfe
426. Beamte
427. Mittelstand im besetzten Gebiet, 1928–29
428/Va. Landesverbände, 1928
428/Va. (Landesverbände) von Dryander
430/Vb. Kreisvereine, 1927–28
06.01 Präsidialkanzlei (Präsi.), by volume number and title:
0/3/7. Persönlicher Schriftwechsel des Herrn Staatssekretärs Dr. Meissner, 1.2.26 bis 25.5.26
0/3/8. Persönlicher Schriftwechsel des Herrn Staatssekretärs Dr. Meissner, 25.5.26 bis 6.8.26
0/3/9. Persönlicher Schriftwechsel des Herrn Staatssekretärs Dr. Meissner, 7.8.26 bis 5.11.26
0/3/10. Persönlicher Schriftwechsel des Herrn Staatssekretärs Dr. Meissner, 6.11.26 bis 2.1.27
0/3/11. Persönlicher Schriftwechsel des Herrn Staatssekretärs Dr. Meissner, 10.1.27 bis 28.2.27
41. Kabinettsbildung
42. Kabinettsbildung
43. Kabinettsbildung, 1.12.25 bis 16.12.26

44. Kabinettsbildung, 17.12.26 bis 7.6.28
45. Kabinettsbildung, 31.5.28 bis 31.12.29
680. Ausführungen des Friedensvertrags, 8.9.23 bis 30.3.24
681. Ausführungen des Friedensvertrags, 1.4.24 bis 8.5.25
682. Ausführungen des Friedensvertrags, 1925–27
687/1. Sicherheitspakt . . .
689. Verhandlungen über Reparationen, 1924
695. Eintritt Deutschlands in den Völkerbund, 1925–26
696. Völkerbund, allgemeine
699. Kriegsachtungspakt, Weltfriedenspakt, 1928–34
700. Frankreich, 1919–26 (Zwischenstaatliche Abkommen)
701. Frankreich, 1919–26 (Zwischenstaatliche Abkommen)
702. Frankreich, 1919–26 (Zwischenstaatliche Abkommen)
703. Frankreich, 1919–26 (Zwischenstaatliche Abkommen)
708. Sowjetunion, 1919–27
61 Re 1 Reichslandbund (RLB), by volume number and title:
120a. Volksbegehren gegen den Young Plan: Presseauseinander-
    setzungen, verschiedene Zeitungen u. Zeitschriften, Nov.
    1928–Feb. 1930
120b. Volksbegehren gegen den Young Plan: RLB, Agrarpoli-
    tische Wochenschrift, Grüne Wochenschau des Reichs-
    landbunds Rundschreiben. April 1929 bis Feb. 1930
121. Behinderungen des Volksentscheids, Aug.–Okt. 1931
122. Reichsreform u. Verwaltungsreform, Nov. 1927–Aug.
    1931
123. [Abänderung des geltenden Aufwertungsgesetz], Juni
    1924–März 1927
124a. Zoll- u. handelspolitische Fragen, Sommer 1924–Sommer
    1925
124b. Zollfragen, Juli 1925–Dez. 1925
125. Bodenreform
126. Rede: "Industrie oder Agrarstaat"
127. Kooperation Landwirtschaft und Christlich-Nationale
    Arbeiterschaft
128. Allgemeine politische u. wirtschaftliche Lage im Ruhr-
    gebiet
129. Ruhrhilfe: Lebensmittelspende des RLB u. der Mitglieds-
    vorstände für das Ruhrgebiet
130. Unruhen auf dem Lande, Erntestreiks, Ernteplunder-
    ungen: Anhalt, Braunschweig, Mecklenburg-Schwerin,
    Sachsen, Thüringen, Verschiedenes, Aug. 1923–März 1924
131. Unruhen auf dem Lande, Erntestreiks, Ernteplunder-
    ungen: Preussen, Aug. 1923–März 1924
132a. Kundgebungen u. Entschliessungen v. Landbünden usw.

133. Fall Achtermann in Land-Bund Pommern, 1928
134. Präsidialabteilung, Bauernschutzgemeinschaft
136a. Kommunalsachen, Allgemeines
137. Kommunalpolitik
138. Tätigkeit des Kommunalpolitischen Ausschusses, Oct. 1930–31
139. Tätigkeit des Kommunalpolitischen Ausschusses, Aug. 1931 ff.
140a. Preussische Landegemeinde-Ordnung, Sept. 1921–Apr. 1922
141. Kommunale Neuregelung im Westen
142a. Schulwesen u. ländliches Bauwesen, Eingaben, Verschiedenes
144. Angelegenheiten des Bundesvorstandes: Rundschreiben Präsidialabteilung
145. Angelegenheiten des Bundesvorstandes: Rundschreiben u. Berichte der Präsidialabteilung über Sitzungen Mitteilungen für Mitglieder, Juni–Dez. 1931
146. Angelegenheiten des Bundesvorstandes, Jan. 1932–April 1933
147a. Sitzungen des Zoll- u. Handelspolitischen Ausschusses u. Kreditausschusses
148. Wirtschaftskuratorium: Berichte, 1921–25
149a. Personalangelegenheiten des Reichslandbunds, Dez. 1920–Mai 1922
149b. Personalangelegenheiten des Reichslandbunds, Juni 1922–Dez. 1928
61 Ve 1 Alldeutscher Verband, by volume number and title:
135. Sitzung des Geschäftsführenden Ausschusses, 1.9.1922, Essen
136. Sitzung des Geschäftsführenden Ausschusses, 21 & 22.4.1923, Berlin
137. Sitzung des Geschäftsführenden Ausschusses, 16 & 17. Feb.1924
138. Sitzung des Geschäftsführenden Ausschusses, 26 & 27. April.1924, Jena
139. Sitzung des Geschäftsführenden Ausschusses, 29.Aug. 1924, Stuttgart
140. Sitzung des Geschäftsführenden Ausschusses, 25 & 26. Okt.1924, Berlin
141. Sitzung des Geschäftsführenden Ausschusses, 31.Jan. & 1.Feb.1925, Berlin
142. Sitzung des Geschäftsführenden Ausschusses, 21.März. 1925, Dresden

143. Sitzung des Geschäftsführenden Ausschusses, 4. & 5.July. 1925, Berlin
144. Sitzung des Geschäftsführenden Ausschusses, 4.Sept.1925, Detmold
145. Sitzung des Geschäftsführenden Ausschusses, 12.Dez.1925, Berlin
146. Sitzung des Geschäftsführenden Ausschusses, 10.April. 1926, Bremen
147. Sitzung des Geschäftsführenden Ausschusses, 3.Sept.1926, Bayreuth
148. Sitzung des Geschäftsführenden Ausschusses, 4. & 5.Dez. 1926, Berlin
149. Sitzung des Geschäftsführenden Ausschusses, 12. & 13. Feb.1927, Berlin
150. Sitzung des Geschäftsführenden Ausschusses, 23.April. 1927, Kothen
151. Sitzung des Geschäftsführenden Ausschusses, 2.Sept.1927, Halberstadt
152. Sitzung des Geschäftsführenden Ausschusses, 26. & 27. Nov.1927, Berlin
153. Sitzung des Geschäftsführenden Ausschusses, 4.März. 1928, Berlin
154. Sitzung des Geschäftsführenden Ausschusses, 21.April. 1928, Eisenach
155. Sitzung des Geschäftsführenden Ausschusses, 7.Sept.1828, Plauen
156. Sitzung des Geschäftsführenden Ausschusses, 1./2/Dez. 1928, Berlin
157. Sitzung des Geschäftsführenden Ausschusses, 19.Jan.1929, Berlin
158. Sitzung des Geschäftsführenden Ausschusses, 20.April. 1929, Essen
159. Sitzung des Geschäftsführenden Ausschusses, 30.Aug. 1929, Würzburg
212. Allgemeine Schriftwechsel
213. Allgemeine Schriftwechsel, 1927
216. Allgemeine Schriftwechsel, 1930
282. Angriffe u. Abwehr: Anker, Major a.D. Kurt
283. Dr. Arning: Deutschnationaler Landestagsabgeordnete Hannover
284. Angriffe u. Abwehr: Asch, Ludwig
286. Angriffe u. Abwehr: Dr. Bachem, 1916
288. Hauptleitung, Einzelne Mitglieder, Oberfinanzrat Dr. Bang

394. Angriffe u. Abwehr: Personen: Hülsmann-Freiburg
395. Hugenberg, Mai 1906–26
397. Einzelne Mitglieder: Hugenberg
489. Dr. Irmgard Wrede, Geschäftsführerin des BDV f. Ober- u. Niederschlesien
490. Korrespondenz, 1920–21
491. Korrespondenz, 1920–21
685. Innere Politik: Preussen—Bildung eines neuen Kabinetts, 31.3/25
686. Einzelne Schriften
687. Zusammenkunft m. Österreich-Hungarn (Politiker u. Freunde)

15.01 Reichsministerium des Innern:
Frieden Generalis, by registry number and title:
    5717–18. Die Reparationsleistungen
    5721.   Das Dawes Gutachten und die Londoner Konferenz, 1924–26
    5722.   Der Völkerbund, 1925–27
Politik, by volume number and title:
    13,332–418. Politische Lage in Deutschland und den deutschen Ländern sowie in anderen Ländern, 1920–28, e.g.:
    13,356.   Politische Lage in Frankreich, 1921–26
    13,358.   Politische Lage in Gross Britannien, 1921–26
    13,344.   Politische Lage in Bayern, Nov.–Dez.1925
    13,547–60. Besetzung des Ruhrgebietes und des Rheinlandes, 1923–27
    25,038.   Zusammenarbeit zwischen Regierung und Reichstag, Regierungsmehrheit und Opposition

15.07 Reichskommission für Überwachung der Öffenlichen Ordnung, by volume number and title:
    197–197/1a. Politische, innerpolitische und wirtschaftliche Bewegungen u.a. Separationsbestrebungen (Rheinprovinzen), 3 vols., 1920–29
208. Umsturzbewegung (Kapp Putsch), 1920–28
237. Wahlen, Wahlergebnisse, Regierungsbildung im Reich
238. Wahlen im Mai 1924
239. Wahlen im Dez.1924
240. Reichspräsidentenwahl, 1925
241. Wahlen, Mai 1928
241/1. Wahlen, Wahlergebnisse, Regierungsbildungen der Länder, Allg.
242. Wahlen usw, Preussen

243. Wahlen usw, Bayern
243/1. Wahlen usw, Sachsen
243/2. Wahlen usw, Württemberg
243/3. Wahlen usw, Baden
243/4. Wahlen usw, Hessen
244. Wahlen usw, Braunschweig
244/1. Wahlen usw, Thüringen
245. Wahlen usw, Oldenburg
246. Wahlen usw, Meklenburg-Strelitz und Schwerin
246/1. Wahlen usw, Bremen
246/2. Wahlen usw, Lübeck
246/3. Wahlen usw, Hamburg
283. Akten betr. Deutschnationale Volkspartei, Bayerische Mittelpartei, Württembergische Bürgerpartei, 1921–28
284. Akten betr. Deutschnationale Volkspartei, Bayerische Mittelpartei, Württembergische Bürgerpartei, Jan.1929–Feb.1930
488–94. Besetzte und abgetrennte Gebiete, 1922–26
16.01 Reichsministerium für die besetzte Gebiete, 1923–30
16.02 Reichministerium für die besetzte rheinische Gebiete, 1919–30
30.01 Reichsjustizministerium, by number and title:
7232–35. Locarno-Vertrag, 1925–29
7247–60. Besatzungskonvention, Rheinlandabkommen, 1923–29
7406–33. Friedensvertrag, Wiedergutmachungen, Reparationsplan, 1920–33

Great Britain
London
British Museum
Private Papers of Edgar Vincent, Lord D'Abernon

Part 2
Published and Nonarchival Materials

Albrecht-Carrié, René. *France, Europe and the Two World Wars.* New York: Harper, 1961.

Barraclough, Geoffrey. *An Introduction to Contemporary History.* Baltimore, Md.: Penguin Books, 1964.

Baumont, Maurice. *La Faillite de la paix (1918–1939).* 3d ed., 2 vols. Paris: Presses universitaires de France, 1951.

Becker, Josef. "Joseph Wirth und die Krise des Zentrums während des IV.

Kabinetts Marx (1927–1928)." *Zeitschrift für die Geschichte des Oberrheins* 109 (1961): 361–482.

———. "Zur Politik der Wehrmachtabteilung in der Regierungskrise 1926/27." *Vierteljahrshefte für Zeitgeschichte* 14 (1966): 69–78.

Behrens, Reinhard. "Die Deutschnationalen in Hamburg, 1918–1933." Ph.D. dissertation, University of Hamburg, 1973.

Bergsträsser, Ludwig. *Geschichte der politischen Parteien in Deutschland.* 10th ed. Munich: Günter Olzog Verlag, 1960.

Berndorff, Hans Rudolf. *General zwischen Ost und West.* Hamburg: Hoffmann & Campe, 1951.

Bernhard, Ludwig. *Der "Hugenberg-Konzern": Psychologie und Technik einer Grossorganisation der Presse.* Berlin: J. Springer, 1928.

Bertelsmann, Heinz Otto Bernhard. "The Role of the German Parliament in Foreign Affairs, 1919–1926: Four Tests of the Weimar Republic." Ph.D. dissertation, Columbia University, 1956.

Besson, Waldemar. "Zur Frage der Staatsführung in der Weimarer Republik." *Vierteljahrshefte für Zeitgeschichte* 7 (1959): 85–111.

Bieligk, Fritz K. *Stresemann: The German Liberals' Foreign Policy.* Translated by E. Fitzgerald. London: Hutchinson & Co., 1944.

Boas, George. "Stresemann: Object Lesson in Post-War Leadership." *Public Opinion Quarterly* 8 (1944): 232–43.

Bonnet, Georges Étienne. *Quai d'Orsay.* Isle of Man: Times Press and Anthony Gibbs and Phillips, translation copyright, 1965.

Bracher, Karl Dietrich. *Die Auflösung der Weimarer Republik.* 4th ed. Villingen/Schwarzwald: Ring Verlag, 1964.

———. *The German Dictatorship: The Origins, Structure, and Effects of National Socialism.* Translated by Jean Steinberg, with an introduction by Peter Gay. New York: Praeger, 1970.

Brecht, Arnold. *Aus nächster Nähe: Lebenserinnerungen, 1884–1927.* Stuttgart: Deutsche Verlags-Anstalt, 1966.

———. "Bureaucratic Sabotage." *Annals of the American Academy of Political and Social Science* 189 (1937): 48–57.

———. *Mit der Kraft des Geistes: Lebenserinnerungen, 1927–1967.* Stuttgart: Deutsche Verlags-Anstalt, 1967.

———. *The Political Education of Arnold Brecht: An Autobiography, 1884–1970.* Princeton, N.J.: Princeton University Press, 1970.

———. *Prelude to Silence: The End of the German Republic.* New York: H. Fertig, 1968.

Bretton, Henry L. *Stresemann and the Revision of Versailles: A Fight for Reason.* Stanford, Calif.: Stanford University Press, 1953.

Carsten, Francis Ludwig. *The Reichswehr and Politics, 1918–1933.* Oxford: Clarendon Press, 1966.

Castellan, Georges. *L'Allemagne de Weimar, 1918–1933.* Paris: Librairie Armand Colin, 1969.

Cerny, Jochen. "Reichs-Landbund (RLB), 1921–1933." In *Die bürgerlichen Parteien in Deutschland*, edited by Dieter Fricke, vol. 2, pp. 521–40. Berlin: Verlag Enzyklopädie Leipzig, 1970.

Chamberlin, Brewster S. "The Enemy on the Right: The *Alldeutschen Verband* in the Weimar Republic, 1918–1926." Ph.D. dissertation, University of Maryland, 1972.

Chanady, Attila A. "Anton Erkelenz and Erich Koch-Weser: A Portrait of Two German Democrats." *Historical Studies, Australia and New Zealand* 12 (1967): 491–505.

———. "The Disintegration of the German National Peoples' Party, 1924–1930." *Journal of Modern History* 39 (1967): 65–91.

Chastenet, Jacques. *Histoire de la Troisième République*. Vol. 5: *Les années d'illusions, 1918–1931*. Paris: Librairie Hachette, 1960.

Clark, Robert T. *The Fall of the German Republic: A Political Study*. London: George Allen & Unwin Ltd., 1935.

Class, Heinrich. *Wider den Strom: Vom Werden und Wachsen der nationalen Opposition im alten Reich*. Leipzig: K. F. Koehler, [ca. 1932].

Coker, Francis W. *Recent Political Thought*. New York and London: D. Appleton-Century, 1934.

Cornebise, Alfred E. "Gustav Stresemann and Ruhr Occupation: The Making of a Statesman." *European Studies Review* 2 (1972): 43–67.

Craig, Gordon. *From Bismarck to Adenauer: Aspects of German Statecraft*. Baltimore, Md.: Johns Hopkins University Press, 1958.

———. *The Politics of the Prussian Army, 1640–1945*. New York: Oxford University Press, 1956.

Curtius, Julius. *Sechs Jahre Minister der deutschen Republik*. Heidelberg: Carl Winter Universitätsverlag, 1948.

D'Abernon, Edgar Vincent, First Viscount. *An Ambassador of Peace: Pages from the Diary of Viscount D'Abernon (Berlin, 1920–1926)*. 3 vols. London: Hodder & Stoughton, 1929–30. The U.S. edition, entitled *The Diary of an Ambassador*, has different pagination.

Dahrendorf, Ralf. *Society and Democracy in Germany*. Garden City, N.Y.: Doubleday Anchor, 1967.

David, Eduard. *Die Berichte Eduard Davids als Reichsvertreter in Hessen, 1921–1927*. Edited by Friedrich P. Kahlenberg. Wiesbaden: Steiner, 1970.

Dichtl, Klaus, and Ruge, Wolfgang. "Dokumentation: Zu den Auseinandersetzungen innerhalb der Reichsregierung über den Locarnopakt 1925." *Zeitschrift für Geschichtswissenschaft* 22 (1974): 64–88.

Dietrich, Valeska. *Alfred Hugenberg: Ein Manager in der Publizistik*. Berlin: By the author, 1960.

Documents diplomatiques belges, 1920–1940: La Politique de sécurité extérieure. Edited by Ch. de Visscher and F. Vanlangenhove. 5 vols. Brussels: Palais des Académies, 1964.

Döhn, Lothar. *Politik und Interesse: Die Interessenstruktur der Deutschen Volkspartei.* Meisenheim am Glan: Hain, 1970.

Dörr, Manfred. "Die Deutschnationale Volkspartei, 1925 bis 1928." Ph.D. dissertation, University of Marburg, published by its author, 1964.

Dorpalen, Andreas. *Hindenburg and the Weimar Republic.* Princeton, N.J.: Princeton University Press, 1964.

Enssle, Manfred. "Germany and Belgium, 1919–1929: A Study of German Foreign Policy." Ph.D. dissertation, University of Colorado, 1970.

Epstein, Fritz T. "Hoetzsch, Otto." In *Neue deutsche Biographie*, vol. 9, pp. 371–72. Berlin: Duncker & Humblot, 1972.

Erdmann, Karl Dietrich. "Die Geschichte der Weimarer Republik als Problem der Wissenschaft." *Vierteljahrshefte für Zeitgeschichte* 3 (1955): 1–19.

——. "Das Problem der Ost- und Westorientierung in der Locarno-Politik Stresemanns." *Geschichte in Wissenschaft und Unterricht* 6 (1955): 133–62.

Eyck, Erich. *A History of the Weimar Republic.* Translated by Harlan P. Hanson and Robert G. L. Waite. 2 vols. Cambridge, Mass.: Harvard University Press, 1962–63.

Feldhaus, Friedrich W. "Die Deutschnationale Volkspartei im Wahlkreis Weser-Ems von 1918–1933." Essay for civil-service examination. Münster, March 21, 1968.

Feuchtwanger, E. J. *Prussia, Myth and Reality: The Role of Prussia in German History.* London: O. Wolff, 1970.

Freytagh-Loringhoven, Axel Freiherr von. *Die Deutschnationale Volkspartei.* Berlin: Pan-Verlags-Gesellschaft, 1931.

Fricke, Dieter, ed. *Die bürgerlichen Parteien in Duetschland: Handbuch der Geschichte der bürgerlichen Parteien und anderer bürgerlicher Interessenorganisationen vom Vormärz bis zum Jahre 1945.* 2 vols. Berlin: Verlag Enzyklopädie Leipzig, 1968, 1970.

Friedrich, Otto. *Before the Deluge: A Portrait of Berlin in the 1920's.* New York: Avon Books, 1973.

Gasiorowski, Zygmunt J. "The Russian Overture to Germany of December 1924." *Journal of Modern History* 30 (1958): 99–117.

——. "Stresemann and Poland after Locarno." *Journal of Central European Affairs* 18 (1958): 292–317.

——. "Stresemann and Poland before Locarno." *Journal of Central European Affairs* 18 (1958): 25–47.

Gathorne-Hardy, Geoffrey Malcolm. *A Short History of International Affairs, 1920–1939.* 4th ed. London: Oxford University Press, 1950.

Gatzke, Hans W. "Gustav Stresemann: A Bibliographical Article." *Journal of Modern History* 36 (1964): 1–13.

——. "The Republic of Weimar." *Current History* 28 (1955): 217–22.

——. "Russo-German Military Collaboration during the Weimar Republic." *American Historical Review* 63 (1958): 565–97.

————. *Stresemann and the Rearmament of Germany.* Baltimore, Md.: Johns Hopkins University Press, 1954.

————. "The Stresemann Papers." *Journal of Modern History* 26 (1954): 49–59.

————. "Von Rapallo nach Berlin: Stresemann und die deutsche Russlandpolitik." *Vierteljahrshefte für Zeitgeschichte* 4 (1956): 1–29.

Gay, Peter. *Weimar Culture: The Outsider as Insider.* London: Secker & Warburg, 1969.

Geigenmüller, Ernst. "Botschafter von Hoesch und die Räumungsfrage." *Historische Zeitschrift* 200 (1965): 606–20.

Gemein, Gisberg Jörg. "Die DNVP in Düsseldorf, 1918–1933." Ph.D. dissertation, University of Cologne, 1969.

Gereke, Günther. *Ich war königlich-preussischer Landrat.* Berlin (DDR): Union Verlag, 1970.

German Democratic Republic, Foreign Ministry. *Locarno-Konferenz 1925: Eine Dokumentensammlung.* Berlin: Rütten & Loening, 1962.

Germany, Büro des Reichstags. *Verhandlungen des Reichstags.*

Germany, Federal Republic of, Foreign Office. *Akten zur deutschen auswärtigen Politik, 1918–1945.* Ser. B, 1925–33.

Gessler, Otto. *Reichswehrpolitik in der Weimarer Zeit.* Stuttgart: Deutsche Verlags-Anstalt, 1958.

Gordon, Harold J., Jr. *The Reichswehr and the German Republic, 1919–1926.* Princeton, N.J.: Princeton University Press, 1957.

Gossweiler, Kurt. *Grossbanken, Industriemonopole, Staat: Ökonomie und Politik des staatsmonopolistischen Kapitalismus in Deutschland, 1914–1932.* Berlin: Deutscher Verlag der Wissenschaften, 1971.

Graef-Anklam, Walter. "Der Werdegang der Deutschnationalen Volkspartei, 1918–1928." In *Der nationale Wille,* edited by Max Weiss. Leipzig: Vaterländischer Buchvertrieb T. Rudolph, 1928.

Graml, Hermann. *Europa zwischen den Kriegen.* Munich: Deutscher Taschenbuch-Verlag, 1969.

Grathwol, Robert. "Die Deutschnationale Volkspartei, Stresemann und die Einladung nach Locarno." In *Tradition und Neubeginn: Internationale Forschungen zur deutschen Geschichte im 20. Jahrhundert,* edited by Joachim Hütter, Reinhard Meyers, and Dietrich Papenfuss, pp. 89–99. Cologne, Berlin, Bonn, Munich: Carl Heymanns Verlag, 1975.

————. "Germany and the Eupen-Malmédy Affair, 1924–26: 'Here Lies the Spirit of Locarno.'" *Central European History* 8 (1975): 221–50.

————. "Gustav Stresemann: Reflections on His Foreign Policy." *Journal of Modern History* 45 (1973): 52–70.

————. "Stresemann Revisited." *European Studies Review* 7 (1977): 341–52.

Great Britain, Foreign Office. *Documents on British Foreign Policy, 1919–1939,* edited by W. N. Medlicott, Douglas Dakin, and M. E. Lambert. Ser. I A, 1925–29. London: Her Majesty's Stationery Office, 1966–.

Great Britain, Parliament. *Debates* (House of Commons), vols. 169–223.

Bibliography

Grewe, Wilhelm. "Zum Begriff der politischen Partei." In *Um Recht und Gerechtigkeit.* Stuttgart: W. Kohlhammer, 1950.

Grün, George A. "Locarno: Idea and Reality." *International Affairs* 31 (1955): 477–85.

Günther, Fritz, and Ohlsen, Manfred. "Reichsverband der Deutschen Industrie (RDI), 1919–1933." In *Die bürgerlichen Parteien in Deutschland,* edited by Dieter Fricke, vol. 2, pp. 580–619. Berlin: Verlag Enzyklopädie Leipzig, 1970.

Halperin, Samuel William. *Germany Tried Democracy: A Political History of the Reich from 1918 to 1933.* New York: W. W. Norton & Co., 1965.

Hartwig, Edgar. "Alldeutscher Verband (ADV), 1891–1939." In *Die bürgerlichen Parteien in Deutschland,* edited by Dieter Fricke, vol. 1, pp. 1–26. Berlin: Verlag Enzyklopädie Leipzig, 1968.

Haungs, Peter. *Reichspräsident und parlamentarische Kabinettsregierung: Eine Studie zum Regierungssystem der Weimarer Republik in den Jahren 1924 bis 1929.* Cologne and Opladen: Westdeutscher Verlag, 1968.

Helfferich, Karl, and Reichert, [Wilhelm]. *Das zweite Versailles: Das Reparationsgutachten der allierten Experten.* Berlin: Deutschnationale Schriftenvertriebsstelle, 1924.

Hertzman, Lewis. *DNVP: Right-Wing Opposition in the Weimar Republic, 1918–1924.* Lincoln. University of Nebraska Press, 1963.

———. "Gustav Stresemann: The Problem of Political Leadership in the Weimar Republic." *International Review of Social History* 5 (1960): 361–77.

Hildebrand, Klaus. *The Foreign Policy of the Third Reich.* Translated by Anthony Fothergill. Berkeley: University of California Press, 1973.

Hilger, Gustav, and Meyer, Alfred G. *The Incompatible Allies.* New York: Macmillan, 1953.

Hiller von Gaertringen, Friedrich Frhr. "Deutschnationale Volkspartei (DNVP)." In *Lexikon zur Geschichte und Politik im 20. Jahrhundert,* edited by Carola Stern, Thilo Vogelsang, et al., vol. 1, p. 184. 2 vols. Cologne: Kiepenheuer & Witsch, 1971.

Hillgruber, Andreas. *Kontinuität und Diskontinuität in der deutschen Aussenpolitik von Bismarck bis Hitler.* Düsseldorf: Droste Verlag, 1969.

Hirsch, Felix E. *Gustav Stresemann: Patriot und Europäer.* Göttingen: Musterschmidt-Verlag, 1964.

———. "Stresemann and Adenauer: Two Great Leaders of German Democracy in Times of Crisis." In *Studies in Diplomatic History and Historiography in Honour of G. P. Gooch, C.H.,* edited by A. O. Sarkissian, pp. 266–80. London: Longmans, 1961.

———. "Stresemann und die deutsche Gegenwart." *Heidelberger Jahrbücher* 7 (1963): 111–20.

Hoepke, Klaus-Peter. "Alfred Hugenberg als Vermittler zwischen grossindustriellen Interessen und Deutschnationaler Volkspartei." In *Industrielles System und politische Entwicklung in der Weimarer Republik,* edited by Hans

Mommsen, Dietmar Petzina, and Bernd Weisbrod, pp. 907–19. Düsseldorf: Droste Verlag, 1974.

———. "Hugenberg, Alfred." In *Neue deutsche Biographie*, vol. 10, pp. 10–13. Berlin: Duncker & Humblot, 1974.

Hoetzsch, Otto. "Die Aussenpolitik der Deutschnationalen Volkspartei." *Europäische Gespräche* 6 (1926): 339–51.

———. *Germany's Domestic and Foreign Policies*. New Haven, Conn.: Yale University Press, 1929.

Holborn, Hajo. "Diplomats and Diplomacy in the Early Weimar Republic." In *The Diplomats, 1919–1939*, edited by Gordon A. Craig and Felix Gilbert, pp. 123–71. Princeton, N.J.: Princeton University Press, 1953.

———. *The Political Collapse of Europe*. New York: Alfred A. Knopf, 1951.

Holtje, Christian. *Die Weimarer Republik und das Ostlocarno-Problem, 1919–1934*. Würzburg: Holzner-Verlag, 1958.

Horkenbach, Cuno, ed. *Das deutsche Reich von 1918 bis heute*. 2 vols. Berlin: Verlag für Presse, Wirtschaft & Politik, 1931–.

Hubatsch, Walther. *Hindenburg und der Staat: Aus den Papieren des Generalfeldmarschalls und Reichspräsidenten von 1878 bis 1934*. Göttingen: Musterschmidt-Verlag, 1966.

Hugenberg, Alfred. *Streiflichter aus Vergangenheit und Gegenwart*. Berlin: A. Scherl, 1927.

Hunt, Richard N. *German Social Democracy, 1918–1933*. Chicago: Quadrangle Paperbacks, 1970.

Jacobson, Jon. *Locarno Diplomacy: Germany and the West, 1925–1929*. Princeton, N.J.: Princeton University Press, 1972.

———, and Walker, John T. "The Impulse for a Franco-German Entente: The Origins of the Thoiry Conference, 1926." *Journal of Contemporary History* 10 (1975): 157–81.

Jasper, Gotthard, comp. *Von Weimar zu Hitler, 1930–1933*. Cologne: Kiepenheuer & Witsch, 1968.

Johnson, Douglas. "Austen Chamberlain and the Locarno Agreements." *University of Birmingham Historical Journal* 8 (1961): 62–81.

Jonas, Erasmus. *Die Volkskonservativen, 1928–1933*. Düsseldorf: Droste Verlag, 1965.

Jones, Larry Eugene. " 'The Dying Middle': Weimar Germany and the Failure of Bourgeois Unity, 1924–1930." Ph.D. dissertation, University of Wisconsin, 1970.

———. " 'The Dying Middle': Weimar Germany and the Fragmentation of Bourgeois Politics." *Central European History* 5 (1972): 23–54.

———. "Gustav Stresemann and the Crisis of German Liberalism." *European Studies Review* 4 (1974): 141–63.

Jordan, William M. *Great Britain, France, and the German Problem, 1918–1939*. London and New York: Oxford University Press, 1943.

Kaack, Heino. *Geschichte und Struktur des deutschen Parteisystems.* Opladen: Westdeutscher Verlag, 1971.

Die Kabinette Luther I und II: 15. Januar 1925 bis 20. Januar 1926; 20. Januar bis 17. Mai 1926. Edited by Karl-Heinz Minuth. Akten der Reichskanzlei, Weimarer Republik. 2 vols. Boppard: Harald Boldt Verlag, 1977.

Die Kabinette Marx I und II: 30. November 1923 bis 3. Juni 1924; 3. Juni 1924 bis 15. Januar 1925. Edited by Günther Abramowski. Akten der Reichskanzlei, Weimarer Republik. 2 vols. Boppard: Harald Boldt Verlag, 1973.

Kele, Max H. *Nazis and Workers: National Socialist Appeals to German Labor, 1919–1933.* Chapel Hill: University of North Carolina Press, 1972.

Kent, George O., comp. and ed. *A Catalog of Files and Microfilms of the German Foreign Ministry Archives, 1920–1945.* 4 vols. Stanford, Calif.: The Hoover Institution, Stanford University, 1962–72.

Klotzbücher, Alois. "Der politische Weg des Stahlhelms, Bund der Frontensoldaten, in der Weimarer Republik: Ein Beitrag zur Geschichte der 'Nationalen Opposition,' 1918–1933." Ph.D. dissertation, Friedrich-Alexander University, Erlangen-Nürnberg, 1964.

Kochan, Lionel. "Stresemann and the Historians." *Wiener Library Bulletin* 7 (1953): 35.

Koch-Weser, Erich. *Deutschlands Aussenpolitik in der Nachkriegszeit, 1919–1929.* Berlin: K. Vowinckel, 1929.

Kordt, Erich. *Nicht aus den Akten . . . Die Wilhelmstrasse im Frieden und Krieg: Erlebnisse, Begegnungen und Eindrücke, 1928–1945.* Stuttgart: Union Deutsche Verlagsgesellschaft, 1950.

Korrespondenz der Deutschnationalen Volkspartei, 1924–26. In October 1926 this party newspaper was converted to the Täglicher Dienst für Nationale Zeitungen, or TDNA, a news service bureau. Subscribers to the newspaper had their subscriptions completed with issues of the weekly *Unsere Partei,* which I have consulted for the later years of my study, i.e., from October 1926 through 1928.

Koszyk, Kurt. "Paul Reusch und die 'Münchner Neueste Nachrichten': Zum Problem Industrie und Presse in der Endphase der Weimarer Republik." *Vierteljahrshefte für Zeitgeschichte* 20 (1972): 75–103.

Koza, Ingeborg. *Die erste deutsche Republik im Spiegel des politischen Memoirenschrifttums: Untersuchungen zum Selbstverständnis und zur Selbstkritik bei den politischen Handelnden aus den Reihen der staatsbejahenden Parteien zur Zeit der 1. deutschen Republik.* Wuppertal: Henn, 1971.

Kruck, Alfred. *Geschichte des Alldeutschen Verbandes, 1890–1934.* Wiesbaden: Franz Steiner Verlag, 1954.

Krüger, Peter. "Friedenssicherung und deutsche Revisionspolitik: Die deutsche Aussenpolitik und die Verhandlungen über den Kellogg-Pakt." *Vierteljahrshefte für Zeitgeschichte* 22 (1974): 227–57.

Kulski, Wladyslaw Wszebór [W. M. Knight-Patterson]. *Germany from Defeat to Conquest, 1913–1933.* London: George Allen & Unwin, 1945.

Lambach, Walther, *Die Herrschaft der Fünfhundert: Ein Bild des parlamentarischen Lebens im neuen Deutschland*. Hamburg: Hanseatische Verlagsanstalt, 1926.

————, ed. *Politische Praxis. 1926*. Hamburg: Hanseatische Verlagsanstalt, 1926.

————, ed. *Politische Praxis, 1927*. Hamburg: Hanseatische Verlagsanstalt, 1927.

Lebovics, Herman. *Social Conservatism and the Middle Classes in Germany, 1914–1933*. Princeton, N.J.: Princeton University Press, 1969.

Leopold, John A. "Alfred Hugenberg and German Politics." Ph.D. dissertation, Catholic University of America, 1970.

Lexicon zur Geschichte und Politik im 20. Jahrhundert. Edited by Carola Stern, Thilo Vogelsang, Erhard Klöss, and Albert Graff. 2 vols. Cologne: Kiepenheuer & Witsch, 1971.

L'Huillier, Fernand. *Dialogues franco-allemands, 1925–1933*. Publications de la Faculté des lettres de l'Université de Strasbourg. [Paris]: Diffusion Ophrys, 1971.

————. "La politique de Stresemann de 1921 à 1925 d'après l'historiographie allemande la plus récente." *Cahiers de L'Association interuniversitaire de l'est*, vol. 3 (1961): *Relations internationales*, pp. 89–100.

Liebe, Werner. *Die Deutschnationale Volkspartei, 1918–1924*. Düsseldorf: Droste Verlag, 1956.

Link, Werner. *Die amerikanische Stabilisierungspolitik in Deutschland, 1921–1932*. Düsseldorf: Droste Verlag, 1970.

————. "Die aussenpolitische Rolle des Parlaments und das Konzept der kombinierten auswärtigen Gewalt." In *Politische Vierteljahresschrift*, vol. 2: *Probleme der Demokratie heute*. Opladen: Westdeutscher Verlag, 1971.

Lochner, Louis P. *Always the Unexpected: A Book of Reminiscences*. New York: Macmillan, 1956.

Loewenstein, Karl. *Political Power and the Government Process*. Chicago: University of Chicago Press, 1957.

Luther, Hans. *Politiker ohne Partei: Erinnerungen*. Stuttgart: Deutsche Verlags-Anstalt, 1960.

Maier, Charles S. *Recasting Bourgeois Europe: Stabilization in France, Germany, and Italy in the Decade after World War I*. Princeton, N.J.: Princeton University Press, 1975.

Marx, Wilhelm. *Der Nachlass des Reichskanzlers Wilhelm Marx*. Edited by Hugo Stehkämper. 4 vols. Cologne: Verlag von Paul Neubner, 1968.

Matthias, Erich, and Morsey, Rudolf, eds. *Das Ende der Parteien, 1933*. Düsseldorf: Droste Verlag, 1960.

Maxelon, Michael-Olaf. *Stresemann und Frankreich: Deutsche Politik der Ost-West-Balance*. Düsseldorf: Droste Verlag, 1972.

Mayer, Arno J. *Political Origins of the New Diplomacy, 1917–1918*. New York: Vintage Books, 1970.

Meier-Welcker, Hans. "Seeckt in der Kritik." *Wehrwissenschaftliche Rundschau* 19 (1969): 268–84.

Meissner, Otto. *Staatssekretär unter Ebert, Hindenburg, Hitler.* Hamburg: Hoffmann & Campe, 1950.

Meyer, Richard Hemmig. *Bankers' Diplomacy: Monetary Stabilization in the Twenties.* New York: Columbia University Press, 1970.

Miller, Jane Kathryn. *Belgian Foreign Policy between the Two Wars, 1919–1940.* New York: Bookman Associates, 1951.

Mommsen, Hans; Petzina, Dietmar; and Weisbrod, Bernd, eds. *Industrielles System und politische Entwicklung in der Weimarer Republik.* Düsseldorf: Droste Verlag, 1974.

Moulton, Harold G., and Pasvolsky, Leo. *War Debts and World Prosperity.* New York: Century Co., for Brookings Institution Publications, 1932.

Muth, Heinrich. "Zeitgeschichte: Innenpolitik, 1918–1933." *Geschichte in Wissenschaft und Unterricht* 22 (1971): 562–76 and 623–40.

Netzband, Karl-Bernhard, and Widmaier, Hans Peter. *Währungs- und Finanzpolitik der Ära Luther, 1923–1925.* Basel: Kyklos-Verlag, 1964.

Neumann, Sigmund. *Modern Political Parties: Approaches to Comparative Politics.* Chicago: University of Chicago Press, 1956.

Nocken, Ulrich. "Inter-Industrial Conflicts and Alliances as Exemplified by the AVI-Agreement." In *Industrielles System und politische Entwicklung in der Weimarer Republik,* edited by Hans Mommsen, Dietmar Petzina, and Bernd Weisbrod, pp. 693–704. Düsseldorf: Droste Verlag, 1974.

Oldenburg-Januschau, Elard. *Erinnerungen.* Leipzig: Koehler & Amelang, 1936.

Organisation des Reichs-Landbundes, Die. Berlin: Reichs-Landbund, 1927.

Pabst, Klaus. *Eupen-Malmedy in der belgischen Regierungs- und Parteienpolitik, 1914–1940.* Aachen: Taken from *Zeitschrift des Aachener Geschichtsvereins* 76 (1964): 218–514.

Peterson, Edward Norman. *Hjalmar Schacht: For and against Hitler: A Political-economic Study of Germany, 1923–1945.* Boston: Christopher Publishing House, 1954.

Politischer Almanach, 1925: Jahrbuch des öffentlichen Lebens, der Wirtschaft und der Organisationen . . . . Edited by Maximilian Müller-Jabusch. Berlin: Verlag K. F. Koehler, 1925.

Poljakow, Wladimir [Augur]. "France and Germany." *Fortnightly Review* 126 (1926): 177–84.

Post, Gaines, Jr. *The Civil-Military Fabric of the Weimar Foreign Policy.* Princeton, N.J.: Princeton University Press, 1973.

————. "German Foreign Policy and Military Planning: The Polish Question, 1924–1929." Ph.D. dissertation, Stanford University, 1969.

Pünder, Hermann. *Politik in der Reichskanzlei: Aufzeichnungen aus den Jahren 1929–1932.* Edited by Thilo Vogelsang. Stuttgart: Deutsche Verlags-Anstalt, 1961.

Quabbe, Georg. *Tar a Ri: Variationen über konservatives Thema.* Berlin: Verlag für Politik & Wirtschaft, 1927.

Rabenau, Friedrich von, ed. *Seeckt: Aus seinem Leben, 1918–1936.* Leipzig: Hase & Koehler, [1940].

Reichshandbuch der deutschen Gesellschaft: Das Handbuch der Persönlichkeiten in Wort und Bild. 2 vols. Berlin: Deutscher Wirtschaftsverlag, [1930–].

Rheinbaben, Werner Karl Ferdinand Freiherr von. *Kaiser, Kanzler, Präsidenten: Erinnerungen.* Mainz: von Hase & Koehler, 1968.

Roloff, Ernst. *Braunschweig und der Staat von Weimar: Politik, Wirtschaft und Gesellschaft, 1918–1933.* Braunschweig: Waisenhaus Buchdruckerei & Verlag, 1964.

Ruge, Wolfgang. "Deutschnationale Volkspartei (DNVP), 1918–1933." In *Die bürgerlichen Parteien in Deutschland,* edited by Dieter Fricke, vol. 1, pp. 715–53. Berlin: Verlag Enzyklopädie Leipzig, 1968.

———. *Stresemann: Ein Lebensbild.* Berlin (DDR): Deutscher Verlag der Wissenschaft, 1965.

Runge, Wolfgang. *Politik und Beamtentum im Parteienstaat: Die Demokratisierung der politischen Beamten in Preussen zwischen 1918 und 1933.* Stuttgart: E. Klett, 1965.

Rusconi, Gian Enrico. *La crisi di Weimar: Crisi di sistema e sconfitta operaia.* Turin: Einaudi, 1977.

Salewski, Michael. *Entwaffnung und Militärkontrolle in Deutschland, 1919–1927.* Munich: R. Oldenbourg Verlag, 1966.

Scheele, Godfrey. *The Weimar Republic: Overture to the Third Reich.* London: Faber & Faber Ltd., 1946.

Schinkel, Harald. "Entstehung und Zerfall der Regierung Luther." Ph.D. dissertation, University of Berlin, 1959, published by its author.

Schlange-Schöningen, Hans. *Am Tage danach.* Hamburg: Hammerich & Lesser, 1946.

Schmacke, Ernst. "Die Aussenpolitik der Weimarer Republik, 1922–1925, unter Berücksichtigung der Innenpolitik (von Rapallo nach Locarno)." Ph.D. dissertation, University of Hamburg, 1951.

Schmidt, Paul. *Statist auf diplomatischer Bühne.* Bonn: Athenäum-Verlag, 1949.

Schmidt, Royal J. *Versailles and the Ruhr: Seedbed of World War II.* The Hague: Martinus Nijhoff, 1968.

Schmidt-Hannover, Otto. *Umdenken oder Anarchie: Männer, Schicksale, Lehren.* Göttingen: Göttinger Verlagsanstalt, 1959.

Schöne, Siegfried. *Von der Reichskanzlei zum Bundeskanzleramt: Eine Untersuchung zum Problem der Führung und Koordination in der jüngeren deutschen Geschichte.* Berlin: Duncker & Humblot, 1968.

Schüddekopf, Otto-Ernst. *Das Heer und die Republik: Quellen zur Politik der Reichswehrführung, 1918 bis 1933.* Hanover: Norddeutsche Verlagsanstalt O. Goedel, 1955.

Schulthess' Europäischer Geschichtskalender. Edited by Ulrich Thürauf. Vols. 65–69. Munich: C. H. Beck'sche Verlagsbuchhandlung, 1924–28.

Schumacher, Martin. *Mittelstandsfront und Republik: Die Wirtschaftspartei,*

Reichspartei des deutschen Mittelstandes, 1919–1933. Düsseldorf: Droste Verlag, 1972.

Shepherd, Henry L. *The Monetary Experiences of Belgium, 1914–1936.* Princeton, N.J.: Princeton University Press, 1936.

Sieburg, Heinz-Otto. "Les Entretiens de Thoiry (1926): Le Sommet de la politique de rapprochement franco-allemand à l'epoque Stresemann-Briand." In *Cent ans de rapports franco-allemands, 1871–1971: Actes du Colloque de Strasbourg, novembre 1971. Revue d'Allemagne*, vol. 4 (1972).

————. "Das Gespräch zu Thoiry 1926." In *Gedenkschrift Martin Göhring*, edited by Ernst Schulin, pp. 317–37. Wiesbaden: Steiner Verlag, 1968.

Sontag, Franz [Junius Alter]. *Nationalisten: Deutschlands nationales Führertum der Nachkriegszeit.* Leipzig: K. F. Koehler, [ca. 1930].

Sontheimer, Kurt. *Antidemokratisches Denken in der Weimarer Republik: Die politischen Ideen des deutschen Nationalismus zwischen 1918 und 1933.* Munich: Nymphenburger Verlagshandlung, 1962.

Spenz, Jürgen. *Die diplomatische Vorgeschichte des Beitritts Deutschlands zum Völkerbund, 1924–1926.* Göttingen: Musterschmidt-Verlag, 1966.

Stambrook, F. G. " 'Das Kind'—Lord D'Abernon and the Origins of the Locarno Pact." *Central European History* 1 (1968): 233–63.

Stampfer, Friedrich. *Die vierzehn Jahre der ersten deutschen Republik.* Karlsbad: Graphia, 1936.

Starkulla, Heinz. "Organisation und Technik der Pressepolitik des Staatsmannes Gustav Stresemann (1923 bis 1929)." Ph.D. dissertation, University of Munich, 1952.

Stegmann, Dirk. "Deutsche Zoll- und Handelspolitik 1924/5–1929 unter besonderer Berücksichtigung agrarischer und industrieller Interessen." In *Industrielles System und politische Entwicklung in der Weimarer Republik*, edited by Hans Mommsen, Dietmar Petzina, and Bernd Weisbrod, pp. 499–513. Düsseldorf: Droste Verlag, 1974.

————. "Die Silverberg-Kontroverse 1926: Unternehmerpolitik zwischen Reform und Restauration." In *Sozialgeschichte heute: Festschrift für Hans Rosenberg zum 70. Geburtstag*, edited by Hans-Ulrich Wehler, pp. 594–610. Göttingen: Vandenhoek & Ruprecht, 1974.

Stephan, Werner. *Aufstieg und Verfall des Linksliberalismus, 1918–1933: Geschichte der Deutschen Demokratischen Partei.* Göttingen: Vandenhoeck & Ruprecht, 1973.

Stockhausen, Max von. *Sechs Jahre Reichskanzlei: Von Rapallo bis Locarno: Erinnerungen und Tagebuchnotizen, 1922–1927.* Edited by Walther Görlitz. Bonn: Athenäum-Verlag, 1954

Stolper, Gustav. *The German Economy: 1870 to the Present.* Translated from the German by Toni Stolper. New ed., continued by Karl Häuser and Knut Borchardt. London: Weidenfeld & Nicolson, 1967.

Stresemann, Gustav. *Vermächtnis: Der Nachlass in drei Bänden.* Edited by Henry Bernhard. 3 vols. Berlin: Im Verlag Ullstein, 1932–33.

Stürmer, Michael. *Koalition und Opposition in der Weimarer Republik, 1924–1928.* Düsseldorf: Droste Verlag, 1967.

Survey of International Affairs. Arnold J. Toynbee et al. London: Oxford University Press, irregularly from 1925.

Suval, Stanley. "Overcoming *Kleindeutschland*: The Politics of Historical Mythmaking in the Weimar Republic." *Central European History* 2 (1969): 312–30.

Teipel, Heinrich. *Graf von Westarp: Der Parlamentarier Wider den Parlamentarismus.* Berlin: Historisch-Politischer Verlag, 1932.

Thimme, Annelise. *Flucht in den Mythos: Die Deutsnationale Volkspartei und die Niederlage von 1918.* Göttingen: Vandenhoeck & Ruprecht, 1969.

———. *Gustav Stresemann: Eine politische Biographie zur Geschichte der Weimarer Republik.* Hanover/Frankfurt a.M.: Norddeutsche-Verlags-Anstalt Goedel, 1957.

———. "Gustav Stresemann: Legende und Wirklichkeit." *Historische Zeitschrift* 181 (1956): 287–338.

———. "Die Locarnopolitik im Lichte des Stresemann-Nachlasses." *Zeitschrift für Politik* 3 (1956): 42–63.

———. "Stresemann als Reichskanzler." *Die Welt als Geschichte* 17 (1957): 9–25.

Thimme, Roland. *Stresemann und die Deutsche Volkspartei, 1923–1925.* Lübeck: Matthiesen, 1961.

Tormin, Walter. *Geschichte der deutschen Parteien seit 1848.* Stuttgart: W. Kohlhammer Verlag, [1966].

Treviranus, Gottfried Reinhold. *Das Ende von Weimar: Heinrich Brüning und seine Zeit.* Düsseldorf and Vienna: Econ-Verlag, 1968.

Turner, Henry A. *Stresemann and the Politics of the Weimar Republic.* Princeton, N.J.: Princeton University Press, 1963.

Übersicht über die Bestände des Deutschen Zentralarchivs, Potsdam. Edited by Helmut Lötzke and Hans-Stephan Brather. Berlin: Rütten & Loening, 1957.

United States, Department of State. *The Treaty of Versailles and After: Annotations of the Text of the Treaty.* Washington, D.C.: U.S. Government Printing Office, 1947.

Unsere Partei. See entry *Korrespondez der Deutschnationalen Volkspartei.*

Vermeil, Edmond. *L'Allemagne contemporaine.* Vol. 2: *La République de Weimar et le troisième Reich, 1918–1950.* Paris: Aubier, 1953.

von Riekhoff, Harald. *German-Polish Relations, 1918–1933.* Baltimore, Md.: Johns Hopkins University Press, 1971.

Walsdorff, Martin. *Westorientierung und Ostpolitik: Stresemanns Russlandpolitik in der Locarno-Ära.* Bremen: Schünemann Universitätsverlag, 1971.

Weidenfeld, Werner. *Die Englandpolitik Gustav Stresemanns.* Mainz: von Hase & Koehler, 1972.

Weiss, Max. "Organisation." In *Der nationale Wille*, edited by Max Weiss. Berlin: Wilhelm Andermann Verlag, 1928.

————, ed. *Politisches Handwörterbuch (Führer-ABC)*. Berlin: Deutschnationale Schriftenvertriebstelle, 1928.

————. "Der Werdegang der Deutschnationalen Volkspartei, 1918–1928." In *Der nationale Wille*, edited by Max Weiss. Berlin: Wilhelm Andermann Verlag, 1928.

Westarp, Kuno (Graf von). *Am Grabe der Parteiherrschaft*. Berlin: G. Stilke, 1932.

————. "Ein Jahr Aussenpolitik." In *Politische Praxis, 1926*, edited by Walther Lambach, pp. 26–47. Hamburg: Hanseatische Verlagsanstalt, 1926.

Winkler, Heinrich August. *Mittelstand, Demokratie und Nationalsozialismus: Die politische Entwicklung von Handwerk und Kleinhandel in der Weimarer Republik*. Cologne: Kiepenheuer & Witsch, 1972.

Zechlin, Walter, *Pressechef bei Ebert, Hindenburg und Kopf*. Hanover: Schlutersche Verlagsanstalt und Buchdruckerei, 1956.

Zimmermann, Ludwig. *Deutsche Aussenpolitik in der Ära der Weimarer Republik*. Göttingen: Musterschmidt-Verlag, 1958.

Zwoch, Gerhard. "Die Erfüllungs- und Verständigungspolitik der Weimarer Republik und die deutsche öffentliche Meinung." Ph.D. dissertation, University of Kiel, 1950.

INDEX

ADV. *See* All-deutscher Verband

All-deutscher Verband (Pan-German League, or ADV), 11, 22, 102–3, 200, 215, 247 n.5; and DNVP radicals, 21; and DNVP power struggle, 54, 192–93; and Rhineland security-pact initiative, 70, 76; and Stresemann, 74; anti-Locarno protests of, 142; DNVP tries to silence, 191

Allied Conference of Ambassadors, 32–34, 153, 181

Alsace-Lorraine: possible renunciation of, 67, 69, 70, 78–79, 86, 137; Stresemann willing to concede, 71, 143–44, 206–7; Hindenburg on, 154

Associated Press, 3

Bainville, Jacques, 101

Bayerische Volkspartei (Bavarian People's Party, or BVP), 27, 61, 156, 158, 159, 191

Bazille, Wilhelm, 237 n.24

Behrens, Franz, 11

Belgium, 18, 68, 178, 179; and Ruhr occupation, 16, 46; and German war guilt, 53; and Eupen-Malmédy, 79, 80, 86; at Locarno Conference, 124; and League of Nations, 168

Beneš, Edward, 75

Berlin Treaty, 195–96

Bernsdorff, Count Johann-Heinrich von, 240 n.3

Berthelot, Philippe, 152

Bonn Republic, 219

Bracht, Franz, 7

Brauns, Heinrich, 131, 254 n.9; hopes for coalition, 23, 61; on Dawes plan, 25; and Rhineland security-pact initiative, 59, 87, 88, 97; and Locarno accords, 105, 121, 125–26, 129–30, 134, 136; on DNVP split, 202–3

Brazil, 168, 171

Breitscheid, Rudolf, 91, 96, 240 n.3

Briand, Aristide: in French cabinet, 80, 85, 115; and German war guilt, 119, 250 n.35; at Locarno Conference, 123; and French Rhineland occupation, 132–33, 194, 197; and Locarno accords, 152; and Germany's league entry, 168, 171–72, 173, 179, 180; and Thoiry meeting with Stresemann, 180–85; and French concessions, 199, 201

Bülow, Bernhard W. von, 108, 264 n.2

BVP. *See* Bayerische Volkspartei

Center Party. *See* Zentrum

Chamberlain, Austen, 196, 199; and Rhineland security-pact initiative, 64, 66, 73; and German war guilt, 115, 250 n.35; and Locarno accords, 123, 131, 133; and League of Nations talks, 168, 172; and Rhineland evacuation, 194, 197

Class, Heinrich, 103, 171, 192, 215, 262 n.52

Coalition possibilities, charts of, 17

Cologne zone of occupation, evacuation of, 61–71 passim, 82, 95, 109–14 passim, 119, 122, 123, 128, 136. *See also* Rhineland,

occupation and evacuation of
Communists, 52, 69, 70, 169, 189, 202
Cuno, Wilhelm, 15, 62, 67
Curtius, Julius, 181–82, 184–85, 189, 190
Czechoslovakia, 74–75, 87, 172, 173

D'Abernon, Edgar Vincent, Lord, 62, 63, 74, 104, 131
Dahrendorff, Ralf, 107
Dawes, Charles G., 18
Dawes plan: committee, 18–20; DNVP opposition to, 21, 22, 23–25, 34–35, 36, 37; as foreign-policy basis, 28; Stresemann on, 30; jeopardized by disarmament issue, 32–33; final negotiations on, 35–36; DNVP demands on, 37–39, 40, 46; cabinet approval of, 39–40, 41; conference on, 42–46; and Allies' military inspection, 42; and DNVP, 47–51, 210; and Reichslandbund, 48–49; vote on, 51–52; acknowledged by DNVP, 55, 56, 57
DDP. *See* Deutsche Demokratische Partei
Deutsche Demokratische Partei (German Democratic Party, or DDP), 27; in Weimar Coalition, 14–15; and Dawes plan, 56; and Rhineland occupation, 59, 91, 92; and Luther, 149, 155, 176, 255–56 n.52; votes for Locarno accords, 155, 156; and Koch-Weser, 157
Deutsche Volkspartei (German People's Party, or DVP), 55, 61, 156, 157, 158, 191; supports policy of reconciliation, 8; in Weimar Coalition, 15; and DNVP, 22, 25–26, 27, 188; and Dawes plan, 48, 50; calls for foreign-policy debate, 91, 94–96; and Locarno accords, 124; and rightist coalition, 189
Deutsche Zeitung, 91, 93; anti-Stresemann campaign of, 103
Deutschkonservativen (German Conservative Party), 12–13, 22, 83
Deutschnationaler Arbeiterbund (German National Labor Federation), 11
Deutschnationaler Handlungsgehilfenverband (German National Federation of Clerks), 11
Deutschnationale Volkspartei (German National People's Party, or DNVP), 4; conservatism of, 8; and policy of reconciliation, 8, 143, 180; myths of, 8–10; foreign policy approach of, 9, 13–14, 25;
and Treaty of Versailles, 9, 20; strength of, 10; composition of, 10–11; heterogeneous following of, 11; interest groups associated with, 11-12; moderates, 12, 28, 54–55; radicals in, 12, 13–14, 21–23, 25, 28; structure of, 12; chairmen of, 12–13; daily functioning of, 14; its aversion to Marxism, 15; antidemocratic penchant of, 15; exclusion of, from cabinets, 15–16; and 1924 success of, 16, 20, 26; and Dawes Committee's report, 19–20; opposes Dawes plan, 21, 22, 23–25, 34–35, 36, 37; and the government, 22–23, 30, 142–43, 147–48, 193; and nomination of chancellor, 24; and cabinet-coalition negotiations, 25–26, 55–56; leadership failure in cabinet negotiations, 28; conciliatory on Dawes plan, 30–31; and German war guilt, 32, 37, 39, 46, 47, 53–54, 75, 77, 100, 116–18, 127, 207; and disarmament inspection, 34; and Dawes-plan demands, 37–39, 40, 46; failure of leadership of, 41; and Dawes plan, 47–51, 210; and Dawes-plan vote, 51–52; split in, 52, 54; Ja-Sager in, 54; Nein-Sager in, 54, 55, 56; acknowledges Dawes plan as binding, 55, 56, 57; gains in Reichstag, 56–57; and "cabinet of personalities," 59; in cabinet, 60; and Rhineland security-pact initiative, 70–75, 76–77, 83–84, 88–89, 90, 210–12; opposes Stresemann, 72, 74–75, 76–77, 81, 82–83, 84, 90–91, 157, 160–61, 206–9; split in, portended, 75, 202–3; and Luther's cabinet, 76, 84, 90, 165, 206; cooperation in, 82–83; ADV pressures, 102–3; and Locarno Conference, 105–7, 109, 110–11, 113, 114, 121, 207; dilemma of, 114–15, 118–20; its approach to diplomacy, 119; and Locarno accords, 124, 125–26, 135–36, 137–39, 140–41, 146–47, 155, 161–62, 175, 212–13; and German entry into League of Nations, 127–28, 163, 165, 166, 167, 169, 174, 175, 213; and perception of Stresemann, 143–44; tensions within, 145, 150–51, 161; press policy of, 145–46; reaction to withdrawal of, 150; alliance of, with Hindenburg, 151, 162, 164, 166, 189, 191, 205, 207; anticoalition forces within, 161; moderation of, 177, 178–79, 180, 185–86, 190–92, 195, 196, 198, 199, 209; moderation and Westarp, 185–86, 191–92; opposes Marx's cabinet, 186–87; and DVP coalition, 188; evolution of, 204,

205-6, 214–16; Stresemann's success
with, 205; failure of, 216–17; and Nazis,
219–21; leadership of, listed, 223–25;
decision-making in, 230 n.26
Disarmament, 62, 66–67, 79, 84, 98, 99, 109,
110, 122, 123, 124, 128, 133, 136, 138,
151, 153, 160, 182, 198; Dawes plan and,
32–33; and IMCC, 32, 33, 58–59, 80,
181; Poincáre and, 32–33; Westarp and,
34; DNVP on inspection of, 34; Locarno
accords on, 132
DNVP. *See* Deutschnationale Volkspartei
DVP. *See* Deutsche Volkspartei

Ebert, Friedrich, 8, 16, 26, 27; death of, 76
Eiserne Blätter, 76
Engel, Eduard, 217, 265 n.22
England. *See* Great Britain
Eupen-Malmédy, 78–79, 80, 86, 137, 165,
181, 206; and Stresemann, 177–78

Fatherland Societies. *See* Vereinigte Vater–
ländische Verbände
Fehrenbach, Konstantin, 39–40
France, 7, 31; and policy of reconciliation, 5;
postwar position of, 5; and Ruhr occupation, 16, 18–20, 32, 58; and Dawes plan,
28; and Rhineland security-pact initiative,
63, 64–66, 80, 85; and Poland's security,
108; and German war guilt, 115–16; and
Locarno accords, 125; on League of
Nations, 168; and concessions to Germany,
193–95, 196–98
Frederick the Great, 5
Frenken, Joseph, 86, 97, 115; and Rhineland
security-pact initiative, 88, 89; attacks
Stresemann, 93; and Locarno accords,
112–13, 129
Freytagh-Loringhoven, Axel Freiherr von, 14,
22, 83, 96, 103, 200, 201; on Rhineland
security-pact initiative, 71–72; and Locarno
Conference, 105

Gaus, Friedrich, 89, 91, 139; and policy of
reconciliation, 6–7; and Locarno Confer-
ence, 104, 105, 106, 107–8
Geneva Protocol, 59, 65, 66, 75
German Conservative Party. *See*
Deutschkonservativen
German Democratic Party. *See* Deutsche

Demokratische Partei
German Manufacturers' Union (Vereinigung
deutscher Industrieller), 11
German National Federation of Clerks
(Deutschnationaler Handlungsgehilfen-
verband), 11
German National Labor Federation (Deutschnationaler Arbeiterbund), 11
German National People's Party. *See*
Deutschnationale Volkspartei
German People's Party. *See* Deutsche
Volkspartei
German war guilt, 31, 42, 46, 144, 238 n.55;
and DNVP, 9, 30, 37, 39, 47, 50–51,
75, 77, 100, 127, 207; Allies' insistence on,
53–54; Schiele on, 109–110, 111, 113–14,
116–18, 127; Stresemann on, 110, 111,
116–17; Hindenburg on, 113; French and
British reaction to, 115–16; Luther on,
116, 117-18; Westarp on, 116, 117–18,
127; and Locarno accords, 122–23, 132
Gesamtverband der christlichen Gewerkschaften Deutschlands (United Alliance of
German Christian Trade Unions), 11
Gessler, Otto, 61, 88, 97, 108, 149, 202,
245 n.9; on Locarno accords, 126, 134, 136,
154; as possible dictator, 170–71
Goldacker, Hans von, 54
Graef-Anklam, Walther, 209
Grand Coalition, 15, 16, 17, 156, 157, 158,
187, 188
Great Britain, 7, 18, 31, 68; and policy of
reconciliation, 5; and Ruhr occupation, 16;
and Rhineland security-pact initiative, 64;
and Locarno Conference, 104; and German
war guilt, 115–16; and Russia, 195

Hamburg Fremdenblatt, 150
Hartwig, Emil, 11
Helfferich, Karl, 20
Hergt, Oskar, 60, 148, 255 n.41, 263 n.55;
career of, 12; contrasted with Westarp,
12–13; and DNVP moderates, 21; and
DNVP entry into government, 22; and
DNVP coalition demands, 26–27; and
Dawes plan, 37, 48, 49–50, 51; on DNVP
Dawes-plan demands, 39; leadership of,
discredited, 54, 55; and Rhineland security-
pact initiative, 70; and Locarno Conference, 109, 114; and DNVP moderation,
185; and Rhineland evacuation, 194,
197–98, 200, 202

Herriot, Edouard, 31, 32, 33, 53, 59; on Dawes plan and Versailles Treaty, 35; and Ruhr evacuation, 42–46; and Rhineland security-pact initiative, 65–66

Hesnard, Oswald, 152

Hilpert, Hans, 175, 185

Hindenburg, Oskar, 171

Hindenburg, Paul von, 8, 80, 136, 149, 192, 220, 255 n.41, 259 n.52; Stresemann supports, 5; on German war guilt, 113; and Locarno accords, 113, 126–27, 135, 151, 153, 154, 155; favors DNVP, 148, 151, 162, 164, 166, 189, 191, 205, 207; promotes minority coalition, 156–58, 159, 162; and League of Nations petition, 166–67, 170, 171; and rumors of dictatorship, 170–71; and rightist coalition, 176–77, 189, 190; and Schiele, 249 n.29

Hitler, Adolf, 22, 219, 220, 264 n.2

Hoesch, Leopold von, 65, 67–68, 99, 104, 152, 153; career of, 7; and Rhineland occupation, 59

Hoetzsch, Otto, 77, 81, 198, 237 n.24; career of, 14; and Dawes plan, 40, 47; on Rhineland security-pact initiative, 70, 71; on Locarno accords, 160; and League of Nations, 177–78; supports Stresemann, 196, 201

Holborn, Hajo, 220

Holland, 173

Houghton, Alanson B., 48, 234 n.33

Hugenberg, Alfred, 106, 220, 262 n.54; and DNVP radical right wing, 13, 103; anti-Locarno protests of, 142; as possible dictator, 171; and Nationalist press, 186, 191, 201; opposes DNVP cabinet entrance, 192, 193; chairs DNVP, 218–19

Interallied Military Control Commission (IMCC), 49; and German armament inspection, 32, 33, 58–59, 80, 181; withdrawal of, 153, 159, 188, 189, 194; abolition of, 183

Italy, 16, 18, 68, 124, 168

Jarres, Karl, 25, 45, 47

Ja-Sager, 54

Kanitz, Gerhard von, 16, 134

Kapp *Putsch* (led by Wolfgang Kapp), 13, 15, 215

Kempner, Franz, 7–8, 47, 94, 250 n.4, 251 n.7; and Locarno accords, 124, 125, 126–27

Keudell, Walther von, 54, 263 n.55

Koch-Eberfeld, Wilhelm, 263 n.55

Koch-Weser, Eric, 157–58, 159, 256 nn.6, 52

Kommunistische Partei Deutschlands (German Communist Party, or KPD), 176

Korrespondenz der Deutschnationalen Volkspartei, 64, 74, 77, 82–83, 108, 118, 145–46, 214

Krohne, Rudolf, 88, 149

Lambach, Walter, 11, 218

Laverrenz, Wilhelm, 54

League of Nations, 32, 59; German entry into, 66, 78–85 passim, 99, 109, 123–24, 132, 163–74, 180; charter of, 124; DNVP opposes German entry into, 125, 163, 165, 166, 167, 174, 175, 213; Reichstag approves German entry into, 155, 156

League of Nations Council, 111; expansion of, 167–68, 169, 180; substitutions on, 172–73; Stresemann chairs, 194

Lindeiner-Wildau, Hans-Erdmann von, 13, 21, 108, 148, 193; attacks Stresemann, 91, 94; and Locarno accords, 105, 106, 140–41

Lindner, Wilhelm, 11

Locarno accords: Gaus and, 6–7; German reaction to, 124–30; initialed, 130; compared with guidelines, 131; and Luther's cabinet, 131–35, 149, 151; disarmament in, 132; German war guilt in, 132; DNVP opposes, 135–41 passim, 146–47, 155, 161–62, 212–13; and Luther, 148, 149–50, 153–55; Hindenburg on, 151, 153, 154, 155; Allied conditions on, 152–53; Gessler on, 154; Reichstag approves, 155, 156; effects of, 159-60; Hoetzsch on, 160; Germany's reaffirmation of, 174; and Eupen-Malmédy dispute, 178-79; French disregard of, 193–202. *See also* Locarno Conference

Locarno Conference, 54; Allied invitation to, 104–6; British suggest, 104; Germans consider, 104, 105, 106, 107–8, 115–16; and DNVP, 105–7, 110–11, 114, 207; Luther's cabinet in, 109–10; guidelines, 111–12, 113, 121–22; delegation to, 112; Stresemann and Luther at, 121–31 passim; League of Nations issue at, 123–24; signing of accords at, 130; France's de-

mands at, 131–32. *See also* Locarno
accords
Lochner, Louis, 3
Logan, James, 234 n.33
London Conference, 42–46, 59. *See also*
Dawes plan
Ludendorff, Erich Friedrich Wilhelm, 5
Luther, Hans, 78, 256 n.6; position of, weakened, 7–8; and Dawes Conference, 42–45;
and coalition formation, 56; and "cabinet
of personalities," 61; and Rhineland
security-pact initiative, 63, 71, 72–73,
87–88, 89, 97; and DNVP, 82, 135, 140–
41, 148; and Stresemann, 87–88, 92, 93–94,
100, 246 n.46; on the United States,
87–88; and foreign-policy debate, 95, 96;
and Locarno Conference, 104, 105, 109,
112, 114, 121–31 passim; and German war
guilt, 116, 117–18, 122–23; and Locarno
accords, 130, 133–34, 148, 149–50, 153–55;
Stresemann on, 150; and minority
coalition, 158–59, 162; on Poland, 169–70;
at League of Nations talks, 171–74
Luther Cabinet (first): formation of, 61; and
DNVP, 64, 76, 144, 147, 148, 149, 206;
and Rhineland security-pact initiative, 65,
89–90; Stresemann's position in, jeopardized, 92–94; and Locarno Conference,
109–10, 112; on German war guilt,
116–18; and Locarno accords, 130, 134–35,
136, 149, 151; resignation of, 155, 156;
and DDP, 256 n.52
Luther Cabinet (second), 256 n.60; vote of
confidence for, 164, 165; DNVP opposes,
165; foreign policy of, 165–66; on League
of Nations entry, 166–68; fall of, 175–76

MacDonald, James Ramsay, 31, 32, 33, 53,
59; and Dawes Conference, 42, 43, 44, 45,
46
Maltzan, Ago von, 6, 47, 53
Margerie, Baron François Marie Pierre de, 131
Marx, Wilhelm, 8, 16, 23, 25, 26–27, 59;
and formation of new government, 26-28;
and Dawes Conference, 42, 44, 45, 46;
and German war guilt, 51, 111, 122; as
chancellor again, 176; on Thoiry talks, 184;
attempts minority coalition, 189, 190
Marx Cabinet, 22–23; and Dawes Committee's report, 18–20; and DNVP, 23, 31,
186-87; reconstituted, 27; and Ruhr evacuation, 45, 46; and coalition negotiations,

55–56; resignation of, 60, 189, 202;
and SPD, 187, 188–89, 191
Marxism, 9
Marxist Socialists, 15
Meissner, Otto, 8, 166–67, 170, 173, 190, 192
Middle bloc, 15, 16, 25, 156, 157, 158,
189, 190
Mission interalliée de contrôles des usines
et des mines (MICUM), treaties of, 16, 18
München-Augsburger Abendzeitung, 76

National Federation of German Industry
(Reichsverband der deutschen Industrie),
11
Nationalists. *See* Deutschnationale Volkspartei
National Socialists, 52, 217, 219
Nazis, 219. *See also* Hitler, Adolf; National
Socialists
Nein-Sager, 54, 55, 56
Neuhaus, Albert, 86, 125, 148, 254 n.9

Painlévé, Paul, 80, 115
Pan-German League. *See* All-deutscher
Verband
Papen, Franz von, 220
Poincaré, Raymond, 7, 31, 178, 186, 193–94,
197; and German disarmament, 32–33;
attacks Herriot, 35; and hard line against
Germany, 181
Poland, 66, 80, 87, 154; border question, 5,
67, 68, 78, 81, 82, 201; security of, 108;
and League of Nations Council, 168,
169–70, 171, 172, 173
Pünder, Hermann, 7, 8; and Locarno accords,
124, 125, 126–27, 129; on Thoiry talks,
184, 185

Quaatz, Reinhold, 77, 200–201

Racists, 21, 69
Rapallo Pact, 195–96
RDI (Reichsverband der deutschen In-
dustrie), 11
Reichslandbund (Reichsland Federation, or
RLB), 11, 16, 31, 48–49, 145, 150
Reichstag elections: of May 1924, 10, 16, 21,
204, 209; of December 1924, 56–57, 60,
202; of May 1928, 10, 202, 204, 218
Reichsverband der deutschen Industrie

National Federation of German Industry, or RDI), 11
Reichswehr, 33, 187, 189, 215, 216
Reparations, 6, 19–20, 24–25, 28, 31–32, 35, 39, 46, 119
Rhineland, occupation and evacuation of, 18, 24–25, 34, 37, 45, 46, 53, 58, 63, 85, 98, 99, 104, 109, 110, 114–15, 119, 122, 123, 128, 153, 154, 160, 181, 182, 183, 199, 200, 202, 217; SPD and, 59; DDP and, 59, 91, 92; Briand and, 132–33, 194, 197; Chamberlain and, 194, 197; Hergt and, 194, 197–98. *See also* Cologne zone of occupation
Rhineland security-pact initiative, 83–84; announced, 62–63, 66–69; and DNVP, 70–77 passim, 88–89, 90, 210–12; Stresemann on, 73, 85–86; Allied response to, 76–77, 81–82; French response to, 80, 85; Westarp on, 81–82, 91, 98–99; German answer on, 86–87, 97, 98, 99; Schiele on, 86–87, 88–89, 90; Seeckt on, 86; Brauns on, 87; Luther on, 87–88, 89; Luther's cabinet on, 89–90. *See also* Locarno accords; Locarno Conference
RLB. *See* Reichslandbund
Ruhr: occupation of, 16, 18–20, 47; evacuation of, 42–46
Russia, 5, 87, 195–96

Schacht, Hjalmar, 40, 41
Scheidemann, Philipp, 188
Schiele, Martin, 60, 61, 103, 108, 196, 211, 252 n.37, 254 n.9, 263 n.55; and Rhineland security-pact initiative, 71, 86–87, 88–89, 90; and Luther, 72; and foreign-policy debate, 97–98; and Locarno Conference, 105, 106, 111–12, 113, 114, 121; on German war guilt, 109–10, 111, 113–14, 116–18, 127; and Locarno accords, 124, 125, 127, 128, 129, 134–35, 136, 140–41, 252 n.30; resignation of, 142; and DNVP "distancing," 148; on minority coalition, 157, 158–59; on League of Nations entry, 164, 208; criticizes Stresemann's foreign policy, 198–99; and Hindenburg, 249 n.29
Schlange-Schöningen, Hans, 13, 180, 215
Schleicher, Kurt von, 49
Schlieben, Otto von, 125, 148, 254 n.9
Scholz, Ernst, 26, 90, 95, 176; and DNVP coalition, 188, 189, 191
Schubert, Carl von, 6, 7, 63, 78, 89, 91, 108, 172

Schultz-Bromberg, Georg, 72, 73
Seeckt, Hans von, 33–34, 49, 68, 108; on Rhineland security-pact initiative, 86; attacks Stresemann, 93, 96; and Locarno Conference, 114; on Locarno accords, 125
Social Democratic Party. *See* Sozialdemokratische Partei Deutschlands
Societies for the Fatherland. *See* Vereinigte Vaterländische Verbände
Sozialdemokratische Partei Deutschlands (Social Democratic Party, or SPD), 27–28, 52, 91–92, 139, 158, 195, 256 n.6; supports policy of reconcilation, 8; as strong party, 10, 57, 202; in Weimar Coalition, 14–15; on coalition, 55–56, 57, 157, 188; and Rhineland occupation, 59; and League of Nations entry, 66, 165, 169, 175; and Rhineland security-pact initiative, 96; mistrusts Luther, 149, 155, 156; votes for Locarno accords, 155, 156; and 1926 referendum on expropriation of princes' property, 176; and Marx's cabinet, 187, 188–89, 191
SPD. *See* Sozialdemokratische Partei Deutschlands
Stahlhelm (Steel Helmet), 11
Sthamer, Friedrich, 7, 64
Stingl, Karl, 61
Stresemann, Gustav: death of, 3; and policy of reconciliation, 4–5, 77–78, 143–44, 167, 204; as annexationist, 5; Eastern policy of, 5–6; Western policy of, 5, 6; and Hans Luther, 7–8, 87–88, 92, 93–94, 100, 246 n.46; on World War defeat, 8; and Grand Coalition, 15–16; and inclusion of DNVP in government, 15–16, 22, 189–90; and Dawes plan, 18–20, 24–25, 30, 35–36, 42–46, 52–53; and DNVP opposition, 23, 34, 38–39, 72, 76–77, 160–61, 206–8; DNVP demands resignation of, 27, 90–91; and German war guilt, 50–51, 110, 111, 116–17, 122–23, 144; foreign-policy aims of, 53, 228 n.2; and rightist coalition, 60, 176; and "cabinet of personalities," 61; and Rhineland security-pact initiative, 62–63, 65, 66–69, 71, 73, 74, 85–86, 89–90, 97, 98, 99, 196–200, 201–2; and renunciation of German land, 78–79; and Eupen-Malmédy, 79, 177–78; and DNVP leadership strain, 81, 82–83, 84; DNVP compromise with, 82–83, 108, 185–87, 205; attacked by Lindeiner-Wildau, 91; attacked by Westarp, 91, 93, 94; removal of, threatened, 92–94, 96, 157;

attacked by Frenken, 93; attacked by Seeckt, 93, 96; on foreign-policy debate, 95–96; opposed by ADV, 102–3; and Locarno Conference, 104–5, 106, 109, 110, 111-12, 113, 121–31 passim; and policy of adjustment, 119; and Locarno accords, 130, 131-33, 136, 152–53, 160, 207; concessions of, to DNVP, 143–44; on Luther, 150; resists DNVP, 155, 208–9; and League of Nations entry, 163, 168–70, 171–74; and Thoiry meeting with Briand, 180–85; chairs League of Nations Council, 194; effectiveness of, 196; Schiele criticizes, 198–99; on Polish-German border, 201; conduct of politics by, 204–5; and Hitler, 264 n.2
Sweden, 168, 171, 172, 173

Thoiry, talks at, 180–85
Tirpitz, Alfred von, 24, 26, 47–48, 61, 264 n.2
Traub, Gottfried, 76
Treviranus, Gottfried, 13, 178

Union of Soviet Socialist Republics, 5, 87, 195–96
United Alliance of Christian Trade Unions (Gesamtverband der christlichen Gewerkschaften Deutschlands), 11
United Societies for the Fatherland (Vereinigte Vaterländische Verbände), 11, 25, 70, 76, 83
United States, 5, 16, 18, 87–88, 186

VDI (Vereinigung deutscher Industrieller), 11
Vereinigte Vaterländische Verbände (United Societies for the Fatherland), 11, 25, 70, 76, 83
Vereinigung deutscher Industrieller (German Manufacturers' Union, or VDI), 11
Versailles, Treaty of: revision of, 4, 5, 6, 67; and DNVP, 9, 20; disarmament clauses in, 32; and French security, 35, 58, 85, 99;

and German war guilt, 39; Stresemann on, 44; and trade arrangements, 60; and Eupen-Malmédy, 79; interpretation of, disputed, 108; and Locarno accords, 133, 138; and civil aviation, 159
Vorwärts, 68

Wallraf, Max, 13, 16, 54, 114
Weimar Coalition, 14–15
Weimar Constitution, 39
Weimar Republic, 214–15, 216, 219; Stresemann and, 3; and DNVP, 9, 15; stable years of, 10; and Kapp *Putsch*, 13; 1920 coalition in, 14–15; ferment in, 229 n.20
Weiss, Max, 14
Westarp, Count Kuno von, 96, 108, 148, 255 n.41; career of, 12–13; and Dawes plan, 19, 48, 49, 50; appeal of, 21–22; on foreign policy, 29–30; denounces disarmaments inspection, 34; and DNVP moderates, 54–55; on Rhineland security-pact initiative, 59–60, 81–82, 91, 98–99; and Stresemann, 91, 93, 94, 196; and DNVP opposition, 102, 103, 142, 143, 211–12, 215, 220–21; and Locarno Conference, 106–7, 109, 113–14, 128–29; and German war guilt, 116, 117–18, 127; on Locarno accords, 127–29, 135, 137–39, 140–41; on a minority coalition, 156–57; on League of Nations entry, 164–65, 166; and rightist coalition, 176–77; and DNVP moderation, 185–86, 187, 191–92; and correspondence with Engel, 217; refuses to oppose Hugenberg for chairmanship of DNVP, 218
William (crown prince), 6, 119, 228 n.10
Wilson's Fourteen Points, 9
Winckler, Friedrich, 12

Zentrum (Center Party), 27, 156, 158, 176, 189, 191; in Weimar Coalition, 14–15; and Dawes plan, 48, 50, 55; and "cabinet of personalities," 61; mistrusts Luther, 149